Does It Really Say That in the Bible?

KATIE HOYT MCNABB

WESTBOW·
PRESS
A DIVISION OF THOMAS NELSON
& ZONDERVAN

Scripture taken from the King James Version of the Bible.

Scriptures taken from the Holy Bible, New International Version®, NIV®.
Copyright © 1973, 1978, 1984, 2011 by Biblica, Inc.™ Used by permission of
Zondervan. All rights reserved worldwide. www.zondervan.com The "NIV"
and "New International Version" are trademarks registered in the United
States Patent and Trademark Office by Biblica, Inc.™ All rights reserved.

All Scripture quotations in this publications are from **The Message**.
Copyright (c) by Eugene H. Peterson 1993, 1994, 1995, 1996, 2000,
2001, 2002. Used by permission of NavPress Publishing Group.

WestBow Press books may be ordered through booksellers or by contacting:

WestBow Press
A Division of Thomas Nelson & Zondervan
1663 Liberty Drive
Bloomington, IN 47403
www.westbowpress.com
1 (866) 928-1240

Cover art by Callum Backstrom
Author photo by Linda Walters

Library of Congress Control Number: 2014911802

ISBN: 978-1-4908-4319-3 (sc)
ISBN: 978-1-4908-4321-6 (hc)
ISBN: 978-1-4908-4320-9 (e)

Printed in the United States of America.

WestBow Press rev. date: 07/22/2014

Contents

A First Thought: Fate, Destiny, and the Meaning of Life............. xi

Part One: An Introduction to the Bible and the Old Testament (Genesis – Ruth) 1

Chapter 1: Does It Really Say That God Created the
World in Six Days?.. 11

Chapter 2: Does It Really Say That Eve Ruined the
World by Eating the Apple?............................. 21

Chapter 3: Does It Really Say That Abraham Is the
Father of Three Faiths?..................................... 31

Chapter 4: Does It Really Say That Moses Parted
the Red Sea? 75

    Exodus.. 76

    Leviticus.. 93

    Numbers.. 99

    Deuteronomy 103

Chapter 5: Does It Really Say That Joshua Fought
the Battle of Jericho and the Walls Came
Tumbling Down?... 111

    Joshua... 113

    Judges 122

    Ruth... 135

Part Two: The Old Testament (1 Samuel – Malachi) 139

Chapter 6: Does It Really Say That David Killed the
          Giant Goliath?..145
    Samuel.. 146
    Kings..161
    Chronicles... 170
    Ezra and Nehemiah 174
    Esther.. 178

Chapter 7: Does It Really Say That Job Was Patient? 183
    Job.. 185
    Psalms.. 192
    Proverbs.. 197
    Ecclesiastes... 201
    Song of Songs 205

Chapter 8: Does It Really Say That God Would
          Send a Messiah? 209
    Isaiah 217
    Jeremiah 226
    Lamentations 231
    Ezekiel.. 233
    Daniel.. 239
    The Twelve (Minor Prophets) 244

Part Three: The New Testament 259

Chapter 9: Does It Really Say That Jesus Was the Messiah?. 269
    Matthew 272
    Mark.. 290
    Luke.. 299
    John... 309

Chapter 10: Does It Really Say That Christians Should
             Spread the Gospel All over the Globe? 325
     Acts 327

Chapter 11: Does It Really Say That Believing in Christ Is
             All There Is to Being a Christian? 351
     The Pauline Letters 352
     Romans 353
     1 Corinthians 362
     2 Corinthians 368
     Galatians 372
     Ephesians 377
     Philippians 380
     Colossians 383
     Thessalonians 386
     1 Timothy 389
     2 Timothy 392
     Titus 393
     Philemon 394
     Hebrews 399
     James 403
     1 Peter 407
     2 Peter 409
     John 1, 2, and 3 410
     Jude 412

Chapter 12: Does It Really Say That the World Will End? 415
     Revelation 418

Afterword 429

Appendix 1: Literary Devices 433
Appendix 2: Comparing the Hebrew and Christian Canons .. 439

Appendix 3: Deities of Israel's Neighbors.. 441
Appendix 4: Herod's Dynasty.. 443
Appendix 5: Jesus' Fulfillment of Messianic Markers............... 445
Appendix 6: Women and Slaves Mentioned
          in Paul's Epistles 453

Bibliography.. 457

Acknowledgements.. 459

About the Author 461

To

Brevard S. Childs,

who made my heart burn
when he opened the Scriptures,

and

Irené Totton Wagner,

who showed me
I could open the Scriptures for others.

A First Thought: Fate, Destiny, and the Meaning of Life

Whether we talk about it or not, all humans find themselves contemplating the meaning of life at one time or another. Picking up a book about the Bible is bound to stir up some of that thinking in your mind. So before we begin, I'm going to suggest that instead we think about two words that color our understanding of the meaning of life from a different angle, namely *fate* and *destiny*. At first glance you will say, "But aren't these synonyms?" and I will agree that they are in this respect. They both direct our attention to the question of how much control we have over our lives. Are we masters of our own *fate*, or are we merely the pawns of *destiny* with no real ability to determine the shape or outcome of our lives?

Let's look at each word separately and see what associations we make with each. When we speak of *fate*, our thinking runs along two tracks of thought. In one vein *fate* simply equates to *chance*—the randomness of life that puts us sometimes in the right place at the right time or just as easily in the reverse. When we think of life's unpredictable disasters like the tornado that hits some homes and spares others, we don't say that the person who was spared or was hurt has actually done something to deserve this result. Rather we chalk it up to good or bad *luck*. Since this idea of *fate* can be used to explain the very existence of life, it carries with it the notion that much of life is under no one's control. In this sense the word *fate* connotes neutrality. The universe is neither for us nor against us. It just is.

But there is another nuance to *fate*. Events that appear to be random but come to a negative end are often deemed *ill-fated.* We would more often say that it was someone's *fate* to be in one of the Twin Towers on September 11 rather than his or her *destiny*. All thinking that *the world is out to get us* falls into this category. Of course, it is illogical to blame the universe for these events, but our emotions take us down that path from time to time.

We have established that the neutral sense of *fate*, and its synonyms *chance* and *luck* bring us no particular help in discovering a meaning to life except a relative one where each individual can assign his or her own significance to life; however, that person still has no standard by which to call his or hers better or worse than another's. What about the word *destiny*? Generally *destiny* carries a more positive connotation than *fate. Destiny* has embedded within it the idea that someone or something has a plan, a purpose, and a *destination* in mind with regard to our lives. Just who/what this person/force is makes for a great debate among people of different ideologies and religions. It could still be a random plan, as it is within Greek mythology where the *Fates* are imagined as three women—one who spins the thread of life, a second who passes out the *lots* of *destiny*, and the last who mercilessly brings death with her shears. It could also be a plan over which we have no control as in the idea that some are *destined* to receive paradise and others are condemned to hell. Or it could be that the someone with the plan is actually rooting for us but has left the choice of *destination* in our hands.

I lay out these possibilities for you as you begin to look at what the Bible really says. Of course, it will be valuable to anyone to know what the Bible says as part of one's education, but I'm guessing that the most interesting question the Bible can answer for you runs more along the lines of these musings. If so, the Bible stands ready for your inquiry.

Part One: An Introduction to the Bible and the Old Testament (Genesis – Ruth)

So you've decided it's time to find out what the Bible *really* says as opposed to what you might think it says or what you hear other people say it says. But how to begin? The Bible is not only a long book. It is also not simple. In actuality, the Christian[1] Bible comprises sixty-six books written during a period of 1,500 years by at least forty separate authors and then copied, edited, recopied, canonized, and passed down for generations without benefit of printing, and it still remained surprising intact by archeological standards. While biblical scholarship has expended much energy attempting to uncover the process by which the Bible evolved from its earliest oral traditions into the masterwork of literature we have today, it has not necessarily simplified the reading of the Bible.

If you begin reading in Genesis it's easy to get bogged down with lists of genealogies. Once you get to an actual story you find the narrative will start and stop and restart in places, repeating a similar plotline but with a different perspective. Some accounts offer too many details, and others make you wish for more information. Interestingly, the most important stories appear more than once, yet without comment over discrepancies

---

[1] The Hebrew Bible is roughly equivalent to the Christian's Old Testament, although the order of the books differs in some places. See appendix 2. Roman Catholic and Orthodox Christians also include the books of the Apocrypha (a series of books written between the Old and New Testaments) as part of their Bibles, though we will not be looking at those books in this study.

of description. We will find two creation stories, two renditions of the Ten Commandments and four gospels testifying about the life of Jesus. You might ask why didn't the editors clean up all these loose ends?

Suffice it to say that the Bible is not an easy-to-read book for the casual reader. But of course, it is not meant to be. In the first place it is literature. Any good English teacher will remind you that you get the most out of your reading of a book when you wrestle with it. There is nothing to be gained by being precious or sanctimonious. A fresh and sharp eye, an open mind, and a brain functioning at full wattage are your best aids. Those literary devices you may or may not remember learning about in English class will come in handy as well. (If you're rusty on these, see appendix 1 for a quick refresher.) A writer will use mechanisms like metaphor and foreshadowing the same way a speaker employs body language and tone of voice to get the message across. If you don't pick up on it, you miss a lot of the meaning.

Now it seems like this Bible reading is going to be a lot of work. What is the carrot that will make all this worth the effort? Beyond the benefit of broadening your education lies another reason to read the Bible and read it closely. We need to check out its claim that it is divine revelation—God speaking to us about Himself,[2] who He is, what He thinks about us, what He has done in history, and what He plans to do in the future. It is an offer of *inside* information. If you ever wonder about the meaning of life,

---

[2] I will use the masculine pronouns (capitalized) for God in this book. Clearly God transcends the categories of gender. The Deity created both male and female and therefore knows each intimately. The Lord even uses male and female examples to describe Himself. English, however, does not have a singular pronoun indicating either male or female (except perhaps *one*, but this becomes stilted with frequent use) and traditionally defers to the masculine in such cases. I will maintain that practice referring to God as well as any general reference to a person.

why it is so good and so bad, and what your place in this universe is, it's a great idea to hear what God's side of the story is.

Before We Begin

I need to make two points before we start. The first involves a brief introduction on how the Bible came to be, and the second concerns why believers find it authoritative.

There are many ways of interpreting the origins of the Bible. Some people maintain that Scripture is literally God's dictated words. Muslims believe this about the Koran. Koran, which translates to *reciting*, refers to the messages that Mohammed received during a period of years directly from the angel Gabriel, who spoke directly for God. Although Mohammed himself could not write, the faithful Muslim believes that his memory preserved the messages perfectly until scribes were able to transpose them. However, the inerrancy of the Koran is only preserved in Arabic. Translating the verses subjects them to error and misunderstanding, rendering the work no longer the precise revelation of God.

Believers in the authority of the Bible have been ticklish about translations as well. Practicing Jews will still send their children to Hebrew school as part of their preparation for their bar and bat mitzvahs. But historically, as interest in the Bible grew outside the region of Israel, language became a barrier. By the third century BCE the Hebrew Scriptures began to be translated into Greek, the version known as the Septuagint, because it was the common tongue of the eastern Mediterranean. With the same thinking in mind the various authors of the New Testament wrote in Greek. In the early fifth century CE, Jerome translated the Bible into Latin, the Vulgate version, again because it was the language known to all who were educated and literate in Europe. Eventually some believers felt the need for people to hear Scripture in their native language superseded the advantage of having a unified Latin translation. As early as 1380, John Wycliffe began his translation of the Bible into English. When Martin Luther spearheaded the Protestant movement in the early sixteenth century, one of his primary claims was that people should be able to read the Bible for themselves. Thus, with the aid of the newly invented printing press, the translations of the Bible multiplied. We can also point to the concern for people being able to read the Bible as the impetus for the literacy movement in the British colonies of North America that vastly increased the number of children taught to read. The potential downside of all these translations, however, hinges on whether they render the message faithfully. Add to this that before the printing press, the Scriptures were copied by hand. Evidence from the Dead Sea Scrolls indicates that the Jewish community did a very good job preserving its texts through the copying process, but can the same be said of the extended canon of the Christians where the copying involved multiple languages and often less durable writing materials (papyrus instead of the more resilient parchment or vellum)? Is what we read today still God's Word?

The question we need to address is whether it is necessary for Scripture to be God's exact words for it to be the authoritative Word of God. When scholars examine the Bible, they perceive a patchwork of sources. It leads them to surmise that the Bible, like all ancient literatures, began as an oral tradition that was kept alive in memory and handed down. You will notice the effects of preserving the memory of this oral tradition when you see the narrative stop to add a footnote of explanation ("This is why—") or when the story appears to get retold from a slightly different perspective. When the Bible came to be written down, it bore the stamp of the community and the individual recording it. What we have preserved as a sacred text carries the further fingerprints of later editors, and over time a variety of groups charged to determine which of the many writings were in fact

Scripture and which needed to remain outside the canon. That's a great number of human hands. Yet neither the Old Testament nor the New claims to have only one voice. As we read, we can hear different voices telling the stories. With even a little training you can detect the seam lines in the Old Testament where different narratives have been stitched together. In the New Testament, we have four gospel writers each telling his own version of Jesus' ministry with no attempt made to sync them into a single narrative. The interesting thing is that though editing occurred along the way, the editors did not see it as their job to remove all surface inconsistencies. Yet the believing community posits that there is a unity of spirit throughout the entire document. We say that the Holy Spirit has inspired the production, but what does that mean?

My understanding of Scripture is this: God chose to reveal Himself to humans. At the same time the Lord invited humans to participate in the creation of the written revelation, making it one of many examples of how the Deity chooses to interact with humans. God's self-disclosure began with the actual experiences of people who dealt with the Lord one-on-one. They told their stories and eventually these were passed down through word of mouth. When it came time to preserve the narratives in written form, the early authors had to augment the memorized oral tradition with their own words here and there to render a clear and readable text. I presume that it is possible for the Holy Spirit to inspire the writing and leave the character of the author intact. Moreover, the Holy Spirit has worked not just by moving the original authors themselves but by giving guidance to all people who handled the Scriptures—the editors, the copyists, the keepers of the sacred writings, and the councils that determined the canon. The finished product represents the collaboration of all these hands under the Lordship of the Spirit so that the Bible we read truly speaks to us in God's voice of God's story. In this way the Scripture draws its authenticity from its recognizably human recording and compiling and its authority from the consistency of its themes that point to the singular and unchanging[3] author behind the human contributors.

Furthermore, although the Bible covers some common ground with other ancient literature, it contains a noteworthy departure from other works of its type. The Bible stories are all told with an emphasis on the "warts and all" viewpoint. There is no embellishing of characters' virtues and strengths in these pages. The men and women of ancient Israel up to Roman Palestine are not larger than life but rather distinguished in their ordinariness, their humanness. Many have observed that no other culture beside the Hebrew people has kept such a scathing record of its own history. This fact alone should pique your curiosity.

The Scope of This Book

In this book I present myself as a guide. I am familiar with the stories and can point out the sights that you might otherwise miss. Moreover, I should explain that I am a Christian guide and will be interpreting Scripture from that perspective. I recognize that though Jews and Christians share Scripture, we do not always understand it in the same way. Nonetheless, all Christians are forever indebted to the people of Israel for maintaining the Scripture and faith that provide the foundation for our understanding of Jesus.

Because this book is meant to serve as an introduction to the whole of the Bible, I cover more breadth than depth. My hope is that this is sufficient for you to taste the richness of the literature

---

[3] I do not mean here that the Israelites' ideas about God are static throughout the Scriptures. As I will show, Israel's faith in and understanding of God evolve and grow as they become more organized as a people with a theology. Still, that Israel comes to know God more thoroughly over time does not mean that God Himself has changed.

while you can still catch a glimmer of the themes that distill the work of so many contributors into a single voice, specifically God's telling of who He is and what He is doing out of love for the humans He has made.

To this end, I have divided this study into three parts: two for the Old Testament and the last for the New. I lead off with a good amount of depth in the book of Genesis, spending three chapters there. Chapters 1 and 2 cover Genesis 1–3—the story of the creation and the fall, the term used to describe how humans broke their connection to their Creator. These chapters are fundamental because the rest of the Bible is basically the story of God working to reconnect to humans. In chapters 3–6, I outline the religious history of Israel. It begins with Abraham, the Patriarch, and the twin promises God makes to him, referring to descendants and land. As Genesis closes, we see that Abraham has many great-grandchildren but that they have had to move from the physical Israel to Egypt because of a famine. Chapter 4 follows the trials of Moses taking God's people back to Israel, and in chapter 5, we see how Israel regains her ownership of the Promised Land under Joshua's leadership. Chapter 6 deals with Israel's monarchy and how it eventually splits the land into two kingdoms—the north calling itself Israel and the south named for the tribe of Judah. The northern kingdom falls to the Assyrians in about 722 BCE, creating the fabled ten lost tribes of Israel as her citizens became assimilated among the people of their captors. Judah manages to hang on until about 586 BCE, when Babylon overpowered her and forced her inhabitants into exile. From that time forward these Israelites became known as Jews (after their name, Judah). Although some Jews returned to Jerusalem about fifty some years after the exile, most were dispersed into the many lands around the Mediterranean and eventually throughout the earth. We label this scattering of the Jews the Diaspora. Those who did return to their homeland did so under the rule of others, accepting the challenge of remaining true to their faith without political autonomy.[4]

Chapter 7 turns from the chronological history to look at the wisdom literature—the books of Job, Psalms, Proverbs, Ecclesiastes, and the Song of Songs. Chapter 8 deals with Israel's writing prophets—the unenviable ones whom God chose to tell Israel to stop sinning and to whom He also revealed that only a "remnant" of God's people would remain strong in the faith. To these prophets who preached throughout the monarchy and into the exile and the return to Jerusalem, God also gave the promise of the Messiah.

While the books of the Old Testament unfold fairly chronologically as a history, the New Testament focuses on the life of Jesus and its immediate repercussions. Four gospels tell the story of Jesus' life, death, and resurrection, and the book of Acts records the events that follow, involving the spreading of the gospel. The rest of the New Testament is a series of letters plus the book of Revelation, which, among other things, deals with the world's end. Chapter 9 explores how the Gospels invite us to meet Jesus in order to understand how His life, death, and resurrection fulfill God's promise of reconciliation with humans. Chapter 10 covers the book of Acts as it chronicles how Jesus' disciples respond to their Master's commission to teach the meaning of Jesus' life, death, and resurrection to the rest of the world. Chapter 11 takes on the epistles, which show the early believers struggling to map out the details of what the Christian life entails. Finally chapter 12 looks at Revelation, St.

---

[4]   Jews did regain political control of their Holy Land for a brief period from the second to first centuries BCE after the Maccabean Revolt in 165 BCE. (This revolt includes the miracle commemorated in the Hanukkah holiday.) However, the advance of the Roman Empire kept this period of political autonomy relatively short. Jews continued to fight Rome in the first and second centuries CE but were ultimately unsuccessful. The Diaspora (the scattering) of the Jews accelerated with these defeats. Not until 1948 did Jews again rule in Israel.

John's record of the visions he received from Jesus, which offer us the Bible's closing comments on all issues of faith as well as its depiction of the end of the world in symmetry with the account of the beginning in Genesis.

Now that you've reviewed the itinerary, I need to mention something about equipment, particularly your own Bible. As I discuss the biblical stories, I use a lot of quotations from the Bible. Unless otherwise noted, these quotes come from Eugene Peterson's paraphrased translation that he titles *The Message*. I selected it for its use of contemporary English and because it may present verses you may have heard before in a new way. But there are many translations of the Bible in English, and you should choose one that you find accessible. Looking at more than one translation will always improve your odds of *getting* what the passage is saying. And now that we've dispensed with these preliminaries, let's get on with the journey and start discovering what it really says in the Bible.

Chapter 1

Does It Really Say That God Created the World in Six Days?

Did you know that there are actually two versions of the creation in the Bible? Chapter 1 of Genesis tells the story with God creating the world "in six days," whereas chapter 2 gives us the story of Adam and Eve. I'll take up the Adam and Eve story in my own chapter 2 so that we can focus on the lead version of the creation here. Although both treatments of creation set off the science v. religion debate, Genesis 1 comes under scrutiny most often because of the mention of the *days* that it took God to create. Are these real days or mere figures of speech? Instead of getting embroiled in that debate, I suggest that we look at the text itself and see what it has to say to us, utilizing our tools for understanding literature.

I take the following version of Genesis 1–2:3 from *The Message* translated by Eugene Peterson. Read this and compare it to your own Bible. The passage is probably somewhat familiar especially in a more traditional translation.

> *First this: God created the Heavens and the Earth—all you can see, all you don't see. Earth was a soup of nothingness, a bottomless emptiness, an inky blackness. God's Spirit brooded like a bird above the watery abyss.*

God spoke: "Light!"
*   And light appeared.*
God saw that the light was good
*   and separated light from dark.*
God named the light Day,
*   he named the dark Night.*
It was evening, it was morning—
Day One.

God spoke: "Sky! In the middle of the waters;
*   separate water from water!"*
God made sky.
He separated the water under sky
*   from the water above sky.*
And there it was:
*   he named the sky the Heavens;*
It was evening, it was morning—
Day Two.

God spoke: "Separate!
*   Water-beneath-Heaven, gather into one place;*
Land appear!"
*   And there it was.*
God named the land Earth.
*   He named the pooled water Ocean.*
God saw that it was good.

God spoke: "Earth, green up! Grow all varieties
*   of seed-bearing plants,*
Every sort of fruit-bearing tree."
*   And there it was.*
Earth produced green seed-bearing plants,
*   all varieties,*

And fruit-bearing trees of all sorts.
  God saw that it was good.
It was evening, it was morning—
Day Three.

God spoke: "Lights! Come out!
  Shine in Heaven's sky!
Separate Day from Night.
  Mark seasons and days and years,
Lights in Heaven's sky to give light to Earth."
  And there it was.

God made two big lights, the larger
  to take charge of Day,
The smaller to be in charge of Night;
  and he made the stars.
God placed them in the heavenly sky
  to light up Earth
And oversee Day and Night,
  to separate light and dark.
God saw that it was good.
It was evening, it was morning—
Day Four.

God spoke: "Swarm, Ocean, with fish and all sea life!
  Birds, fly through the sky over Earth!"
God created the huge whales,
  all the swarm of life in the waters,
And every kind and species of flying birds.
  God saw that it was good.
God blessed them: "Prosper! Reproduce! Fill Ocean!
Birds, reproduce on Earth!"
It was evening, it was morning—
Day Five.

God spoke: "Earth, generate life! Every sort and kind:
cattle and reptiles and wild animals—all kinds."
And there it was:
wild animals of every kind,
Cattle of all kinds, every sort of reptile and bug,
God saw that it was good.

God spoke: "Let us make human beings in our image,
make them reflecting our nature
So they can be responsible for the fish in the sea,
the birds in the air, the cattle,
And, yes, Earth itself,
and every animal that moves on the face of the Earth."
God created human beings;
he created them godlike,
Reflecting God's nature.
He created them male and female.
God blessed them:
"Prosper! Reproduce! Fill Earth! Take charge!
Be responsible for fish in the sea and birds in the air,
for every living thing that moves on the face of Earth."

Then God said, "I've given you
every sort of seed-bearing plant on Earth
And every kind of fruit-bearing tree,
given them to you for food.
To all animals and all birds,
everything that moves and breathes,
I give whatever grows out of the ground for food."
And there it was.

God looked over everything he had made;
it was so good, so very good!

It was evening, it was morning—
Day Six.

Heaven and Earth were finished,
down to the last detail.

By the seventh day
God had finished his work.
On the seventh day
he rested from all his work.
God blessed the seventh day.
He made it a Holy Day
Because on that day he rested from his work,
all the creating God had done.

This is the story of how it all started,
of Heaven and Earth when they were created.

Although most translations write these verses as prose, I agree with Peterson's presentation of them as poetry. Here is where I put on my English teacher hat. We need to ask ourselves why the author chose poetry over prose. Prose is the language of complete sentences and therefore complete thoughts. It makes an excellent mode of communication for narrative, explicative, and persuasive writing. In contrast, poetry addresses us in the language of images, offering cues to our senses as well as our cognition. Poetry frequently employs the sounds, rhythms, and repetition of words or phrases to speak to us. Notice how Genesis 1 expresses the creation formulaically.

1. God spoke, or God said—
2. The thing God spoke came into existence—
3. God saw that it was good—
4. It was evening. It was morning.

While poetry comes in a wide variety of formats (e.g., rhyming schemes, prescribed meter, etc.), different cultures have historically developed their own characteristic styles. For instance, parallelism[5] is prominent in Hebrew poetry, and we can see the parallels drawn in the creation story quite easily in the six days.

Day 1: God creates light.	Day 4: God defines the light as the sun, the moon, and the stars.
Day 2: God separates the waters of the sky and the ocean.	Day 5: God fills the sky with birds and fish swim in the oceans.
Day 3: God calls for dry land and vegetation.	Day 6: God makes land dwelling creatures, and finally, humans.

Poetry serves this telling in several ways. First it serves as an aid to memory. You learn the formula and only need to remember the different days. The parallelism makes an excellent teaching tool and also works to highlight the unmatched seventh day, the day God rested and set aside as the Sabbath. Moreover, the flow of the words and the escalation of the number of things created each successive day build anticipation about what God is making the world into and why. Notice how, beginning in day three and also in day six, God personifies the Earth and metaphorically delegates to it the task of bringing forth an assortment of vegetation and then creatures, each according to variations of the land. The Lord has such confidence in what

---

[5] In his *Reflections on the Psalms* (pp. 3–5), C. S. Lewis observes that while many features of poetry (e.g., alliteration, rhyme, meter) do not translate well from one language to another, parallelism continues to function in any language.

He has called into being that He downplays His own role in managing it. But what comes next—the creation of humans, the beings the Deity fashions in God's own image, male and female—the Lord proclaims as the climax. Now the world is a completed picture. Everything God made before the humans was designed *for* them. The Lord will entrust them with the keeping of the earth. Thus, the poetry casts a spell of wonder on us. How amazing this creator God is! There was nothing—chaos, in fact— and methodically the Lord weaved order out of the mess and blessed it with life. God shined forth as an artist filling a blank canvas with masterful skill. After each day the Lord stood back and admired the work. From the beginning God had a plan, but the hearer could not see it until it was completely unfolded and punctuated. "God looked over everything he had made; it was so good, so very good" (Genesis 1:31).

The poet here places us at God's elbow where we can watch the mysterious cosmos come into being. We are even privy to God's thoughts—His pleasure as He produces His work, His particular interest in humankind, to whom He has connected Himself in a special way because they are like Him. We know immediately that God expects humans to prosper, to grow in numbers, and to be in charge of the creation. Some translations will say, "To fill the earth and subdue it," but we can tell from the context that this edict from God is no sanction for abusing the earth. Rather humans are responsible for the earth and need to see that within creation God has given them the means to support themselves and grow themselves into communities. The *very good* expressed at the end of the sixth day shows us God's excitement about what He has made.

Chapter 1 ends with the sixth day, but the writing of this creation story spills into the first three verses of chapter 2. Here is the climax beyond the climax of creation—the Sabbath. Perhaps God, being omnipotent, could have chosen to snap His fingers and bring the whole of the universe to be at once. Instead, this creation version shows us God working at creation, allowing it to evolve over a period of time. Was the period of time six days? Everything in the context here indicates that God's use of six days to create the earth is meant to model for humans how their labors run for six days with rest like God's on the seventh. The text is not dealing in science here (how long did it take God to make the world?) but rather in example. The Hebrews were to live in terms of weeks. Ancient societies quickly learned to account for time in years (trying to approximate the revolution of the earth around the sun) and months (corresponding to the cycles of the moon), but there is no astronomical rationale for the creation of weeks.[6] God supplies it in this version of creation.

In summation, the creation poetry of Genesis 1–2:3 reveals to us that God made the world according to His own design and that what the Lord made was very good. In the evolution debate this remains the only point in which the Bible can be said to contradict theories of scientific cosmology that hypothesize that the world came into existence as a random or unplanned event. Theists can assert that God actually created the universe using the schedule and time frame cosmologists continue to uncover. Genesis, however, is more concerned with the whys of creation. God makes the earth full of wonder and beauty. Science exposes the magnitude of this truth. But for all the amazing forms of life and the intricacies of the balance of nature, Genesis reminds us that humanity emerges as God's quintessential act of creativity. The narrative frames the creation as the gift the Lord presents

---

[6] The origin of the seven-day week probably predates this writing of Genesis. Ancient humans could see seven heavenly bodies in the sky—the Sun, the Moon, and five planets (Mercury, Venus, Mars, Jupiter, and Saturn). That we can even see in English the evidence of naming the days of the week for these bodies (Sun day, Mo[o]n day, and Satur[n] day) points away from the biblical account inventing the week. Still, Genesis frames the observance of the week in the context of God's creation and intention for humans to keep a Sabbath. This is further corroborated by the Hebrew naming of the days of the week by their number (first, second, and so forth) rather than the names of the planets.

to humans to enable their flourishing as the inhabitants and stewards of the earth. In addition, humans' link to God differs from the rest of nature because humans would also be able to know their maker. Like their Creator, their lives would involve work, and they needed the model of a day of rest that renews their bodies and reminds them to appreciate the giver. The seven days of creation are relevant to the explanation of the week. Trying to use them in the category of science is like the fatal math error of comparing apples to oranges. Instead of wondering if the Bible is literally true, we ought to ask ourselves first what it is communicating as literature. If all we can come up with at the end of this poem is "Did it really take God only six days to make the world?" we have missed the point.

Chapter 2

Does It Really Say That Eve Ruined the World by Eating the Apple?

This question gets us way ahead of ourselves. Yes, Eve eating the apple[7] or the forbidden fruit probably is what you think about first when I mention the garden of Eden. You may also remember something about nudity, and that probably begs the question of whether sex is involved in the story. There is a lot of work to be done to bring the story of the garden of Eden back to what the Bible really says.

Let's start with what I mentioned in chapter 1 about there being two creation stories. The first story is the magnificent poem of God calling the world into existence with the power of His voice. The second version of creation appears in Genesis 2:4–25 as the beginning of the garden of Eden story.

As you read this passage in English, it probably does not occur to you that it uses a different name for God.[8] The poet of Genesis

---

[7]   The confusion over the apple stems from the Latin (Vulgate) translation. In Hebrew and Greek, we read the *fruit* from the Tree of the Knowledge of Good and Evil. When this gets translated into Latin, "of evil" becomes *malum* (think of our word *malice*) and gets mistaken for its homonym *malum*, which also means apple.

[8]   In *The Message*, Peterson uses the following device to distinguish between the two Hebrew words for god. The Hebrew word *elohim*, sometimes shortened to *el*, is the generic name of god, capable of referring to Israel's God or any other god or gods. Peterson renders it God when referring to the Bible's deity and god for pagan deities. The other Hebrew word for god is specific to Israel's God and was considered so precious that is was never

1 uses the Hebrew word *Elohim* for God, whereas in this second version of the creation, the word for God in Hebrew is the special name of God indicated by the four consonants transliterated as *YHWH*. Because Hebrews considered it sacrilegious to pronounce God's name, they traditionally substituted the words *the Lord* (*Adonai* in Hebrew) whenever YHWH appeared in the text. Peterson uses GOD to translate YHWH, but many other translators use the LORD to differentiate from the translation of *elohim* as *God*.

From this detail most scholars theorize that the garden of Eden story represents the work of a different author than Genesis 1 and a separate oral tradition. This new scribe writes in prose and at first does not seem to know the account offered in Genesis 1, especially since he appears unaware that, according to that version, his events are out of order.

Here God creates a single man before He brings rain or any plants and animals. The Hebrew verb for God's *making* of man is the same used to describe how a potter molds a pot from clay. God *forms* the man from the dust of the ground, and when the Lord gives him a name, it is simply Adam, originating from the Hebrew *adamah*, meaning dirt. God breathes into the man, implying that his life comes directly from God or God's Spirit.[9]

Having created man, God prepares a special place for him to live. He plants a garden in Eden with all kinds of trees both "beautiful to look at and good to eat" (Genesis 2:9). In this garden

---

spoken aloud. Scholars will often refer to Yahweh as an approximation of how the letters could be pronounced. It was represented in Hebrew by four consonants that transliterate to YHWH. Biblical Hebrew spells words by consonants and applies various smaller points to indicate vowels, but no vowels were ever included in the name of God, lest it be a temptation to pronunciation. It became tradition in many translations to substitute "the Lord" (often written the LORD) whenever YHWH appeared in the text. Peterson translates YHWH as GOD.

[9]   The root of the English word *spirit* is the same used for *breath*. Think of words like *respiration* and *inspiration*.

there are two trees with peculiar names—the Tree of Life and the Tree of Knowledge of Good and Evil. This is when a distant memory of an English teacher past should be making you wonder whether these trees are meant to be symbols.

The next paragraph seems straightforward enough. Verses 10 to 14 describe the four rivers flowing out of Eden, and the detail here makes us think the writer is referring to places his original audience might recognize. It takes us aback a bit to meet this touch of reality after the dose of symbolism.

The narrative now returns us to the man whom God has placed in the garden so that he can "work the ground and keep it in order" (Genesis 2:15). This sounds like the charge placed on all the humans in Genesis 1:28–30. The only thing the man can't do is eat the fruit of the Tree of Knowledge of Good and Evil because "the moment you eat from that tree, you're dead" (Genesis 2:17). The author also notes that the man is alone and God determines that this is *not* good—another reference to Genesis 1. Now it seems the narrator does know about the first version. This is where scholars conjecture that the editors come in. We can suppose that the editors are loathe to tamper too much with the preserved oral tradition, but when they see a chance to echo the first creation version, they do so. The details we observe standing in contradiction, such as the order of creation, must not be critical, but the essential notions, such as God's making the creation *good*, require reinforcement.

To return to the narrative in Genesis 2:19, God makes *the animals of the field and birds of the air* and asks the man to aid the Lord by naming the creatures. Yet none of this assuages the pain of the man's loneliness. To meet this need, God creates woman. In Hebrew the verb to define her creation is *fashions* or *sculpts*, indicating great care in contrast to the mere forming of the man.

When the man beholds her, he is so overwhelmed with wonder and joy that he bursts into poetry and declares, "At last, someone like me!" Notice how the emphasis here differs from the Genesis 1 presentation of the two sexes where God's encouragement is to reproduce. Genesis 2 stresses companionship—what the man and woman give to each other as partners. It prompts the author to editorialize. This is why people marry (not merely for procreation). Therefore, a man leaves his father and mother (even though the wife joining her husband's family was the common practice in Hebrew culture) and embraces his wife. They become one flesh (Genesis 2:24). The man and woman were also naked but felt no shame. This segues into what went wrong in the garden.

What should we learn from the differences in these two creation stories? In Genesis 1, we see the creation from God's perspective. In Genesis 2, the writer places us at ground level, standing in the dirt with the man called Adam. We see more closely that the creation was made specifically with the man (and the woman) in mind. We see that God encourages the human to participate in God's work, even giving the man the job of naming the animals (Genesis 2:19–20).

If something is not as it should be, God tweaks it until it is right. God seeks man's response to signal that the creation is now good as God intends it. And so by the end of Genesis 2 as at the end of the seventh day, all is well with the new creation.

But the author of Genesis 2 is not finished with his story. Let's look at Genesis 3:1–13. First, let's note that while the writer continues to use *YHWH* (Peterson's GOD), he records the Serpent and the woman referring to *Elohim* (Peterson's God). Does the author mean to imply by this that the man and woman do not yet know God as intimately as the people Israel will?

Next, observe how swiftly and deftly the author takes us through the unraveling of this idyllic scene. With no preamble he states that the clever Serpent approaches the woman as if to check whether he understands the garden rules correctly. Presumably the woman knew this commandment because she is well aware of it when the crafty Serpent queries her. As a matter of interest, she takes it upon herself to embellish the commandment by adding, "We're not even to *touch* it or we will die" (Genesis 3:3).

But the Serpent knows he can make the woman see otherwise. With only two lines of dialogue he subtly questions God's motivation for the dictum, suggesting that God's commandment is not uttered out of concern for the man and the woman's safety and welfare but rather as a means of protecting the Deity from their advancement to God's own level. What the Serpent is really calling into question is God's trustworthiness. Is the Deity actually good? The Serpent's rebuttal that God's warning is untrue—they won't die if they eat the fruit, and perhaps he even corroborates it by eating the fruit in front of her—convinces the woman. She eats the fruit and offers it to her husband, who does the same. They do not die, but they feel ashamed of their nakedness and seek to cover themselves.

In verse 8, the author presents God walking in the garden, calling to the couple. When God specifically asks the man, "Where are you?" (Genesis 3:9–10), the man answers that his nakedness has made him afraid. Of course, this response tells God exactly what has happened, but the Lord chooses to extract the facts from the man out of his own mouth. "Have you eaten from the tree I commanded you not to eat?" (Genesis 3:11 NIV).

The man responds rather poorly, "The woman you put here with me," implying that it is really God's fault as well as hers, "gave me the fruit and I ate it" (Genesis 3:12 NIV).

Turning to the woman, God receives more of the same, "The serpent deceived me" (Genesis 3:13 NIV). What makes these responses so interesting is that once God confronts the man and woman, neither one takes this opportunity to rebut the commandment. They don't even try out the Serpent's argument on the Deity (so much for being as wise as God). With their excuses and blame passing, they are indeed acknowledging the wrongness of their act—though not their responsibility for it—as well as the legitimacy of God's ordinance.

God dispenses with questioning the Serpent and instead immediately launches into a pronouncement of consequences that will bear on each party in reverse order of His interrogation. Henceforth, the Serpent will crawl on his belly. The woman will have pain in childbirth and be ruled by her husband and the man will have to toil to work the land to get his livelihood. Finally they will all die—not immediately, as the Serpent led them to believe the commandment stated, but eventually. God puts it rather ingloriously, "You started out as dirt, you'll end up dirt" (Genesis 3:19).

Still, God doesn't abandon the man and woman, now named Adam and Eve. The Lord furnishes them with clothing and then drives them out of the garden because for some reason it would be disastrous if they now ate from the Tree of Life. Perhaps if they ate from that eternal fruit now, they would live forever in a state of sin, but the text does not really explain God's action. Adam and Eve have exchanged their carefree existence for a life of hard work.

Christian theology calls this the story of the fall, meaning that the disobedient behavior of the first man and woman explains why the world is no longer good. Milton dubbed it "paradise lost." It is not that God is untrustworthy, as the Serpent suggests, but that humans are. They have broken the contract they had with God. The beautiful creation of Genesis 1 has been set out of kilter, and nothing is quite as God planned it to be. But if God is indeed an all-knowing deity, didn't He realize that this would happen?

This is when we go back to the text of Genesis 2–3 to search for clues in answer to our questions. The narrative unfolds in broad and concise strokes. The man and woman are not named as they commit the first sin. This encourages us to see them as symbols of every man and woman. The commandment not to eat from the Tree of Knowledge of Good and Evil seems somewhat arbitrary.

Why should the knowledge of good and evil be something the humans should avoid? Why would it cause death? The Serpent surmises that the fault lies with God, that the Deity is afraid of competition. Yet we know from Genesis 1 that God explicitly creates humans in His own image. Why should the Lord now be worried about that likeness? What we do see in the story is that God's character is truly benevolent. The Lord centers the creation on the man and then makes the woman so that the two can be companions together. God gives them a beautiful garden to care for where the labor is not arduous. The Deity is available for their questions because God walks through the garden and talks to the humans. Yet the man and the woman still mistrust God despite all the Lord has done. They are still vulnerable to the idea that they could be not just *like* God but *equal* to Him. When God confronts them in their hiding place, their concern for their nakedness can also be understood as their awareness of their transparency before God. They are no longer comfortable in God's presence, not because of God's shaming but because of their own guilt.

The Eden story allows us to perceive the fall of the first man and woman as the pattern for every human's sense of disconnection from God. It is not because of Adam and Eve that the rest of us live in a broken, fallen world. It is because each of us is susceptible both to the suggestion that God is not on our side and, though not logically consistent, the idea that we can be our own god. Yet as long as God makes humans with free will, they will reliably fail this test of obedience. But what was God's alternative? Clearly the testimony from the first three chapters of Genesis shows us a Creator who wants a relationship with humans, a relationship of love. But love cannot be compelled and remain love. How can the Lord, leaving free will intact, transform humans who defy Him (even if it's just occasionally) into beings who choose to love Him and live consistently by God's code of holiness?

In the first three chapters of Genesis, God outlines for us the incredible worthiness of this creation project and also the reason it seems to have a fatal flaw. The flaw is not in God's design so much as it is fallout from God's daring move to give humans their own minds and by extension the possibility of having a loving relationship with their maker. Notice how, contrary to our common method of storytelling that uses a single narrative, the skillful juxtaposition of these two creation stories—one told from God's perspective contrasted with one viewed from the human level—work together to offer the ultimate explanation for why the world we live in is such an agonizing mixture of good and bad. Think how often the bad seems to outweigh the good and how easy it becomes to question whether there is a God behind creation. But then we must remember that this is the beginning of God's story. Herein is the cipher the Lord has set for Himself to solve: How can God effect a change in humans that will prompt them to choose to obey the Deity out of their trust and love for the Lord and therefore live the good existence of God's intention?

Looked at one way, the story of the garden of Eden forms the template for the plot of the rest of the Old Testament.

Comparing the Eden Story to Israel's History

What happens in Eden	What happens in Israel
1. God provides the garden of Eden for Adam and Eve.	1. God provides a Promised Land for His chosen people.
2. God gives Adam and Eve a rule, "Don't eat from this tree."	2. God gives Ten Commandments through Moses to His people.
3. Adam and Eve disobey.	3. Israel disobeys.
4. God sends Adam and Eve out from the garden.	4. After a long history, God sends His people into exile.
5. God continues to care for Adam and Eve until the time is ripe to reconnect the broken bonds.	5. God continues to care for His people until the time is ripe to reconnect the broken bonds.

As we will follow in chapter 3, the stories beginning with Abraham in Genesis 12 form the prequel to the above history by telling how God chooses for Himself the people Israel. Then God provides for His people Israel the land Israel—the Promised Land and the new Eden. This begins with Abraham's purchase of a burial plot for his wife in the land of Canaan in Genesis 23 and is realized fully in the conquest of Canaan narrated in the book of Joshua. In this new Eden there is not just one arbitrary dictum but ten great commandments and 613 smaller ones. In short order it will be very clear that God's people do not keep the Lord's rules but are more than a little prone to blatant disobedience. After much time, and many warnings, Israel will find itself banished from the Promised Land. Although some Jews return to the land of Israel, most are dispersed among the various peoples of the earth.

Yet while the stories and writings of the Old Testament seem to flesh out the pessimistic inevitability of the garden of Eden parable with the lives of real individuals and the history of Israel, it is by no means the whole story. Within the tale of the Israelites' failure to honor their duty to their maker and their fellow beings, God weaves the story of His own counterstrike. God is not willing to let the breach between Himself and humanity be the last word. Unrealistic as it seems to us even now, God not only believes there can be a different outcome. The Lord has always had a plan to accomplish it. What this plan is and how it will work is embedded throughout the narrative, poetry, parables, letters, and prophecy that make up the Bible. As we journey through the biblical landscape from book to book, we will also be looking for clues to answer this question: How will God restore His broken relationship with us? Like a giant math problem, Genesis 1–3 has defined the dilemma, but it will take the rest of the Bible to show the work that leads to the answer. I'd say it's time we begin.

For comparison, the tradition of blaming the presence of evil in the world on womankind probably comes more directly from the Greek myth of Pandora. Zeus, the king of the gods, was angry with Prometheus, one of his allies in his victory over his father, the former king of the gods, because Prometheus had given men the secret of fire. In retaliation, Zeus designed Pandora, the first woman, to be the undoing of mankind (even though men were merely the recipients of fire and not the violators of Zeus' province). All the other gods bestowed gifts on her (hence, her name meaning the gift of all) to enhance her beauty. Still more prominent than her beauty was her curiosity. When she received a box that she was told not to open, she could not restrain herself from discovering what was inside and thereby unleashed onto the earth all the evils known to humankind. It is important to note here the distinction from the biblical first woman. Zeus creates Pandora in order to punish men, knowing that he has built her to obey her curious nature over any edict he might deliver. She is not given any consequence to fear if she cannot contain her inquisitiveness. Nor is she given any purpose to her life beyond being the pawn of the gods. In contrast, the woman who becomes Eve is created to be the companion and helper of the first man and an equal partner in the care of the garden. Both know the dire consequences of disobedience up front but allow the Serpent to persuade them nonetheless. While the woman is the first to eat the fruit, God begins His confrontation with the man. Even though they receive different consequences as a result of their disobedience, there is no implication that God holds one party more responsible than the other. The man and woman together bring God's punishment on themselves. From the beginning God has only acted for their good.

Chapter 3

Does It Really Say That Abraham Is the Father of Three Faiths?

If you've heard of the biblical Abraham lately, it was probably in the aftermath of the September 11 attacks. Suddenly Islam was on the front page of our nation's consciousness, and most Americans realized that they knew very little about this religion. In this context magazines published articles about the Abrahamic faiths, namely Judaism, Christianity, and Islam, which all take Abraham for their father and also claim to worship the same one God.[10] But is this what the Bible says about Abraham?

Again we need to backtrack. Anyone who has ever studied anthropology knows that one characteristic of human societies is that they all develop religions. In ancient times religions claimed to explain things about nature that humans couldn't understand. Most civilizations worshiped gods and goddesses that managed the parts of life that humans couldn't control—their crops, their hunts, their fertility, and their success in war. The hope of religion was to remove the factor of chance or randomness in life and assign it to a deity. Then all one had to do was to appease or placate the deity usually with some kind of sacrifice that the humans who were "in the know" about the deity, the priests and the priestesses, decided the god wanted. Of course, the best that

---

[10] Strictly speaking, there are five major religions in the world today. All three Abrahamic faiths originated in the Middle East. The two eastern religions, Hinduism and Buddhism, began in India.

this could offer was only the illusion of control because between the politics of the power brokers (the priests and the kings) and the reality that man-made gods and goddesses couldn't change the weather or open wombs or certify victory, humans really weren't in control. Even among the ancients, deities were always suffering from poor or at least testy public relations.

Now God created humans and knew ahead of time that they were bound to create their own gods. This was partly because of the human tendency to crave control but also because as our maker, the Lord knew that there was something in us that desired God, that needed to be in a worship relationship with the Lord. Yet there was no way that humans could ever create any religion out of their own minds that was not too confining to apprehend what the real God was like. The best they could come up with was what is described in the preceding paragraph. God had to reveal Himself to people in order to be known. But this was difficult. God is so huge, so beyond our ability to take in. How could such a revelation work? This is where Abraham comes in.[11]

The Bible doesn't begin the story of Abraham until Genesis 12. Scholars name the interim stories of Genesis 4 to 11 "prehistory" and find there much that resembles other contemporary writings in the area of Mesopotamia in terms of plot and style. This section leads off with our first concrete demonstration of the consequences of the fall when, out of jealousy, Cain murders his brother, Abel, and delivers his famous retort (when God asks him what happened to his brother), "Am I my brother's keeper?" (Genesis 4:9 NIV). In common with other Near-Eastern records, we have many genealogies incorporated into the text, but with this important difference: Neighboring cultures' preservation of family lineages guarded (or fabricated) the legitimacy of political rulers, whereas the concern within the Bible rests in keeping

---

[11] I am not saying here that God never revealed Himself to peoples other than the Israelites.

track of the ancestors of God's chosen people through whom the Lord will work.[12] While chapters 4 through 11 make note of the first time *men and women began praying and worshiping in the name of GOD* (Genesis 4:26), they primarily show us a picture of how wicked and increasingly chaotic God's world was becoming as a result of the fall—what we see in the account of Noah and the flood (Genesis 6–8) and the building of the Tower of Babel (Genesis 11).

Among the many people named in Genesis 4–11, the author distinguishes a few with the description that they *walked with God*. Enoch (Genesis 5:21–24) is the first of these; the narrator adds that Enoch "walked steadily with God. And then one day he was simply gone: God took him" (Genesis 5:24), implying that Enoch went to heaven without dying. Noah also walks with God, giving God a reason to save him and his family from the flood that the Lord uses to cleanse the world of its many wicked humans.[13] At first look, the flood story may appear to be a godly attempt to resolve the world's sinfulness by simply getting rid of all the bad actors and working only with the descendants of one who walked with the Lord, but quickly enough we will see that evil abounds among men again. God's plan to convince humans to choose holiness runs in a different line.

Abraham is this different line. At the end of chapter 11, we are introduced to a descendant of Noah named Terah who fathers three sons—Abram (Abraham's name before God changes it), Nahor, and Haran. At some point in Abram's adult life his father, Terah, moved the family from Ur of the Chaldeans (a rather sophisticated city probably along the southeastern end of the Euphrates as the river empties into the Persian Gulf) northwest

---

[12] Brevard Childs, *Introduction to the Old Testament as Scripture,* p. 153.

[13] The author of the flood story records God's voice in direction to Noah but never Noah speaking back. We know that Noah was obedient to God's commands but not whether he ever wondered, for example, *What about the little children who will die in the flood?* Abraham's story will fill this gap.

along the Euphrates to the caravan city called Haran (just south of modern-day Turkey). In both places the worship of a moon god was common. What was uncommon was what happened to Abram and his barren wife, Sarai, after they had settled in Haran for some time.

In a departure from the genealogical recording of chapter 11, chapter 12 begins with God speaking to Abram the following command and promise:

> *Leave your country, your family, and your father's home*
>   *for a land that I will show you.*
> *I'll make you a great nation*
> *And bless you.*
> *I'll make you famous;*
> *You'll be a blessing.*
> *I'll bless those who bless you;*
> *Those who curse you I'll curse.*
> *All the families of the Earth will be blessed through you.*
> (Genesis 12:1–3)

In verse 4, the narrator tells us simply, "So Abram left, just as God said." We see two points immediately. Firstly Abram, like Noah, is readily obedient to God's command. We are not told what convinced Abram to comply; just that he did, packing up his whole household, even including his nephew, Lot, and his family. The second point is that this indeed is God's first move in this master plan. The plan begins with a promise to Abram that he will be a great nation—an interesting pledge to make to a man with no descendants. But the ending promise is more far-reaching. "All the families of Earth will be blessed through you." I point this out here because it shows God as a master strategist who knows from His first move what His last move will be.

Abram is said to be seventy-five in Genesis 12:4, when God first calls him. The land the Lord shows him is the land of Canaan, what would later become Israel. There are a couple of problems with Canaan, however. First Canaan already has inhabitants, and though there is room enough for Abram and company to move in, the space isn't limitless. In addition, the land is prone to times of famine. A famine breaks out shortly after Abram moves there, and he and his entourage have to seek food in Egypt. Pharaoh, ruler of Egypt, keeps a harem, and Abram fears that he will be expendable if the monarch looks on his beautiful wife, Sarai, and desires her. In anticipation of this dilemma, he instructs Sarai to agree to say that she is merely his sister.

It turns out that Abram is correct in his assessment of Sarai's attractiveness, and once they arrive in Egypt, she is immediately taken into the royal house. Abram profits from having a lovely "sister," and he accumulates both servants and animals to increase his wealth. But where Abram sees in a crafty lie an expedient strategy for saving his neck, God views a pollution of His plan. God has already told Abram in 12:7 that the land of Canaan would go to Abram's offspring, but Abram with his barren wife probably assumes that God is speaking metaphorically. Moreover, Abram likely presumes that Pharaoh will not be able to impregnate Sarai because of her infertility. But God plans to open Sarai's womb, and the Lord is not going to let it be said that anyone but Abram has fathered the child. Interestingly enough, God does not take Abram to task for the lie. Instead, the household of Pharaoh becomes seriously sick, and Pharaoh knows immediately that it is because Abram has played him falsely. (Perhaps a little bird named God has told him.) Pharaoh gives Abram the tongue-lashing he deserves for lying and sends him packing with all his acquired wealth and personnel inexplicably intact.

When Abram and company return to Canaan, they are rich. But now the animals are too many to graze together on the land they have been sharing with nephew Lot, and moreover, fights keep breaking out among the household shepherds. Acknowledging the need to split the family apart, Abram magnanimously offers the choice to Lot, "Isn't there plenty of land here? Let's separate. If you go left, I'll go right; if you go right, I'll go left" (Genesis 13:9). Lot takes the plain of the Jordan since it recalls to him verdant Egypt and the *garden of the Lord* where the water is plentiful. Still, our narrator indicates foreboding when he reminds us that the city of Sodom lies here. Lot's choice leaves Abram with the land of Canaan. God takes this moment to share with Abram a restatement of His initial promise, "Open your eyes, look around. ... Everything you see ... I will give you and your children forever. I'll make your descendants like dust—counting your descendants will be as impossible as counting the dust of the Earth" (Genesis 13:14–16). So Abram builds an altar to God.

Time passes. There is some local infighting and Abram shows himself to be a good military strategist and manages to save Lot from neighboring kings (Genesis 14:14–16). But still there is no child. Finally the beginning of chapter 15 records a conversation between Abram and God. God appears to Abram in a vision and says, "Don't be afraid, Abram. I'm your shield. Your reward will be grand!" (Genesis 15:1). But now we hear Abram speak back, "God, Master, what use are your gifts as long as I'm childless and Eliezer of Damascus is going to inherit everything? See, you've given me no children, and now a mere house servant is going to get it all" (Genesis 15:2-3). It's the first time we've heard anyone talking back to God since the Cain story, and we have to agree that Abram's point is well taken. But God responds, "Don't worry, he won't be your heir; a son from your body will be your heir" (Genesis 15:4). Then God leads Abram outside to look up at the sky, and reformulating His previous vow, the Lord tells Abram, "Can you count the stars? Neither will you be able to count your descendants" (Genesis 15:5). The narrative then reports simply that Abram believed God (and clearly this belief was based on nothing but trust), and God counted Abram's faith in the Lord as righteousness (Genesis 15:6).

Once Abram's trust in the person of God is established, the conversation opens up further. God explains to Abram that He is the same God who originally called his father, Terah, to move out of Ur. All was done so that God could give Abram this land to own. In a world where every community has its own gods, this is an important revelation to Abram. This God that Abram is speaking to has been at work directing him for a long time and has powers beyond the gods Abram had grown up knowing. Yet despite this God's extraordinariness, Abram feels comfortable enough to question him. "Master God, how I am to know this, that it will all be mine?" (Genesis 15:8). Even faith can ask for confirmation. God instructs Abram to make an animal sacrifice (a familiar practice of worship for Abram) to the Lord. As Abram tends the sacrifice ceremony, a sleep overcomes him, and he is filled with a sense of dread. In this dreamy state God speaks the future to Abram. "Know this: your descendants will live as outsiders in a land not theirs; they'll be enslaved and beaten down for 400 years. Then I'll punish their slave masters; your offspring will march out of there loaded with plunder. But not you; you'll have a long and full life and die a good and peaceful death" (Genesis 15:13–15).

Whatever exhilaration Abram may have felt after this encounter, when he came inside to tell Sarai, it is unlikely that she could have shared in it. A woman's infertility was a problem in the ancient world. With no birth control it would be obvious to all that something was wrong with a married woman who did not become pregnant. Moreover, remaining childless carried with it a huge social stigma. But women tend to be resourceful, and in that world it was a common practice for a barren wife wealthy enough to have a maidservant to offer that woman to her husband in the hopes of having a child through her. In chapter 16, we learn that Abram has lived in Canaan for ten years, meaning that God's initial promise is that old as well. What the narrative doesn't reveal is how much time elapses between Abram's conversations with God in chapter 15 and Sarai's proposal in the beginning of chapter 16 to have Abram sleep with her Egyptian maid, Hagar. Possibly when Abram shared the God encounter with Sarai, she took note of God's word to Abram, "A child of your own body," and figured that the offspring could come through a surrogate. Perhaps she was thinking, too, that "God helps him who helps himself," a line that doesn't show up anywhere in the Bible despite how many people misquote it. It seems logical enough even to us. But humans don't operate on logic alone.

Hagar does become pregnant and immediately begins to lord it over Sarai. This is more than Sarai bargained for, and she complains to Abram, who dismisses her with a "do what you want with your maidservant" (Genesis 16:8). With this license, Sarai abuses Hagar, and Hagar resorts to running away. Now God intervenes. The Lord sends to Hagar an angel who tells her that she must put up with her mistress' mistreatment because this child is part of God's plan. God will give her a large family, and the child she now bears will be a "bucking bronco of a man, a real fighter, fighting and being fought, always stirring up trouble, always at odds with his family" (Genesis 16:12). Despite this fairly disturbing prophecy, Hagar deems the God who spoke to her the "God who sees me" and derives from this encounter enough courage to return to the Abram household and give Abram his firstborn son, Ishmael. Abram was eighty-six years old.

Again there is a lapse in the narrative perhaps corresponding to a hiatus in Abram's contact from the Lord. Chapter 17 picks up thirteen years later when Abram is ninety-nine. More or less out of the blue God appears on the scene and announces to Abram, "I am The Strong God, live entirely before me, live to the hilt! I'll make a covenant between us and I'll give you a huge family" (Genesis 17:1–2). Appropriately Abram prostrates himself before the Deity. Though they have talked in the past, hearing the Lord's voice is not something that happens every day for Abram. Moreover, he has probably considered that God has made good on His promise in his son, Ishmael. What is God doing showing up now?

God proceeds to explain Himself,

> This is my covenant with you: You'll be the father of many nations. Your name will no longer be Abram, but Abraham, meaning that I'm making you a father of fathers—I'll make nations from you, kings will issue from you. I'm establishing my covenant between me and you, a covenant that includes your descendants, a covenant that goes on and on and on, a covenant that commits me to be your God and the God of your descendants. (Genesis 17:4–7)

The covenant will include the ownership of the land of Canaan. Abraham's sign that he agrees to this covenant is the rite of circumcision to be performed on every male, slave or free, insider or outsider, who joins his household. The circumcision provides a permanent mark in the body to correspond to the permanence of God's promises.

Perhaps Abraham is thinking this is well and good. Circumcision is a relatively small price to pay for what God is offering in return. He must have been amazed when God continued, "And Sarai your wife: Don't call her Sarai any longer; call her Sarah. I will bless her—yes! I'll give you a son by her! Nations will come from her; kings of nations will come from her" (Genesis 17:15–16). This was over the top. The narrator even tells us that Abraham laughs at such a preposterous idea. "Can a hundred-year-old man father a son? And can Sarah, at ninety years, have a baby?" (Genesis 17:17). He attempts to bring God back to reality, "Oh, keep Ishmael alive and well before you!" (Genesis 17:18). Why should God offer something so ridiculous now when Ishmael was already a boy growing to manhood and beloved by Abraham? But the Lord persists, "That's not what I mean. Your wife, Sarah, will have a baby, a son. Name him Isaac (Laughter). I'll establish my covenant with him and his descendants, a covenant that lasts forever" (Genesis 17:19). Anticipating a father's concern, God then adds, "And Ishmael? Yes, I heard your prayer for him. I'll also bless him; I'll make sure he has plenty of children—a huge family. He'll father twelve princes; I'll make him a great nation. But I'll establish my covenant with Isaac whom Sarah will give you about this time next year" (Genesis 17:20-21). By God's own words we see Abraham fathering both Jewish and Arab peoples. Perhaps you begin to see why relations in the current Middle East are still so complicated.

Apparently the notion that old postmenopausal Sarah would produce a child was so shocking to Abraham that he had to hear the news twice. The second telling takes place in chapter 18 when three visitors approach Abraham's camp in the heat of the day. As was the custom of most ancient societies, strangers were treated as honored guests. You never want to be caught being unkind to someone you don't know. The person could always be a god or one of his messengers (an angel)! Abraham greets the trio with full courtesy and makes a hurried aside to Sarah within their tent that she needs to start making bread. How astounding that these visitors should ask for Sarah when they finish eating! One of the three spells it out for Sarah's benefit this time. "I'm coming back about this time next year. When I arrive, your wife Sarah will have a son" (Genesis 18:10). Sarah has been listening from within the tent. Like Abraham, she is unable to contain her incredulity and laughs to herself as she says, "An old woman like me? Get pregnant? With this old man of a husband?" (Genesis 18:12). But now God speaks again to Abraham, "Why did Sarah laugh? ... Is anything too hard for God?" (Genesis 18:14). Sarah tries to deny it, but God confirms, "Yes you did; you laughed" (Genesis 18:15). What seems like a joke will bring to Abraham and Sarah the laughter (Isaac) of joy.

What happens next proves to be an interesting turn of events in terms of the development of Abraham's relationship with God. In Genesis 18:16, the three heavenly visitors get up to leave and Abraham walks out with them to see them off. Suddenly we hear God's voice again as He says,

> Shall I keep back from Abraham what I'm about to do? Abraham is going to become a large and strong nation; all the nations of the world are going to find themselves blessed through him. Yes, I've settled on him as the one to train his children and future family to observe God's way of life, live kindly and generously and fairly so that God can complete in Abraham what he promised him. (Genesis 18:17–19)

God certainly sounds mysterious. It is as if the Deity is consulting with someone else but within Abraham's hearing. When the Lord continues, God speaks directly to Abraham and says, "The cries of the victims in Sodom and Gomorrah are deafening; the sin of those cities is immense. I'm going down to see for myself, see if what they're doing is as bad as it sounds. Then I'll know" (Genesis 18:20–21).

Something in God's manner must have also indicated to Abraham how God planned to resolve this outrage because Abraham's response is to block God's path.

> Are you serious? Are you planning on getting rid of all the good people right along with the bad? What if there are fifty good people left in the city; would you lump the good with the bad and get rid of the lot? Wouldn't you spare the city for the sake of those fifty innocents? I can't believe you'd do that, kill off the good and the bad alike as if there were no difference between them. Doesn't the judge of all the Earth judge with justice? (Genesis 18:23–25)

We find ourselves agreeing enthusiastically with Abraham. Far be it from God not to be both just and merciful. Hasn't God just stated that He is counting on Abraham to teach the upcoming generations to live *kindly, generously, and fairly?*

Yet God's response to Abraham surprises us further. The Deity enters into a negotiation ritual with Abraham almost as if they were haggling at a bazaar. "If I find fifty decent people in the city of Sodom, I'll spare the place just for them" (Genesis 18:26). Abraham picks up the cue and, with proper humility, rejoins, "Do I, a mere mortal made from a handful of dirt, dare to open my mouth again to my Master? What if the fifty fall short by five—would you destroy the city because of those missing five?" (Genesis 18:27–28). So begins a series of bartering exchanges between Abraham and God with God always agreeing to Abraham's insistence that the threshold number of good people be lowered until they stop at ten. We don't know why Abraham neglects to press God further, but God does agree to spare the city for even ten good souls.

What does this exchange show us about God, Abraham, and their relationship? Some skeptics will look at this scene and say that the Hebrews have anthropomorphized their deity (the act of humans making God into their own image). On the other hand, is it not just as credible that God dons a human manner for the purpose of facilitating this conversation with Abraham? In the first place God must have known what Abraham's response to the proposed destruction of Sodom and Gomorrah would be. The out-loud wondering whether or not to share this information with Abraham shows that somehow God thinks it is important for Abraham to weigh in on the situation. Since God is planning on Abraham's descendants being a blessing to the world's future generations, the Lord must be pleased with Abraham's revulsion to rampant destruction and particularly to his concern that good and bad be punished alike as if it doesn't matter how people behave.

In this encounter we see Abraham speaking rather boldly to God. It is interesting that his spoken reasons for objecting to the decimation of Sodom do not include the fate of his nephew, Lot, although that could have been in his mind. Despite his temerity in challenging the Lord, Abraham takes care to demonstrate his awareness of his humble status as a human before the Almighty. But his tone is still one of placation, as though he was thinking that if he could only say the right words, he would get the Lord to do what he wanted. Abraham does get what he wants, but we, the listeners, don't get the sense that Abraham has actually bent God's will. Yet knowing the huge plans God has for Abraham, it is good to hear that Abraham is capable of caring about moral righteousness. But by now what you really want to know is this: "What's so bad about Sodom?" Chapter 19 gives us an excellent example of what God is so fed up about, and it works particularly well in juxtaposition to Abraham's recent reception of God's three visitors.

After the Lord finishes speaking with Abraham, two angels approach the city of Sodom. At the city gate they meet Abraham's nephew, Lot, who, showing good manners because the apparent men are strangers to the city, insists on preparing them a good meal and taking them in for the night. Before long, however, the men of the town gather around Lot's home, pressing in on all sides. They call out, "Where are the men who are staying with you for the night? Bring them out so we can have our sport with them" (Genesis 19:5). (Note that the NIV translates more bluntly, "So that we can have sex with them.") Appalled that the menfolk of Sodom would flout the code of hospitality so brutally, Lot steps outside and tries to appease them by saying, "Brothers, please, don't be vile! Look, I have two daughters, virgins; let me bring them out; you can take your pleasure with them, but don't touch these men—they're my guests" (Genesis 19:7–8). But the townsmen respond, "Get lost! You drop in from nowhere and now you're going to tell us how to run our lives.

We'll treat you worse than them!" (Genesis 19:9). Immediately they attempt to barge into the house, but the angels pull Lot inside, lock the door, and strike all the offenders blind. Next they instruct Lot to gather his family so that they might survive the destruction they will momentarily rain down on Sodom. The narrator notes, "Lot was dragging his feet. The men grabbed Lot's arm, and the arms of his wife and daughters—God was so merciful to them!—and dragged them to safety outside the city" (Genesis 19:16). The rescuers warn the family not to look back, but Lot's wife does anyway and becomes a pillar of salt. We are left thinking that if Lot, who was willing to sacrifice his daughters, merits saving, the standard of righteousness must have been set fairly low.

Now the narrative takes us back to Abraham and Sarah to what sounds like a replay of their trip to Egypt in chapter 12. As we read through this second version of Abraham playing loose with the truth, we have to wonder what purpose it serves at this point in the narrative. In chapter 20, Abraham and Sarah have migrated for a while into Gerar, and Abraham has again taken the precaution of calling Sarah his sister. The king of Gerar, Abimelech, sends for Sarah and takes her into his house. But before he can sleep with her, God comes to him in a dream and tells him that Sarah is indeed Abraham's wife. Abimelech protests to God that it isn't his fault. Both Abraham and Sarah have lied to him. God confirms that He knows this and that is precisely why the Lord is giving Abimelech this warning. Note how God's tone with Abimelech in verses 6–7 comes across as almost apologetic as if He's saying, "Sorry, but this is the only prophet I have to work with." He continues saying that Abraham will pray to save Abimelech's life and household as long as Sarah is returned. Abimelech wakes early in the morning in order to put Sarah back in Abraham's hands. Abraham does not escape a thorough recrimination for his lie, and we can't be very impressed with his defense. "I just assumed that there was no fear of God in this place and that they'd kill me to get my wife. Besides the truth is that she is my half sister" (Genesis 20:11–12). Abraham's impulse to scatter the blame is deeply reminiscent of the Eden story.

If we try to interpret this episode within the chronology of the events just described, the ages of Abraham and Sarah strain our believability. Therefore, the story serves a different purpose than mere historical record. Let's note what it points out about Abraham's character. If we were tempted to accord virtue to Abraham based on his favorable comparison with Lot and the Sodomites, the repeat of this deception story reminds us that Abraham is not yet a stunning example of righteousness. It looks as if not much progress has really been made in human moral evolution. But still the story does serve to underline the legitimacy of Sarah's offspring, who is right around the corner.

Isaac arrives in chapter 21, and there is understandably much rejoicing. But eventually there is another showdown between Sarah and Hagar. Sometime after Isaac's weaning, Sarah has caught Ishmael, now in his late teens, making fun of Isaac. Perhaps it was the last straw for her. She comes to Abraham and demands, "Get rid of this slave woman and her son. No child of this slave is going to share inheritance with my son Isaac!" (Genesis 21:10). Since Abraham has never stopped loving Ishmael as his son, Sarah's edict cuts him to the quick. But God consoles him, "Don't feel badly about the boy and your maid. Do whatever Sarah tells you. Your descendants will come through Isaac. Regarding your maid's son, be assured that I'll also develop a great nation from him—he's your son too" (Genesis 21:12–13).

Despite his pain at their parting, Abraham obediently sees Hagar and Ishmael off early the next morning. Again God ministers to the Egyptian woman, showing her a well when she feared that she and her son would die of thirst. An angel speaks to her as well and reassures her of the good future God has planned. "What's wrong, Hagar? Don't be afraid. God has heard the boy and knows the fix he's in. Up now, go get the boy. Hold him tight. I'm going to make of him a great nation" (Genesis 21:17–18).

After this loss of Ishmael, life appears to return to normal for Abraham. He continues to prosper. He conducts business with his neighbors, negotiates for well rights, watches Isaac grow, and worships his Lord. But actually something extraordinary has been happening inside Abraham, a transformation of his relationship with God that the author exposits by means of the story told in chapter 22. Without any real introduction, the narrator begins, "After all this, God tested Abraham" (Genesis 22:1). The word *test* immediately sets us, the listeners, on edge. We're back in a classroom with the teacher passing out exam papers, and we're protesting, "We didn't know there was going to be a test!" What can a test mean? Why does Abraham need to be tested? With all this churning in our minds we hear the exchange between God and Abraham. God calls, "Abraham!" and Abraham answers, "Yes? I'm listening." Despite our anxiety, God seems not to have startled Abraham this time. God doesn't have to say immediately, "Don't be afraid!" and Abraham has not fallen on his face in terror. Perhaps in the time that has passed, they've talked more frequently. Still, they are not equals. Abraham's response anticipates God asking something of him. He is ready to act.

God does have a burden to place on Abraham. "Take your dear son Isaac whom you love and go to the land of Moriah. Sacrifice him there as a burnt offering on one of the mountains that I'll point out to you" (Genesis 22:2). We want to say, "What!" This makes no sense to us. Why would God require a human sacrifice? Moreover, why would the Lord require the sacrifice of this long-promised son, in whom rests nearly all the promises God has made to Abraham? Let us look again at what God has said. "Take your dear son Isaac *whom you love*." God is well aware of the cost of what He is asking. How can God mix compassion with such an outrageous request? Yet the author takes us through none of these heart-wrenching emotions. Read how concisely the narrative of 22:3–19 speaks the rest of the story to us. What seems at the beginning to be a negation of everything that God has promised and stood for ends up resolved as we have not been led to anticipate. The refusal of the narrator to second-guess the action with moral or emotional commentary allows the story to unfold with maximum impact. If anything, when we, the listeners, are full of anxiety for Abraham, it is he who keeps our unrest at bay with his swift and determined acceptance of God's bidding. He leaves the servants and tells them *we* will return after our worship. He tells Isaac that God will provide the sacrifice. For a moment we may wonder, *Does he know something we do not?* But at the climax Abraham must still tie Isaac up and place him on the altar and lift the knife with the intention to kill. And God calls it off. It was God's intention not to have Isaac become a burnt offering but to expose Abraham's faith. Actually Abraham has passed this test of trust in every way that we can imagine. He has not delayed to do God's will. He has not unburdened his own pain at the prospect of sacrificing his son to anyone concerned—not to Sarah, not to the servants, and not even to Isaac. He does not rage against God as if the Deity is forcing his hand. He does not cower out of fear that God will harm him if he refuses what God asks. Instead, his tone throughout the ordeal is one of peaceful and courageous trust, of feeling the leading of God in every step, no matter the cost or pain.

What is the outcome of the test? The text shows us the words of God rejoicing at Abraham's obedience. Clearly this is meant as a reversal of that original flagrant renunciation of God's commandment in Eden. But still we may wonder why God would put Abraham through a test, especially since God must have already known how he would perform. Clearly then the test is not for God. It is for Abraham, who does not even know that it is a test, a chance to realize how far his faith has grown. And the test is for us, the listeners. We need to see what it looks like for a human to choose to trust God above all else. Abraham, this mere human, without being perfect, is able to show God the kind of obedience that allows God not only to bless him but to build a people who will bless the world as well.

What do we learn from Abraham's obedience? Abraham trusts God to be good. Even though what is asked is abhorrent, Abraham believes that doing as God says will render a good outcome no matter how strange the request might seem. This is a far cry from a man and a woman in paradise being told they can do anything except for this one thing. But the main difference between the sin of Eden and the binding of Isaac involves the depth of the relationship established between the parties. In Eden God gave the man and the woman everything and required little of them, and even the little proved too much. With Abraham, God worked with time, allowing the relationship with Abraham to grow and develop. From the very beginning God also asks Abraham to do things, and Abraham obeys. First it is a matter of leaving his home to go to a place God will show him. We do not really know why Abraham trusts God in this first instance. Christians call this mysterious ability to believe "grace." But we can see how over time each episode of God asking something from Abraham and eventually delivering something to Abraham strengthens Abraham's trust in God. It is noteworthy that though Abraham grows more comfortable with God over time (he ceases to fall on his face in fear every time God speaks to him), God never loses His mystery in Abraham's eyes. Abraham seems to accept God's otherness, His beyondness. When he sets out to sacrifice Isaac, he puts aside his questions as if to say, "I cannot expect to understand God, but this need not stop me from loving and serving him." Later authors of Scripture in the New Testament sum it up by calling Abraham a "friend of God."

Our original question asked if the Bible sees Abraham as the father of many faiths, three faiths specifically. We know that the Bible is very aware of Abraham's status as the father of many nations. Abraham means *father of fathers*. As we will see, the descendants of Abraham become the fathers of many peoples. By tradition, Islam claims Ishmael for its father, and Jacob, the second son of Isaac, whose name God changes to Israel, is the last of the three Patriarchs of Judaism. Christianity traces itself through Judaism back to the faith of Abraham. In fact, all three religions see the near sacrifice of Isaac story as an example of their understanding of faith. For Christianity it takes on added meaning in the story of Jesus, God's own Son, whose sacrifice on the cross is not called off.

A further dimension to the binding of Isaac story remains. The author of Chronicles maintains that the site of Abraham's test, the region of Moriah (Genesis 22:2), is actually the Mount Moriah, on which Solomon built the original temple of Judaism. The Babylonians destroyed this first temple during their routing of Jerusalem in 586 BCE, but some fifty years later Ezra and the returning Jews would rebuild it on the same spot. This second temple fell to the Romans in 70 CE. In 691 CE, Muslims built the Dome of the Rock at this same location in order to commemorate Abraham's near sacrifice of Ishmael (as their tradition teaches). It still stands there today, giving us another clue in understanding the tensions between Israel and Islam.

Though we have answered this chapter's question, we need to continue our journey through the remainder of Genesis to gather more insight into what God is seeking to accomplish by befriending Abraham and his family. After God averts Abraham's sacrifice of Isaac, the text reminds us that the promises God has made to Abraham—the promise of the land and progeny—have yet to be fully delivered. The land comes first. In chapter 23, we learn that Sarah dies, and Abraham purchases a burial plot for her from the Hittites. Chapter 24 follows with the tale of how Abraham sends his servant off to Haran, the city Abraham had moved to with his father so many years before. Abraham wants to find a bride for Isaac from amongst his own people, not the local Canaanites. Observe how the nervous servant charged with this daunting task calls upon Abraham's God to lead him to the right woman (Genesis 24:12–25). Just as he has prayed, the servant finds Rebekah, Abraham's grandniece through his brother, Nahor. Nahor's son, Bethuel, Rebekah's father, as well as her brother Laban acknowledge to the servant, "This is totally from GOD … Rebekah is yours" (Genesis 24:50–51). Interestingly Rebekah also gets asked if she is willing to go, and she responds enthusiastically, "I'm ready to go" (Genesis 24:58). Then in the Bible's first mention of love in marriage, our narrator explains, "He (Isaac) married Rebekah and she became his wife and he loved her" (Genesis 24:67). This marriage added to the burial plot purchase brings Abraham two steps closer to the fulfillment of God's promises. Thus, Abraham is able to die in peace, having lived a long and full life as God predicted he would (Genesis 15:15). We are pleased to hear that both his sons join to bury him beside his wife Sarah (Genesis 25:9–10).

Although Isaac is the second Patriarch of Judaism, Genesis gives us considerably less information about him than about his father Abraham. We learn in Genesis 24:67 that he marries Rebekah, and in Genesis 25:21, we see him praying to the Lord on behalf of his wife because she is barren. This time God answers the fertility prayer with twins, two sons named Esau (meaning *hairy*) and Jacob (meaning *heel* since he is born grasping his brother's heel and also meaning *deceiver*). Yet before they are even born, God tells Rebekah, "Two nations are in your womb, two peoples butting heads while still in your body. One people will overpower the other, and the older will serve the younger" (Genesis 25:23). Sure enough, God's Word begins its fulfillment in the attitude of the parents. Once the twins arrive, Isaac favors firstborn Esau, while Rebekah connects deeply with Jacob.

For any parent of more than one child, it will come as no surprise that Esau and Jacob emerge from the womb as utterly different children. Drawn to the outdoors, Esau becomes an excellent hunter and pleases Isaac with the game he catches. On the other hand, Jacob tends to stay by Rebekah and learns to cook. In their first piece of recorded rivalry, Jacob has been making a stew at home when Esau comes in from hunting, starving. Esau demands, "Give me some of that red stew—I'm starved" (Genesis 25:30). Jacob retorts, "Make me a trade: my stew for your rights as the firstborn" (Genesis 25:31). Does it sound to you like Jacob has been planning this? In characteristic haste, Esau replies, "I'm starving! What good is a birthright if I'm dead?" (Genesis 25:32). Jacob makes Esau swear in Genesis 25:33, and with that stroke Esau yields up his right as the firstborn to receive the family inheritance. We, the listeners, see Esau's rash behavior as problematic, but we also know that Jacob has taken unfair advantage.

With this introduction to Isaac and Rebekah's family life, the stage returns to Isaac who, in chapter 26, replays some of his father's experiences. During a famine he and Rebekah visit another Abimelech in Gerar. God appears to him in this moment of stress and repeats the promises given to Abraham,

> Stay here in this land and I'll be with you and bless you. I'm giving you and your children all these lands, fulfilling the oath that I swore to your father Abraham. I'll make your descendants as many as the stars in the sky and give them all these lands. All the nations of the Earth will get a blessing for themselves through your descendants. And why? Because Abraham obeyed my summons and kept my charge—my commands, my guidelines and my teachings. (Genesis 26:3–5)

But even with this reassurance, Isaac stumbles just as his father did. Once they move to Gerar, he claims Rebekah is his sister. Although she is not taken into the harem, when Abimelech observes Isaac caressing Rebekah one day, he calls him on the carpet. Again it is the foreign king who delivers the reprimand for lying. Nonetheless, Isaac accumulates wealth, so much that Abimelech asks him to leave. He returns to the territory of Abraham, and God appears to him again saying, "I am the God of Abraham your father; don't fear a thing because I'm with you. I'll bless you and make your children flourish because of Abraham my servant" (Genesis 26:24). Like Abraham, Isaac builds an altar to the Lord. From this point on, however, though Isaac continues on the stage, our text shifts focus to Jacob, the one God has selected to become the namesake of the people of Israel.

Jacob and Esau continue at odds with each other. After Jacob's appropriation of his brother's birthright, their next encounter begins in Genesis 27:1 at what we are told is Isaac's deathbed. Isaac calls Esau to his side and bids him go out and hunt down some fine game for Isaac to eat. When Esau serves it to his father, Isaac will pronounce his blessing on his firstborn before he passes away. Dutifully Esau sets out to obey his father. Meanwhile, Rebekah has eavesdropped on the conversation. Not content that her favorite has already acquired his elder brother's birthright, she will now conspire with Jacob to steal the blessing as well. Rebekah sends Jacob out to the household flock to pick out two choice goats that she will prepare just as Isaac prefers. Jacob is then to serve them to his father as though he were Esau and therefore obtain the paternal blessing. Not opposed to the idea of the mission, Jacob's only concern is getting caught, especially since his brother is hairy. Rebekah has already considered this contingency and has saved out some of Esau's good clothing for Jacob to dress in, and then she places goatskins on Jacob's hands and neck so that when Isaac (whose eyesight is failing) touches him, Jacob will feel hairy like Esau. Quite an elaborate plot.

As the scheme unwinds in Genesis 27:18–27, we observe Isaac pronouncing his personal blessing on the son he thinks is Esau only to have the real Esau turn up as the last words leave his mouth. According to the thinking of the day, once Isaac has given the blessing, regardless of the deceptive circumstances, the blessing sticks. In a fury Isaac proclaims that the sneaky Jacob has now been made the master of his brother. Aghast, Esau vows to kill Jacob as soon as Isaac has been properly mourned. As neither Rebekah nor Jacob finds an empty threat in Esau's words, Jacob must now run for his life. Ironically for all her conspiring to assure Jacob's financial and political security within the family, Rebekah now sends her beloved son off basically empty-handed. Still, she is careful to supply Isaac with a plausible reason for Jacob's flight. Seemingly out of the blue she announces to Isaac, "I'm sick to death of these Hittite women. If Jacob also marries a native Hittite woman, why live?" (Genesis 27:46). This touches a nerve with Isaac because Esau has already married two local Hittite women in Genesis 26:34–35, and Isaac and Rebekah actually agreed that this was a bad idea. With Rebekah's maneuvering, Jacob now receives even more from his father—the blessing-laden bidding to travel to his mother's birth city of Haran, where her brother, Laban, lives. Rebekah and Isaac both want Jacob to marry one of his cousins. Esau also finds this a credible explanation of Jacob's flight and shows his bitterness toward his parents' disapproval of his Canaanite spouses by marrying one of Ishmael's daughters (Genesis 28:8–9).

Despite acquiring what amounts to a triple blessing—the birthright, Isaac's personal blessing meant for Esau, and finally his father's sanction on his running away—when Jacob gets on the road, he is alone. The first night camping out he dreams of angels walking up and down a stairway that leads from the ground up to the sky. Perhaps you have heard of this referred to as Jacob's ladder. Then the Lord appears to Jacob and repeats the words the Lord spoke first to Abraham and then to Isaac,

> I am GOD, the God of Abraham your father and the God of Isaac. I'm giving the ground on which you are sleeping to you and to your descendants. Your descendants will be

as the dust of the Earth; they'll stretch from east to west and from north to south. All the families of the Earth will bless themselves in you and your descendants. Yes, I'll stay with you, I'll protect you wherever you go, and I'll bring you back to this very ground. I'll stick with you until I've done everything I promised you. (Genesis 28:13–15)

With these words, God introduces Himself to Jacob and offers to be his God as He has been God to Isaac and Abraham. It is important to note here the enactment of God's plan. God knows that faith is not something a person can inherit. Just because Abraham believed does not mean that Isaac or Jacob will. We can see from the stealing of the blessing story that Jacob knows about his father's God because he uses the line "*Your* God cleared the way for me" (Genesis 27:20) when Isaac questions the speedy delivery of his meal. But Jacob has no personal relationship with this God. Nor does he appear to have much interest. After the dream, however, Jacob is impressed. He awakes from his vision full of fear and awe, remarking, "GOD is in this place—truly. And I didn't even know it" (Genesis 28:16). Awash with newly felt solemnity, he converts the stone he had made into a pillow the night before into a pillar that he anoints with oil. Then he dubs the place "Bethel" (God's house) (Genesis 28:18–19). Yet his first foray into faith abounds in conditions. He vows, "If God stands by me and protects me on this journey on which I'm setting out, keeps me in food and clothing, and brings me back in one piece to my father's house, this GOD will be my God" (Genesis 28:20–21). Apparently this was enough of a beginning for God.

Jacob does make it safely to Haran, and whom should he meet upon entering the town but his very own first cousin, Rachel. Jacob had been making conversation with some men at the well when he notes Rachel's arrival with her father's sheep. Her beauty moves him to gallantry, and he single-handedly rolls the stone over the well away in order to water the sheep for her. Knowing from the men that she is his mother's niece, he kisses her in greeting and then breaks into tears. Rachel runs to her father, Laban, with the news of his sister's son, and Jacob is welcomed into the family with ready embraces (Genesis 29:1–12). After a month's hospitality, however, Laban has tired of feeding his nephew for nothing. He offers Jacob a job and asks him to name how Laban shall pay him. Probably Laban had already figured out that he was in love with Rachel. Magnanimously Jacob offers to work for Laban for seven years in return for leave to marry Rachel. Laban agrees, and the author records this observation: "So Jacob worked seven years for Rachel. But it seemed like a few days, he loved her so much" (Genesis 29:20).

When the momentous wedding day arrives, Laban throws a huge feast. Jacob goes through the marriage ceremony only to find Rachel's older sister, Leah, in the marriage bed with him. Needless to say, Jacob is not pleased. Laban explains that since Leah is the older sister, he could hardly be expected to marry Rachel off before her. Jacob is not happy but bows to inevitability. He must finish the honeymoon week with Leah and then would be allowed to marry Rachel as well, though he would still have to work an additional seven years to pay the bride price for two wives (Genesis 29:22–30). As Jacob cheated Esau, now he knows what it is like to be on the receiving end of another's deception.

We don't have to work hard to imagine the complicated love triangle begotten by Laban's bait and switch. Leah knows that Jacob prefers her sister. But Leah is fertile, and she takes her ability to bear sons as a sign that God understands her misery. On the other hand, Rachel has Jacob's love but cannot get pregnant. By the time Leah brings four sons into the world—Reuben, Simeon, Levi, and Judah—jealousy drives Rachel into supplying a surrogate to Jacob as Sarah had once done with her maid, Hagar. Rachel's maid, Bilhah, gives Jacob two more sons—Dan and Naphtali—and now it is Leah's turn to become jealous. What worked for her sister now works for her. She presents her maid, Zilpah, to Jacob, and sons seven, Gad, and eight, Asher, arrive (Genesis 29:31–30:13).

By this time Rachel is utterly frustrated. When she sees her nephew, Reuben, Leah's eldest, harvesting mandrakes (also called love apples because of the superstition that they would enhance a woman's fertility) and bringing them to his mother, she asks her sister to share. Leah is ready with her retort, "Wasn't it enough that you got my husband away from me? And now you also want my son's mandrakes?" (Genesis 30:15). Rachel concedes, "All right. I'll let him sleep with you tonight in exchange for your son's love-apples" (Genesis 30:15). Thus, Jacob returns to Leah's bed and in time gives her two more sons—Issachar and Zebulun—as well as a daughter named Dinah. After all this, God remembers Rachel and opens her womb. Joseph becomes Jacob's eleventh son as well as his favorite (Genesis 30:16–24).

Having finally gotten a son on Rachel, Jacob now feels that he would like to return home. But it is complicated. He cannot just pick up and leave with all his wives and children. It is not lost on Uncle Laban that he has enjoyed tremendous prosperity ever since he has had Jacob in his employ. Twenty years have passed since Jacob's arrival, six years beyond the two sets of seven years that counted as payments for Leah and Rachel, and still Laban has never settled on what property properly belongs to Jacob. So the negotiations begin. Jacob suggests that they divide up the herds. Laban could keep the white sheep and goats (which were more plentiful) while Jacob would claim the ones that were spotted or black. But Laban was greedy. He gave the speckled sheep to his sons and sent them off on a three-day journey so that they could not mate with Jacob's herd. Even so, Jacob's herds mated and produced the nonwhite sheep bountifully. Laban's sons began to gripe about Jacob stealing their inheritance. It was becoming clear to Jacob that he had outstayed his welcome (Genesis 30:25–31:2).

Interestingly Jacob consults both Rachel and Leah with his plans to leave. He explains how often their father has tried to cheat him but adds that his God has seen fit to protect him. He even relates to them the dream he has had in which God showed him the spotted and speckled sheep mating and told him it was time to return to his home in Canaan. God reminds Jacob that He is the same God that Jacob vowed conditionally to serve while on the way to his mother's family. Jacob had to acknowledge that indeed this God has stood by him. Jacob must obey the Lord's call to move on. Rachel and Leah agree wholeheartedly with Jacob's assessment of their situation and immediately prepare to depart. But Rachel does one thing more. She steals her father's household gods. Even though Laban and his father, Bethuel, acknowledged the authority of this God of Abraham, Isaac, and now Jacob as far back as the arrangements for Rebekah's marriage to Isaac (Genesis 24:50), that did not mean that they worshiped the Lord exclusively. Household gods and other forms of idols were commonplace among the various peoples contemporary with Jacob. Apparently Rachel, who was superstitious enough to think mandrakes would make her fertile, fears to go away from her home without these glorified good luck charms (Genesis 31:3–21).

Jacob and his company go off in stealth. It is three days before Laban realizes that they have actually left. Of course, Laban is angry, and the discovery of the stolen gods fuels his fury and gives him a ready excuse to pursue Jacob. Within a week they overtake Jacob's camp. But by now God has sent Laban a cautionary dream. "Be careful what you do to Jacob, whether good or bad" (Genesis 31:24).

Laban begins by making nice.

> Why didn't you tell me? Why, I would have sent you off with a great celebration—music, timbrels, flutes! But you wouldn't permit me so much as a kiss for my daughters

and grandchildren. It was a stupid thing for you to do. If I had a mind to, I could destroy you right now but the God of your father spoke to me last night, ... and I understand. You left because you are homesick. But why did you steal my household gods? (Genesis 31:27–30)

Jacob replies honestly, "I was afraid. I thought you would take your daughters away from me by brute force. But as far as your gods are concerned, if you find that anyone here has them, that person dies" (Genesis 31:31–32). Jacob is unaware of Rachel's thievery. Laban sets to work, going through every tent, but Rachel avoids discovery by sitting on the idols and then claiming to be unable to stand because she is menstruating. Now it was Jacob's turn to register his anger, and he proceeds to vent twenty years' worth of frustration with his father-in-law. Amazingly in the end the two tricksters call it a day and even make a monument to immortalize their agreement to part amicably. At the site of the designated stone pillar, Laban even intones, "The God of Abraham and the God of Nahor (the God of their ancestor) will keep things straight between us" (Genesis 31:53), but Jacob offers a sacrifice only to the God of his father Isaac (Genesis 31:53–54). "Laban got up early the next morning, kissed his grandchildren and his daughters, blessed them, and set off for home" (Genesis 31:55).

Dealing with Laban is just the first hurdle for Jacob. Now that he has set his face toward home, another looms—his brother Esau, last seen vowing to kill him. It is encouraging then when Jacob meets God's angels along the way. He makes bold and sends messengers forth to Esau with the following missive: "A message from your servant Jacob: I've been staying with Laban and couldn't get away until now. I've acquired cattle and donkeys and sheep; also men and women servants. I'm telling you all this, my master, hoping for your approval" (Genesis 32:4–5). Perhaps he sighed and felt for that moment optimistic about the coming reunion. But then the messengers returned and said, "We talked to your brother Esau and he's on his way to meet you. But he has 400 men with him" (Genesis 32:6).

The news escalates Jacob's anxiety to panic mode. First he divides his company into two groups—the better for one to escape if the first is attacked. But immediately after this maneuver he falls on his face in desperate prayer.

> God of my father Abraham, God of my father Isaac, God who told me, "Go back to your parents' homeland and I'll treat you well." I don't deserve all the love and loyalty you've shown me. When I left here and crossed the Jordan I only had the clothes on my back, and now look at me—two camps! Save me, please, from the violence of my brother, my angry brother! I'm afraid he'll come and attack us all, me, the mothers, and the children. You yourself said, "I will treat you well; I'll make your descendants like the sands of the sea, far too many to count." (Genesis 32:9–12)

Hearing Jacob make this prayer combined with his recent worship of God at the place where he parted from Laban, we are momentarily led to believe that Jacob has finally become a true God believer—maybe not up to the level of trust for his grandfather's binding of Isaac—but he was certainly no longer the swaggering young man who basically challenged God to prove Himself worthy of allegiance back in chapter 28. But as the narrative shows us, there is more to come in Jacob's faith journey. In his prayer Jacob owns up to being undeserving and acknowledges that God has actually come through better than advertised. Jacob does have two camps after all (Genesis 32:10). But like us, now that he is in a crisis, he still pleads for some assurance that God will help him out of the current jam (Genesis 32:11). Though he reminds himself of God's repeated promises in Genesis 32:12, we notice that he continues to busy himself with further action. He prepares a gift for his brother—three sets of livestock to be sent forth in succession, probably a bit more than customary ritualized gift-giving since Jacob hopes to soften Esau up before they meet face-to-face. Next he tries to settle down for the night, but still fraught with fear, he wakes his camp and sends his wives and children and all his possessions across the Jabbok, a brook easily forded (Genesis 32:23).

Jacob himself, however, remains on the far side of the Jabbok for the balance of the night. Perhaps he had planned to rest alone on that shore and try to get a grip on his fear. But it was not to be. Instead he spends the night wrestling with a stranger. The two appear to be evenly matched because the clash continues until daybreak, when the opponent, according to the text, "saw that he couldn't get the best of Jacob as they wrestled, [and] deliberately threw Jacob's hip out of joint" (Genesis 33:25). Let's examine the exchange that follows the wrestling match in Genesis 32:26–30.

What has actually happened to Jacob? Clearly there is more here than a simple "let's settle this man-to-man" type of altercation. In the first place we don't know why Jacob agrees to fight an unnamed stranger. Even if he were attacked and merely defending himself, we would expect the narrative to include his protests. Questions like, "Why are you wrestling me?" seem natural enough, but there are none. Instead the two stay engaged in fisticuffs all night long. At daybreak it is the stranger, not Jacob, who calls it quits, easily dislocating Jacob's hip, a move he could have made at any point in the encounter. But here Jacob startles us by insisting on a blessing, unmindful of the pain of his hip injury. The blessing takes an interesting form—a name change. Jacob, the Heel, the Deceiver, has become Israel, the God-Wrestler. We can see how Jacob needs to shed his conniving ways in order to follow God, but it is surprising that his new persona is one that struggles with God. For all its mystery the story shows us a picture of God wanting an intimate, honest relationship with Jacob. Although we don't usually associate intimacy with fighting, Jacob's wrestling match shows us a God welcoming those who get in His face and grapple with His commands. God keeps it a fair fight. (The stranger did not best Jacob until He deemed it over.) And blessing is there for the asking. No wonder Jacob exclaims with amazement that he has seen God face-to-face (Peniel) and survived (Genesis 32:30). What an incredible metaphor—Israel, God-Wrestler—God has chosen for the people He is bringing into being through these three Patriarchs, specifically Abraham, Isaac, and Jacob.

Thus, we see how Jacob in his own way comes to believe in this mysterious single God who has taken such an interest in his family. Our next site will be to observe the course of Jacob's life after this momentous night. The narrative does not make us wait. When Jacob, who is alone again, scans the horizon in the dawn's light, he immediately sees Esau's four hundred. Quickly he divides his family among the four mothers, placing the concubines' children first and then lining up Leah and her seven and finally keeping Rachel and Joseph in the rear. Then he walks to the front and performs the ritual seven bows that indicate his total submission to Esau. "But Esau ran up and embraced him, held him tight and kissed him. And they both wept" (Genesis 33:4). The feared reunion has a happy outcome. Each brother is impressed with the other's wealth, and they haggle a bit over whether Esau ought to accept Jacob's gifts. In the end each goes on his own way—Esau back to Seir and Jacob and company making their way to the city of Shechem in Canaan, where Jacob is able to purchase lands for his tents outside of town (Genesis 33:5–19).

Shechem proves to be a troubled spot for the new Israel and his family. Although God has called Jacob to shed the old deceiving self at Peniel, we are now to be reminded that it was the original Jacob who raised his sons, and as the expression goes, "The apple does not fall far from the tree." While the family makes their campsite on the land Jacob has bought from

Hamor, the city's chieftain, Dinah, Leah's daughter, goes into Shechem to visit with some other young women there. During her excursion in the city one of Hamor's sons, a young man named Shechem (like the town), sees Dinah and first rapes her and then claims that he loves her and wishes her to be his wife. During the negotiations that follow, Jacob's sons insist that the only way they will even contemplate legitimizing this union would be for Shechem and all his household to submit to circumcision. Amazingly Shechem's family agrees. Apparently, however, this was merely a ruse on the brothers' part. Three days after the circumcisions while the men are still sore, Dinah's brothers, Simeon and Levi, barge into the compound and murder the entire lot. The rest of the brothers proceed to loot and ransack the homes (Genesis 34:1–29). Though the narrator notes Jacob's lament over the boys' actions (Genesis 34:30), it remains to the reader to pass judgment on their behavior. Nonetheless, we will shortly see how this passage foreshadows the sons' deeds that follow.

When we get to chapter 35, we will observe a bit of patching of one narrative strain to another and see quickly what points in the ongoing narrative merit repetition. A passing reference to Shechem in Genesis 35:4 helps our transition to this telling of God's instruction to Jacob to travel back to Bethel, the site of his initial experience with God. We find Jacob speaking to God and building altars to the Lord while warning his company to throw out any alien gods and lucky charms they have horded en route (Genesis 35:1–4). God reiterates the changing of Jacob's name to Israel and restates the Lord's promise that Jacob's descendants will multiply and count kings and nations in their number and that they will inherit the land pledged to Abraham and Isaac (Genesis 35:6–15). We learn at this time that Rachel is pregnant again, but unfortunately she suffers a hard labor and dies giving birth. The circumstance forces Jacob to bury her on the roadside at a place called Bethlehem, with a pillar to mark her grave.

But she has given him his twelfth son, and Jacob names him Benjamin (Genesis 35:16–20).

Just as the twelfth son is born, the first betrays his father. While en route from Bethel back to the family homestead, Reuben sleeps with Bilhah, and Israel finds out (Genesis 35:22). We'll see what it costs Reuben farther down the road. In the meantime the company does makes it back to Jacob's childhood home, and incredibly Isaac is still alive but on his deathbed. Clearly our editors are not as concerned over chronological details as they are over the reasons behind our characters' actions. Whenever Isaac actually died, it is important to note that his funeral serves as an echo to Abraham's (Genesis 25:9), his two once-estranged sons also burying him together (Genesis 35:29).

After a chapter of genealogies the narrative returns to Jacob, but now it tells us the story of his sons and particularly his son Joseph, firstborn of Rachel. Remembering how Jacob favored Rachel, it becomes no surprise to us that he esteems her son similarly. He even gives him a specially embroidered coat. Of course, favoritism is a double-edged sword. What Joseph gained from his father he paid for tenfold from his jealous brothers. The coat ignites a hatred that becomes further inflamed when, as a late teenager, Joseph shares his dreams with his brethren. There are two dreams, each with a simple and obvious interpretation. In the first Joseph proclaims that he and his brothers were out in the field gathering bundles of wheat. "All of a sudden my bundle stood straight up and your bundles circled around it and bowed down to mine" (Genesis 37:7). In the next dream Joseph sees the sun and moon (his parents) and eleven stars bowing before him (Genesis 37:9). Even Jacob has to reprimand his son for these crazy dreams, but he still does not refrain from sending Joseph off to gather progress reports on his brothers' grazing of the flocks.

From the Dinah story we already know what kind of men these brothers are. When they see Joseph on the horizon coming to check on them, knowing they are in a remote area far from their father's eyes, the brothers easily concoct a plot to commit fratricide. No sooner does Joseph come upon them than they are ripping off his coat and throwing him into a nearby cistern so that they can consider the method of his murder over their supper. Reuben is against murder and secretly plans to retrieve Joseph from the cistern later (perhaps to get back in his father's good graces). But as he fails to stay and sup with the younger boys, his chance to play the hero with his father runs awry. While the remaining brothers are eating, a caravan of Ishmaelites passes by on its way to Egypt. Judah hits a brain wave. "Brothers, what are we going to get out of killing our brother and concealing the evidence? Let's sell him to the Ishmaelites, but let's not kill him— he is, after all, our brother, our own flesh and blood" (Genesis 37:27). Together they plan their cover story. They take Joseph's fancy robe and smear it with goat's blood and take it back to their father. Naturally Jacob believes a vicious animal has slaughtered Joseph, and he quickly submerges into prolonged grief.

Having informed us that Joseph was sold in Egypt, the narrative shifts to his brother Judah, the one whose counsel has spared Joseph from fratricide. This tale tells of Judah's marriage to a Canaanite woman. By her he has three sons, and when the oldest, Er, is of marriageable age, Judah weds him to a woman named Tamar. But Er's ways were wicked, and God kills him. Here is where we learn of the custom that we now label "levirate (meaning brother-in-law) marriage." When Er dies childless, Judah demands of Onan, his second son, "Go and sleep with your brother's widow; it's the duty of a brother-in-law to keep your brother's line alive" (Genesis 38:8). Onan, however, is not interested in fathering children in his brother's name. Though he sleeps with Tamar, he fails to impregnate her by spilling his semen on the ground. For this God takes Onan's life as well. By this time Judah fears for the life of his third son. He puts Tamar off, saying he will give her to the youngest boy when he grows up. She goes to live with her father (Genesis 38:8–11).

Time passes, and Judah's wife dies. He forgets about his obligation to Tamar, but she does not. By now she has figured out that the third son, Shelah, though certainly old enough, is not going to be made her husband. She devises a strategy. Taking off her widow's garb, she veils herself as a prostitute and waits by the road, where she knows Judah will pass by. He engages her services for the price of a kid goat and leaves with her his personal seal and cord and his staff as a pledge of his future payment. When Judah sends the goat via messenger, the woman is nowhere to be found, and the people nearby claim there has never been a prostitute in their location. Judah feels satisfied that he has done his best to make good on his word and thinks no more on the incident. But three months later the rumor mill informs him that his daughter-in-law has behaved shamelessly and gotten herself pregnant. Judah is ready to condemn her to be burned (the penalty for prostitution) when she produces his staff, seal, and cord. Interestingly he acknowledges his own wrongdoing. "She's in the right; I'm in the wrong—I wouldn't let her marry Shelah" (Genesis 38:26). Like Rebekah, Tamar gives birth to twins with one son beating out his brother to be firstborn (Genesis 38:28–30).

The story exposes an interesting piece of irony. Though the story of Judah and Tamar highlights the emphasis on male hereditary lines in Hebrew society, here it is the woman who goes to considerable lengths to ensure that Judah has descendants, seemingly caring more about Judah's line than he does. As Genesis closes, we will see why it is so important that Judah has sons and how his progeny will figure in God's plan.

Meanwhile, we go back to Joseph in Egypt, where an official of the Pharaoh named Potiphar purchases him. Though his brothers have abandoned him, Joseph soon finds that God has not. Everything he does for Potiphar turns to gold as God blesses Potiphar's household for Joseph's sake. Quickly Joseph wins Potiphar's trust and affection with his skillful and diligent attention to the requirements of his position, and in no time Potiphar places him in charge of all his business and household affairs.

But Joseph is not only a savvy manager. He is "strikingly handsome" (Genesis 39:6) as well. As he rises in Potiphar's esteem, he does not escape the attention of Mrs. Potiphar. She begins to badger him to sleep with her, but he remains stalwart, saying, "Look, with me here, my master doesn't give a second thought to anything that goes on here—he's put me in charge of everything he owns. He treats me as an equal. The only thing he hasn't turned over to me is you. You're his wife, after all! How could I violate his trust and sin against God?" (Genesis 39:8–9).

In character for a woman spurned, Potiphar's wife eventually falsely accuses Joseph of rape. Because he ends up leaving his coat in her hands as he tries to escape her advances, she uses it as evidence of his attempted violation. Potiphar understandably feels betrayed and immediately throws Joseph in prison. But again God does not abandon him. The warden spots Joseph's intelligence immediately and soon turns over the management of the jail to Joseph (Genesis 39:11–23).

While Joseph is still incarcerated, two of Pharaoh's officials, the head baker and head cupbearer, land in the slammer. After some time has passed, Joseph is making his morning rounds, checking on all the prisoners when he notices that the cupbearer and the baker seem particularly dispirited. It turns out that each has had a disturbing dream the previous night and regrets that no one is present to interpret for them. Joseph's response probably takes them by surprise. "Don't interpretations come from God?" (Genesis 40:8). With that piece of evangelism he proceeds to offer the interpretation God gives him for each dream. The cupbearer will be recalled to service in three days, but in three days the baker will be executed. Joseph is quick to beseech the cupbearer to keep Joseph in mind when he returns to the palace. Within the three days both prisoners are called to the throne room, and things play out as Joseph has predicted; however, for the time the cupbearer forgets about Joseph (Genesis 40:9–23).

Two years pass. Now it is Pharaoh having dreams, and none of his interpreters can make sense of them. At last the cupbearer remembers Joseph and encourages Pharaoh to send for him. When Joseph comes into the royal presence, Pharaoh addresses him, "I have dreamed a dream. Nobody can interpret it. But I've heard that just by hearing a dream you can interpret it." Joseph answered, "Not I, but God. God will set Pharaoh's mind at ease" (Genesis 41:15–16).

Pharaoh has dreamed twice, making this the third pairing of dreams in Joseph's story. In the first dream seven scrawny cows eat seven healthy ones. In the second seven sickly stalks swallow up seven full stalks of grain. Joseph reveals that both dreams impart the same meaning. "God is telling Pharaoh what he is going to do" (Genesis 41:25). The seven healthy cows and ears of grain represent seven years of plenty that will be followed by seven years of famine. In light of this interpretation Joseph offers the following advice:

> Pharaoh needs to look for a wise and experienced man and put him in charge of the country. Then Pharaoh needs to appoint managers throughout the country of Egypt to organize it during the years of plenty. Their job will be to collect all the food produced in the good years ahead and stockpile the grain under Pharaoh's authority, storing it in the towns for food. This grain will be held back to be used later during the seven years of famine that are coming on Egypt. This way the country won't be devastated by the famine. (Genesis 41:33–36)

Naturally the plan makes sense to Pharaoh, and when he discusses it with his council, they all agree that Joseph is the man for the job. So Pharaoh says to Joseph, "You're the man for us. God has given you the inside story—no one is as qualified as you in experience and wisdom. From now on, you're in charge of my affairs; all my people will report to you. Only as king will I be over you" (Genesis 41:39–40).

In this way Joseph at the age of thirty comes to be in charge of the entire country of Egypt. Pharaoh gives him an Egyptian name, Zaphenath-Paneah, as well as an Egyptian wife through whom he eventually fathers two sons (Genesis 41:45, 50). What a reversal! Though Joseph meets injustice at the hands of his brothers, his first master and mistress, and even the prisoner he helps, God converts all his woes into the makings of a spectacular résumé. Ironically all his misfortune has served to prepare him to undertake this daunting assignment, where even the Egyptians feel at a loss. In Joseph we see no trace of the family trait of deceitfulness, though he has the wily Jacob for his father, the sneaky idol-smuggler Rachel for his mother, and the double-talking, backstabbing sackers of Shechem for his brothers. Instead we see a man deeply aware and trusting of his God, speaking about the Lord readily even among foreigners. That he is able to rise from every downturn in his circumstances he attributes to God's hand in his life. But he also feels a pull to an unknown destiny. He knows he doesn't belong in prison and doesn't hesitate to beg for the good word of the cupbearer so that he might be delivered, but he is also able to be patient, buoyed by God's care through the many years that pass from his brothers' betrayal to his current election to Pharaoh's right hand.

During the years of plenty Joseph stockpiles the surplus grain. When the famine comes seven years later, Egypt stands as the only country in the region prepared. Moreover, the famine is far-reaching. In Canaan, Jacob and his family hear that Egypt has bread. The patriarch sends his ten older sons to that country to buy food. He keeps Benjamin at home lest another mishap should befall his last son of Rachel. When the Hebrew brothers arrive to make their purchase, they pay obeisance to the Egyptian manager, never recognizing him as their long-lost relative. But Joseph spots them immediately. Here is his childhood dream coming true. Nonetheless, he refrains from revealing himself. Instead he accuses the group of spying out Egypt's weaknesses. When they protest that they are merely ten of now eleven brothers from Canaan, Joseph allows that they can prove their innocence by returning to Canaan to retrieve the last brother as long as one of them remains hostage in jail. The ten discuss the matter in Hebrew, unaware that Joseph understands their speech. Led by Reuben (with his own "I told you so!"), they all interpret their dilemma as their payback for what they did to Joseph. For the first time we, the listeners, hear their memories of Joseph pleading with them for mercy when they throw him in the cistern. Joseph has to turn away so that he can weep. When he is able to compose himself, Joseph gives the order for Simeon to be held as prisoner (Genesis 42:1–24).

The nine set off with their sacks full of grain, but when they stop for the night, they discover that their money has been returned along with the grain. Now they are all so frightened that they ask one another, "What's God doing to us?" Not knowing what else to do, they continue to Canaan and lay the problem before their father. Jacob, though equally distressed over the boys' circumstances, is adamant that Benjamin may not go. Reuben offers his own sons as hostages, but Israel remains emphatic. "My son will not go down with you. His brother is dead and he is all I have left. If something bad happens to him on the road, you'll put my gray, sorrowing head in the grave" (Genesis 42:38).

As time goes on, the famine worsens. The brothers appeal to Jacob again to give them leave to take Benjamin to Egypt lest they all starve. Judah pledges his own life if Benjamin comes to harm. They pack themselves up loaded with gifts as well as double the money for new grain and embark. This time they enjoy a warm reception before Joseph. Joseph orders a steward to prepare a banquet for the Hebrews in his own home. But the brothers take this sudden hospitality as a ruse for their capture. They take the steward aside and plead their case, explaining how the money had appeared in their sacks, claiming that they had never meant not to pay for the grain they had picked up in Egypt on their last visit. The steward, however, reassures them, "Everything's in order. Don't worry. Your God and the God of your father must have given you a bonus. I was paid in full" (Genesis 43:23). He then proceeds to bring out Simeon as well. Unable to fathom what will happen next, the Hebrew men await Joseph's arrival at the meal. They lay all their gifts out to show him. When Joseph arrives, he pays little heed to the gifts but is ready with questions about their father, Jacob. "How is he? Is he still alive?" (Genesis 43:27). Then when he beholds his full brother, Benjamin, he has to excuse himself for a moment, again to burst into tears.

The meal goes well, though the brothers find it odd that their seats are arranged in the order of their ages. Still, with their grain and their hostaged brother in tow, they are happy to depart for home. They do not check their saddlebags, and so they are amazed when the Egyptian house steward steals upon them and accuses them of thievery. Not only has Joseph returned their money again to their sacks, he has had his silver chalice planted in Benjamin's bag. The steward berates them, "Why did you pay me back evil for good? This is the chalice my master drinks from" (Genesis 44:4–5). Of course Jacob's sons are aghast at the accusation. "What is my master talking about? We would never do anything like that! Why, the money we found in our bags earlier, we brought back all the way from Canaan—do you think we'd turn right around and steal it back from your master? If the chalice is found on any of us, he'll die, and the rest of us will be your master's slaves" (Genesis 44:7–9).

When the chalice shows up among Benjamin's belongings, all the brothers begin to despair. In their audience before Joseph,

Judah pleads for Benjamin's life. He does not even attempt to deny the charges but instead explains that the loss of Benjamin will put their father in his grave. He offers to remain as Joseph's slave in Benjamin's place. The speech takes Joseph to the end of his endurance. He orders his servants from his chamber in barely enough time before he breaks into sobs. "I am Joseph," he confesses in Hebrew. Though the news strikes his brothers speechless, he proceeds to explain to them, "I am Joseph your brother whom you sold into Egypt. But don't feel bad; don't blame yourselves for selling me. God was behind it. God send me ahead of you to save lives" (Genesis 45:4–5).

Joseph hurries them off to retrieve Jacob. The Egyptians, upon hearing that Joseph has discovered his family, sends them home with carts for bringing their wives and their children back to Egypt, as there remain five years of famine ahead. Though it is hard for Jacob to believe the news when his traveling sons return to him, God confirms it for him. "I am the God of your father. Don't be afraid of going down to Egypt. I'm going to make you a great nation there. I'll go with you down to Egypt; I'll also bring you back here. And when you die, Joseph will be with you; with his own hand he'll close your eyes" (Genesis 46:3–4).

In this way it comes to pass that Jacob and all his family leave Canaan, the land of God's promise, and settle in Goshen in Egypt, the land Joseph has procured from Pharaoh for his family to call its own. The famine continues to intensify in severity so much that even the Egyptian citizens have to sell themselves into slavery to Pharaoh to pay for food. Joseph keeps Pharaoh strong with his disciplined management of the grain and adds considerably to Pharaoh's land and wealth. The Hebrews thrive in Goshen, where they continue to shepherd their flocks.

After seventeen years Jacob, now 147, makes his final blessings on his children. He leaves behind him twelve sons who now lead twelve tribes. Passing over the first three born—Reuben because of his affair with Jacob's concubine Bilhah (Genesis 35:22) and

Simeon and Levi because of their hotheadedness in Shechem
(Genesis 34:25)—he appoints as family head Judah, the fourth
born, the one who directly prevented Joseph's murder and also
agreed to substitute himself in place of the accused Benjamin.
In his blessing Jacob proclaims,

> *The scepter shall not leave Judah;*
>> *He'll keep a firm grip on the command staff*
> *Until the ultimate ruler comes*
>> *And the nations obey him.* (Genesis 49:10)

Thus, he echoes God's original pledge to Abraham that this
line of descendants will bless all the world's peoples (Genesis
12:3) and hints at what will become the promise of the Messiah to
Israel. Perhaps you wonder with me why the ultimate ruler would
not come through Joseph's line since Joseph has demonstrated
such persevering faith. My only intuition about why Judah is
chosen draws from the Tamar story. When Tamar confronts
Judah with the truth of his own culpability in denying her his son
in marriage, he readily acknowledges his fault (Genesis 38:26).
That trait coupled with his willingness to sacrifice even his own
life the second time a son of Rachel falls under a death threat
shows us a man capable of growth and transformation. As we go
forward, let us watch for these characteristics in Judah's progeny.

Jacob also blesses Joseph's two boys, Manasseh and Ephraim.
He puts his right hand on Ephraim, the younger, foreseeing that
he will be greater than his brother. This keeps intact the Genesis
theme that younger sons supersede their elders in contrast to the
tradition of primogeniture that so many cultures have observed
throughout history.

When Israel does breathe his last breath, all the sons return
his body to the family burial ground in Canaan, where he joins his
wife, Leah, as well as forebears Isaac and Rebekah and Abraham
and Sarah. Even after the years of living together in Egypt, the

brothers fear reprisal from Joseph now that their father is gone. Together they throw themselves on the ground before Joseph and offer to be his slaves in compensation for their sin of selling him into slavery. But Joseph replies, "Don't be afraid. Do I act for God? Don't you see, you planned evil against me but God used those same plans for good?" (Genesis 50:19–20). From that time on they continue to live together in Egypt. As Joseph approaches his death, he reminds his surviving brothers of God's promise to bring the family back to Canaan. "God will most certainly pay you a visit and take you out of this land and back to the land he so solemnly promised to Abraham, Isaac and Jacob. When God makes this visitation, make sure you take my bones with you as you leave here" (Genesis 50:24–25).

We have now reviewed the stories of Genesis—four generations of people God chose to approach one-on-one. God's first task was to reveal Himself as a God unlike any others. The Lord is not a God to be placated and then manipulated. God's blessings flow from God's own agenda, not as a result of the magnificence of the sacrifices made to the Deity. Yet despite God's omnipotence, the Lord has sought to be intimate with Abraham and his sons. The Patriarchs and Joseph are rightly called *friends* of God.

We have seen in these pages the birth of at least three nations of peoples all stemming from Abraham—the Ishmaelites, the Edomites (from Esau), and of course, the Israelites. Though the text is careful to state that God is not forgetting the sons of Ishmael and Esau, it is clear that the thrust of the Lord's story will run through Israel. Jacob's twelve sons, flawed as they are, will go forward as the promise bearers. God's plan to bless all the families of the earth will be worked through their lines. Keeping in mind the Tamar story, we note from the passage of fatherly blessings (Genesis 49:1–27) Jacob's prediction that an "ultimate ruler" (Genesis 49:10) will come from Judah's line, though little else is disclosed about that person here. What is interesting to reflect on is what these histories reveal about God. First the Lord is dependable. God's promises always come through. Abraham and Sarah have a son and buy a piece of land in Canaan, the first step of God's grand promise. Isaac and Rebekah bring forth two sons, each very different but both very prosperous, and Jacob, leaving home in fear for his life, returns to Canaan aware that it has been the God of his fathers who has blessed him and kept him safe. Yet God never accomplishes these promises in the manner one might expect. When Sarah laughs to think she could bear a son, we stagger with her to learn that nothing is impossible for God. Each patriarch has his patience tried, and each suffers personal anguish as a result of the complicated family dynamics that erupt as he tries to see God's plan. Abraham is tested with the proposed sacrifice of Isaac, and Jacob even wrestles with God and survives. Although we never hear God and Joseph converse, we have seen that Joseph's faith in God permeates everything he does and says throughout his life. It is he who offers us the insight that God's ability to do the impossible extends even to taking an act one person has meant for evil and using it to provide for good. In these characters we see enacted the working out of God's self-imposed challenge—finding humans who choose to love and trust Him out of their free will to carry out the Lord's plans.

Genesis closes with the embalming of Joseph's body and its placement in a coffin. When Joseph dies, the Israelites are a small but growing population in Egypt. Most of Egypt's own citizens have chosen to enslave themselves to Pharaoh because of the famine, but the Hebrews are free shepherds. As we turn the page to Exodus, the tables will turn as well for Israel as God sets the stage for the Lord's signature act, namely the deliverance of God's people from the bondage of slavery.

Chapter 4

Does It Really Say That Moses Parted the Red Sea?

Years ago *Saturday Night Live* ran a sketch in which it claimed to encapsulate a college education in two minutes by pointing out how little people retain of what they learn. For instance, what do you remember about economics? *Supply and demand!* It's a little like that with Moses. You might recall the story of baby Moses adrift in a basket on the Nile, or better yet, you might associate him with the Ten Commandments; however, the main thing that springs to mind about Moses is the parting of the Red Sea. But what does the Bible actually say about Moses?

The Moses story spans four books of the Bible—Exodus, Leviticus, Numbers, and Deuteronomy. Together with Genesis these five books form the Pentateuch (Greek for five books) or the Torah in Hebrew, meaning God's Law, the Lord's code of holiness that informs us on how to treat the Deity and our fellow human beings. Whereas Genesis reads as a mostly chronological narrative, the remaining books of the Pentateuch weave a tapestry of narration, exposition, and sermon. It is helpful to begin our examination of Exodus through Deuteronomy with this overarching theme in mind. Having established a genetic line through the Patriarchs of Genesis, God's next step in His plan is to make a Genesis project out of His people, Israel. In chapter 1 of Genesis, God uses speech to create. Here God will use Moses to help Him mold and breathe life into the people Israel,

His firstborn child. In this context we should see Moses as the midwife[14] who assists God in the birth and then the nursemaid charged with overseeing the rearing of this child so that Israel will grow to see herself as a nation set apart that can become the vehicle of God's reconnection with all humankind. This is why we find the narrative of the Moses story braided together with the explanation of the laws and the exposition of the rituals of worship in these books. Israel's history is inseparable from her worship of God and her mandate to practice the Lord's ways.

Exodus

Exodus begins with an artful liaison to the end of Genesis. Verse 1:8 reads, "A new king came to power in Egypt who didn't know Joseph." As we are quickly told, the Hebrews have suffered a complete reversal of their fortunes since the days of Joseph. At that time much of Egypt was enslaved to Pharaoh. At present it is the Israelites who serve the Egyptian monarch under duress. They have lost their land and status, but their women have remained fertile. Now their sheer numbers make the Egyptians anxious lest they move to rise up against their oppressors. In the face of this perceived threat Pharaoh resorts to making a law that all Hebrew boy babies be drowned.

While this edict is in effect, Moses is born into the tribe of Levi. His mother "saw that there was something special about him" (Exodus 2:2) and manages to keep him hidden for three months. Afraid every day that he would be discovered and killed, she resolves to place him in a papyrus basket and sets it afloat among the reeds at the river's edge. Ironically Pharaoh's daughter ends up drawing the crying babe from the Nile, exclaiming, with compassion, "This must be one of the Hebrew babies" (Genesis 2:6). Thus, Moses, the future liberator of the Hebrews and

---

[14] Eugene Peterson, *The Message,* p. 16.

nemesis of Pharaoh, escapes the monarch's death sentence by growing up in the royal residence.

Fast-forward to Moses as an adult when he has somehow learned of his Hebrew heritage and had his consciousness raised about the slaves' hard lot. In righteous indignation upon seeing an Egyptian hit a Hebrew, he kills the man, and thinking no one has seen, he hides the body in the sand. The next day when he returns to the Hebrew workplace, he tries to intervene in a fight between two slaves. But one slave shocks him by saying, "Who do you think you are, telling us what to do? Are you going to kill me the way you killed that Egyptian?" (Exodus 2:14). Knowing himself to be in trouble now, Moses runs to the land of Midian in order to dodge Pharaoh's attempts to have him killed a second time (Exodus 2:15).

Upon his arrival in Midian, Moses takes a rest by a well. The well scene will function again as a romantic venue recalling Abraham's servant coming upon Rebekah (Genesis 24) and Jacob meeting Rachel (Genesis 29) as we observe in chapter 2. The priest of Midian, a man alternately called Reuel and Jethro, has seven daughters who approach the well to water their father's sheep. Some shepherds come and try to run the girls off, but Moses rises to their defense and ends up helping them with the watering. In no time Moses decides to make Midian his home. He marries Zipporrah, one of the daughters, and together they begin a family (Exodus 2:21–22).

Meanwhile back in Egypt the old Pharaoh has died, but the new king does nothing to relieve the Israelites' misery. The Hebrews cry out to God to save them. Chapter 2 concludes with God's response to His people's groaning.

> *God remembered his covenant with Abraham, Isaac, and with Jacob.*
> *God saw what was going on with Israel.*
> *God understood.* (Exodus 2:24–25)

With that piece of foreshadowing, chapter 3 returns to Moses' life in Midian and his first encounter with God. Let us see it as a kind of courtship. We find Moses shepherding his father-in-law's flock when God's angel appears to him in a burning bush that burns but does not burn up. That's a pretty good opening line as well as an amazing metaphor for God—endless energy that never exhausts itself. Curious, Moses stops to investigate and hears God call him by name. Moses answers God's call with an eager "Yes? I'm right here" (Exodus 3:4), but his enthusiasm bursts once he hears what God is calling him to do.

> God said, "I've taken a good long look at the affliction of my people in Egypt. I've heard their cries for deliverance from their slave masters; I know all about their pain. And now I have come down to help them, pry them loose from the grip of Egypt, get them out of that country and bring them to a good land with wide-open spaces, a land lush with milk and honey ... It's time for you to go back: I'm sending you to bring my people, the People of Israel, out of Egypt." (Exodus 3:7–10)

We can scarcely blame Moses for blurting out, "But why me?" (Exodus 3:10). He has no particular ties with the Hebrews. When he tried to be true to his heritage in chapter 2, it had gone badly. He left Egypt without any real ethnic allegiances and has made a happy life for himself in the quiet of Midian as a family man. But God, undaunted, continues to press His suit. "I'll be with you" (Exodus 3:12). Doesn't God realize that Moses hasn't really been brought up in the Hebrew faith and doesn't really know God? Frustrated, Moses stalls for time. If he goes to the people of Israel, how will he identify God? (Exodus 3:13). All the gods and goddesses Moses has heard of have names. But this is where things get interesting. Already God has identified Himself as the God of Moses' father and the Patriarchs, specifically Abraham,

Isaac, and Jacob (Exodus 3:6). Now for the first time the Lord answers in a new way. "I Am Who I Am. Tell the People of Israel, I-AM sent me to you" (Exodus 3:14). We have already seen this special name for God represented by the four letters YHWH sprinkled throughout Genesis along with the generic *Elohim.* The name pronounced might be rendered "Yahweh," but because the name of God is too sacred to be spoken, Israel substitutes *the Lord* whenever YHWH shows up. Here, however, we get an insight into the meaning of God's name. The Deity has named Himself "the one who exists, the one who really is." The form of the Hebrew verb *to be* utilized in the name of God implies all its tenses—past, present, and future—in order to combine the notion that God's lead characteristic is not only His realness but also His presence in all time. Most gods want to bill their omnipotence. We will see that God does not shrink from showing godly might, but the Lord's name speaks a different message, one that will eventually lead Israel to proclaim monotheism.

God makes this revelation about His name but is not willing to let Moses tarry in ruminations. The Lord acknowledges that what He asks will not be an easy task. Egypt will object and will not let the people go until God performs many miracles that will send them reeling! Moreover, the Israelites will not leave Egypt empty-handed, but God will provide the circumstances that will enable them to receive from Egypt all sorts of valuables (Exodus 3:21–22) just as God had foretold to Abraham (Genesis 15:13–16). At this point Moses continues to protest with a string of excuses. God deals with him patiently, attempting to buoy his confidence by teaching him "magic tricks" that will impress the Egyptians (Exodus 4:1–9). When Moses complains that he stutters (Exodus 4:10), God shows impatience, but even so, He relents and allows that Moses' brother, Aaron, can do the talking to Pharaoh (Exodus 4:14).

This final accommodation somehow clinches it for Moses. Like Abraham before him, he accepts his destiny and sets off for Egypt. Yet even with Moses finally on board, God refuses to sugarcoat the job ahead. The Lord's parting word to His new servant foreshadows a deadly resolution to the predicted hard-heartedness of Pharaoh. "Tell Pharaoh ... 'Israel is my son, my firstborn! I told you, "Free my son so that he can serve me." But you refused to free him. So now I'm going to kill *your* son, *your* firstborn'" (Exodus 4:22–23).

Aaron and Moses' confrontation with Pharaoh falls out as God knew it would in a very elongated battle of wills—God's and Pharaoh's. God sends a succession of ten plagues against Egypt, each escalating in severity. With each pass Pharaoh promises to release the Israelites if Moses will get rid of the scourge only to renege on that promise once the danger has been lifted. As you read through the plagues (Exodus 7:14–11:10), you might find them needlessly repetitious. This is when we have to dig deeper. What is actually changing throughout the plagues? One thing to observe is how Aaron's voice fades against Moses' growing self-assurance and increasing vehemence. By the pronouncement of the final plague we find that "Moses, seething with anger, left Pharaoh" (Exodus 11:8). Another typical question is why God "hardens Pharaoh's heart" throughout. Is God usurping the Egyptian's free will? Or is the Deity using the monarch's natural stubbornness to demonstrate God's might not only to Egypt but to the Hebrews as well?

In chapter 11, we think we are coming to the climax with the tenth plague when God pauses to tell Moses to have the Hebrews ask for silver and gold from their neighboring Egyptians. Far from what we would expect, the narrative informs us, "God saw to it that the Egyptians liked the people. Also, Moses was greatly admired by the Egyptians, a respected public servant among both Pharaoh's servants and the people at large" (Exodus 11:3). Having completed this parenthesis, the story setting returns to the stormy last encounter between Pharaoh and Moses wherein Moses pronounces God's final verdict of death to the firstborn of

Egypt—even to the households that have recently paid out the Hebrews with their treasure. Yet just as we are getting to the height of the drama, the story line stops abruptly in chapter 12 to explain the ritual that commemorates the event. Why does this happen? What better way to remind the practitioner of the faith to place himself in the shoes of those not yet liberated Hebrews whenever he performs the rites? The Passover is celebrated in *anticipation* of God's saving action, and thus, it becomes Israel's first major lesson (of many) in trusting God. While the Hebrews listen to the Egyptians' wails through that night, they hold faith that the blood of the unblemished lamb smeared on the lintel and the doorposts of their homes (Exodus 12:7, 22) will keep them safe. The name Passover refers to the literal image that death *passes over* the houses identified by the blood on the door. The evening meal must include unleavened bread (Exodus 12:8) since the Hebrews have to leave early the next morning to go out from Egypt and do not have time to let the bread rise. Bitter herbs (Exodus 12:8) round out the menu to remind the Israelites of the bitterness of the slavery that they are leaving behind them. The family eats fully dressed and with sandals on in order to be ready for the exodus to come (Exodus 12:11). When the storytelling resumes in Exodus 12:29–39, the Hebrews are in a hurry to leave, and the Egyptians are hastening them on their way. God has bested the seemingly immoveable Pharaoh and won Israel's manumission from slavery.

Thus, the Israelites leave Egypt. They bring their flocks and even the gold and silver of their Egyptian neighbors. Moses also remembers to bring Joseph's bones per his dying request so that they can be buried in the land of Canaan. Of course, none of them really knows the way to the Promised Land, but it is no problem because God's angel leads them. A pillar of cloud proceeds in front of the company during the day and then changes to a pillar of fire through the night, giving Israel both light and warmth (Exodus 13:19–22).

It is not long, however, before Pharaoh forgets his terror before this foreign God. The scandal of Egypt's defeat rankles quickly and Pharaoh sends his warriors in pursuit of the slaves. The mighty foot soldiers and chariots of Pharaoh's army catch up to the Israelites as they are encamped at the seaside with nowhere to advance. The sight and sound of the approaching Egyptians strike absolute terror in the hearts of the Hebrews. Though they cry out to God, they complain bitterly to Moses, "What have you done to us, taking us out of Egypt? Back in Egypt didn't we tell you this would happen? Didn't we tell you, 'Leave us alone here in Egypt—we're better off as slaves in Egypt than as corpses in the wilderness'" (Exodus 14:11–12).

Nonetheless, Moses' faith remains firm. He tells the people, "Don't be afraid. Stand firm and watch God do his work of salvation for you today" (Exodus 14:13). Moses' statement of trust sounds the overture of God's upcoming actions where the Lord will put His glory on display. First the pillar of the cloud moves from the seashore in front of Israel to a spot between the Hebrew and Egyptian camps, giving light to Israel but plunging the Egyptians into darkness. Then God instructs Moses to stretch out his staff and hand over the Red Sea while "God, with a terrific east wind all night long, made the sea go back ... The Israelites walked through the sea on dry ground with the waters a wall to the right and to the left" (Exodus 14:21–22). But when the Egyptians try to follow them, God bids Moses stretch his hands out again, this time to bring the waters down on the Egyptian Army. All who have pursued Israel perish that day.

This incredible feat—the parting of the Red Sea—has fascinated readers throughout history. People have developed many theories trying to get their heads around what happened there and then. Most scholars agree it couldn't have been the huge Red Sea, and some have speculated it was really the Reed Sea instead. The Reed Sea was much smaller and even had a raised pathway of sorts where people could have perhaps crossed on foot but where chariots would have been mired in mud. These theories, however, are not germane to our purposes here. Our concern lies with how the Bible understands this phenomenon. What is clear from the narrative is that God actually planned to put the Hebrews in this dire situation so that the Lord could rescue them. They come up to the firm land on the other side of the sea "in reverent awe before God, trusting in him and his servant Moses" (Exodus 14:31). For Israel the parting of the sea is a complete wonder, a clear demonstration of the mightiness of their God. If we try to minimize the miraculous nature of this event in order to suit our own sense of what could really happen, we will completely misconstrue the indelible imprint it left on the people of Israel. Moreover, we need to appreciate that the Israelites understand the parting of the sea both literally and figuratively. God saves their lives from the waters and the Egyptians, but in the same motion the Lord also liberates them from the psychological death of slavery. Salvation thus becomes God's signature act throughout the Bible and will always be conceived as multilayered. God's parting of the sea will be recalled by all future generations of Israel in times when they face physical danger and disaster as well as in times when they find themselves haunted by despair because the God of Israel is the "God who acts in history." See this as a derivative of God's name: God's realness as the *God who is* translates to the *God who acts*. God hears the misery of His people in Egypt and sends Moses to get them released from their bonds. Then the Deity purposely leads them to the brink of disaster, exposing their thorough lack of faith in God, and proceeds to save them by doing the impossible—splitting the sea. In the days of these Hebrews, every people had their own gods, but Israel's God is a God who does what cannot even be wished for. The Lord's power is beyond compare, causing even foreign peoples to acclaim His supremacy. Moreover, if we try to give the credit to Moses either for his bravery or his brilliant military strategy, as some documentary films do, we lose sight of the only thing the Bible does credit Moses with, namely his faith. It is Moses who explains the context within which God's acts are to be understood. While it is true that God was displaying His might with the parting of the sea, the key for Israel is to see that their God was using His considerable strength to preserve them. We will see in the stories that follow that Israel will found her faith on the precious memory of God's many deeds of salvation.

We began this chapter with the notion that God is using Moses to complete a *Genesis project* with His people Israel. In *The Message*, Peterson encourages us to understand the plagues as the labor pains and passing through the sea as the metaphorical birth of God's first child. But Israel though born alive, is still very much a people in chaos, and thus Moses' role will shift subtly from midwife to nursemaid. Up to this point his job has mainly revolved around confronting Pharaoh. Now he has to contend with Israel herself. If you thought Pharaoh was a trial for him, the Egyptian doesn't hold a candle to the frustration greeting Moses on the next horizon.

With Egypt now forever behind them, the Hebrews plod along in the wilderness. Here again we will observe the biblical tactic of speaking in multiple layers. The wilderness where Israel wanders after God's routing of the Egyptians operates as both a literal and figurative image. It is literally wilderness because the Israelites live a nomadic existence, doing no farming and little hunting there. Yet they are also in limbo spiritually. They have lost their identity as slaves but still not gained an identity as a people. The Hebrews God sends Moses to liberate know little more about God than the fact that He is the Deity of their progenitors. Because of the promises God made to the Patriarchs, the Lord intends for them to inherit the Promised Land as free men. But when the Hebrews leave Egypt, they are not ready to rule themselves. Long years of slavery have eroded their self-reliance. Moreover, God will be asking them to modify their code of right and wrong in order to align it with His ordinance. This will require them to change in ways that will prove difficult for them. At the heart of these changes will be God's desire for His people to trust their Lord. As the story of Israel's history will prove, it is one thing to be able to brag that your God is stronger than all the other gods when events proceed in your favor. But what good is a powerful God when that Deity doesn't give you everything you want or think you need? In other words, what good is a mighty God that you cannot control? That is the challenge that the Lord now undertakes through His mediator Moses. God will seek to win Israel's trust while He makes it clear that their Deity cannot be manipulated. The Lord will show mercy to the Hebrews out of love for them but will still expect their obedience to His ways. As the narrative will show, this will be a tall task.

A song written in the afterglow of the parted sea reminds Israel to consider, "Who compares with you among gods, O God?" (Exodus 15:11). But soon the starkness of the desert deflates the people, and even slavery in Egypt looks good compared to the prospect of thirst and starvation. Three days into the journey when they could only find brackish water, they fall back on their moaning to Moses that life was better in Egypt (Exodus 15:25). Having anticipated these traveling trials, God proceeds to turn them into lessons to teach and test His people. Still, it will be Moses who will explain what God is doing. Speaking for God, Moses informs the people that each evening God will cause quail to fly into the camp to provide the Hebrews with meat (Exodus 16:13). Likewise, each morning as the dew evaporates, the Israelites will find a fine, flaky substance on the ground. At first, they can't even identify it, asking one another, "What is it?" (*man-hu*). But Moses teaches the Hebrews to collect this *manna* every morning to make their bread. Each family is to gather only what it needs for one day until the sixth day, when a double portion will be garnered in order to allow rest on the Sabbath. Anyone who takes in more than his or her share or tries to save a portion for the morrow will find the bread rotten and wormy the following morning (Exodus 16:14–30). By these means God seeks to teach His people to trust the Lord with a daily proof of God's dependability. It was also the beginning of training in keeping the Sabbath holy.

But God is not only there to provide their daily sustenance. God's care extends to protection against enemies. When Amalekites attack Israel shortly after her exodus from Egypt, Moses puts Joshua in charge of the battlefront but places himself on a hilltop, lifting God's staff. As long as Moses' keeps the staff aloft, beseeching God, the fight favors the Hebrews (Exodus 17:8–13). This image of Moses' raised arms demonstrates how Israel's survival is a collaborative effort of Israelite soldiering and God's will.

After three months the pillar of the cloud has led the Israelites back to the mountain in the wilderness of Sinai, where Moses first heard the voice of God. Camp is set up facing the mountain, and Moses proceeds to ascend to meet with the Deity. On the way up God calls out to him,

> Tell the people of Israel: "You have seen what I did to Egypt and how I carried you on eagles' wings and brought you to me. If you will listen obediently to what I say and keep my covenant, out of all peoples you'll be my special treasure. The whole Earth is mine to choose from, but you're special: a kingdom of priests, a holy nation." (Exodus 19:4–6)

When Moses conveys this message to the people, they answer unanimously, "Everything God says we will do" (Exodus 19:8). Having taken this vote of confidence back to the Lord, Moses returns down the mountain to prepare the people to hear directly from God in three days. The Israelites scrub themselves clean in readiness, but when they hear the thunder and trumpet blast and see the lightning and the mountain smoking that herald God's presence, they cry out to Moses to speak in the Lord's place. They are sure that they will die if they hear God's voice. Thus, Moses repeats to Israel God's Ten Words, the Ten Commandments (Exodus 20:1–17).

We see that the commandments[15] divide between obligations to God and duties to one's fellow man. God begins by defining Himself in terms of His actions. "I am GOD, your God, who brought you out of the land of Egypt, out of a life of slavery" (Exodus 20:1). The first commandment follows: Israel is to worship God (Yahweh) exclusively. Notice that God does not here deal with the existence of other gods. The way this statement probably translated to Israel at this time was more like, "Other peoples may have other gods, but you are to worship me alone." The second law—the ban against idols—demonstrates God's insistence that just as Israel's God was different than those of other nations, so were they to worship the Deity differently. God has made Himself manifest in a voice and words, not an image. In the same vein the edict against profanity, swearing with God's name in "curses or silly banter" again serves to distinguish the Hebrews' relationship with their God from the way other people relate to their deities. To invoke a god's name in an oath was a way of summoning that god's power for oneself, but Israel's God wields might according to His own plans. Finally the fourth commandment, the observance of the Sabbath, also sets Israel apart from her neighbors. Just as God rested from His work of creation, they are to rest. The commandment includes even their servants, slaves, and animals, presaging an understanding of

---

[15] I number the Ten Commandments according to the Protestant order. The Catholic Church uses the same text but combines the Protestant first two ordinances and makes two of the Protestant tenth.

human equality that would take centuries for humans themselves to accept. In this law God shows concern for people's general welfare at the same time that the Lord links that well-being to the importance of worship.

Ten Commandments

Worship only GOD.	Honor your parents.	Don't murder.
Have no idols.		Don't commit adultery.
Do not swear.		Don't steal.
Keep the Sabbath.		Don't lie.
		Don't covet.

Commandment five—honor your father and mother—forms the hinge that unites the two sorts of statutes. It is the only truly positive statement, explaining that obedience to this law renders long (and presumably good) life. The remaining directives are a series of don'ts and cover generally every aspect of potential human conflict, with the tenth law gathering all the miscellaneous sources of friction under the rubric of "don't compare yourself to your neighbor and lust for what he has." Of course, Israel was not unique in delineating these last commandments as similar laws appear among other cultures. Still, it is important to grasp the strategy these laws employ to regulate human relations. Clearly they represent an effort to discourage the rule of "might makes right" and pave the way for swapping the ideology of "I will do what I want" with "I will do what is right in God's eyes." Notice, too, that though the Hebrew culture of this era is highly patriarchal, the commands are not gender-specific but apply to men and women alike.[16]

Having delivered the Decalogue, Moses returns up the mountain to receive further instructions from God. He stays for a long time as God teaches him more specifically how His people are to relate to each other and to their Lord. Exodus 21–31 covers the array of topics that God presents in this first extended tutoring session. Regarding laws governing the community of Israel, God speaks first about the handling of slaves/servants, personal injuries, and property rights before He then moves on to the more general issues of social responsibility and justice. (See chart of Torah teachings under Leviticus.) Rules for the observance of the Sabbath and the three annual festivals, the Feast of Unleavened Bread (Passover), the Feast of Harvest or Weeks (later known as Pentecost) in the spring, and the Feast of Tabernacles in the fall form the transition into the discussion of the rituals of worship. God explains to Moses how to build the tabernacle, a portable sanctuary where Israel can worship and make offerings. The tabernacle will also hold, in a special chamber called the Holy of Holies, the ark of the covenant, wherein the stone tablets engraved with the ten laws written by the finger of God can be housed. Only a priest can enter the Holy of Holies, and even he can only enter once a year on the Day of Atonement, when he makes expiation for his own and the people's sins (Exodus 30:10).

However, while Moses sits in rapt attention to God's lessons, the Hebrews camping at the base of the mountain start to believe that their leader is not returning to them. Chapter 32 returns to narration in order to highlight the irony of Israel's faithlessness against the solemnity of Moses' instructions from God. In their restless fear, the Hebrews have turned to Aaron, who apparently is skilled in the craft of idol making, and begged him to construct

---

[16] While the tenth commandment's masculine language forms a technical exception, the spirit of the edict is gender-free.

gods for them. Note that though they had agreed to obey God's commandments and had just listened to the recitation of the law against idols only weeks before, they are desperate for the old kind of god. When their golden calf is complete, the people responded with enthusiasm, "These are your gods, O Israel, who brought you up from Egypt" (Exodus 32:4). The incident echoes loudly from Eden's original transgression. Humans are so easily seduced by the idea that we can make our own gods—not a far leap from being our own gods. When God interrupts His tutelage of Moses to send him down the mountain to tend to the out-of-control Israelites, we get a more personal picture of the divine frustration and disappointment than we saw in Genesis 3. Within the confidence of a conversation with Moses, we see God consider disowning Israel.

> *Your* people whom *you* brought up from the land of Egypt have fallen to pieces. In no time they've turned away from the way I commanded them: They made a molten calf and worshiped it. They've sacrificed to it and said, "These are the gods, O Israel, that brought you up from the land of Egypt!" I look at this people—oh! what a stubborn, hard-headed people! Let me alone now, give my anger free reign to burst into flames and incinerate them. But I'll make a great nation of you. (Exodus 32:7–10)

Moses refuses to take God's leave to abandon Israel, however. Instead he cajoles God into quieting His fury.

> Why, GOD, would you lose your temper with your people? Why, you brought them out of Egypt in a tremendous demonstration of power and strength. Why let the Egyptians say, "He had it in for them—he brought them out so he could kill them in the mountains, wipe them right off the face of the Earth." Stop your anger. Think

twice about bringing evil against your people! Think about Abraham, Isaac, and Israel, your servants to whom you gave your word, telling them "I will give you many children, as many as the stars in the sky, and I'll give this land to your children as their land forever." (Exodus 32:11–13)

Here we see clearly the unique and unenviable role that Moses is called to play in this drama. Moses may have served as the midwife overseeing Israel's birth in her laborious departure from Egypt. From now on, however, he will stand as the mediator between God and Israel, alternately speaking for one and then the other through the long period of frustrating wrestling that precedes the entrance into the Promised Land. Sometimes it will even seem as if Moses and God are two spouses arguing over what it to be done with their children.

Moses has no trouble seeing the big picture while he advises God to calm His indignation, but he is unable keep his own counsel for long. When he goes down the mountain himself, carrying the God-made tablets of the Law, and sees the Hebrews in a frenzied orgy, bowing down to their golden calf, he ends up having the temper tantrum he has just talked God out of. Enraged, he smashes the tablets and melts down the golden calf. Then he turns to Aaron and says, "What on Earth did these people ever do to you that you involved them in this huge sin?" (Exodus 32:21). In yet another echo of the Eden pass-the-blame game, Aaron protests that Moses knows what an evil people the Hebrews are and that when Moses didn't come down off the mountain, they begged him for a god. Then he threw their gold in the fire and "out came this calf" (Exodus 32:24).

In the midst of this chaos Moses addresses the camp, enlisting the aid of all who are on God's side. The Levites, members of Moses' own tribe, sign up, and Moses gives them license to go through the camp and slaughter the idol worshipers, though they be "brother, friend, and neighbor" (Exodus 32:27). As a result, three thousand are killed. The next day Moses ascends the mountain again to try to atone for the people's great sin. He and God come to the following arrangement. Since the Israelites shrink in terror at the sound of God's voice and since God fears He might destroy them if He has to listen to all their complaints (Exodus 33:3), Moses agrees to be the go-between for God and Israel. This routine is established. God is present in the Hebrew camp in a cloud above Moses' tent where God and Moses speak face-to-face "as a man speaks with his friend" (Exodus 33:11 NIV). God seals the arrangement by allowing Moses to see "His glory" (Exodus 33:19–23). Moses calls out to Israel to remind them who their God is, "a God of mercy and grace, endlessly patient—so much love, so deeply true—loyal in love for a thousand generations, forgiving iniquity, rebellion, and sin. Still, he doesn't ignore sin. He holds sons and grandsons responsible for a father's sin to the third and even fourth generation" (Exodus 34:6–7). Before Israel leaves Mount Sinai, Moses spends forty days and nights fasting on the mountain while God allows him to restore the tablets with the Ten Commandments. Moses' face glows with the radiance of having spoken to God when he brings the precious laws down from the mountaintop this time (Exodus 34:27–29).

For the balance of that first year God tasks the Israelites with the building of the tabernacle—a moveable tent where God can dwell among His people and where they can worship Him. What a contrast it makes with Aaron's golden fabrication of a god. Whereas the calf was Israel's idea, God initiates the Tent of Meeting concept. Because the tabernacle is a place to meet God, it must be carefully cleansed and made sacred. God's specifications are quite precise. The Lord even tells Moses the names of the craftsmen He wants to do the work (Exodus 35:30–35). Since this is done in the wilderness, all the materials for the construction come out of contributions the Hebrews make out of their own possessions. They prove so generous that Moses eventually has to tell them to stop making offerings (Exodus 36:6–7). But fundamental to all this effort stands the fact that the structure does not contain God. The rule against idols exists to reinforce the notion of God's invisibility and intangibility, and therefore, it underscores that the Deity cannot be manipulated. When the work is finally finished and the tablets are laid in the ark of the covenant, the cloud of God's presence fills the structure (Exodus 40:34–35). This image makes a fitting tableau for the close of Exodus.

The year Israel spends camped at Mt. Sinai is not solely for the building of the tabernacle, however. It is also school time. The directions for constructing the Tent of Meeting are embedded with lessons of godly behavior. Note how in Exodus these passages of detailed instruction (chapters 21 to 31 and 34 to 40) form parentheses around the golden calf story (chapters 32 to 33). This arrangement works metaphorically to demonstrate that only God's law can keep humans' sinful nature in check.

Leviticus

The center book of the Pentateuch—Leviticus, named for the tribe of Levi, whom God designates as Israel's priests—contains the intensive course in understanding God's code of holiness. After all, becoming a holy people who will show the world God's character by how they live is to be the centerpiece of Israel's identity. Almost entirely devoid of narration, Leviticus focuses on all aspects of proper worship (the Levitical code that includes explanation on sacrifices, priestly duties, dietary and other health restrictions, as well as the rules for practicing the Day of Atonement) and godly living (the holiness code that covers rules for daily interaction with one's fellow humans). We should note here that the detail specified in each facet of worship indicates the degree of care and discipline God would expect in Israel's piety. Likewise, the expansion of the second tablet of the Ten Commandments involving the duties owed to others anticipates the extenuating circumstances that make compliance with these laws so difficult (e.g., differentiating between purposeful and accidental death).

Reading the legal code of any people is never light fare. Some have suggested that parts of Leviticus may even cure insomnia. Though our modern eyes may glaze over the sections on the exact specifications of the tabernacle, what makes food ritually unclean, and how to deal with infectious skin diseases, it is important to examine the Mosaic code from the perspective of what it does differently from the norms of the ancient world. Any new form of government must always take into account what people have been used to doing. For example, take a look at Leviticus 18 and the regulations concerning sexual and marital relations. This chapter gives us a snapshot of what kind of behavior has been the standard in a society where women are largely treated as property and there is a high rate of mortality. Notice the chaos of blended family relations that these prohibitions seek to rein in. Drawing from Exodus through Deuteronomy, let's take inventory of the ways that the Torah modified the practices that the surrounding culture took for granted.

Worship: The elaborate system of sacrifices and offerings may have had some of the comfort of familiarity with what the Hebrews had seen other peoples practice. But there were no human sacrifices and no idols. Worship was not a casual thing where you could quickly bring in your animal offerings and get your godly brownie points. Making the execution of worship intricate may have helped to deepen the Israelites' sense of piety.

Vengeance: The rule of blood vengeance already had the authority of a long history in the Middle East of

Moses' day. The law of retaliation, "Anyone who injures his neighbor will get back whatever he gave: fracture for fracture, eye for eye, tooth for tooth. What he did to hurt that person will be done to him" (Leviticus 24:19–20; also Exodus 21:23–25; Deuteronomy 19:21), is often misinterpreted as a statement of the brutality of the Hebrew culture (often drawn as a contrast to the Christian God of love). This is completely erroneous, however. The law of retaliation was a law to limit the blood vengeance so that mere injury could not be grounds for justifiable homicide. Further, the Mosaic code dictated that in the new Israel cities of asylum be established so that people guilty of accidental death had the recourse of mercy available to them if they could prove the unintentionality of their killing. Finally Moses will quote God warning Israel not to be obsessed with the sin of others because the Lord assumes authority for the execution of vengeance. "I'm in charge of vengeance and payback" (Deuteronomy 32:35).

Slavery: Slavery also was (and continued for centuries thereafter) an established institution in Moses' day. For the Hebrews a countryman could become a slave if he is unable to pay his debts, but he was to be released after six years of service (Exodus 21:2). Moreover, the practice of rest from all labor on the Sabbath always applied to slaves as well as free men and women.

War: Although very specific instruction is given regarding the total destruction of the peoples who inhabited the land God meant for Israel to have in Canaan, war engaged under ordinary circumstances was always to include the offer of peace before attack (Deuteronomy 20:10–12). Before battle, army officers were to query the troops about their readiness for the fight. "Is there a man here who has built a new house but hasn't yet dedicated it? Let him go home right now lest he die in battle and another man dedicate it ... Is there here a man engaged to marry who hasn't yet taken his wife? Let him go home right now lest he die in battle and another man take her" (Deuteronomy 20:5–7). "When a man takes a new wife, he is not to go out with the army or be given any business or work duties. He gets one year off simply to be at home making his wife happy" (Deuteronomy 24:5).

In other respects the Torah makes many general statements regarding social responsibility and personal integrity that break new ethical ground in its cultural milieu.

Poverty: "There are always going to be poor and needy people around you. So I command you: Always be generous, open purse and hands, give to your neighbors in trouble" (Deuteronomy 15:11). Yet the goal is that "there must be no poor people among you because God is going to bless you lavishly" (Deuteronomy 15:4). Israelites were not to charge interest when lending money to the needy (Exodus 22:25). When reaping the harvest, they were to leave some for the alien and the poor to glean (Leviticus 19:9–10). Likewise, it was the community's responsibility to protect the poor from being denied justice in a lawsuit because of their economic status (Exodus 23:6).

Economics: It was the responsibility of the Hebrew community to support the temple priests financially (Deuteronomy 14:29). God required the people to tithe, paying one tenth of everything earned in a year as an offering (Leviticus 27:30). Every seven years the farmland was to lie fallow (Exodus 23:10–11), and all debts within the community of Israel were to be written off (Deuteronomy 15:1).

Justice: The concern for general fairness was paramount. False testimony was the enemy of justice, and leniency was not given to those who followed the crowd in doing wrong (Exodus 23:1–2). There were to be no bribes (Exodus 23:8) and no cheating in business dealings (Leviticus 19:35). The law applied the same to rich and poor (Leviticus 19:15). The Israelites were not to take advantage of widows and orphans (Leviticus 25:36) and not to mistreat foreigners. Instead, "remember you were once strangers in Egypt" (Exodus 22:21). Justice included, "If you find your enemy's ox or donkey loose, take it back to him" (Exodus 23:4). Neither should parents suffer for the crimes of their children nor vice versa. "Each person should be put to death for his own sin" (Deuteronomy 24:16). Capital crimes could only be punished on the testimony of two or three witnesses, and while all executions were to be committed corporately (usually by stoning), these witnesses were to cast the first stones (Deuteronomy 17:6–7). The rationale for all legal punishment stemmed not from vengeance but from the need to keep Israel pure as a community (Deuteronomy 17:7).

The Mosaic code in all its length, breadth, and depth filled Israel with tremendous pride and joy. Their doctors of the law spent hours discussing its implications in every aspect of life. Eventually the Talmud would collect the oral tradition around these debates over the meaning of the Torah. But over time two lines stood out as a summary of all the statutes. "Do not seek revenge or carry a grudge against any of your people. Love your neighbor as yourself" (Leviticus 19:18). Then universalizing this teaching to all people, "When a foreigner lives in your land, don't take advantage of him. Treat the foreigner the same as the native. Love him like one of your own. Remember that you were once foreigners in Egypt" (Leviticus 19:34).

In the first century BCE, tradition has it that a Gentile wishing to convert to Judaism asked the rabbi Hillel to tell him the sum of the Law standing on one foot. Rabbi Hillel replied, "That which is hateful to you, do not do to your fellow. That is the whole Torah; the rest is the explanation; go and learn."[17] Similarly when a religious scholar of the day asked Jesus to name the greatest commandment of the Law, He replied, adding Deuteronomy 6:5, "'Love the Lord your God with all your heart and with all your soul and with all your mind.' This is the first and greatest commandment. And the second is like it: 'Love your neighbor as yourself.' All the Law and the Prophets hang on these two commandments" (Matthew 22:37–39 NIV).

In the end Leviticus makes it clear that God is serious about worship and holiness. Unlike pagan gods, Israel's God does not crave worship for the aroma of the sacrifices but because it aids His people in understanding who God is and allows them to demonstrate their appreciation of God's gifts. Again departing from the religions of her neighbors, Israel's obligation to worship does not bind God to any particular course of action. Better attention to the details of piety did not accumulate credit for Israel in God's accounting books. Instead, worship was always construed as the privilege of Israel for the sake of the love they bore the God who first loved and saved them. Long into the future after Israel had lost the Promised Land,

---

[17] This famous maxim ascribed to Hillel is found in the Pirkei Avoth (the Chapter of the Fathers) in the Talmud. Compiled between 200 and 500 CE, the Talmud contains the written version of centuries of oral tradition recounting Jewish theologians' discourses on the precise meaning of the Torah.

she would still count it a privilege to serve and worship the Lord according to the Torah.

Numbers

If it seems hard to follow what is going on in the book of Numbers, consider that its mishmash of census lists, additional ordinances and rites, and stuttering storytelling match right up with the forty-year history of disorganized wandering that the book is covering. We open with the new configuration of twelve tribes. Since Levi has become the tribe of priests, the tribe of Joseph has been split between Joseph's two sons, Ephraim and Manasseh. Picking up where the narrative left off at the end of Exodus with the completion of the tabernacle, Israel's moveable tent of worship, it would seem that Israel is poised to tackle the next thing on God's agenda—the Promised Land itself. Quickly, however, we will see that while God is ready to give Israel the land, she is not ready to take it. A year's training in God's law and the gift of the rituals of worship will prove insufficient for the Hebrews to trust God in taking them into war. The tale of Numbers will track Israel's extended sojourn in the wilderness—the forty years it will take the new generation, those unacquainted with a life in Egypt, to grow up. We must particularly observe the relationship of God and Moses as it develops through these difficult times, which Peterson calls Israel's teenage years.

At God's command, Moses assembles the tribes with the flag of Judah in the lead (Numbers 10:11–14). The cloud signifying God's presence lifts from above the tabernacle to indicate that Israel is to leave Sinai. Thus, with God's teaching supposedly fresh in their minds, the tribes of Israel set forth for their new home. Three whole days pass before the complaining begins (Numbers 11:1). Though God continues to provide manna and quail, the Israelites gripe that they want something else to eat.

Some even echo the refrain that they were better off back in Egypt (Numbers 11:4–6). When it gets too much for Moses, he takes his honest exasperation to God in a passage that substantiates our suggestion of his role as Israel's nanny/mother.

> Why are you treating me this way? What did I ever do to you that I deserve this? Did I conceive them (the Israelites)? Was I their mother? So why dump the responsibility of this people on me? Why tell me to carry them around like a nursing mother ... I can't do this myself—it's too much! If this is how you intend to treat me, do me a favor and kill me." (Numbers 11:11–15)

Next Moses has to deal with squabbles in his own family. In chapter 12, we find sister Miriam and brother Aaron with their noses out of joint, complaining that Moses is unfairly getting all the credit for speaking for God (Numbers 12:2). God settles this by making Miriam leprous. Aaron immediately repents on behalf of both of them, and while God accedes to Moses' prayer for Miriam's healing, it is clear that God is unwilling for either to presume equality with Moses' position.

By chapter 13, we discover that though God means for Israel to have the Promised Land, the Lord is not handing it over to them on a silver platter. Logically a scouting mission must precede the conquest. Led by Moses' right hand, Joshua, representatives from each of the twelve tribes go forth to spy out the land and return after forty days with a mixed report. The land is beautiful, but the people are giants and therefore unbeatable (Numbers 13:27, 31). Only Joshua and Caleb of Judah dissent out of faith. "If God is pleased with us, he will lead us into that land ... He'll just give it to us. Just don't rebel against God! ... They have no protection and God is on our side. Don't be afraid of them!" (Numbers 14:8–9).

Nonetheless, the people's fear has carried the day. There is talk of stoning Joshua and Caleb, and many are singing the "let's go back to Egypt" tune. God is furious: "How long will these people treat me like dirt? How long refuse to trust me? And with all these signs I've done among them," and again tells Moses He will make a better nation through him (Numbers 14:11–12). But Moses remains steadfast in his defense of Israel, talking God down from His anger by quoting His own self-description in Exodus 34:6–7. "GOD, slow to get angry and huge in loyal love, forgiving iniquity and rebellion and sin ..." (Numbers 14:18). The Lord pronounces the divine verdict on the matter. God will honor Moses and forgive Israel, but the Promised Land will be off limits to the entire generation who rejected the Deity (Numbers 14:20–23). The only exceptions will be all children under twenty and the two who filed the minority report, Joshua and Caleb.

Thus, the Israelites end up roving the wilderness of the Sinai Peninsula for forty years while the older age bracket dies off. It is significant that these rising adults have no experience of living as slaves. Similarly they have spent their lives relying on God's providence for their daily food and water. God meets regularly with Moses. The Deity provides manna and quail and continues to draw water from rocks when no fresh water is otherwise available. The camp moves when the cloud above the tabernacle rises and stays put when it descends. Led by Aaron, priests are ordained from the tribe of Levi.

Mostly it is schooling that continues. Examples are made of disobedience. When Israel sees God's wrath over their fear regarding the attack of Canaan, they try to make it up to the Lord the next day by going into battle against the Amalekites and Canaanites. But as Moses forewarned them, there would be no victory without God's direct leading (Numbers 14:40–45). Similarly when a man gathers wood on the Sabbath, he is stoned to death in keeping with the sanctity of the commandment (Numbers 15:32–36). A group of rebel leaders attempt to muster the Hebrews against Moses, saying the

Promised Land was actually Egypt. God has the earth swallow them (Numbers 16:13–32). Because of yet another whining session, God sends venomous snakes among the Israelites. Those afflicted had to demonstrate their renewed faith by gazing at a bronze snake Moses set up on a pole (Numbers 21:4–9). Men engaging in sex with Moabite women as part of their Baal worship are killed, and their bodies are put on public display (Numbers 25:1–4).

In time God begins to prepare Israel for the conquest of Canaan with skirmishes amongst the peoples of the desert they are traversing on their way to the Promised Land. When the Hebrews consult with God before their attack and promise to dedicate their spoils to the Lord, they enjoy victory (Numbers 21:1–3). Moses negotiates with kings for passage through their territories. Some kings attack Israel to their woe (Numbers 21:21–35). Balak, King of Moab, even tries to hire a soothsayer named Balaam to put a curse on Israel to no avail (chapters 22–24). Moses leads a campaign against Midian, resulting in the first territory that Israel takes as a possession for two and a half of the twelve tribes (chapter 31).

In summation, Numbers demonstrates the devilishness of the details in remaking a people's identity. Israel's wilderness wanderings are a messy, uneven time. It is a book full of squabbles and grumpiness with instructions having to be repeated and lessons learned more than once. In particular, we see God and Moses constantly getting exasperated with the subpar performance of the Israelites. Yet the brunt falls upon Moses. He is the glue reminding God and Israel that they are family and need to stick with God's program. In this section we have already looked at some of the instances of his frustration with the task God has set before him, but we have also seen how his honest venting of his grievances to God has enabled him to endure pressure that would easily crush an ordinary human leader. Moses has come a long way since his first encounter with

God in the burning bush, but the final portrait of Moses waits to be revealed in the book of Deuteronomy.

Deuteronomy

Numbers ends rather unceremoniously with Moses tweaking a legal issue of land inheritance for the daughters of Zelophehad, a man who had no son to be his heir (Numbers 36). There is no particular climax that leads into Deuteronomy, nothing that says, "Now at long last Israel is ready to embark on her destiny to become landowners in the site of God's promise to Abraham." Even so, the time has come. We open the last book of the Pentateuch to find Moses poised to say his good-byes to Israel. We will find him something like a parent launching a child from the homestead, knowing that it is time for the son or daughter to be on his or her own but nonetheless nervous for the trials the young one will face.

Basically Israel has her game plan set. By God's Word to Moses (Numbers 27:18–22) Joshua will be in command. The Hebrews will enter Canaan from the east side of the Jordan River, having just captured the territory to the east and deeding it to Gad, Reuben, and half of the Manasseh (Numbers 34). All the adults of the generation that doubted God one too many times have passed away. Even Moses' siblings are gone. Moreover, God has told Moses that his days are numbered and that he will not be allowed to see the Promised Land that he has spent the last third of his life seeking. Ostensibly Moses is barred because he lost his temper over the people's complaint about water while in Kadesh in the Desert of Zin (Numbers 20:2–12). However, because God has a habit of forgiving people, this explanation doesn't really ring true. When Moses tries to talk to God about it one more time as he looks across the Jordan, God cuts him off, "Enough of that. Not another word from you on this ... [Instead] command Joshua. Give him courage. Give him strength. Single-handed he will lead this people across the river. Single-handed he'll cause them to inherit the land at which you can only look" (Deuteronomy 3:26–28). Moses has completed the job God set before him. Joshua's time to serve comes next.

Nonetheless, as Moses gazes across the Jordan, it occurs to him that he still has one last service to render. The people are ready for battle; the leadership of the twelve tribes has been set. The tension of eagerness combined with fear-tainted anticipation fills the camp. Joshua is more than equal to the task ahead of him. But only Moses can capture for Israel what she has learned since God has freed the Hebrews from their bondage in Egypt. No one else has the perspective of having talked one-on-one to God, of being privy to the Lord's great plans, the anger that has been tempered with patience and forgiveness, and the huge love that lies behind it all. Somehow Moses must put all this into the people's hearts so that they do not forget who they are and whose they are.

Moses rises to speak to his people. In a series of three sermons he reiterates for them first their history—the trials they have endured, the sins their forefathers committed, and over it all the wonders they have seen God do (Deuteronomy 1:6–4:43). Second he addresses their new beliefs—God's gift of the Torah that will set Israel apart as a holy nation (Deuteronomy 4:44–11:32 plus chapters 12–26). Finally he explains how it lies with each Israelite to decide to embrace this destiny that God has so generously made available to the people Israel (Deuteronomy 29–30). Notice as you read how Moses begins by referring to God as "our God" and then increasingly as "your God" throughout his addresses. In this way he entreats Israel to begin owning their relationship to their Lord for themselves instead of merely relying on his mediation.

In the first sermon Moses organizes Israel's memory of her history. Against our expectations his review of Israel's past does not begin in Egypt but in the wilderness, the part that the present group of Hebrews has actually lived through. As Moses recaps the story line of Numbers, he pauses to lament Israel's unfaithfulness to her God, who fought for her in Egypt and "who carried you as a father carries his child" (Deuteronomy 1:32) through all these years of hardship. Anticipating the second treatise, Moses urges Israel,

> Pay attention: I'm teaching you the regulations that GOD commanded me, so that you may live by them in the land you are entering to take up ownership. Keep them. Practice them. ... What other great nation has gods that are intimate with them the way GOD, our God, is with us, always ready to listen to us? And what other nation has rules and regulations as good and fair as this Revelation that I'm setting before you today? ... Don't forget anything of what you've seen. ... Teach what you've seen and heard to your children and grandchildren. (Deuteronomy 4:5–9)

But the exhortation includes several ominous warnings.

> When the time comes that you ... become corrupt and make any carved images ... you'll be kicked off the land that you are about to cross over the Jordan to possess (the Exile). ... GOD will scatter you far and wide (the Diaspora). ... But even there, if you seek GOD, your God, you'll be able to find him if you're serious, ... GOD, your God, is above all a compassionate God. In the end he will not abandon you. (Deuteronomy 4:25–31)

Only now does Moses harken back to the incredible works God did for Israel in Egypt (Deuteronomy 4:32–34) in order to lead the Israelites to the great truth they need to see as they receive the land promised. God is not merely the God of Israel. "You were shown all this so that you would know that GOD is, well, God. He's the only God there is" (Deuteronomy 4:35). Thus, Israel's monotheism begins in earnest.

Having reminded Israel of what God has done, Moses focuses the second sermon on God's great gift of the Law. Moses repeats the Ten Commandments (Deuteronomy 5:6–21) and crowns this part of his sermon with the *Shema*, Israel's ultimate statement of faith, which says, "Hear, O Israel, the Lord our God, the Lord is One" (Deuteronomy 6:4 NIV). Next follows the reminder to "love, GOD, your God, with your whole heart: love him with all that's in you, love him with all you've got" (Deuteronomy 6:5). It is this radicalization of Israel's faith—the bold pronouncement that God is the only god—that becomes the rationale behind Israel's war policy in conquering Canaan. If the faith of Israel is to survive, the Hebrews must "completely destroy" (Deuteronomy 7:2) the current residents of the land so that their paganism does not lead God's people away from the beliefs that set them apart from others.

Of course, it will not be enough simply to eliminate the influence of foreign gods and worship. Israel will need to assert her faith constantly. God will give Israel the land, but it will be tempting for the Hebrews to congratulate themselves for their victories. Moses advises them to make a litany of God's great deeds as their mantra.

1. God delivered Israel from Egypt.
2. God led the Hebrews through the wilderness.
3. God saved His people from snakes and scorpions.
4. God saved His people from thirst (water from the rocks).
5. And God saved His people from hunger (manna) (Deuteronomy 8:15–16)

These acts not only demonstrated God's faithfulness but also prepared Israel for the hardship of making the land their own.

Chapters 12 to 26 form what is called the Deuteronomic code and serve as a summary not only of the laws derived from the Ten Commandments but also the practice of worship and holiness that were to define the cult of Israel. As we discussed in the section on Leviticus, these laws run the gamut from the nitpicky details of kosher nutrition (Deuteronomy 14:3–21) to socially progressive admonitions to be generous to the poor (Deuteronomy 15:7–11) and give time off to new husbands (Deuteronomy 24:5). As in Jacob's address at the end of Genesis, Moses refers to a prophet whom God will raise up out of the house of Israel and who will continue to lead God's people. But even though the Hebrews should seek this prophet, they must be wary about individuals making false claims of speaking for God (Deuteronomy 18:15–22). While it would be easy to get bogged down in the complexity of all these ordinances and admonitions, the bottom line is clear. If Israel will live obediently according to God's ways, she will enjoy God's blessings. If she does not, curses will abound (chapter 28).

In the final sermon Moses makes the contrast between curse and blessing paramount.

> I command you today: Love GOD, your God. Walk in his ways. Keep his commandments, regulations and rules so that you will live, really live, live exuberantly, blessed by GOD, your God, in the land you are about to enter and possess. But I warn you: If you have a change of heart, refuse to listen obediently, and willfully go off to serve and worship other gods, you will most certainly die … I place before you Life and Death, Blessing and Curse. Choose life so that you and your children will live. And love GOD, your God, listening obediently to him, firmly embracing him. (Deuteronomy 30:16–20)

Notice here the parallels with the garden of Eden. Israel is about to enter the Promised Land, which "flows with milk and honey" but which bears with it very serious injunctions against disobedience. But unlike the Eden story, where the edict against eating from the Tree of Knowledge of Good and Evil seemed like an arbitrary rule, the spirit of the laws of the Torah (if not all of the specific statutes) make good sense to us. What would be wrong in a society where people actually kept the Ten Commandments? We can imagine it, but we have never witnessed it.

Let this reality check help us feel the pathos of Moses' good-bye. In chapter 32, he teaches the people a song chronicling God's frustrating love affair with Israel. After that, Moses hands the priests the revelation he has written out, held by tradition to be the five books of the Torah (Deuteronomy 32:44–47). Chapter 33 follows with blessings to the individual tribes in parallel with Jacob's words to his sons at the end of Genesis. Then Moses climbs from the plains of Moab to Mount Nebo and takes his last look at the land he will not walk in life. Deuteronomy closes by saying that Moses died there in the land of Moab but that no one knew his burial site. At 120 years old "his eyesight was sharp and he still walked with a spring in his step" (Deuteronomy 34:7). Israel mourns him for thirty days and leaves him this epitaph: "No prophet has risen since in Israel like Moses, whom God knew face-to-face" (Deuteronomy 34:10).

Like Abraham, Moses was a friend to God. The man who began his service so reluctantly in Exodus ends up in Deuteronomy with a strength to his faith analogous to the transformation we observed in Abraham in the binding of Isaac story (Genesis 22). Let us look at what the Moses story teaches us about this transformation process.

The job God gave Moses was arduous, and Moses did not perform it without his moments of straightforward complaint and frustration. Neither did God reward him in this life for all the hardship he endured on the Lord's behalf. Yet even God's denial of Moses' last heart's desire—to see the Promised Land—did not harm their mutual understanding. Perhaps what is most illuminating in the God-Moses relationship is their frequent bantering. Some may ask if seeing Moses talk God out of decisions doesn't bring God down a peg, making the Deity subject to Moses' influence. Yet if we consider the nature of any relationship operating between unequal parties, someone has to be the one who accommodates the other. God must come to Moses' level of understanding since the reverse is impossible. Thus, we see God interacting with Moses in an honest expression of human emotions. The Lord takes the first step by sharing with Moses His name, an intimacy God had not allotted to the Patriarchs. In keeping with the name of Israel, God presents Himself to Moses as one who can be wrestled with. The Lord listens to Moses and allows Moses the dignity of putting forward arguments that God can buy. This is not an abdication of divine sovereignty. Rather it is the means by which God facilitates the forging of His relationship with Moses.

As a result of all this effort on God's part, Moses changes from a simple man tentative in his willingness to do a job (how do you say no to God?) to an impassioned leader nurturing Israel with all the painstaking devotion of a parent raising a child. It is with honest zeal that Moses preaches his parting words to his people just because it is one more thing he can do to serve them and serve his Lord. Because of that passion and his patience and shared purpose with God, God is able to use Moses' leadership to shepherd the children of Israel out of their bondage to their slave mentality toward becoming free people who are able to make a nation of themselves. The Genesis project is accomplished. God has created a people as a foothold among humanity. The divine connection is not merely with a single human but with a people who are beginning to be able to see who the Lord is, the God no one could imagine, unlike any pagan ideas about deity. God, self-named I Am, is the only God. He is all-powerful and impervious to manipulation but open to sincere argument. While God is capable of great anger, that wrath is never arbitrary and more importantly, never stronger than the divine compassion. Because Israel knows God and knows the Torah, the Lord can begin to demonstrate holiness to all the peoples of the earth. If the Law is followed, life will indeed be the good thing God created it to be back in Genesis 1.

The rules have been explained. The new Eden awaits God's new creation.

Chapter 5

Does It Really Say That Joshua Fought the Battle of Jericho and the Walls Came Tumbling Down?

> Joshua fit de battle of Jericho, Jericho, Jericho
> Joshua fit de battle of Jericho,
> And the walls came a tumblin' down
>
> You may talk about the man Gideon,
> You may talk about the man Saul,
> There's none like good ole Joshua, and the battle of Jericho
>
> Up to the walls of Jericho
> He marched with spear in hand;
> "Go blow them ram horns," Joshua cried, "for the battle is in my hand.
>
> —African-American Spiritual

If you've heard of Joshua at all, it may be because of this song heard sometime in your childhood. It's more likely that you've heard of Jericho, the city Israel was able to capture because the walls crumbled before her. Let's see how the song and the story of Jericho fit into the history of how Israel takes up residence on the land bridge between two ancient civilizations—Egypt and Mesopotamia—as it is recorded in Joshua, Judges, and Ruth.

Reading Exodus through Deuteronomy, we watched how God created the people Israel by means of a mediator named Moses. Moses has said his good-byes and turned over the leadership of Israel to Joshua, the man who has stood by him since the parting of the Red Sea and knows intimately what it has taken to get Israel to this juncture. This changing of the guard appears to be part of Israel's growing-up process and is probably at the root of God's denial to let Moses see the Promised Land. Whereas Moses emerged as a parent to Israel, Joshua's role will be more that of a military chief, thus, allowing Israel to continue to transition into adult independence.

Before we begin our tour of Joshua, Judges, and Ruth and their description of Israel establishing ownership of the Promised Land, we need to discuss up front the military policy of total war or "holy curse," as Peterson labels it in *The Message,* that will characterize the conquest of Canaan. We have already seen this required obliteration of life (men, women, children, and animals) in the battles fought east of the Jordan with Moses at the helm (Numbers 31). In the book of Joshua, we will find it implemented in full force. But why is this God's policy? Our first thought is that it seems to run counter to the teachings of fairness and compassion that comprise the Torah. But we need to remember that we discuss a time in world history where animosity between neighboring peoples always involved military action accompanied by horrific lack of mercy and loss of life. Even though we still have a passage in Deuteronomy that reminds Israel to make an offer of peace to a city she plans to attack (Deuteronomy 20:10–12), this ordinance will not apply to the taking of the Promised Land. As we will see throughout the rest of the history books of the Old Testament, Israel will be at war with her neighbors much of the time. For a period she will enjoy victory. Later her success will ebb and flow with the strength of her leaders. What will distinguish Israel from her contemporaries in her notions about war will be the perspective she gains by categorizing her exploits as either God-sanctioned or selfishly motivated. We will need to ask ourselves if the notion that "God made me do such and such" is simply an excuse that Israel concocts to justify her aggrandizement or if God's commands end up causing Israel to behave in ways that seem unusual for this period in history. If God's point in adopting a people is to show the world what the Deity and His ways look like, we should be on the lookout for what makes this history of Israel's rise to power different from that of other peoples of the ancient world.

Joshua

Deuteronomy ends with Israel poised for battle but stopping to mourn Moses. Joshua picks up on that same note. Taking up where the Lord left off with Moses, God speaks to Joshua, "Moses my servant is dead. [You need to] get going. Cross to the country I'm giving to the People of Israel ... just as I promised Moses ... In the same way I was with Moses I'll be with you" (Joshua 1:1–5). God means for Israel to have the land of Canaan, the land flowing with milk and honey where Abraham, Isaac, and Jacob had all lived and been buried. But by now the land is occupied by others—idol worshipers whose practices include sacred prostitution and child sacrifice, practices that are antithetical to everything that God has taught the Hebrews in their years in the desert. Because of the threat these foreign people's ideas represent to Israel's ability to live according to God's newly revealed Torah, God has commanded that the enemy be completely destroyed—women, children, and livestock as well as all the artifacts of their religion. The degree of Israel's obedience to God would correspond directly to their level of success.

Having gotten the go-ahead pep talk from God (Joshua 1:2–9), Joshua addresses his people. "Pack your bags. In three days you will cross this Jordon River to enter and take the land GOD, your God, is giving you to possess" (Joshua 1:11). The city of Jericho lies on the west side of the Jordan. As a good military strategist, Joshua sends scouts to assess the battle situation. The spies manage to get themselves in the good graces of a local prostitute whose house is conveniently located on the wall of the city. Even when the king of Jericho warns his citizens about the coming Israelite attack, Rahab does not betray the Hebrews. Instead, she lies to the regal messenger that the men seen entering her house had left when the city gates were about to be shut. In reality, she has them hidden on her roof. With the king's men befuddled, she approaches the strangers and reveals to them what she and all Jericho have heard about the Israelites, "I know that GOD has given you the land. We're all afraid. . . . We heard how GOD dried up the waters of the Red Sea before you when you left Egypt" (Joshua 2:9–10). In exchange for a guarantee of her family's safety, Rahab releases the scouts out over the wall on a rope. The spies return to Joshua with this encouraging insight and acquaint him with their promises to the woman who helped them.

Meanwhile, the people of Israel are packed and ready. Never mind that there is no bridge across the Jordan. On the eve of their embarking Joshua tells them, "Sanctify yourselves. Tomorrow GOD will work miracle-wonders among you" (Joshua 3:5). As the morning dawns, God whispers to Joshua how the Lord will seal the people's trust in his leadership, "This very day I will make you great in the eyes of all Israel. They'll see for themselves that I'm with you in the same way I was with Moses" (Joshua 3:7). Prompted by God's Word, Joshua instructs the priests to carry the ark of the covenant into the center of the Jordan River. But as soon as the priests' feet hit the water, the flow of the river stops and dams itself somewhere upstream. In a stunning reenactment of the parting of the Red Sea for this new generation, Joshua leads his people to the west side. Joshua asks a representative from each tribe to pick up a stone from the riverbed, and these are gathered to make a commemorative monument on the far side. Once everyone else is across, the priests bring the ark back from the midpoint of the river, and the water flows again as they touch the western bank. Indeed, "GOD made Joshua great that day in sight of all Israel. They were in awe of him just as they had been in awe of Moses all his life" (Joshua 4:14).

Though the people of Israel are now in the Promised Land, there remain some items to address before the conquering begins. During the forty years of wandering the practice of circumcision has apparently been in hiatus. Making sure this new generation is properly included in this covenant, which began with Abraham, becomes the first order of business. While their men heal, the nation holds together in the campsite and prepares to celebrate the Passover. For the first time since Egypt manna is off the menu, and the people eat from the food grown in their new homeland (Joshua 5:2–12).

Following these happy festivities, Joshua is preparing for the battle of Jericho when he notices a stranger holding a drawn sword. Joshua approaches him to inquire if he be friend or foe. The man says, "Neither. I'm commander of God's army" (Joshua 5:14). This messenger from God makes it clear that the Lord is not merely the hired god of the Israelites. Israel is to fight for God, not the other way around. Joshua falls down in obeisance and begs, "What orders does my Master have for his servant?" The commander responds just as God had once spoken to Moses from the burning bush, "Take your sandals off your feet. The place you are standing is holy" (Joshua 5:14-15, compare to Exodus 3:5). The conference Joshua has with God at this juncture concerns some unorthodox battle strategy. In this battle it will be clear that God *gives* Jericho to Israel. With seven priests blowing trumpets and bearing the ark of the covenant embedded in their midst, Israel's troops are to make a single circuit of the circumference of Jericho's walls for six days followed by seven circuits on the seventh day. With the final march, Israel is to add their shouts to the blaring of the trumpets, and this will cause the walls of Jericho to crash down (Joshua 6:2–5).

Of course, the plan works. The walls crumble, and the city is put to the sword. Only Rahab and her family are spared that day. Joshua's soldiers obey the command to destroy everything alive in Jericho. Yet God has forbidden any Israelite to gain personally from this victory. All valuables—gold, silver, and the like—are to be deposited in the treasury of God's house. This is our first indication of God requiring Israel to obey a command inconsistent with customary warfare practices. Our horror at the annihilation of the people of Jericho is not something that would resonate with the Israelites, who would see this as a common consequence of conquest. But denying soldiers the right to plunder in victory is another story. As we might expect, not everyone complies with this last edict. Achan of the tribe of Judah has looted on his own behalf. This has made God angry.

Unaware of Achan's violation, Joshua plans his next battle against the city of Ai. The scouts judge this city an easy mark and advise their leader not to bother sending his whole army. But when the three thousand attack the city gate, immediately thirty-six Israelites fall, and the rest turn tail and run. Joshua takes his angst to God, "Oh, Master God. Why did you insist on bringing this people across the Jordan? … Why didn't we just settle on the east side of the Jordan?" (Joshua 7:7–9). Before we dismiss Joshua for being as faithless as the Hebrews wishing to return to Egypt, we need to see that Joshua's lament stems from his deep faith that God would, of course, grant them continuous victory in battle. Suddenly this defeat makes him wonder if God is indeed guaranteeing Israel's success. A horrific thought hatches inside him. Has God capriciously played him false, taking away the charm of victory when He knew Joshua was counting on it? Surely any human can identify with the deep wound Joshua feels considering the ramifications if God is not as trustworthy as one has always believed. Still, we, the readers, already know that the problem is not God but Achan. It is interesting that though God could have taken Joshua's accusations as a serious insult, the Lord's actual response is to set the record straight with mere annoyance. "Get up. Why are you groveling? Israel has sinned" (Joshua 7:10–11).

Rescued now from his spiritual crisis, Joshua has only to assemble the people by tribes and allow God to point out the guilty party. When Achan is found out, he makes a full confession and tells where he has hidden the valuables. Nonetheless, an example is made of him. The community of Israel stones him, his entire family, and his livestock. All that he had owned, including the ill-gotten booty, is then burned. The Torah endorses the stoning of Achan for his violation against God's command (Deuteronomy 17:2–7), but it does not call for the family to suffer for the patriarch's sin (Deuteronomy 24:16). What we see here is the holy curse being applied with equal fervor within Israel as without. God means to have the divine ways obeyed. With the debt for the sin paid, Joshua can return to his battle strategy with renewed confidence in God's help as well as sobering consciousness of God's standards of obedience.

Although God reasserts the guarantee of Israel's victory (Joshua 8:1), we should note that in the second strike against Ai Joshua utilizes what he learned militarily from the failed attempt in planning his new strategy. Apparently only the battle of Jericho is to be a bona fide gift. The remaining battles would have to be won with military acumen. An advance guard of Joshua's army pose themselves as sitting ducks before the soldiers within the walled city. The king takes the bait, and the armed forces of Ai move out to chase away the Israelites. In the meantime the bulk of Joshua's men prepare to storm the city itself. Joshua signals this ambush by raising a javelin and keeping it lifted until the battle concludes (Joshua 8:18, 26), an act reminiscent of Moses holding his hands up during the fight with the Amalekites shortly after the parting of the Red Sea (Exodus 17:11). Israel takes Ai and burns the city to the ground, killing all twelve thousand inhabitants in battle, save the king, whom they assassinate after the fact. With irony, this time God allows the collection of personal booty and livestock. Following the win, Joshua builds an altar according to the instructions Moses has left in the book of Revelation (the Torah). There Israel makes offerings and sacrifices while Joshua writes out a copy of Moses' book and then reads it aloud to the people (Joshua 8:32–35).

As word of the conquering Israelites gathers in the region, many tribes decide to band together to challenge the Hebrew menace with the greater strength of numbers. The Gibeonites, however, choose a less obvious strategy. They determine to save their necks by styling themselves as faraway foreigners. In this way they hoodwink Joshua into granting them a peace treaty, even though, the narrative notes, the Israelites who checked out their story did not consult God regarding their findings (Joshua 9:14). When the truth comes out that indeed the Gibeonites are natives of Canaan, Joshua does not kill them because of his oath. He does, however, consign them to menial jobs within Israel— woodcutting and water carrying—on account of their deception. Although not addressed specifically here, we can begin to see that sometimes it is difficult to prioritize God's commands. Here Joshua believes that he must uphold his oath (Numbers 30:2) over God's general command to destroy the neighboring peoples.

At length, those peoples who are working the alliance stratagem become proactive and attack. Five kings of the Amorites, located in the south, move against Gibeon, knowing of its treaty with Israel. The Gibeonites call in Joshua's troops who travel by night and take their enemies by surprise. The would-be Israelite challengers disperse in retreat. God joins the battle by raining hailstones on the foe and then, at Joshua's request, causing the sun to stop "in its tracks in mid sky ... all day" (Joshua 10:13). Not only is the battle won handily, but the five kings are also discovered holed up in a cave. Joshua makes an object lesson of the futility of testing Israel by executing the disgraced monarchs publicly. Even so, another coalition of kings from the north sets upon Israel, but they are also stymied against the favor of Israel's God. In the end Joshua and his Israelites take down thirty-one kings, massacring all their subjects according to the holy curse God had commanded. And then "Israel had rest from war" (Joshua 11:23).

Only three chapters narrate the bulk of the conquest of Canaan. In contrast, it will take most of the second half of Joshua to describe how Israel's leader endeavors to apportion the newly won land equitably among the tribes. This imbalance of emphasis underscores how unusual this account of history is. Clearly Israel did not deem the prowess of her military worthy of extended chronicling. Yes, Israel fought these battles. Even though God told the Israelites they would be victorious, the Lord did not make any more city walls tumble down after the battle of Jericho. When Joshua asked for the sun to stop in the sky, it was not because Israel was losing that particular battle. What the narrative does show is collaboration between God and Israel to get the job of freeing the land for Israel's use accomplished. Israel does not sing her own praises but God's. "And so GOD gave Israel the entire land that he had so solemnly vowed to give their ancestors. ... Not a single one of their enemies was able to stand up to them—GOD handed over all their enemies to them. ... Everything came out right" (Joshua 21:43–45). The war was a means to an end. The important part was getting Israel settled in the new land.

The nation of Israel begins as a loose confederacy with each tribe governing its own people and lands according to the Law given by Moses. When the time comes for Joshua's farewell to his people, his address will closely follow the sermon Moses delivered before his death.

> I'm an old man. I've lived a long time. You have seen everything that GOD has done to these nations because of you. He did it because he's GOD, your God. ... Now, stay strong and steady. Obediently do everything written in the Book of the Revelation of Moses—don't miss a detail. Don't get mixed up with the nations that are still around. Don't so much as speak the names of their gods or swear by them. And by all means don't worship or pray to them. Hold tight to GOD, your God. (Joshua 23:1–8)

Like Moses, Joshua then proceeds to detail the history of God's relationship with Israel, but he takes the history further back to God's call to Abraham's father, Terah, to move from Ur. This recitation of God's deeds again highlights for Israel the depth of God's care for the Hebrews while it also affirms their identity as a people chosen to reveal God's holiness in the living of their lives. Through Joshua, God reminds Israel, "I handed you a land for which you did not work, towns you did not build. And here you are now living in them and eating from vineyards and olive groves you did not plant" (Joshua 24:13). All this Joshua uses to build to this crescendo: "So now: Fear GOD. Worship him in total commitment. ... If you decide that it's a bad thing to worship GOD, then choose a god you'd rather serve—and do it today. ... As for me and my family, we'll worship GOD" (Joshua 24:14–15).

Just as they did when Moses asked if they would promise to obey God's commandments, the Israelites readily answer, "Count us in: We too are going to worship GOD. He's our God" (Joshua 24:18). Joshua hears how easily his people assent to a commitment to the Lord and warns prophetically, "You can't do it; you're not able to worship GOD. He is a holy God. He is a jealous God. He won't put up with your fooling around and sinning. When you leave GOD and take up the worship of foreign gods, he'll turn around and come down on you hard. He'll put an end to you—and after all the good he has done for you" (Joshua 24:19–20). But the people protest. They will worship God. Joshua dismisses them. Shortly thereafter he dies and is buried in the land of his inheritance.

In this way the book of Joshua ends on a high note. The conquest has been accomplished with as much ease as God had promised. Except for his momentary faltering after the first battle of Ai, Joshua has proved himself a paragon of faithfulness and obedience to the instructions God has given him. He has led this new generation with all the strength and good habits Moses mentored into him. God has provided that Joshua would hold the allegiance of his people just as Moses did before him.

God has come through with all His promises as well. The Israelites have survived the hundreds of years of slavery in Egypt and the forty years in the wilderness, and their numbers have only increased. Now they possess the land—the land flowing with milk and honey—fulfilling the vow God made first to a childless nomad whom He had settled upon to be the father of His people.

While the biblical narrative never questions the method by which Israel comes to rule the erstwhile Canaan—the placing of whole peoples under the holy curse of total destruction—we cannot help but note what a departure this practice seems from the ethics of the Torah. The only explanation implied is that somehow the fledgling faith of Israel would not have withstood the side-by-side exposure to the pagan worship of the Canaanites. The remainder of the Old Testament corroborates the truth of this contention with an abundance of anecdotal incidences of Israel abandoning the Torah's teachings. Still, why God chose that means to give Israel to His people remains a conundrum of Jewish and Christian theology.

If we set aside our concern over the multiple massacres, we see that the book of Joshua chronicles a new beginning for Israel. Under the steady leadership of Joshua the people are mostly compliant to God's commands. They are aware of the connection between obeying God and having life go well—what theologians will call the "Deuteronomic code." They have organized their practice of formal worship and structured their local tribal government. They have the Torah and the reminder to hold close to their hearts all that is written therein as well as all that is inscribed in their memories about the saving acts of their God. As is noted at the end of chapter 21, everything has come out right. It is like a reprise of the garden of Eden story told not in metaphoric symbols but with real characters in a real place within human history. God has set Israel up in a land she did not work for with laws (the Torah) that will demonstrate to the world who the Lord of the universe is and what God expects of humans. But even Joshua knows with deep regret how hard it will be to keep evil out of this new Eden.

Judges

Whereas the book of Joshua presents the conquest of the Promised Land as a kind of "Paradise Gained" recovery from Israel's chaotic life in slavery and then in the wilderness, the order created in the apportioning of the tribal lands erodes quickly. For all the good that came Israel's way via the providence of God in Joshua, the book of Judges answers with an uncomfortable *but*. Moses had groomed Joshua as his heir apparent, but no leader emerges after Joshua's death. Peace reigned as Joshua passed, but after his death border skirmishes spark a state of unrest. The various tribes have some moderate success in these smaller battles, but in many cases they fail to drive out the remaining Canaanites and end up living beside them. And living in close proximity with foreign cults leads Israel to start worshiping alongside her neighbors as well.

The book of Judges paints the time following Joshua's death as a dark age. Even the chronology of the events described is left murky. The major thrust of the narrative explains that after those who had lived through the conquest die off, "another generation grew up that didn't know anything of GOD or the work he had done for Israel. The People of Israel did evil in GOD's sight; they served Baal-gods" (Judges 2:10–11). Thus, God's presence in the narrative becomes more distant. Like a human parent, God seems to be giving Israel more space. "Because these people have thrown out my covenant that I commanded their parents and haven't listened to me, I'm not driving out one more person from the nations that Joshua left behind when he died. I'll use them to test Israel and see whether they stay on GOD's road and walk down it as their parents did" (Judges 2:20–22). In short order a pattern of *foxhole faith* develops. As the Israelites start to worship with idols, their neighbors begin to threaten and subjugate them. Israel calls out to God in repentance, pleading for rescue, and in mercy, God raises up a judge—a savior—who enables Israel to regain her autonomy for a time. But then Israel begins to stray again, and the cycle repeats.

The judges function largely as warrior chiefs and prove a mixed lot. The first one, Othniel, Caleb's nephew, emerges after

Israel has endured eight years of servitude to Naharaim, the king of Aram. Othniel leads the tribes in battle, and with the Spirit of God upon him, he brings Israel her freedom and forty years of quiet. But Israel goes back to her evil ways, and God delivers His people to Moab. This time judge Ehud comes to Israel's aid with a trick up his sleeve … or his thigh actually. While bearing the ransom money to the Moabite king, he asks to speak to him privately. Once Eglon sends his guards away, Ehud pulls out a double-edged short sword he has secreted against his thigh and stabs the king in the stomach.

Then God shows Himself an equal-opportunity employer by raising up the prophetess Deborah as judge. When Israel again wanders from God, God allows the tribes to fall under the power of a Canaanite king named Jabin. The people beseech Deborah's help in this calamity, and Deborah calls her officer Barak to lead Israel against Jabin and his military commander, Sisera. Though Deborah promises God's assurance of victory, Barak refuses to go to war without her at his side. Her retort to his insistence, "Of course, I'll go with you. But understand that with an attitude like that, there'll be no glory in it for you. GOD will use a woman's hand to take care of Sisera" (Judges 4:9). With that Israel heads into battle. Deborah calls, "Charge!" to Barak's troops. When the fighting runs in Barak's favor, Sisera makes his escape into what he thinks is a safe tent only to have his friend's wife, Jael, dupe him with kindness and then ram a tent peg into his temple as he sleeps (Judges 4:14–22). Chapter 5 records the victory song Deborah composes—one of the oldest poems in the Bible and a pretty bloodthirsty one at that. Note the female perspective displayed in Judges 5:28, where the poet imagines Sisera's mother waiting anxiously for his return. This episode of both feminine leadership and bloodlust occurs without self-conscious awareness of breaking the norms of female behavior.

But it is not until the judgeship of Gideon that we receive a clear insider's picture of life in this time. As chapter 6 begins, Israel has again done *evil in God's eyes*, and now Midian is having its turn placing Israel at its mercy. Midianites have camped in Israel's fields, destroying her crops and livestock and leaving God's people to seek refuge in caves and hideouts with no means of supporting themselves (Judges 6:2–5). When an angel calls to Gideon in response to Israel's prayers, Gideon responds candidly, "With *me*, my master? If GOD is with us, why has all this happened to us? Where are all the miracle-wonders our parents and grandparents told us about, telling us, 'Didn't GOD deliver us from Egypt?' The fact is GOD has nothing to do with us—he has turned us over to Midian" (Judges 6:13). It is interesting that while Gideon sees no culpability on his own or Israel's part for the current state of affairs, God does not choose to address this point. Instead, God only presses Gideon further until he protests with temerity, "*Me*, my master? How and with what could I ever save Israel? Look at me. My clan's the weakest in Manasseh and I'm the runt of the litter" (Judges 6:15). As the Lord did when Moses tried to present himself as unworthy of the divine call, God reminds Gideon that the Lord will be beside him in battle; God will certify the defeat of Midian. No longer able to dismiss this messenger, Gideon persists in his boldness and asks God to provide a sign while Gideon prepares a gift for the Lord. When the angel touches the food offering, fire breaks out on the rock, burning everything up. This proves so strong a sign that Gideon sincerely regrets his mouthiness with God. "Oh no! Master, GOD! I have seen the angel of God face to face" (Judges 6:22). God calms Gideon's fears but takes him back to the task. Gideon is to tear down his father's altar to Baal and the Asherah fertility pole beside it. For the first time we get a concrete vision of the extent of Israel's unfaithfulness to God. The common man has pagan paraphernalia in his home. With these evil items removed, Gideon is to sacrifice his father's prime bull on a newly made altar with the chopped-up Asherah pole as the firewood beneath the offering. While Gideon follows the instructions to the letter, he still makes the sacrifice at night out of fear of community reprisals.

By Judges 6:34, we note that God's Spirit has come on Gideon, and he solicits troops with success. Nonetheless he craves further confirmation from God. "If this is right, if you are using me to save Israel as you've said, then look: I'm placing a fleece of wool on the threshing floor. If dew is on the fleece only, but the floor is dry, then I know that you will use me to save Israel as you said" (Judges 6:36–37). God not only honors his request, but the Lord even repeats the sign in reverse in response to Gideon's persistent lack of confidence. The next morning, however, when Gideon gathers the troops for battle, God interrupts him and says, "You have too large an army with you. I can't turn Midian over to them like this—they'll take all the credit, saying 'I did it all myself,' and forget about me" (Judges 7:2). By various means God gets Gideon to cull thirty-two companies of men down to three hundred. Perhaps Gideon feels somewhat chagrined after all his recruiting, but he obeys God and situates the three hundred in view of the huge campsite of Midian (Judges 7:2–8). In the night as Israel awaits the morning battle, God offers Gideon yet another glimpse of the righteousness of his rekindled faith in the God of his forefathers. The Lord suggests that if Gideon has any last-minute anxiety about the success of this venture God has put him on, he should go with his armor bearer to eavesdrop on the conversation of the Midianite sentries. Hidden in the night shadows, Gideon hears a soldier relate his recent dream to his partner who immediately interprets it to mean that Israel's God will turn Midian over to Gideon. Immediately Gideon falls to his knees in prayer (Judges 7:9–15). The three hundred defeat their Midian foes with ease, but it is clear to Gideon that God has orchestrated Israel's success (Judges 7:15–21).

Once the Israelites have relished their victory over Midian, their first impulse is to make Gideon their king. They implore their champion, "Rule over us, you and your son and your grandson. You have saved us from Midian's tyranny." But Gideon responds appropriately, "I most certainly will not rule over you, nor will my son. God will reign over you" (Judges 8:22–23). Thus, Gideon becomes a portrait for this era of a faithful warrior for God. His story demonstrates that given a person's allegiance and trust, God can make any leader equal to the job of keeping Israel safe. It does not take a Moses or a Joshua to keep Israel a holy nation, only a people willing to be obedient and humble before their Lord.

It is with dramatic contrast that the narrative turns next to the case of one of Gideon's bastard sons. Abimelech slays all but the youngest of his seventy brothers and proclaims himself king (Judges 9:5–6). Heavy violence stains his three-year rule, and in the end Abimelech suffers the ignominy of being killed by a woman who drops a millstone on his head from a balcony (Judges 9:51–54). In this way "God avenged the evil Abimelech has done to his father, murdering his seventy brothers" (Judges 9:56).

Yet despite these vibrant object lessons, Israel returns to her unfaithful ways. This time the Ammonites threaten God's people, setting up camp in Gilead. Lacking an established leader, the Gileadites turn to Jephthah, a mighty warrior but also an illegitimate son whose family has put him aside to protect their own inheritance. When the elders call him back on the eve of war, Jephthah proposes, "So, if you bring me back home to fight the Ammonites and God gives them to me, I'll be your head—is that right?" (Judges 11:9). His terms accepted, Jephthah next moves to parley with the Ammonite king. Failing in these negotiations,

Jephthah prepares for battle, and the Spirit of God comes upon him. Caught in the moment, he makes the following vow to God. If God gives him victory, he will sacrifice the first thing that meets him on his return home. And of course, God puts the Ammonites into his hands, but the triumph tastes bitter because rather than the expected goat, it is his only child, his daughter, who first rushes out to greet him at his homecoming. Though Jephthah rips his clothing, saying, "Ah, dearest daughter—I'm dirt. I'm despicable. My heart is torn to shreds," his daughter insists, "Dear father, if you made a vow to GOD, do to me what you vowed: GOD did his part and saved you from your Ammonite enemies" (Judges 11:35–36). The daughter is correct in terms of the law, which in Numbers 30:2 states, "When a man makes a vow to GOD or binds himself by an oath to do something, he must not break his word; he must do exactly what he has said." (See also Deuteronomy 23:21–23 and Ecclesiastes 5:4–5.) On the other hand, the Torah specifically taught Israel to stay away from the Ammonite cult of Molech because of its practice of sacrificing children (Leviticus 18:21). It is hard to conceive how Jephthah could not have believed that the edict against child sacrifice would trump the requirement to keep one's oath. Apparently as we also saw with Joshua and the Gibeonites (Joshua 9) and even back to Isaac and his blessing mistakenly spoken over Jacob (Genesis 27), ancient Israel imbues taking oaths with an authority approaching superstition. But where is the Levite community of priests who should have been called upon to settle or at least weigh in on such an ethical dilemma? This story becomes yet another anecdote demonstrating Israel's descent into chaos in the period covered in the book of Judges. Notice that while the narrative has generally delivered plenty of uncensored blood and gore up to this point, in this tale the details of the death of Jephthah's daughter remain inexplicit, covered by the description of her retreat into the hills, mourning her virginity.

Yet what is called a "custom in Israel" (Judges 11:39) appears nowhere else in the Scriptures. Perhaps even the editor of Judges was aghast.

Jephthah dies after he judges Israel for six years. A series of shorter-lived judgeships follow, and within a few decades Israel is back to doing evil in God's eyes. This now commonplace scenario forms the backdrop for the story of Samson, the judge with the longest story and undoubtedly the most fame. Samson is born to a previously barren woman whom an angel visits to alert her to the special requirements of this child. He will be a Nazirite, which means no razor is to touch his head, and he is to abstain from alcohol and all unclean foods. His destiny lies in delivering Israel from the Philistines (Judges 13:1–5).

It is ironic then when the grown-up Samson decides to marry a Philistine woman in chapter 14. He selects his foreign bride without concern for his parents' preference for an Israelite woman (Judges 14:3). Moreover, while the narrative immediately introduces us to Samson's extraordinary strength, especially when the Spirit of the Lord comes upon him (he kills a lion with his bare hands in Judges 14:6), it goes on to prove him lacking both in wisdom and self-restraint. For entertainment at his wedding feast Samson wagers that his guests cannot solve a riddle he fashions but ends up giving the answer away because he can't stand up to his new wife's nagging (Judges 14:12–18). The narrative of the Samson cycle recounts an appalling level of tit-for-tat violence attending the story. The wedding guests threaten to burn the bride and her household to death if she does not extract the riddle's key from Samson (Judges 14:15). Samson murders thirty innocent bystanders in order to obtain the thirty garments as payment for the bet (Judges 14:19). When Samson discovers that his erstwhile father-in-law had given his bride to Samson's best man, he avenges himself by setting fire to the Philistine grain, even though the father offers another daughter (Judges 15:1–5). Inexplicably the Philistines choose to blame the wedding host rather than Samson for their aborted harvest and resort to burning both father and bride at the stake (Judges 15:6). But Samson also takes offense at this act and storms the local Philistines, tearing all of them "limb from limb" (Judges 15:7–8).

All the previously outlined bedlam serves to explain how Samson and the Philistines make a hate match between themselves. Still, it is unclear how Samson merits acclaim as a savior of Israel, especially when we find the tribe of Judah selling Samson out to the Philistines to save their own necks (Judges 15:9–13). Only in his response to this capture do we finally see Samson using his God-given power to defeat the Philistines rather than merely toying with them (Judges 15:14–16). For the first time Samson calls upon God—were you wondering if he even knew about God?—and even here, though he acknowledges that God has given him victory, he is mainly interested in getting a drink. And God provides water bursting from a rock as the Lord did for Israel in the wilderness (Judges 15:18–19). Perhaps we need to think of Samson as a sort of wilderness judge appropriate to sum up the dark age of the Judges.

Let us look at the last episode in the Samson cycle to check whether this evaluation fits. Here at last is the story for which Samson remains famous—the Delilah encounter. Aware of Samson's womanizing tendencies, the Philistines approach Samson's current lover, Delilah, with a cash proposal. If she can connive to learn the secret of Samson's Herculean strength as well as provide the Philistines the means to undo his powers, they will pay her handsomely. Apparently it proves an enticing deal for Delilah, and she immediately sets to work on her seduction techniques. We remember from the first Samson episode that he is fairly vulnerable to a woman's charms, but in this instance he deludes Delilah fully three times. Each time she asks for the secret of his strength, he invents a plausible story upon which she quickly acts while he sleeps. Then having subdued Samson by whatever method he has suggested to her, she calls in the Philistines, awakening her lover with the warning, "The Philistines are on you, Samson." But each time he breaks his bonds in seconds, and the Philistines retreat with egg on their faces and their silver still in their pockets. Now Delilah goes for broke, using the same wiles that won Samson's first bride her ill-fated success. "How can you say 'I love you' when you won't even trust me?" (Judges 16:15). With this she nags him until in exasperation he blurts out, "A razor has never touched my head ... If I were shaved my strength would leave me" (Judges 16:17).

Knowing Samson has now told the truth, Delilah prevails upon the doubting Philistines one more time to make their ambush after she cuts off the seven braids of her lover's hair. Again she stirs him with her cry, "The Philistines are on you, Samson," and he thinks he will go through his usual routine and shake loose of her ties. The narrator notes here, "He didn't realize GOD had abandoned him" (16:21). In short order his captors have him, and we see that their real desire is not Samson's immediate death but his slow torture. They gouge out his eyes and set him in chains to do the work of grinding in the prison. Time passes, and Samson's hair grows again. As the Philistines gather to celebrate the presentation of a sacrifice to their god Dagon, someone suggests bringing in their prize prisoner, Samson, to be paraded and mocked through the proceedings. But the tables are about to be turned on the Philistines. In the midst of the following hoopla Samson cries out to God,

> "*Master* GOD!
>> *Oh, please, look on me again.*
>> *Oh, please, give strength yet once more.*

God!
With one avenging blow let me be avenged
On the Philistines for my two eyes!" (Judges 16:28)

Then as he grabs onto the two central pillars of the temple, Samson collapses the building on himself and all the Philistines present so that in his death he kills more of the enemy than he had in life (Judges 16:29–30).

What are we to make of this tale of the Hebrew Hercules? Compared to the Greek hero whose life deeds were dogged by guilt, Samson seems a rather cavalier brute, more concerned with his own pleasures than matters of right and wrong. He becomes a judge based solely on a résumé of savagely massacring Philistines, and there is no commentary on the effectiveness of his judgeship. As many as he kills, more Philistines remain. When he finally falls to his enemies at Delilah's machinations, his own foolishness undercuts any sympathy we might feel for him. Only when we go on to observe the brutality of the Philistines does our opinion soften toward Samson. Then when he turns back to God, acknowledging the Lord as the source of his strength, he redeems himself after a fashion. That his final act is yet another slaughter the narrator congratulates with irony. His death accomplishes more than his life. Theologically, however, Samson goes from taking God for granted and paying for that hubris when God abandons him (symbolically in the cutting of his hair) to then returning to faith (as his hair grows back) by asking for God's favor in terms relevant to his time so that he might smite Israel's enemy.

After Samson, Judges no longer records the stories of any more leaders in Israel. Instead an interesting refrain surfaces, "In those days there was no king in Israel. People did whatever they felt like doing" (Judges 1 ':6; 18:1; 19:1; 21:25). This complaint, the absence of a mona, ch, stands as the only defense against the reprehensible behavior discussed in these closing chapters. In chapters 17 and 18, a Levite priest leads people into idol worship. Another Levite in chapter 19 takes a concubine and allows her to be gang-raped while on an overnight stay in Benjaminite country. Unthinkably the would-be husband does nothing to rescue the woman during her nightlong assault, but when he finds her dead on the doorstep the next morning, he cuts her body into twelve pieces that he sends throughout Israel. He charges the men he hires to distribute her parts to say to Israel, "Has such a thing as this ever happened from the time the Israelites came up from the land of Egypt until now? Think about it! Talk it over. Do something!" (Judges 19:30). The people of Israel do assemble and decide to take on the tribe of Benjamin. Civil war breaks out, but when the combined forces of Israel defeat the tribe of Benjamin, the people lament the loss of one of their tribes. The congregation of Israel decides to reinstate the Benjaminites and even helps them kidnap Shiloh girls to be their wives when the war has left the men shy of enough women. As Judges caps off this last story with the thematic refrain repeated, "At that time there was no king in Israel. People did whatever they felt like doing" (Judges 21:25), note that it is a series of crimes against women (chapters 19–21) that crystallize the essence of Israel's depravity.

We remember that earlier in the book Gideon had the perfect retort for those who sought a king for Israel. Israel already has a king—the Lord. By the end of Judges, however, this idea no longer prevails as the consensus. Judges contrasts with Joshua as the book where everything starts to fall apart. Everything Joshua has foretold is occurring. The people worship idols. They forget to rely on the Torah, book of the Revelation Moses had bequeathed to them, and they only call on God when they're in trouble. Likewise, the judges themselves fall far short of heroic glory. Any amazing feats they are able to accomplish can generally be traced to their receipt of the Spirit of the Lord. As always, God honors anyone who puts his trust in the Deity. The Lord actively works with Gideon to build up his faith, and in turn, Gideon demonstrates that he really *gets* what being called to serve God involves—the refusal of personal glory (the kingship) in order to praise God's gift of victory. Yet even Gideon makes a golden ephod out of his battle's plunder, and he and all Israel bow down to it (Judges 8:27).

Even though Joshua presented us with the holy curse, demanding the relentless killing off of Israel's enemies, it is the book of Judges that delivers the real murder and mayhem. In these pages, though the foes of Israel are not obliterated, the escapades of the judges somehow involve more gore and more gloating (e.g., Deborah's victory song in chapter 5). Israel cries out to God when she needs something, the way Samson grudgingly acknowledges God's help in defeating the Philistines but accuses the Lord of letting him die of thirst in the same breath (Judges 15:18).

What remains particularly interesting in the book of Judges is the neutral tone of the narration. We find no finger-wagging here. The facts of the stories are presented with only occasional commentary (as in Judges 9:56, when God avenges Abimelech's wickedness). Likewise the chronicling expends little effort in indicting Israel's enemies. Occasionally the narrator notes that the peoples surrounding Israel are wicked, but no litany of their crimes makes it on these pages. We see glimpses, mostly in the Samson story with its eye gouging and burning people at the stake, but nothing indicates that these behaviors shock Israel. We even see Jephthah sacrifice his daughter and an innocent woman gang-raped—reminding us of two incidents that were staved off in Genesis (Genesis 22 and 19)—without a corresponding outcry. In short, the picture Judges draws of Israel shows a people who behave very much the same as her neighbors. The Lord chose

Israel to be set apart and holy in order to show the world God's ways, but Israel has chosen to blend in.

By the end of Judges, it looks like this grand experiment of God's—to take a people unto Himself and rear them in His ways—is no less than a gigantic fiasco. Sure, Israel can do all right when she has a leader who is right with God, but left to her own devices, the nation bears no resemblance to the holy people God purports to make of them. This is where the book of Ruth comes in to offer its own take that there's more to this story than Judges suggests.

Ruth

At first glance the story of Ruth might present itself as a quaint but inconsequential tale of ordinary Hebrew life. Peterson even translates the opening as saying, "Once upon a time," striking a completely appropriate tone for the narrative. But the book of Ruth achieves much more than its four chapters would lead us to expect. On the heels of Judges' ending dose of misogyny, it surprises us first to receive a story about women. During a famine Naomi has emigrated from Israel with her husband and sons and settled in the land of Moab. Circumstances have brought tragedy to her family. Both her husband and sons perish in Moab, and though there are wives, there are no grandchildren. Bereft, Naomi resolves to return to her homeland a broken woman. But her daughter-in-law, Ruth, insists on joining her, vowing to accept that "your people are my people and your God is my god" (Ruth 1:16). Once back in Israel this unlikely pair manages to make their way utilizing the safeguards built into Hebrew society to provide for the widow and the alien. Ruth gleans in the field of Boaz only to discover that he is a distant relative of Naomi's dead husband. Drawing on the law of levirate marriage that we first found referenced in the Judah and Tamar story of Genesis 38, Naomi takes heart in the hope of procuring a marriage contract for Ruth with this kinsman Boaz. Despite a couple of legal tangles, the plan ends up working, and Ruth and Boaz wed and give Naomi a grandson. "And they all lived happily ever after" is the implied ending.

Yet to dismiss this story as a fairy tale would amount to missing many points of its theology. Naomi leaves Moab when she has come to the end of her rope. Because there is yet no teaching about the afterlife, the only way she knows to understand her life continuing is through descendants. When her sons die childless and she is now too old to bear more of her own children, she sees no hope for her future. She even goes so far as to complain that God has "ruined her" (Ruth 1:21). But God nonetheless surprises her with bounty beyond her ability to imagine. How the Lord accomplishes this transformation is the most interesting part. At all points in the story it is the Torah that provides compassion for Naomi. Ruth can go to glean in the fields because as it says, "When you harvest your land, don't harvest right up to the edges of the field or gather the gleanings from the harvest ... Leave them for the poor and the foreigner" (Leviticus 19:9–10). When Boaz learns of this Ruth from Moab, far from being suspicious of her foreign ethnicity, he notes her devotion to Naomi as well as her industry with admiration. Again the custom of levirate marriage provides a respectable means for Ruth to propose marriage to Boaz. Though willing to marry Ruth, Boaz will not assent to the union until the town elders address the rights of a nearer kinsman. (See Deuteronomy 25:7–9.) Yet concern for legality does not hinder the happy ending. Rather it seals it. Thus, between the stalwart affection of her outsider daughter-in-law and the unselfish compassion of a little known relative into whose field Ruth just happens to stumble, God is able to give Naomi practical if not biological descendants. In the same way the Lord further uses the virtues displayed in Ruth and Boaz to build a genetic line to David (Ruth 4:18–22), who would become Israel's greatest king.

It is interesting that in the arrangement of the Hebrew Scriptures, the story of Ruth shows up amongst the wisdom writings gathered after the historical books. But the Greek translation of the Old Testament (the Septuagint, which came into circulation around the third century BCE) placed Ruth in its current position in the Christian canon. Perhaps this was done merely to maintain chronology since the tale claims to have occurred in the time of the Judges. Theologically, however, its placement after Judges makes many important points. Primarily it stands as a foil to the pejorative description of Israel in the years after Joshua's death. It shows God working in the lives of everyday people—even women—with the same compassion and subtlety that we have already observed in the divine relationships with Israel's leaders. Moreover, we get to see the goodness of life lived in harmony with the Torah, the way life could be if God's humans would live according to God's ways.

Yet perhaps the most important service the story of Ruth renders is to foreshadow the events that follow it historically. The biblical books that come next—what we will cover in chapter 6—record the rise and fall of the Israelite kingdom. In contrast to the serenity of Ruth, the monarchy makes a mostly messy story, not unlike Judges in its capacity for unholy behavior and broken promises to God. But the thread begun in Ruth—the line that leads to David—is also the strand that stretches forward to Jesus. Though Judges proclaims the bad news that the Promised Land—the new garden of Eden—is clearly polluted with Israel's rejection of God, its placement between Joshua and Ruth reminds the reader not to give up on God's people and His plan. As Ruth leads into the history of Israel's monarchy, its lessons alert us to the unexpected ways that God will continue to advance that plan to counteract the relentless assault of sin on human life.

Part Two: The Old Testament (1 Samuel – Malachi)

We began with the premise that the Bible is revelation—God's decision of self-disclosure to humans. We saw how God's purpose for the world was "good" (chapter 1) but also how humans' disobedience of God's commands derailed the fulfillment of the Deity's intentions (chapter 2). In chapters 3 through 5, we took up the Bible story of how God resolved to save the spoiled creation not by merely crafting a do-over (Noah and the flood) but by working within the flaws of humans to achieve redemption and transforming what was bad into something good. God initiated a plan of reconciliation by building a relationship with Abraham and his family and providing an example of good coming out of evil in the Joseph story (chapter 3). Next God called Moses to help create (a new Genesis project) from the descendants of Abraham a people to whom the Lord would reveal Himself specifically in terms of saving deeds and a holy code of behavior known as God's Torah (chapter 4). Having made Israel into a people, God reenacted the metaphor of the garden of Eden by leading the Hebrews into the Promised Land, guaranteeing by covenant their victory over their enemies as long as they promised to keep the Lord's commandments. We saw in chapter 5 that Israel's allegiance to that covenant began to waver within a generation of the conquering of Canaan. From the perspective of the book of Judges, the warrant for Israel's exile from the Promised Land was already in God's pocket. But the writer of Judges held out this hope: Israel has no king. Ruth followed, reinforcing this idea that a king may yet set Israel aright again, especially a king descended from the Torah-embracing Boaz and Ruth.

As we have already discussed at the outset, Israel's monarchy does not preserve the nation of Israel. Like all the nations of the earth, Israel emerged as a force on her world stage for a moment in history only to fall from political autonomy for a period of roughly 2,500 years. Nevertheless, we will see in the next three chapters that God was unfolding this plan of redemption within the flaws of Israel's monarchy. This portion of the Old Testament, namely Samuel to Malachi, will reveal God's actions with a heightened degree of intricacy. What we have read from Genesis through Ruth has drawn largely from an oral tradition. In chapters 6 through 8, much of what we will read draws heavily from written material. The writers of the books of chapter 6 make frequent references to ostensibly neutral sources—annuls of kings and other court records—as a means of corroborating their data. In chapter 7, the Wisdom Books present as primary resources—poems by King David and proverbs displaying the wisdom of Solomon. Finally in Chapter 8, we will hear the words of the prophets who actually wrote their sermons and their stories down. In summation, the Bible will use multiple perspectives to explain what happened to Israel (see chart below). We will not be reading a single historical account but a series of renderings, thus requiring the reader to gather understanding by hearing a variety of voices. Through these chapters, expect the Scripture to ask you to ponder why God allows Israel to have a monarchy even though it leads to Israel's demise. Given that God knew that the Promised Land would produce the same disobedience as the garden of Eden, what clues to the divine counterstrike do we see emerging in this amalgam of narrative, poetry, wisdom, and prophecy?

The History of Israel's Monarchy
(in multiple perspectives)

Monarchy Established with Saul in about 1025 BCE[18]

Saul 1025–1005	1 Samuel 9–31	1 Chronicles 10	
David 1005–965	1 Samuel 16–1 Kings 2:12	1 Chronicles 11–29	Psalms
Solomon 968–928	1 Kings 2:13–11:43	2 Chronicles 1–9	Proverbs

The Kingdom Divides 928 BCE

The Kings of Israel

Ahab 873–852	1 Kings 16:29–22:40	2 Chronicles 18	
Jeroboam II 788–747	2 Kings 14:23–29		Jonah, Amos
Zechariah 747	2 Kings 15:8–12		Hosea
Shallum 747	2 Kings 15:13–15		Hosea
Menahem 747–737	2 Kings 15:16–22		Hosea

---

[18] Scholars debate the dating of specific events of Israelite history that the Bible covers. An example of one problem that we can even read in the text is the tendency of monarchs to begin their reigns as the co-regent alongside their fathers, creating an overlap in the years they rule. The dates I offer here are meant as approximate, the *Anchor Bible Dictionary* being the primary source.

Israel Falls to Assyria 722 BCE

The Kings of Judah

Rehoboam 928–911	1 Kings 12:1–24; 14:21–31	2 Chronicles 10–12	
Abijah 911–908	1 Kings 15:1–8	2 Chronicles 13–14:1	
Asa 908–867	1 Kings 15:9–24	2 Chronicles 14:2–16	
Jehoshaphat 870–846	1 Kings 22:41–50	2 Chronicles 17–21:3	
Jehoram 851–843	2 Kings 8:16–24	2 Chronicles 21:4–20	
Ahaziah 843–842	2 Kings 8:25–29; 9:21–29	2 Chronicles 22:1–9	
Athaliah 842–836	2 Kings 11	2 Chronicles 22:10–23	
Joash 836–798	2 Kings 12	2 Chronicles 24	
Amaziah 798–769	2 Kings 14:1–22	2 Chronicles 25	
Azariah /Uzziah 785–733	2 Kings 15:1–7	2 Chronicles 26	Isaiah
Jotham 759–743	2 Kings 15:30–38	2 Chronicles 27	Isaiah, Micah
Ahaz 743–727	2 Kings 16	2 Chronicles 28	Isaiah, Micah
Hezekiah 727–698	2 Kings 18–20	2 Chronicles 29–32	Isaiah, Micah
Manasseh 698–642	2 Kings 21:1–18	2 Chronicles 33:1–20	Nahum
Amon 641–640	2 Kings 21:19–26	2 Chronicles 33:21–25	Nahum
Josiah 639–609	2 Kings 22–23:30	2 Chronicles 34–35	Jeremiah, Zephaniah

Jehoahaz 609	2 Kings 23:31–33	2 Chronicles 36:1–4	Jeremiah, Habakkuk
Jehoiakim 608–598	2 Kings 23:34–24:7	2 Chronicles 36:5–8	Jeremiah, Joel
Jehoiachin 597	2 Kings 24:8–17; 25:27–30	2 Chronicles 36:11–21	Jeremiah
Zedekiah 596–586	2 Kings 24:18–25:26	2 Chronicles 36:11–21	Jeremiah, Obadiah

Jerusalem Falls 586 BCE

Babylonian Exile 598–539 BCE

Going into Exile		Ezekiel
Life in Exile	Esther	Daniel 1–6

Return to Jerusalem

First Returnees 538 BCE	Ezra	Haggai, Zechariah
Second Wave 515 BCE	Nehemiah	Malachi, Isaiah

Chapter 6

Does It Really Say That David Killed the Giant Goliath?

Sportscasters often make an allusion to the David and Goliath story when an underdog team beats one favored to win. In addition, you've probably heard of the Star of David as a symbol of Judaism and Jerusalem as the city of David. Now we'll have a chance to explore just who David was in the biblical record and discover why he is so important both to Judaism and Christianity.

In this chapter we reach the part of the Bible where the story of Israel is more readily found in sources beyond the Scriptures. The research of many historians and archeologists shows that Israel did develop into a unified nation in roughly the same geographic location as the modern state under King David sometime around 1000 BCE. During the reign of David's son, Solomon, Israel enjoyed a golden age of wealth and regional ascendancy from which it proceeded to fall during the succeeding 350 years. At that point Jerusalem fell to Babylon, and her people were deported in exile, the final note in the reenactment of the garden of Eden comparison. Yet ironically it is this exile and the history following it that mark the emergence of the people we now recognize as Jews, one of very few ancient peoples who have survived into the modern era. As we already stated in the introduction, the Bible will cover this story from multiple vantage points. From the books examined in this chapter we will receive a largely historical presentation, although not a history according to our modern ideas of fact-verifying and strict chronology. What we will see instead is a framing of history drawn from written sources (often regal court records), which evaluates the story of Israel's monarchy according to its obedience to Israel's God and His Torah. We should picture the authors of all these books (except perhaps Samuel) holding the Pentateuch, particularly the book of Deuteronomy, in their hands as they write about Israel's rise and fall. Moreover, we will find the narration presented in duplicate—the two paired[19] books of Samuel and Kings, probably completed during the Exile, followed by the two books of Chronicles, which were written after the return to Jerusalem. Another pair of books, Ezra and Nehemiah, then goes on to show us the resolve of the Jews who returned to their homeland, albeit under foreign rule, while the final book, Esther, offers us a look at the lives of Jews who continued to live outside the physical Israel but nonetheless did not depart from practicing their faith.

Samuel

The book of Samuel takes us through Israel's transition from a loose confederacy of tribes intermittently pulled out of their lawless chaos under the leadership of a judge into their formation as a unified nation led by a king. As we consider this material, I find myself reminded of Jane Austen's original title for her novel *Pride and Prejudice*, which was *First Impressions*. Our initial introduction to many of the characters does not lead us to anticipate the surprising ways their tales unwind. The narrator seems anxious to show us that Israel's tendency to

---

[19] The three paired books of the Old Testament—1 and 2 Samuel, 1 and 2 Kings, and 1 and 2 Chronicles—should be read as single books. These histories, originally written on scrolls, were likely split into two because they were too long for a single scroll. Because the division between what now appears as two books was generally not made according to content, I will treat each set as a single story.

want what other peoples have will not render the good results that she expects.

In an echo back to Ruth, Samuel begins with a story of a woman of strong faith named Hannah. Her husband, Elkanah, has two wives. Peninnah has given him many children, but he nonetheless loves Hannah despite her barrenness. With surprise we note his tender sympathy on their annual pilgrimages to Shiloh when he gives Hannah a double portion of the festival sacrifice meat to make up for Peninnah's taunts over her childlessness (1 Samuel 1:5–6). At last he even goes so far as to plead with her, "Hannah, am I not of more worth to you than ten sons?" (1 Samuel 1:8). Moved by her husband's kindness, Hannah resolves to entrust her pain to the Lord with the following pledge: If God will give her a son, she will give the child back to the Lord. Eli, the priest overseeing the worship at Shiloh, observes her impassioned weeping in the temple and mistakes her fervency for drunkenness. She refuses to let his harsh judgment embarrass her and defends her demeanor as the honest expression of her heartfelt prayers to God. Her integrity stirs Eli's compassion, and he sends her out with, "May the God of Israel give you what you have asked" (1 Samuel 1:17). Thus, Samuel is born. In her praise song in chapter 2, Hannah notes with joy how God is the master of reversals, "The barren woman has a houseful of children" (1 Samuel 2:5).

We see God's hand on Samuel shortly after he begins his early apprenticeship to Eli in Shiloh. God calls to Samuel in the night, and Eli has to instruct the confused child how to respond. "Speak, GOD. I'm your servant, ready to listen" (1 Samuel 3:10). Samuel learns immediately the hardship of being God's servant. God's message predicts the demise of Eli's house. Shortly thereafter Eli's already errant sons die in a battle with the Philistines where the ark of the covenant is lost to the enemy. But Samuel grows up strong in his faith and in adulthood becomes Israel's judge.

Twenty years after the ark's hapless capture and return, Samuel calls an assembly of Israel to rally God's people back to their faith. He points to the Philistine threat and reminds the tribes that God is available to help Israel, but she must rid herself of idols and turn back to faithful worship of the Lord. An object lesson brings home the message. While Samuel offers a sacrifice and prayer, God sounds a thunderclap in the Philistine camp, sending the troops into chaos and allowing Israel to carry the day (1 Samuel 7:10–11). For the balance of Samuel's judgeship of Israel, the Philistines are kept largely at bay.

Despite Samuel's solid leadership, his sons fail to follow in his footsteps. When as an older man he tries to instate them as judges, they fall to taking bribes (1 Samuel 8:3). Discouraged, the people begin to clamor for Samuel to find them a king like the other nations around Israel have. Samuel sees the plea as God did. The people were rejecting God as their King. But in his prayer Samuel receives an unexpected answer. God is going to give Israel what she asks for. Samuel is to explain what a human king would mean for Israel. You can't ask for a better summation of the downside of a monarchy than you get from 1 Samuel 8:11–18. Here Samuel itemizes the following predictable actions of a king: conscription of young men as soldiers as well as other forced labor, regal claims put on the best lands as gifts for favored friends, and heavy taxation that will leave common folk no better off than slaves. But the people remain dead set in their desire, and God tells Samuel, "Do what they say. Make them a king" (1 Samuel 8:22).

Chapter 9 introduces us to Saul, the tall and handsome son of Kish of the tribe of Benjamin. The narrative now puts a more positive spin on the finding of the king by describing a convoluted meeting between Samuel and Saul over some lost donkeys that makes it clear that God has selected Saul for Samuel to anoint. We want to remember from Deuteronomy 17:14–15, "When the time comes ... appoint the King your God chooses." But when Samuel makes the anointing of Saul public in an assembly in Mizpah, he doesn't hesitate to get in a couple of digs against the idea of a monarch. "God's personal message to you: ... I delivered you from Egyptian oppression—yes, from all the bullying governments that made your life miserable. And now you want nothing to do with your God, the very God who has a history of getting you out of troubles" (1 Samuel 10:18–19). Nonetheless, Israel cheers Saul as her king, and he quickly earns his people's respect by defeating the brutal Ammonites. He even gives God the glory after the battle, saying, "This is the day GOD saved Israel!" (1 Samuel 11:13).

Samuel still has his misgivings. Like Moses in Deuteronomy, he recounts for Israel the litany of God's saving deeds that were worked through God's handpicked leaders from Moses through himself to prove the adequacy of having God serve as their King (1 Samuel 12:6–11). A king will only work out for Israel if both Israel and the king follow God (1 Samuel 12:14). Samuel even brings home the point by calling on God to make a thundershower in the dry season as proof of the people's sin in asking for a king (1 Samuel 12:17–19). Though he succeeds in making the people fear God's power, Samuel insists that his point is always God's faithfulness. "GOD is not going to walk off and leave his people ... You've seen how greatly he has worked among you! (But) be warned: if you live badly, both you and your king will be thrown out" (1 Samuel 12:22–25). Anticipating his people's future troubles with kings, Samuel also resolves not to walk out on Israel as she transitions to a monarchy. Having abdicated his authority as Israel's last judge, Samuel takes on the new role of prophet. We will see many prophets going forward in the Bible. Let us be clear in our understanding of the office. A biblical prophet is not primarily what we associate with the colloquial *prophets of doom*, although we will see how such a moniker gets attached to the occupation. Instead of predicting the future, the biblical prophet speaks for God. As the monarchy continues, the king's prophet takes the charge of reminding the king of his obligations to God. Samuel embraces this position as Saul assumes the throne.

Qualified by Samuel's concerns for the monarchy, the narrative proceeds to fast-forward to what went wrong under Saul's kingship. Saul rules over Israel for more than forty years, but we learn mostly about the latter years of his reign. Perhaps we should assume that there were actually many good years during which Saul and the people remained faithful to God, Saul seeing himself as a servant of the Lord as Samuel had always seen himself. But at some point Saul's confidence in God falters, and he prefers to rely on his own counsel, eschewing Samuel's advice. Chapter 13 describes a battle with the Philistines where Israel is outnumbered. Saul elects to make a burnt offering for victory without waiting for Samuel's arrival (though Saul does wait the anticipated seven days and only departs from Samuel's advice when the prophet is later than expected). We can empathize with Saul's sense of needing to do something in the face of such low morale, but Samuel judges Saul lacking in faith. "If you had kept the appointment that your GOD commanded, by now GOD would have set a firm and lasting foundation under your kingly rule over Israel" (1 Samuel 13:13). Let us not assume that Samuel is overly harsh, however. His statement may well reflect an observed trend toward religious lassitude in Saul. Samuel's further admonition that God is seeking Saul's replacement tends to corroborate this assessment. However, Samuel's note that God will next seek out a man of His own choosing does not explain why Saul was not also the man of God's choosing.

The narrative then returns to the battle to demonstrate the further wavering of Saul's leadership. The appearance of Saul's son Jonathan in chapter 14 serves as a foil to Saul's waning faith. Attempting to infiltrate the Philistines, Jonathan remarks to his armor bearer, "There's no rule that says GOD can only deliver by using a big army. No one can stop GOD from saving when he sets his mind to it" (1 Samuel 14:6). Jonathan's ambush is effective.

He and the armor bearer kill twenty and send the troops into a panic. The noise of the chaos cues Saul into leading a new charge, but he inexplicably forbids his soldiers to eat anything until the day's slaughter is complete. By evening the men were so hungry they were butchering animals and eating meat with the blood still present, which was a clear violation of kosher rules. "Don't eat meat with blood in it" (Leviticus 19:26). Though Saul hastens to arrest that sacrilege, he is game to loot among the Philistines. But the priests caution him to ask God's opinion first. When the holy men draw a lot for an answer, none comes forth—a sign that God is withholding judgment because of someone's sin. The sin exposed is Jonathan's eating honey while unaware of Saul's ban during the battle. When Saul wants to kill his own son to expunge the sin, his own troops defend Jonathan.

Next Samuel instructs Saul to attack Amalek but to put everyone and everything under a holy ban as in the days of the conquest of Canaan. Yet when the battle is won, Saul keeps back some of the flocks from the slaughter. Confronted by Samuel, he protests that he is merely keeping the best of the animals for sacrifice to *your* God (1 Samuel 15:15 NIV). This proves the final straw for Samuel, who retreats from Saul in prayer. God commiserates with Samuel and explains that the Lord has selected a new king for Samuel to anoint from the family of Jesse in Bethlehem. When Samuel eyes the eldest of Jesse's sons, God interrupts him, "Don't be impressed with his looks and stature … GOD judges persons differently than humans do. Men and women look at the face; GOD looks into the heart" (1 Samuel 16:7). In a scene reminiscent of the Cinderella story, Samuel sizes up Jesse's seven sons and asks, "Is this it? Are there no more sons?" (1 Samuel 16:11). Thus, they fetch the youngster, David, from tending the sheep, and God confirms that this is Saul's replacement, "the man after his own heart" (1 Samuel 13:14). And then "the Spirit of GOD entered David like a rush of wind, God vitally empowering him for the rest of his life" (1 Samuel 16:13).

Although this private anointing of David has no immediate repercussions on Saul's authority as king, the narrative explains that the Spirit of God leaves Saul at the very moment it enters David and that Saul plunges into a deep depression. The eruption of these black moods causes the royal advisors to seek out a musician who can calm the king's melancholy with his harp. In this way David is introduced into the court of Saul. "Saul liked him immediately and made him his right-hand man," sending word back to Jesse that he was very impressed with David (1 Samuel 16:21–22).

What follows next in the narrative serves as almost an alternate history to David's introduction to Saul—the famous story of Goliath. Here we picture David, still a shepherd for his father, charged with bringing supplies to his brothers in Saul's army while they are again fighting the Philistines. Each day he enters the camp, he hears the derisive insults of the mammoth Philistine leader taunting Saul to send out an Israelite champion for single combat. Though his brothers accuse David of hanging around to get a glimpse of battle gore, David is sincerely outraged by the giant's mockery and listens in earnest to the other soldiers musing over the rewards to be garnered by the one who could slay Goliath. His interest in the challenge draws Saul's attention. When David gains an audience with the king, he asks permission to take on the menace, claiming confidence from his shepherding experience in which he has taken down lions and bears. Saul attempts to dissuade him, but in the end Saul relents and offers him a suit of soldier's armor for his protection. But David rejects the armor, saying the he can't even move inside it, and he approaches the battlefield with only his shepherd's staff and slingshot and five smooth stones. Goliath ridicules the boy, but David stands firm and says, "You come at me with sword and spear and battle-ax. I come at you in the name of GOD-of-the-Angel-Armies, the God of Israel's troops, whom you curse and mock. This very day GOD is handing you over to me ... The whole earth will know there's an extraordinary God in Israel" (1 Samuel 17:45-46). Here we enjoy a real Hollywood moment. Remember our jolt of surprise when the very intimidating sword brandishing foe in *Raiders of the Lost Ark* confronts Indiana Jones and Indy simply pulls out a gun and shoots him dead. Now consider that David delivers this same shock with a single burst of his slingshot! Next David uses Goliath's own sword to cut off the Philistine's head. After this stunning victory Saul sends his army commander, Abner, to vet David as a prelude to inviting him to serve as a soldier.

The upshot of this double introduction is to show how extraordinary David is. The Goliath incident demonstrates the depth of his faith in God, particularly for such a young man. It immediately reminds us of the trust Saul's son Jonathan exhibited in the battle of chapter 14 and is likely at the heart of the bond of friendship forged between the pair as chapter 18 opens. That David is also a musician rounds out his character with human sensitivities that instantly win him the favor of the court and army. Joseph from Genesis (see Genesis 39:3–4, 21–23; 41:39–20) springs to mind when we read, "Whatever Saul gave David to do, he did it—and did it well. So well that Saul put him in charge of his military operations. Everybody, both the people in general and Saul's servants, approved of and admired David's leadership" (1 Samuel 18:5).

Yet the narrative is quick to remind us that this portion of the book of Samuel is still devoted to Saul and his descent from God's blessing. Now that David has appeared on the scene, Saul's behavior erodes steadily. When the townswomen make up a ditty saying, "Saul kills by the thousand, David by the ten thousand!" (1 Samuel 18:7), Saul ends up throwing a spear at David while he is playing the harp for him (1 Samuel 18:11). Next he offers his daughter Merab in marriage only to renege before the wedding (1 Samuel 18:17–19). When his second daughter, Michal, falls in love with David, Saul agrees to the match because he can make

David fight the Philistines as a means of earning the bride price. (As the eighth son of a humble family, David has no access to riches.) But instead of being killed in battle, David returns with twice the glory (1 Samuel 18:20–28). In short order jealousy transforms Saul's early love for David into a violent hatred.

The remainder of 1 Samuel chronicles David's trials in escaping Saul's wrath. When a "black mood from God" (1 Samuel 19:9) falls upon Saul, he again throws a spear at David during a music session. With the help of Michal (1 Samuel 19:11–17) and Jonathan (1 Samuel 20), David actually flees the royal court and embarks on a life on the run, getting food from a priest named Ahimelech. David covers his unorthodox request, saying that he is on a secret mission. Ahimelech only has consecrated bread on hand but gives it to David after David promises that he and his men are ceremonially clean because "none of us has touched a woman. I always do this when I'm on a mission" (1 Samuel 21:5). When Saul discovers David's escape, he orders the slaughter of the eighty-five priests on duty with Ahimelech. But his men refuse. No one can fathom what Saul has against David. Only Doeg, the Edomite (descendant of Jacob's impulsive brother, Esau), can be commanded to carry out Saul's sentence (1 Samuel 22:17–19). It pains David to have caused such a massacre (1 Samuel 22:22), but he nonetheless gathers his loyal followers when God encourages him to fight the Philistines on behalf of the Israelites in Keilah (1 Samuel 23:1–6). Despite David's good deeds, Saul continues to pursue him. David flees Keilah when God convinces him that the people there will turn him over to Saul (1 Samuel 23:7–12), and with his men, he lives off the land, raiding Israel's neighbors and protecting the Israelite villages. Yet even though the reader knows that Samuel has anointed David to be king after Saul, nothing in David's recorded actions or thoughts betray an attempt to undermine Saul's legitimate authority as king. Instead the narrative gives us two examples when Saul's life is in David's hands (chapters

24 and 26), but David refuses to act against God's anointed king (1 Samuel 24:10; 26:23).

Although Samuel has dropped out of the action ever since he anointed David, we are told of his death in chapter 25 in order to see yet another way that Saul's character declines. Faced with another Philistine battle, Saul becomes so desperate for guidance that he flouts the Torah prohibition against the occult (Leviticus 19:26, 31) and consults a witch in order to speak to the shade of Samuel. All he learns is the truth of his fears. The upcoming clash will be his death. In chapter 31, we find Saul mortally wounded. He falls on his own sword. The Philistines abuse his dead body until soldiers loyal to Saul recover it.

Before Saul's death David's life on the run had come to a crisis. Incredibly, in an effort to throw the king off his trail, he chooses to seek sanctuary among the Philistines, whose leader, Achish, is willing to give him a safe harbor, knowing his opposition to Saul (1 Samuel 27:1–4). David refrains from serving Achish honestly, however. He claims to be raiding towns in Israel while he is actually sacking villages of other neighboring peoples, killing everyone to avoid a witness betraying him to Achish. By God's providence the Philistine commanders refuse to trust David to go into battle against Israel (1 Samuel 29:6–11), and instead he and his men destroy Amalek (1 Samuel 30) while Saul unsuccessfully battles the Philistines. David's flush of victory fades quickly, however, when he learns the news of Saul and Jonathan's deaths (2 Samuel 1:1–16). He then composes of song of lament for both (2 Samuel 1:17–27).

Saul's death clears the way for David to assume leadership in his area of Israel—Judah in the south where his hometown of Bethlehem is located. Saul's second son, Ish-Bosheth, takes over the rule of the north (Israel) for a scant two years, but after his murder David unifies Judah and Israel by making a treaty with the northern kingdom (2 Samuel 5:1–3). Next he conquers the Jebusites and sets up their city of Jerusalem as his own capital.

David is thirty years old when he becomes king of Judah and thirty-seven when he begins his reign in Jerusalem.

Despite the number of murders that pave the way to the throne, David manages to find the high moral ground most of the way. He refuses to congratulate the messenger who claims to have killed Saul (2 Samuel 1:14–16), and he blesses the soldiers who retrieve Saul's body from the Philistines (2 Samuel 2:4–6). Infighting between David's men and Saul's troops follows David's ascension to king of Judah. But when Joab, David's army commander, murders Saul's army commander, Abner, after he had agreed to rally Israel to David's side, David does not consider Joab's plea of blood vengeance legitimate (2 Samuel 3:26–30). Likewise, when two of Ish-Bosheth's raiding captains, hoping to curry favor with David, kill the king in cold blood, David condemns their deed (2 Samuel 4:5–12).

David also earns his kingship in battle against the Philistines but only because of God's help (2 Samuel 5:17–25). Once established in Jerusalem, David decides that it is time for the ark of the covenant to come out from its desert dwelling and reside with him in the capital city. It takes some doing to accomplish (2 Samuel 6:6–15), but when the chest arrives in Jerusalem, David dances with joy (2 Samuel 6:14). The peace that settles after these events gives David a new idea. As he sits in his fine palace, it occurs to him that the ark resides in a simple tent. Why should he not build a house for God's chest? He tests out the notion on Nathan, his prophet, who agrees with him at first. But that night Nathan receives a contradictory word from God. David will not make a house for God. The Lord will make one for David. David's son "will build a house to honor me, and I will guarantee his kingdom's rule permanently" (2 Samuel 7:13). David accepts this revelation in all humility. "What can I possibly say in the face of all this? You know me, Master GOD, just as I am. You've done all this not because of who I am but because of who you are—out of your very heart!" (2 Samuel 7:20–21).

The early part of David's reign continues to involve warfare, and David persists as a warrior king until we come to chapter 11, a turning point in David's career. While the narrative does not shift in tone, what this chapter discloses in its matter-of-fact parlance shakes the reader. David has uncharacteristically stayed home from battle, and his wandering eye has settled on Bathsheba bathing at her home near the palace. Though it is not uncommon for a man of this day, especially for one of David's stature, to have his pick of women for his bed, the Torah commandment against adultery still holds force. Had Bathsheba been single, this would hardly have been a story. She would be added to the list of David's wives or concubines without mention. But she is married to Uriah, who is away fighting the war, and when she becomes pregnant (note how the text clarifies that the child can only be David's in 2 Samuel 11:4), it becomes a problem for the king. Without excuse or explanation, we read how David finds the low road to tackle this dilemma. First he calls Uriah back from the war so that he can sleep with Bathsheba and believe that the child is his. But instead the soldier demonstrates his virtue by refusing to enjoy his wife when his fellows are still enduring the hardships of battle (2 Samuel 11:6–11). We already know that this was a policy David established in the early days of his fighting for Saul (1 Samuel 21:5). Having failed to legitimize Bathsheba's offspring, David resorts to setting Uriah up to be killed in battle. The deed accomplished, Bathsheba moves into the palace after she mourns her husband. Then finally comes a comment from our author, "But GOD was not at all pleased with what David had done" (2 Samuel 11:27).

It is Nathan in his office as prophet who brings God's Word to David, notably not in a lecture but in a parable (2 Samuel 12:1–4). The import of the tale escapes David. Instead he becomes furious with the man in the story who, though wealthy, steals a poor man's only lamb. This allows Nathan to reply with the éclat of understatement, "You are the man!" He follows up with God's argument against David (2 Samuel 12:7–12). But in David's response to this indictment, we see for real why he is the man *after God's heart*. Without hesitation he owns his guilt, "I've sinned against GOD" (12:13). If you peek ahead at Psalm 51, you hear David's full confession. It is interesting how God responds to David's admission of guilt. Through Nathan we learn that God will spare David's life but not that of Bathsheba's child (2 Samuel 12:13-14). Neither will God insulate David from the repercussions of his sin.

Although Bathsheba goes on to give David another son, Solomon, who becomes his heir to the throne, family troubles dog David for the rest of his life. First David's son Ammon brutally rapes his half sister Tamar (2 Samuel 13:1–19). David is angry, but like Eli and Samuel before him, he fails to discipline Ammon for the offense (2 Samuel 13:21–22). In time Tamar's full brother, Absalom, successfully plots to murder Ammon in revenge (2 Samuel 13:23–33) and banishes himself from the royal city for three years. Upon his return Absalom ingratiates himself with the masses by trying cases David has no time to hear (2 Samuel 15:1–6). After four years Absalom hatches his plot to overthrow his father. David flees Jerusalem. Absalom takes the reins in the royal city, even sleeping with his father's concubines to show his dominance (2 Samuel 16:22). Though David's forces rally and eliminate the Absalom threat, David cannot cease his mourning for his lost son, alienating the men who fought hard to put him back on the throne (2 Samuel 19:1–7).

As David's reign winds to its close, we see that he is a broken man in many ways. Perhaps his sons' sins remind him of his own. During his flight from Jerusalem when a clansman of Saul pelts the retreating company with stones and curses David, the king replies, "Don't bother with him; ... he's preaching GOD's word to me" (2 Samuel 16:11). Surely Absalom's betrayal echoes back to David's troubled relationship with Saul. Just as Saul's hatred never made sense to him (1 Samuel 26:18), neither does the loss of his son's love. "O my Absalom, ... Why not me rather than you, my death and not yours" (2 Samuel 18:33).

Although skirmishes with other rebels pepper the remainder of David's reign (2 Samuel 20), we will see when we get to the book of Kings that he has nonetheless elevated the unified Israelite kingdom to a distinguished position of prosperity and regional predominance. Solomon rules Israel in her golden age. Yet the story of David does not end with a reiteration of these successes. Instead what we find in the closing three chapters of Samuel is an appendix that serves as an analysis of David's reign. We can symbolize the three topics covered in this coda in the following way:[20] first, a discussion of God's wrath against Israel to be labeled (a); second, accounts of David's warriors, labeled (b); and finally, examples of David's poetry, labeled (c). If we do so, we observe the coda falling into the following pattern: *a-b-c-c-b-a.* This technique, known as inverted parallelism, occurs frequently in the Old Testament and should be read with the emphasis placed on the center points.[21] In line with this cue we should understand David's reign as beginning with the challenge of cleaning up Saul's mistakes—the famine God brought because of Saul's early attempt to wipe out the Gibeonites (not recorded elsewhere in the biblical record) (a 2 Samuel 21:1–14) and ending with his trial of paying for his own lack of godly trust by calling for a census (a 2 Samuel 24:1–25). The warrior accounts (b 2 Samuel 21:15–22 and 23:8–39) highlight the bona fide prowess of David's men, and we should note the irony of including Uriah, husband of Bathsheba, in the list of David's top thirty (2 Samuel

---

[20] NIV, p. 451.

[21] See appendix 1 for definition. The Pentateuch itself is a form of inverted parallelism. Both Genesis and Deuteronomy focus on God's promise of land for His people (a). Exodus and Numbers highlight God's salvation of Israel from Egypt (Exodus) and the dangers of the wilderness (Numbers) (b). This leaves Leviticus with its instructions on how to worship God and live rightly among humans to represent (c), the center section, and therefore, the focal point of the Torah.

23:39). But in the heart of the passage, we see David's own heart exposed in his songs of praise to the Lord. The first section (c 2 Samuel 22) is also recorded as Psalm 18 and parallels the imagery Hannah uses in her song at the beginning of Samuel. (For example, both refer to God as their Rock.) Here David celebrates God's faithful rescue through the countless attempts on his life in battle and at the hand of Saul. God's steadfast love and reliability amaze David. Many scholars surmise that the ebullient praise of this section predates the Bathsheba incident. In contrast, the tone of the second section (c 2 Samuel 23: 1–7), titled *David's Last Words,* is more sober. While not alluding directly to David's sin, these lines sum up the ideal theocratic king: "Whoever governs fairly and well, who rules in the fear of God is like the first light at daybreak without a cloud in the sky" (2 Samuel 23:3–4).

Clearly David falls short of this description, but it remains the standard to which he aspires for his descendants. Yet we must also factor into our understanding of David's vision of his dynasty the words he speaks when he is dealing with God's wrath over his census taking. An angel of the Lord has given David three options for atoning his guilt in 2 Samuel 24:10–16. Though David selects a plague as the least painful of God's choices, he is not able to bear the angel afflicting his people and cries out, "Please! I am the one who sinned; I, the shepherd, did the wrong. But these sheep, what did they do wrong? Punish me and my family, not them" (2 Samuel 24:17). In this way we get our first glimpse of the paradox that will confound Israel about the Messiah the prophets (chapter 8) will promise. Like David, the Messiah will have a heart for God and be a mighty King unifying God's people. However, though He will be more righteous than David, He will also bear the punishment that David deserves.

The book of Samuel closes on this image of David. I stated at the outset that this narrative reminded me of the fallacy of *first impressions.* We have seen already how Eli had to replace his accusation of Hannah being drunk with a realization that she was a woman of profound faith (1 Samuel 1:12–17) Out of her trust in God, Samuel is born—God's servant tasked with guiding Israel in her transition into monarchy. Samuel deplores Israel's demand for a king, but God sees within this weakness of His people an opportunity to build a vision of their ultimate salvation. Saul looks made for the role of king, but as his victories mount up, his faith begins to wane. It is not even that he fails to follow Samuel's advice on religious matters (1 Samuel 13) but more that he develops no relationship with God apart from what Samuel prescribes for him. Note how he refers to the Lord as Samuel's God, not his own (1 Samuel 15:15). Add to this his rash behavior in battle—demanding the soldiers eat nothing (1 Samuel 14:24) and vowing to put his son Jonathan to death (1 Samuel 14:44). Tragically Saul does not truly understand his paranoid obsession with David stealing his throne as we see in his second apology to his successor (1 Samuel 26:21). Instead it is David, introduced as a mere shepherd boy, the youngest of his clan, who ends up embodying for Israel what a godly king could be. Even David, who begins so stalwart in this faith that he defeats Goliath, soon enough allows the power of his position to corrupt his morals. Certainly in David's time (and even our own) it was common for persons of influence to make their own rules regarding war, riches, and women with impunity. But God calls David to account for breaking the Lord's commandments. In his acknowledgment and readiness to repent of his sins, David demonstrates the kind of man God can work with. Though God does not spare David the consequences of his sin, neither does the Lord leave David's side. Thus, the relationship between David and God becomes the model through which God hones the divine plan for reconciliation with humankind.

Kings

The author of the book of Kings connects his history of Israel's monarchy to the story told in Samuel by beginning with the transition from David's reign to that of his son Solomon. In addition, he matches the ending of 2 Samuel by using the same device of inverted parallelism to tell the story of Solomon's reign.[22]

1. Solomon's succession (1 Kings 1:1–2:12)	9. Rehoboam's succession (1 Kings 12:1–24)
2. Solomon's reign established (1 Kings 2:13–46)	8. Solomon's reign weakened (1 Kings 11:14–43)
3. Solomon's wisdom (1 Kings 3)	7. Solomon's folly (1 Kings 11:1–13)
4. Reign evaluated (1 Kings 4)	6. Reign evaluated (1 Kings 9:10–10:29)
5. What Solomon built (1 Kings 5:1–9:9)	

A quick look at the outlined content of the Solomon story shows us that the narrative seeks to hold up Solomon's building projects, particularly his construction of the temple as central to his reign. We will also see the author apply this model of a monarch's rise and fall to his description of the kings that follow Solomon—a strategy of "I'll give you the good news first and then finish with the bad."

Though the kingdom that David passes on to Solomon is burgeoning with wealth and regional respect, politics splits the palace on the issue of the heir. Adonijah, David's fourth but probably his oldest surviving son, makes a bid for the throne while David is on his deathbed. The prophet Nathan and Queen Bathsheba secure the crown for Solomon by getting David to proclaim Bathsheba's son his choice (1 Kings 1:29–30). At David's suggestion Solomon proceeds to upstage Adonijah's coronation feast by parading into Jerusalem on a mule and having Nathan and the priest, Zadok, formally anoint him king of all Israel (1

---

[22] Adapted from NIV, p. 463.

Kings 1:38-43). Next as David's death approaches, the outgoing king pronounces his farewell blessing to his son first with a charge to keep faith with the Lord, "Do what GOD tells you. Walk in the paths he shows you: Follow the life-map absolutely, keep an eye out for the signposts, his course for life set out in the revelation to Moses" (1 Kings 2:3). David then adds some specific directives about how to deal with certain people adjacent to the throne (1 Kings 2: 5–9). In the early days of his reign, Solomon attends to his father's advice and even augments it by finding an excuse to have Adonijah eliminated (1 Kings 2:13–25). Despite ordering these politically expedient murders, Solomon nonetheless seems to have heard his father's advice on faith. When God appears to the young monarch in a dream, willing to grant his heart's desire, Solomon responds most piously, "You were extraordinarily generous in love with David my father ... and now here I am [on the throne in his place] ... I'm too young for this ... job. Give me a God-listening heart so I can lead your people well, discerning the difference between good and evil" (1 Kings 3:6–9). God is so impressed that Solomon begs for wisdom rather than riches or glory that the Lord vows to grant these as a bonus along with the requested understanding. "And, if you stay on course, keeping your eye on the life-map and the God-signs as your father David did, I'll also give you a long life" (1 Kings 3:10–14).

Thus, early on in his reign Solomon emerges as a most shrewd king. His famous first feat of prudence is to discover the real mother between a pair of prostitutes disputing over the ownership of a baby. Solomon suggests settling the argument by cutting the baby in half, knowing that the real mother will give up the child rather than see it destroyed (1 Kings 3:16–27). The renown of his sharp wits spreads far beyond Israel's borders. He composes three thousand proverbs (some of which we will see in chapter 7) and studies every kind of plant and animal so that people far and wide, including the queen of Sheba (1 Kings

10:1–13), seek his judgment (1 Kings 4:29–34). Add to this that his reputation increases his opportunity to trade, and we have no trouble seeing how easily Solomon also acquires tremendous wealth. That he uses this largess to build an exquisite temple for God is all the more to his credit. Yet we also need to note that God cautions him in the midst of the building, "What's important is that you *live* the way I've set out for you and *do* what I tell you ... Then I'll complete in you the promise I made to David" (1 Kings 6:12).

After seven years the temple is complete. As it did during the dedication of the original tabernacle built under Moses at the end of Exodus, the cloud of God's presence fills the temple as the ark of the covenant is placed within the Holy of Holies (1 Kings 8:6–11). Solomon makes a solemn prayer to God. Even though the temple cannot contain God, he asks that it be the place where God is honored. When God's people sin and God has bad things happen to them, let them come back here to the temple to pray for God's forgiveness and vow not to sin again. Solomon closes by asking for justice for Israel so that "then all the people on earth will know God is the true God; there is no other God" (1 Kings 8:60).

When God appears to Solomon in another dream after the completion of the temple, the Lord formally accepts the terms of Solomon's dedication plea but reminds the king again of the consequences of flouting God's ways, particularly taking up with foreign gods (1 Kings 9:3–9). These comments foreshadow the forthcoming erosion of this golden reign. The narrative now gathers together more negative details of Solomon's life. Though the temple took seven years to complete, the king's palace has consumed thirteen years of construction (1 Kings 7:1). King Hiram of Tyre, one of the chief suppliers of lumber and gold for all of Solomon's projects, winds up less than satisfied with the monarch's payment (1 Kings 9:10–14). The labor force assembled to accomplish these feats consists mainly of non-Israelite slaves, remnants of the old Canaanite nations who have continued to live amongst the people of Israel (1 Kings 9:20–21). But the last straw is Solomon's women. Not only does he accumulate seven hundred wives and three hundred concubines (1 Kings 11:3) for whom he sets up shrines so that they can worship their native gods and goddesses, but he also joins them in sacrificing to their foreign deities. His indiscretion proves anew the foresight of the warnings in the Torah concerning kings. "Make sure [your king] doesn't build up a harem, collecting wives who will divert him from the straight and narrow" (Deuteronomy 17:17).

Although Solomon lives out his forty-year reign without much personal consequence from his fall from faith, the seeds of the eventual disintegration of the unified kingdom are sown on his watch. With no recorded farewell advice from Solomon, Rehoboam, the king's heir, demonstrates an astonishing lack of statecraft when he ascends to the throne. At the initial unification of Israel and Judah, it was the elders of Israel who agreed by contract to anoint, already king of Judah, David as king of the northern kingdom as well (2 Samuel 5:3). But when Rehoboam visits the northern tribes to renegotiate this compact under his leadership, the elders advise him that the people have suffered under Solomon's reign and would likely be more willing to support him if he were to pledge to lighten governmental demands. Instead of heeding this advice, Rehoboam listens to his peers and threatens the people with an even harsher rule. Consequently the people reject Rehoboam and rally behind Jeroboam to become the new king of Israel. Thus, what had been all Israel under one king now becomes two kingdoms—Israel in the north and Judah in the south (1 Kings 12:1–17).

The author of Kings takes pains to make his a comprehensive history now of both kingdoms, proving that in his mind both lands house the people of God. Referencing several official records, he documents the successive reigns of both sets of kings in terms of each other, noting their interactions. Though

God gives Jeroboam the opportunity to rule in Israel (1 Kings 11:29–31, 37–39), Jeroboam abuses this divine privilege by erecting a pair of golden calves as a shrine of worship so that the northerners needn't be troubled with going to Jerusalem for making sacrifices (1 Kings 12:26–30). All the kings that follow in Israel continue this evil practice of unsanctioned worship of foreign deities. Most of the monarchs in the south match the north in ungodly behavior. The narrative evaluates each king succinctly. Either he did evil in God's eyes, or he did what pleased God, demonstrating that the author has the predictions voiced in Deuteronomy in mind. "If you listen obediently to the Voice of GOD ... and heartily obey his commandments ... [you will have] blessings ... If you don't ... curses will come down hard on you" (Deuteronomy 28). This king-by-king chronicle then serves to verify God's legitimate rationale for allowing each kingdom to meet its demise. Judah lasts longer than Israel only because it enjoys a few monarchs who still hold faithful with God.

What was God doing while Israel and Judah were adding nails to their coffins? The Lord sent prophets. While we will hear the words of many of these prophets firsthand in chapter 8, we will take note of some that get incorporated into this royal history. First Elijah enters the scene in the north during the reign of Ahab, one of Israel's most evil kings. Ahab's foreign wife, Jezebel, has added her own shrines and priests dedicated to Baal and Asherah and the pagan worship that already exists in Israel. (See appendix 3.) Elijah calls for a showdown between God and Baal. He gets the 450 prophets of Baal to agree to the following challenge. Two bulls are slaughtered—one for the Baal altar and one for that of God. Neither altar is lit, however, because the god who can light his own fire will be proven the true God. The Baal worshipers pray all morning to no avail. Elijah begins to taunt them. "Maybe you should pray louder. Maybe your god is sleeping. Maybe he is on vacation." Waiting until late in the day, Elijah finally takes his turn. He arranges the wood beneath the altar around twelve stones (for Israel's twelve tribes) and proceeds to douse the area with water three times (thus adding to the drama). Of course, when Elijah prays, God sends a roaring fire that burns up the offering. The onlookers fall on their faces in awe. "GOD is the true God" (1 Kings 18:39). At Elijah's bidding the people massacre the prophets of Baal.

Despite this dramatic demonstration, Elijah fails to inspire either Ahab or Jezebel to mend her ways. The tale of Jezebel aiding her husband in the fraudulent acquisition of citizen Naboth's vineyard (1 Kings 21:1–17) offers a good snapshot of their royal character. Nonetheless, Elijah's devotion to obeying and declaring God's Word along with the continued service of his protégé, Elisha, who takes up God's work after the Lord calls Elijah to heaven in a chariot of fire (2 Kings 2:1–11), testifies to God's efforts to give the tribes of Israel their opportunity to repent. Though Elijah and Elisha fail to win Israel back to God, several women in difficult circumstances witness God's power and compassion through the ministries of these prophets (1 Kings 17:7–24; 2 Kings 4:1–37).

Once the northern kingdom falls to Sargon II of Assyria in 722 BCE, the narrative of Kings closes out with the stories of the last kings of Judah. Only two monarchs from this period stand out as highlights, and God's prophets aid both. Hezekiah rules in Judah when Hoshea, the last king of Israel, falls in Samaria (the capital established in the reign before Ahab). Although Ahaz, Hezekiah's father, had placated the Assyrian threat by paying tribute, Hezekiah, in seeking to rid Judah of her foreign worship, draws the attention of Sennacherib, Sargon's successor, with his assertion of religious independence. Once duly threatened, Hezekiah attempts to pay off Sennacherib with gold from the temple, but now the king wants more, namely the hearts and minds of the Judeans. Sennacherib sends his chief field commander into the heart of Jerusalem to incite the people to abandon Hezekiah. Not only does he promise that their standard of living would improve under his king's rule, he taunts them with a hyperbolic depiction of Assyria's might compared to the puniness of their God. To up the intimidation ante, he even delivers the threat in Hebrew instead of Aramaic, the region's commercial tongue at the time (2 Kings 18:19–35). Upon hearing this news, Hezekiah rips his robes in despair, but he is also proactive, sending messengers to the prophet Isaiah. Isaiah's return message assures Hezekiah that God will take care of the crisis, but it takes great faith on the king's part to believe in the face of a second envoy dispatching more bullying (2 Kings 19:9–13). Hezekiah goes to the temple and lays the letter from Assyria before God. "God, God of Israel, ... You are the one and only God, ... save us from raw Assyrian power; make all the kingdoms on earth know that you are God, the one and only God" (2 Kings 19:15–19). Isaiah sends a further message: God has heard Hezekiah's prayer and will dissolve the Assyrian menace. An angel puts to death the 185,000 troops laying siege outside the gates of Jerusalem so that the Judeans wake up the next morning to a "camp of corpses" (2 Kings 19:35). Upon his retreat Sennacherib winds up murdered by his own sons (2 Kings 19:36–37).

Unfortunately the awe this miracle engenders in Judah does not last. Hezekiah's heir, Manasseh, comes to the throne at twelve and rules for fifty-five years, rebuilding the pagan shrines his father tore down and "setting new records for evil" (2 Kings 21:11) by burning his son as a sacrifice (2 Kings 21:6) and installing an Asherah carving within the temple (2 Kings 21:7). But his heir, Josiah, returns to godly ways. While they are tending to repairs in the temple, the workmen discover a book that turns out to be an old copy of God's Revelation to Moses (either the book of Deuteronomy or perhaps the entire Pentateuch). When Josiah hears its contents, he tears his robes in dismay because he sees readily both that Judah has not been obedient to God's commands and that the consequences of that faltering faith (i.e., exile) have become realistic. The counsel of the prophetess Huldah confirms Josiah's doomsday fear but consoles the king that God acknowledges the monarch's faithfulness. The end of Judah will not come during his reign (2 Kings 22:15–20).

To his credit, Josiah is not willing to rest because of God's promises of his personal safety. He immediately assembles the elders, reads the book of the covenant publicly, and then calls on everyone there to recommit themselves to God's service and the Torah injunctions. The temple receives a major purging followed by the cleansing of pagan idols, prostitutes, and the iron furnaces used for child sacrifice from shrines all over the kingdom. Next they celebrate the Passover according to the directives in the Book. Apparently no one had properly observed this holiday since the time of the book of Judges (2 Kings 23:22). The narrative showers Josiah with praise. "There was no king to compare with Josiah ... who turned in total and repentant obedience to GOD, heart and mind and strength, following the instructions revealed to and written by Moses" (2 Kings 23:25).

Still, when we come to the death throes of the kingdom, the tone of the text remains distant and matter-of-fact. Though meticulous in the details of Judah's last regencies, the narrative pronounces a simple verdict. Babylon's invasion of Judah was not "by chance—it was GOD's judgment as he turned his back on Judah because of the enormity of the sins of Manasseh" (2 Kings 24:3). We might ask why Manasseh's sins get to be the last straw when there have been so many instances of unfaithfulness on the part of God's people. Perhaps God merely allowed Israel and Judah to run out of their own steam. But all through this history the author's presentation has begged the question: What else could you expect from such a people? Often he holds the teachings of the Torah, particularly Deuteronomy, as a banner saying, "God told you this would happen." While we are used to history showing us that nations rise and fall, it is unusual for a native son to tell his people's story with the following bottom line: "You have only yourselves to blame." That is why it deserves our attention that though Israel and Judah disappeared as names on a map at this time, God's people live on and finally learn something from their past. But that story unfolds elsewhere. For the author of Kings, the point to drive home is that in the end, the monarchy failed and that "Judah went into exile, orphaned from her land" (2 Kings 25:21).

Chronicles

When we think of Israel after the exile, it might help to remember Dr. Seuss' fairy tale about the Grinch. Even though the Grinch steals all the trappings of Christmas, the Whos still sing joyfully to ring in the holiday. In the same way when God's people find themselves stripped bare of their land and their temple, they discover that they still have something to celebrate. Chronicles sets out to retell the history we have just heard from Samuel and Kings from the new perspective of people who realize they have not lost everything. Writing in the period when Jews have returned to the environs of Jerusalem under foreign rule and using several resources, including some version of Samuel and Kings, the chronicler seeks to help the Jews both remember and understand their legacy. When we note some of the big details that get omitted in this version (for example, the Bathsheba incident), it would be tempting to assume that the author is merely spinning the history into a more palatable form. If this were really the case, however, we would expect this text to replace the earlier stories. The Hebrew Scriptures gather Chronicles, Ezra-Nehemiah, and Esther (in reverse order) after the Wisdom Literature (subject of chapter 7) into the final section of its Bible known as "the Writings." In that position these stories operate more as an afterthought to the history of the monarchy. In contrast, by placing Chronicles, Ezra-Nehemiah, and Esther immediately after Kings, the Christian canon encourages us to consider that these books have something more important to add to our understanding of the history of the monarchy.

First Chronicles devotes most of its first nine chapters to genealogies—tangible proof that God's people still live and still know their heritage. The actual history begins with the death of Saul, whose downfall is ascribed to disobedience. He sought a witch's help, not God's (1 Chronicles 10:13–14). As the story of David unfolds, we will note the issues that the book of Chronicles deals with differently than the rendering Samuel offers. In chapter 12, observe that the men who help David while he is on the run from Saul come from many tribes and not just from David's own Judah. When the chronicler goes on to relate the history of the monarchy, he will focus solely on the kings of Judah, but he lays the groundwork here to assert that Judah nonetheless represents members of all Israelite tribes. When David finally brings the ark of the covenant into Jerusalem, the narrative adds that the king leads an elaborate worship service to honor its arrival (1 Chronicles 16). The paired accounts run parallel in recording the legacy of God pledging to make a dynasty of David's house and in summarizing David's many victories in battles, but Chronicles refrains from mentioning both the Bathsheba debacle and all other dirty family laundry, such as Tamar and Ammon and Absalom's revolt. It makes a bigger point, however, of David calling for a census, even blaming it on Satan (1 Chronicles 21:1) but matches Samuel in expressing David's deep remorse. (1 Chronicles 21:8, compare to 2 Samuel 24:10).

Where Samuel ends his discussion of David, however, Chronicles goes on at length to explain that though David knew Solomon would be the one to build the temple, he did lay much of the groundwork for its building in his lifetime. He organizes resident aliens skilled in stonecutting and stockpiles materials for the construction since "my son Solomon is too young to plan ahead for this" (1 Chronicles 22:5). In what becomes an ongoing comparison to Moses, David explains that as much as he wanted to build the temple (as Moses wanted to enter the Promised Land as outlined in Deuteronomy 3:23–26), God told him his hands were too bloodied from war. Instead his son, Solomon, whose name is so close to the Hebrew *shalom* (meaning *peace*), would do the job and reign during a period of peace (1 Chronicles 22:8–9). Next while he formally passes the throne to Solomon (with no mention of the rivalry with Adonijah), David, who is now an old man, organizes the Levites into their various temple assignments just as Moses passed out tasks for the original construction of the tabernacle in the wilderness (Exodus 35:30–36:1). David even offers a farewell address to his leaders, exhorting everyone to obey and study God's commandments (1 Chronicles 28:8). It's just not as long as Moses' extended good-bye in Deuteronomy. Finally he turns to the people to ask for contributions for the project after he makes an example of his own offering. Again, like the people under Moses (Exodus 35:4–9; 36:6–7), the leaders of the families and tribes of Israel give generously (1 Chronicles 29:6–9).

When the narrative takes on the ascension of Solomon, echoes of Joshua reverberate. In 2 Chronicles 1:1, we see Solomon with a firm hold of the throne and the full backing of God. Moreover, the following verse where Solomon speaks to *all Israel* corroborates his undivided popular support. Solomon's request for wisdom appears but without the example of his judging the motherhood of the disputed child. The construction of the temple begins with a detail unique to Chronicles, specifically the positioning of the temple on Mount Moriah (2 Chronicles 3:1). Elsewhere in the Old Testament Mount Zion identifies the temple site. By tradition Mount Moriah marks the spot where Abraham binds Isaac (Genesis 22:2, 14). The description of the building process proceeds with only some abridgement from Kings, while the dedication ceremonies come across with somewhat more detail, especially with regard to the duties of the Levites (2 Chronicles

7:6). Note here the reference to the participation of *all the Israelites.* The chronicler persists in emphasizing the unity of the people under Solomon and the religious climax realized in the temple dedication service where a "bolt of lightning out of heaven struck the Whole-Burnt-Offering and sacrifices and the Glory of GOD filled The Temple" (2 Chronicles 7:1). Just as "everything came out right" (Joshua 21:45) when Joshua set up the twelve tribes in their places in the Promised Land, all is good again for God's people once the temple is established.

The history of the monarchy that follows confines itself to the succession of kings in Judah. Whereas the author of Kings took pains to maintain that Israel consists of both kingdoms, the chronicler insists instead that the traditions kept alive in Judah represent the true character of all Israel and are never ethnically exclusive to the tribe of Judah. The reigns of the Judean kings run mostly parallel with the version in Kings. After all the details and extenuating circumstances of each king's term unfold, the author follows the example set in Kings and pronounces a verdict regarding how God viewed the monarch's actions. The faithful obey God's commands. Those who turn away and do evil pave the road to exile exactly as Deuteronomy had foretold it. "Because you didn't serve GOD, your God, out of the joy and goodness of your heart ... you'll have to serve your enemies whom GOD will send against you" (Deuteronomy 28:47–48).

Hezekiah and Josiah again emerge as high points. In the Hezekiah story, the miracle salvation from the Sennacherib siege of Jerusalem plays second fiddle to the discussion of the king's sweeping purifications of the temple worship. After this extensive cleansing Hezekiah sends couriers throughout Israel and Judah to invite God's people to rededicate themselves to God in the Passover celebration (2 Chronicles 30:5–9). Here and in the depiction of Josiah's Passover, the emphasis rests on the roles of the Levites and other priests and musicians. Their performance of their religious duties becomes the key to the chronicler's message. The monarchy has failed, but Israel still exists within the practice of her worship of God. Again, Deuteronomy holds God's promise for Israel's current situation. "While you're out among the nations where GOD has dispersed you and the blessings and curses come … and you … take them seriously and come back to GOD … GOD will restore everything you lost" (Deuteronomy 30:1–3).

Therefore, Chronicles does not end on the despairing note we find at the close of Kings. The narrative concedes the kingdoms' failings. "GOD, … repeatedly sent warning messages to them … to give them every chance possible. But they wouldn't listen; they poked fun at God's messengers, despised the message itself, and in general treated the prophets like idiots" (2 Chronicles 36:15–16). Moreover, it acknowledges that God uses Nebuchadnezzar of Babylon to give His people their just deserts (2 Chronicles 36:17). But that is not the end of the story. God preserves a remnant of people who have maintained their faith. Some of the temple artifacts make it safely into exile as well. When Babylon falls to Cyrus of Persia and Cyrus fulfills the prophecy of Jeremiah by permitting the Jews to return to their homeland and rebuild their temple, the chronicler stands ready to remind God's people of all they have to celebrate. "All who belong to GOD's people are urged to return [to Jerusalem]—and may your GOD be with you!" (2 Chronicles 36:23). They are still alive. Their traditions are still relevant. God is still God. What will happen if they get serious about obeying the Lord's commandments?

Ezra and Nehemiah

The books of Ezra and Nehemiah report on some of the stories of the restoration, the Jews returning from exile in Babylon to rebuild their temple and reclaim their identity as a people of faith, not of political power. Yet these books do not lend themselves easily as documents of history. The chronology gets murky in places. The voice of the narrative shifts from third to first person, and the language even switches between Hebrew and Aramaic. Rather they point us to particular landmarks that occurred in the process by which the Jews who returned to their homeland figured out how to insulate the practice of their faith from the pitfalls that had led the Israelites astray in their past.

In Ezra 1–6, we learn the struggles that accompany the rebuilding of the temple. The new management that has taken over Babylon in the person of Cyrus has not only sanctioned the Jews' return but allows them to rebuild the temple to their God. Perhaps Cyrus subscribed to the theory that local deities retain power in their geographic homes, and it made sense for a conqueror to keep these gods placated with believers' worship rituals. On the other hand, he could simply have reasoned that happy people pay taxes better. Israel, however, interprets this action as God's fulfillment of Jeremiah's prophecy (Ezra 1:1). Although only a minority of Judeans exercises this option, those who do are eager for the opportunity. Their first task after they settle into Jerusalem is to erect the altar in order to begin making sacrifices (Ezra 3:2). The second year sees the foundation of the temple laid. As the construction continues, some of the local residents offer to help with the project, but the returnees reject their assistance. These enemy residents of Jerusalem, called Samaritans after the old capital of the northern kingdom, were probably transplanted from Israel during the Assyrian exile. The Babylonian exiles did not consider them true Jews because they worshiped Israel's God along with other local deities. "Building the Temple of our God is not the same thing to you as to us" (Ezra 4:3). Thus excluded from the temple work, this faction proceeds to harass the construction laborers for the next fifteen years. Ultimately they petition the Persian government to withdraw the building permit on the claim that the Jews have a history of rebellion and will be likely to cease paying tribute once their temple is complete (Ezra 4:12–13). The argument persuades King Artaxerxes, and work on the temple ceases until Darius replaces him. At the urging of the prophets Haggai and Zechariah, the Jews go back to work and this time are able to get the new king to research the original contract for the construction. With the rediscovered edict comes the added bonus of the initially promised financial assistance from the royal treasury (Ezra 6:3–4). By the sixth year of Darius's reign, the temple is complete and the Jews of Jerusalem celebrate the Passover (Ezra 6:19).

The Jews count the resurrection of the temple as merely the first step in their reestablishment of their identity. In Ezra 7–10, we follow the emergence of the scholar priest Ezra, who travels to Jerusalem with the temple artifacts salvaged from the Babylonian sacking of the city in order to lead the congregation at the newly built temple. Though he rejoices in the opportunity and protection God provides (Ezra was too embarrassed to ask for an escort through the bandit laden territory on the route to Jerusalem in Ezra 8:22), Ezra finds the actual scene in Jerusalem deeply disturbing. Many of the Jews living in the city of David have married outside of the faith. Ezra sees no other recourse but to have these offenders divorce their foreign wives. How can they rebuild themselves as a people if they repeat the mistakes that led to their recent exile?

Meanwhile, back in Babylon, Nehemiah is serving as cupbearer to King Artaxerxes when he hears from his brother the sorry state of affairs in Jerusalem. "The wall of Jerusalem is still rubble; the city gates are still cinders" (Nehemiah 1:3). Nehemiah mourns and fasts for days in deep prayer.

> I'm praying day and night in intercession for your servants, the People of Israel, ... We haven't done what you told us ... All the same, remember the warning you posted to your servant Moses: "If you betray me, I'll scatter you to the four winds, but if you come back to me and do what

I tell you, I'll gather up all these scattered people from wherever they ended up and put them back in the place I chose to mark with my Name." (Nehemiah 1:6–9)

God answers this prayer by having Artaxerxes agree to release Nehemiah for a time from his royal duties in order to have him oversee the rebuilding of the Jerusalem walls (Nehemiah 2:7–9).

Nehemiah runs into some of the same problems encountered in the rebuilding of the temple. The workers have to endure mockery from the Samaritans in the midst of their labors (Nehemiah 4:1–3), and Nehemiah ends up posting round-the-clock guards to secure operations against attacks (Nehemiah 4:16). He also has to take the wealthy Jewish leaders to task for sending their brothers into debt slavery with exorbitant interest on loans (Nehemiah 5:1–12) in violation of the Torah (Exodus 22:25). Despite these distractions, it takes only fifty-two days to complete the new city walls. "When all our enemies heard the news ... they knew that God was behind this work" (Nehemiah 6:15–16).

With the walls rebuilt, the people of Israel again gather to celebrate. Families register their names in the temple. Men and women assemble at the water gate to hear Ezra read from the Torah (Nehemiah 8:2–3). In the aftermath of that initial reading, the Levites and all the temple personnel lead the people for a fast and day of repentance. Out of this reflection the Levites deliver a prayer that summarizes their new understanding of their relationship to God in light of the exile. First they acknowledge that God is the only God. Then in a litany of Israel's history so often repeated by Israel's past leaders, they enumerate God saving acts on Israel's behalf—Abraham and his covenant, the rescue from Egypt, the splitting of the Red Sea, the Torah, and the manna. But "our ancestors were arrogant" (9:16) and built a golden calf to worship, causing God to postpone the entry into the Promised

Land with forty years in the wilderness, where, even there, the Lord kept His people alive with divine providence. Even after they received the land, God's people continued to mutiny against the Lord's commandments until they found themselves in exile. "You [God] are not to blame for all that has come down on us; You did everything right, we did everything wrong" (Nehemiah 9:33). Because of the Jews' history of disobedience, they resolve to make a "binding pledge, a sealed document signed by our princes, our Levites, and our priests" (Nehemiah 9:38). Intermarriage with non-Jews is forbidden. No work will be done on the Sabbath. People will pay the temple tax to provide for the upkeep of the worship of Israel (Nehemiah 10:30–39).

Thus, the Jews became a people set apart, identifiable by their radical monotheism with its shunning of idols, their refusal to work on the Sabbath, and their maintenance of specific dietary rules. What they had not been able to achieve when the land was theirs, they now discover they can accomplish because it is all they have left to define themselves. But now they see that what they have left is what really matters after all. Like the Whos singing for joy just because it is Christmas, the Jews could celebrate because God had not abandoned them. They have the Torah from Moses, and they have worship from David, the great king who danced and sang out of his love for his Lord.

Esther

The book of Esther closes out the formal history of Israel. Given that Xerxes succeeded Darius to the Persian throne, we can date these events after the inroads Ezra and Nehemiah made in reclaiming Jerusalem as a worship center for Jews. As we noted in the discussion of the restoration, most Jews did not elect to return to the homeland. Some had assimilated well in their new surroundings and were unwilling or simply uninterested in uprooting families that had made the land of exile a home.

Yet that does not mean that all the transplanted Jews enjoyed a comfortable lifestyle. As Esther will show us, even if the people living around them seem unaware of their religious heritage, the Jews remain keenly cognizant that prejudice against them lies thinly veiled beneath the surface.

Esther's story begins when, in a fit of temper, Xerxes has banned his queen from court for not obeying him. Because his advisors believe that tolerating such insolence on the part of any woman would be a recipe for social chaos (Esther 1:16–18), they are quick to steer him away from this bride once his anger cools. They propose, "Let's begin a search for beautiful young virgins for the king" (Esther 2:2), and the idea captures Xerxes' imagination immediately.

Women are gathered up from around the city, brought to the palace complex, and put through a battery of beauty treatments lasting twelve months. Thus prepared, each one gets her single evening to please the king. Among those chosen is Esther (Hadassah in Hebrew), an orphan who has been raised by Mordecai, an employee within the palace staff whose ancestors had been taken from Jerusalem. Everyone at the palace knows Mordecai is a Jew, but they do not know this about Esther. Esther thrives in the beauty program, and when her time with the king arrives, Xerxes falls in love with her and makes her his new queen. Governed by Mordecai's advice, she has not told anyone in the palace that she is a Jew (Esther 2:10, 17–18).

In the meanwhile the king promotes Haman to head of his officials, and all the palace staff makes a point of honoring him by bowing and kneeling in his presence. When Mordecai refuses to make obeisance for Haman, however, the new boss becomes furious. He decides to exact his revenge on Mordecai by talking Xerxes into ordering a massacre of the Jews and cleverly describing them as an "odd set of people scattered through the provinces of your kingdom who don't fit in" (Esther 3:8). Xerxes never bothers to have Haman identify this group but simply agrees to the stratagem since Haman is willing to fund it out of his own pocket (Esther 3:11).

Insulated within the palace, Esther only learns this horrific news after she sees Mordecai donned in sackcloth and mourning. But Mordecai does more than bring her up to date on current events. He asks her to plead with the king on her people's behalf. The request unnerves Esther because a queen-consort (as opposed to a queen who enjoys co-regent status) is not at liberty to come into the monarch's presence uninvited. Unless the king extends his scepter to a suppliant, death is automatic (Esther 4:11). Moreover, it has been thirty days since Xerxes has called for her. But Mordecai declines to let her off the hook.

> Don't think that just because you live in the king's house you're the one Jew who will get out of this alive. If you persist in staying silent at a time like this, help and deliverance will arrive for the Jews from someplace else … (but) maybe you were made queen for just such a time as this. (Esther 4:13–14)

Esther bravely accepts the challenge, but she begins by asking Mordecai to organize all the Jews in the palace district to join her in a fast lasting three days. After the fast she dresses herself in her royal robes and positions herself in the inner court, where she knows Xerxes will see her. Impressed with her beauty, the king summons her and asks, "What's your desire, Queen Esther? … Ask and it's yours—even if it's half my kingdom!" (Esther 5:3). But all Esther requests is his presence with Haman at a dinner she arranges. Though Xerxes presses her to reveal her real wish, she makes him wait until her second dinner to put forward her plea. Thus, with courage and patience, not only does Esther manage to persuade her husband to renege on the royal sanction of the extermination of the Jews (Esther 8:7–8) but also procures his permission to grant the Jews recourse if people attack them (Esther 8:11). She takes Haman down in the process (Esther 7:6–10) and sees Mordecai elevated to second in command under the king (Esther 8:2; 10:3). Not bad for a woman in a society where the law requires a wife to live under her husband's rule!

It's possible that you did not notice while you were reading Esther that God's name never appears in the story. Sometimes the book has even received criticism on this point. But careful reading reveals God's presence in the vivid faith of Esther and Mordecai. Moreover, there are few places in the Bible that elucidate the tension between God's sovereign will and a human's free will like Mordecai's challenge to Esther in Esther 4:14. Some way or another God will save His people; however, it is Esther's choice that she act on behalf of her fellow Jews. Observe, too, that she never expects to face this challenge alone. Mordecai asks for her help, and she tells him what she needs to accomplish it. When she risks her life to intercede for Israel, she stands fortified by the faithful prayers of her community along with her own trust in God.

As we close this chapter on Israel's monarchy—our first read on what went wrong with God's people—we want to pay attention to the structure of the telling. In using the order of books found in the Christian canon as opposed to the Hebrew Scriptures, we can make some interesting observations. Stories about women of strong faith form the bookends of this history. The monarchy is born because of Hannah's willingness to serve God even at the cost of giving the Lord her firstborn. Esther's risking of her own life to save her people represents God's preservation of Israel against the threat of genocide from foreign peoples. Taken together their stories form the cradle that nurtures the growth of God's plan. Led by God, Samuel, Israel's last and greatest judge, anoints David, the man after God's heart. Under his kingship all Israel becomes a single nation. It is his idea to build the temple that will allow Israel to worship God according to the traditions that began with Moses. The heinous sins of adultery and murder that he commits in hubris become the means by which we measure the hugeness of God's forgiveness and the endurance of David's faith when chastened by humility. While David suffers the consequences of his sins, he never abandons God. Rather he begs of God the opportunity to make restitution for his wrongs through his life and that of his descendants. Though his son, Solomon, reigns over Israel's golden age and actually builds the temple, the practice of worship remains the legacy of David as the books of Chronicles, Ezra, and Nehemiah attest. For all that is lost in the failure of the monarchy—the divided kingdom, the apostasy of the people, and the exile—the memory of David's kingship becomes the basis of God's ongoing counterstrike. God translates the legacy promised to David's line into an even greater sign of divine grace—the Messiah. Though the picture of the Messiah is dim as we leave this history, we will see its image expanded as we delve into the Wisdom Books of chapter 7 and the words of the prophets in chapter 8.

Chapter 7

Does It Really Say That Job Was Patient?

People may refer to the expression, "the patience of Job," less frequently these days. If you're not familiar with its usage, you'll need to imagine a person who is putting up with long and arduous suffering with saintly endurance. My mother used to say, "That woman must have the patience of Job to stay married to that husband," implying there was something both amazing and ridiculous about her misery. As we begin our study of the Wisdom Literature with the book of Job, we'll want to check out whether this expression does a good job of capturing the character of the book's protagonist.

First, however, let's review what lies in store for us in the next five books of the Bible, namely Job, Psalms, Proverbs, Ecclesiastes, and the Song of Songs. The graphic below attempts to give us an overview of what the Wisdom Literature covers.

Wisdom Books[23]
The Truth about Life that Doesn't Fit within the Narrative of Israel's History

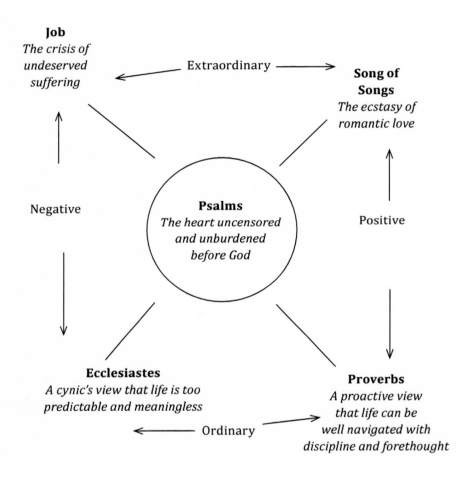

Job
The crisis of undeserved suffering

Extraordinary

Song of Songs
The ecstasy of romantic love

Negative

Psalms
The heart uncensored and unburdened before God

Positive

Ecclesiastes
A cynic's view that life is too predictable and meaningless

Ordinary

Proverbs
A proactive view that life can be well navigated with discipline and forethought

Up to this point in the Bible[24] we have mostly been reading stories—the chronicle of Israel's history with God. But as we know with our own lives, just telling what happened to us is

---

[23] This graphic is an expansion of Eugene Peterson's description in his "Introduction to the Wisdom Books" in *The Message*, pp. 837–838.

[24] Remember that we are using the order of books established in the Christian canon. For a comparison to the Hebrew Scriptures, see appendix 2.

not necessarily the whole story. How we feel as things happen to us is not always easy to describe within the context of a narrative. In fact, prose doesn't often do it justice. It should come as no surprise then that this section of the Bible, the Wisdom Literature, is almost entirely poetry. As the graphic helps us to visualize, these books attempt to encompass the full range of emotions that humans encounter in the course of their lives— the negative and positive, the extraordinary and the ordinary, as well as everything in between. In his book, *Prayer: Does It Make Any Difference?* Philip Yancey[25] points out that the Bible anticipates the import of every argument skeptics mount against God. I would add that most of the questions that challenge God's existence and ultimate concern for humans echo through this wisdom poetry and into the writings of the prophets, which we will cover in chapter 8. As we turn to the book of Job, we hit the query that tops this list with the following question: "Why do bad things happen to good people?"

Job

As we have already seen, when Deuteronomy recapitulates the law of Moses, it often seems to boil the message down to a black-and-white dictum, "If you obey God's commands, life will be a blessing. If you abandon them and fail to repent, you will find life cursed" (as outlined Deuteronomy 28, 30:11–18). Certainly the Jews recovering from exile agreed with this axiom: Israel fell because she had continuously and unabashedly flouted God's commandments particularly by worshiping other gods. The bottom line was this: Israel had no one but herself to blame for losing her land. Yet even though this Deuteronomic code helped to explain Israel's fall, it was not meant to speak for all situations in life. For instance, the code may seem to imply its

---

[25]   Philip Yancey, *Prayer: Does It Make Any Difference?* p. 40.

logical converse. If your life looks like a blessing, you have been obedient. A miserable life must betray sinfulness. But the tale of Job plus the testimony of many of the psalms go to great lengths to show us that this converse is not a valid predictor of a human's allegiance to God. Human suffering is something neither easily understood nor neatly dismissed.

Job becomes our case in point. We are introduced to Job simply as a man who lives in Uz (Job 1:1). The text makes no effort to assign him a place in time, and even the location of the land of Uz is vague—all the classic signs of a parable. The outline of the text bears comment. A prose prologue and epilogue frame the body of the story that chronicles in poetry the dialogue (debate really) between Job and his so-called friends and eventually the conversation between Job and God. These prose bookends provide a context for Job's predicament. Satan, posing here merely as the designated accuser (true to the original derivation of the name and what we mean when we say someone is being the Devil's advocate), submits to God that there is no human who loves the Deity simply for Himself. God suggests His servant Job, a man "honest inside and out" (Job 1:1), but Satan protests that the only reason for Job's devotion is the high degree of blessing he has enjoyed at God's hand. God accepts the challenge with a confident "Game on!" allowing Satan to remove the blessings in Job's life so long as Job's own life is spared. Will this cause Job to deny God? After the first round where Job has lost his property and his children, Job bemoans his sad fate but refuses to blame God. Unwilling to concede defeat, Satan maintains that Job remains faithful only because his health is not impaired. When God removes that caveat, Job develops miserable skin sores and boils. His wife urges him to "curse God and be done with it" (Job 2:9), but Job refuses still to deny God. "We take the good days from God—why not also the bad days?" (Job 2:10). It seems as though God has made His case. If we turn then to the epilogue we see that indeed, despite Job's great suffering, it all comes out right in the end. God restores Job's losses and even doubles his blessings (Job 42:10). The teaching of Deuteronomy is true if one waits long enough. But the prose account is just the wrapping paper. The gift that is Job's tale lies in the poetry (chapters 3–42).

It is clear as we begin chapter 3 that Job has no notion of the wager made between God and Satan. For Job there is no explanation for his sudden rash of tragedy. Even if Job is not cursing God, he is far from meeting his situation with equanimity. He curses the day he was born, wants to "vomit his anguish" (Job 3:24), and wonders, "What's the point of life when it doesn't make sense?" (Job 3:23). Three friends have come to sit with him in his misery. Each will offer his own explanation and advice for his troubled friend. Eliphaz begins by flattering Job, remembering how Job has helped others. But then he begs Job to consider, "Has a truly innocent person ever ended up on the scrap heap?" (Job 4:7). Job should accept it as a blessing when God corrects him (Job 5:17). Bildad chimes in next, confronting Job with the rhetorical, "Does God mess up?" (Job 8:3) and concluding, "There's no way God will reject a good person" (Job 8:20). Zophar summarizes on an upbeat note. If Job would just confess and abandon his sins, God would make everything right again (Job 11).

The friends' testimony demonstrates their acceptance of the converse of the Deuteronomic code. If a person's life looks bad, it's because he or she has disobeyed God's commandments. Somehow Job must deserve the pain he's getting. Of course, Job finds no comfort in their words because he knows he has not committed any sacrilege. He begs God to "show me where I have gone off track" (Job 6:24). "God knows good and well that I'm not guilty" (Job 10:7). "I can only conclude that God destroys the good right along with the bad" (Job 9:22). Sarcastically he responds to his friends, "When you die there will be no one to tell us how to live" (12:12). While he admits their point that God is sovereign, he wants to take his case to God nonetheless. "God and I are not equals" (Job 9:32). "There must be some Attorney who can clear my name—I appeal to the One who represents mortals before God" (Job 16:21).

The friends persist in their insistence on Job's guilt. Eliphaz wonders that Job even dares to challenge God (Job 15:5). People who question God will be paid back for their folly. Besides, can anyone be sinless? (Job 15:14). Bildad and Zophar agree that the evil must answer for their crimes. Indeed Scripture and good sense tell us that this must be so (Job 18, 20). But Job exposes their lack of compassion pleading, "Aren't you appalled by what's happening [to me]?" (Job 21:5). Moreover, the wicked do prosper in this life (Job 21:7). Job asserts his utter frustration, "God has no right to treat me like this—it isn't fair" (Job 23:2). If I confronted God, "Do you think he'd dismiss or bully me? No, he'd take me seriously" (Job 23:6) because I've "not just obeyed his advice—I've *treasured* it" (Job 23:12). Yet as much as Job desires an audience with God, the thought scares him (Job 23:15–17). He acknowledges that terrible things happen in the world, "The wretched cry out for help and God does nothing, acts like nothing's wrong!" (Job 24:12).

Finally Job's friends fall silent. Job takes time to review his life. He agrees that God is incredibly powerful but refuses to confess to false charges (Job 27:4). "I was known for helping people in trouble" (Job 29:12). Earlier he had pleaded with God to reveal the charges against him (Job 10:2) and he will "take whatever I have coming to me" (Job 13:13), but after he searched himself and his past, he can find no wrong. In desperation he cries, "I shout for help, God, and get nothing, no answer! ... What did I do to deserve this?" (Job 30:20, 24). With that plea, Job rests his case.

Here in a small insert of prose we learn of a fourth visitor to Job's misery. Elihu, junior to the elders who have already spoken to Job, sees his opportunity to air his thoughts. He is angry with all parties. The friends have presumed Job's guilt but brought no evidence to support their allegations. Yet he still has a bone to pick with Job. "God is far greater than any human. So how dare you [Job] haul him into court and then complain that he won't answer your charges? God always answers one way or another" (Job 33:12–14). Moreover, "it's impossible for God to do anything evil" (Job 34:10). Elihu claims Job's sin is nothing less than "wickedly talking back to God" (Job 34:36), presuming that God is the one who is punishing him. Does Job know everything about God's ways? "It's unthinkable that he'd treat anyone unfairly. If you're wise, you'll most certainly worship him" (37:23–24).

Elihu's series of speeches segue to God's voice, bringing to life what Elihu has just asserted—that God does answer *one way or another*—and foreshadowing the notion that God's response is not likely to be what we would expect. In chapters 38 to 41, God delivers the divine *answer* with fearsome force directly to Job's ears. Does Job know the mysteries of creation? Does Job have any clue how to keep the universe running? Job cowers in reply, "I babbled on about things far beyond me" (Job 42:3). The poetry closes as Job apologizes and asks God's forgiveness (Job 42:6).

What are we to make of God's answer? Throughout the dialogues we have rooted for Job, proud that he was unwilling to confess to sins he had not committed, pleased that he refused to sell out his integrity in an attempt to placate God. But God's speech blindsides us with its harsh tone. We must concede that God does not accuse Job of wrongdoing. In the epilogue God turns instead to the friends whom He criticizes, "You haven't been honest either with me or about me—not the way my friend Job has" (Job 42:7). From this comment we gather that God is also not angry with Job for speaking up on his own behalf. We should ask further, "Is God even angry with Job at all?" Job has posed the question rhetorically to his friends, "Do you think [God] would dismiss or bully me? No, he'd take me seriously" (Job 23:6). God has taken Job seriously enough to speak to him directly. But does the divine speech serve to bully and dismiss

Job? It is easy for us to hear it that way, but Job seems not to interpret the theophany as negatively as we might. Halfway through God's tirade he admits, "I'm speechless, in awe … I'm ready to shut up and listen" (Job 40:3–4). By quizzing Job on the various particulars of the creation, God has impressed Job with the hugeness of the enterprise. If Job can't understand the intricate secrets of nature, how can God explain the ins and outs of sin and its consequences? Does Job know how to "target the arrogant and bring them to their knees, [or how to] stop the wicked in their tracks" (Job 40:12)? Then how can God explain why the innocent suffer? It is beyond the capacity of human comprehension. Having heard God speak, Job sees things differently. God's perspective has humbled Job not by accusing him of sin or by equating his torment with punishment but by reminding him that he cannot fathom how God makes the world work. As Elihu already surmised, "If you're wise, you'll most certainly worship him" (Job 37:24).

Let's take a moment to reflect further on the book of Job as a whole piece. It is tempting to separate the poetry from the prose. Looking at the prologue alone, we would have to agree that Job is a patient person. The Job of the poetry is clearly exasperated. The prologue doesn't even deal with the issue of unjustified suffering. Instead it questions God's integrity. Does God play favorites, getting people to worship the Lord by blessing them? We can readily see why God would want to dispel such a suggestion, remembering how diligently the Deity worked with Israel to break her of the thinking that her God could be placated or manipulated the way other peoples' gods supposedly could. Still, it remains a hard thing to prove that a person's love for God is not conditioned by the blessings that have come his or her way. Yet Job's willingness to take the bad with the good from God (Job 2:10) goes a long way to demonstrate that his relationship with his Lord is not a simple *quid pro quo* affair. Considering that Satan does not even appear in the epilogue, it would be easy to allow the story of God's wager in the prologue to stand alone. Scholars once thought that the prose portions were written after the poetry in order to frame Job's story within a resolving context. Although there is still no consensus, some academics now suggest that the first version of Job consisted of a folklore legend the prologue and epilogue summarize and that the poetry was composed later to expand on the implications of the wager with Satan.

Whatever its formation history, however, the book of Job speaks to us most clearly as a whole. The prose does contextualize Job's ordeal and offer closure by giving Job a happy ending. But the poetry's honest depiction of Job's agony, not just of loss and physical pain but also of spiritual anguish, address a major gap within the biblical testimony up to this point. Bad things do happen to good people. People get consequences they don't deserve and often don't get to see justice in their lifetime. These ideas need to be voiced within the vacuum of Job's ignorance of God's arrangements because humans are likewise in the dark about what God is doing when tragedy and torment befall us. Taken together, the combined story of Job becomes an opportunity for us to approach the issue of unmerited suffering from both the human and divine perspective. In the midst of our afflictions God does not offer explanations but does promise us divine providence, even when we cannot feel the Lord's presence. Although we don't expect the *answer* Job receives from God, the story helps us to contemplate whether any rationalization of guiltless suffering would satisfy us. Still, where would the Bible be without this sojourn of Job's into the incomprehensible world of innocent anguish? It is immensely important to the integrity of the biblical witness that Job acknowledges both that the righteous do suffer and that their torment is fundamentally different from hardship and misery that come as the consequence of disobedience to God's commands.

Before we move on to the book of Psalms, we should note the series of reflections that Job offers that go unanswered within the immediate text. We'd have to agree that though God addresses Job directly, the voice coming out of a whirlwind (Job 38:1) still paints a scary picture. Early on in his commentary with his friends, Job admits, "God and I are not equals … How I wish we had an arbitrator to step in … some Attorney who can clear my name" (Job 9:32–33; 16:19). And if he has sinned as his friends suggest, "Why don't you [God] just forgive my sins and start me off with a clean slate?" (Job 7:21). He wishes, "My sins will be stuffed in a sack and thrown in the sea" (Job 14:17). He wonders further, "If we humans die, will we live again?" (Job 14:14). Let us keep these questions hanging in our minds and look for other unresolved musings as we continue through the rest of the Old Testament.

Psalms

If you try to open the Bible to its center, more often than not you will find yourself in the book of Psalms. This is a good example of form following function because in many ways the psalms (also known collectively as the Psalter) form the heart of the Bible. Listening to these worship songs and prayer poems allows us to hear the pulse of those who pray. Only here in the Bible do we have a book devoted solely to the human speaking directly to God. As I have said earlier, Scripture in general for Jews and Christians is revelation, God taking the initiative to make Himself known to humans. The psalms, however, supply the response to the Deity's self-disclosure, specifically humans answering back.[26] But don't look for careful piety here. By refusing to be subject to human manipulation, God clears the deck for honest communication between Deity and humans. Without spells and incantations to recite the supplicant must speak in his own voice before God. In this vein the Psalter adopts a strict, no-holds-barred policy. Every category of human emotion finds its

[26] Eugene Peterson titles one of his books about the book of Psalms *Answering God*.

way into these pages—pain (Psalm 38), assurance (Psalm 37), complaint (Psalm 10), gratitude (Psalm 16), trust (Psalm 11), fear (Psalm 57), relief (Psalm 23), anger (Psalm 44), awe (Psalm 8), joy (Psalm 100), desperation (Psalm 102), grief (Psalm 22), remorse (Psalm 51), despair (Psalm 88), vengeance (Psalm 137), celebration (Psalm 81), and praise (Psalm 46).

Although Psalm 1 sounds a reprise of the Deuteronomic code of blessing and curse and there is also a single psalm attributed to Moses (Psalm 90), Scripture primarily associates psalms with David. Whatever you didn't understand about David and his faith as it is chronicled in the books of Samuel gets clarified in the Psalter. Nearly one half of the psalms are attributed to David by headings added on to the beginning of many of the chapters. Thirteen of these give us situational specifics so that we can align the feelings of the poem with the circumstances David was experiencing. Take a look at Psalm 3, where David is crying out to God as his son Absalom's rebellion chases him from Jerusalem (narrated in 2 Samuel 15:13–17:22). Clearly from the first two verses David is afraid and tempted to lose faith. But verses 3 through 6 demonstrate that David's trust in the Lord remains strong despite the dire situation. He is even able to sleep in the midst of the chaos (Psalm 3:5). From verses 7 through 8, we find that God has not yet delivered a rescue, but David is nonetheless strengthened to meet the challenge. The act of praying to God has brought David peace and assurance even before his plight has improved.

In another example, the heading of Psalm 51 tells us that this is what David prayed after his prophet Nathan opened his eyes about his affair with Bathsheba. Notice the deep remorse David displays in the following: "I know how bad I've been; my sins are staring me down" (Psalm 51:3). Observe also David's claim that his sins are against God (Psalm 51:4), not merely, as we would expect, against Uriah or Bathsheba. David sees this event as a turning point in his life when he says to God, "What you're after is truth from the inside out. Enter me, then; conceive a new, true life … God, make a fresh start in me, shape a Genesis week from the chaos of my life" (Psalm 51:6, 10). He also admits that his sin has had the good effect of bringing him back to God. "I learned God-worship when my pride was shattered" (Psalm 51:17). What we learn of David's repentance in the Samuel narrative pales before this stunning confession and its follow-up acceptance of God's restorative forgiveness.

Yet what is particularly interesting about these two examples and the other psalms attributed to parts of David's story is how they serve two purposes at once. In each case it is easy to identify the emotions depicted with the event David is said to be undergoing at the time, but each psalm also remains general enough to speak to the listener's own life and circumstances. Psalm 3 may be interpreted as a prayer for anyone facing a fearful situation. Psalm 51 likewise might be a plea for forgiveness for every sinner. In a stroke we see how these original prayers of the faithful, starting with David himself, evolved into the present Psalter.

As books of the Bible go, Psalms probably has the longest history, beginning first with David's monarchy and continuing with additions and editions through almost the third century BCE. Poems and songs that began as individual's prayers to God grew to give voice to the community at large. Pilgrims entering Jerusalem probably sang Psalms 120–134, dubbed the Psalms of Ascent, as they made the climb to the temple for festival celebrations. In time the psalms became essential to worship as the various instructions to musicians attest. The postexilic writers' frequent mention of music and choirs singing during worship services allows us to imagine that once the Jews had lost the temple in Jerusalem as the focus of worship, they were able to reclaim their heritage in the Psalter.[27] David's kingship, though

---

[27] When we compare the chronicler's narrative of Solomon's dedication of the temple to 1 Kings 8:62–65, we find note taken of the musical portion

still remembered for its glory, became better revered as a witness to David's outstanding faith made clear in his songs to God.

One of the outstanding features of so many of the psalms is their capacity to demonstrate the transformation of the speaker's attitude. Take Psalm 22 as a case in point. The psalmist begins in utter despair, "God, God ... my God! Why did you dump me miles from nowhere? Doubled up with pain, I call to God all the day long. No answer. Nothing" (Psalm 22:1–2). He doubts whether God has any concern for him and bemoans his current state of distress. "Here I am, a nothing—an earthworm, something to step on, to squash" (Psalm 22:6). "Now packs of wild dogs come at me; thugs gang up on me" (Psalm 22:16). In a last gasp, it seems, he exclaims, "You, God—don't put off my rescue!" (Psalm 22:19). But then starting in verse 22, everything changes. Now the complaint becomes a declaration of God's abiding goodness. "[God] has never let you down, never looked the other way when you were being kicked around" (Psalm 22:24). The effect on the listener is to see the act of baring the soul as a means of getting connected to God's assurance of rescue and provision against life's pitfalls. What works for the psalmist promises also to be an answer for the listener. No wonder the psalms continue to serve both Jews and Christians literally thousands of years after their composition.

The editors who established the Psalter in its present form were keenly aware of the utility of its contents both for the worship community and individual devotion. The first two psalms serve as an introduction to the book. Psalm 1 congratulates the reader who meditates on God's Word. The following claim is put forth: If you keep reading these prayers (the psalms that follow),

---

of the ceremony that does not appear in the Kings version. "The choir and orchestra of Levites that David had provided for singing and playing anthems to the praise and love of GOD were all there; across the courtyard the priests blew trumpets" (2 Chronicles 7:6). We find similar remarks about music in Ezra 3:10 and Nehemiah 12:27–46, both making particular reference to music dating from the days of David.

your life will become like the "tree replanted in Eden, bearing fresh fruit each month" (Psalm 1:3). In contrast, Psalm 2 offers a reminder against discouragement. The world at large will often seem at odds with God and His ways, but the Lord will yet anoint a King, a Messiah (literally one who is anointed) to vanquish these enemies. Originally this psalm probably celebrated the coronation of various Davidic kings in recognition of their role as part of God's promise to build David a house. That it was kept in the Psalter and made part of the introduction after the monarchy had fallen bears witness to the transformation of the idea of the Davidic dynasty into the messianic hope, the belief that God would sometime in the future anoint an heir to David's kingdom who would redeem Israel. Several other psalms testify to the growth of this messianic hope. (Psalms 72, 110, and 132 are some examples according the NIV notes.)

At first glance the book of Psalms may appear to be arranged rather randomly. While the editors clearly did not develop a rigid system for organizing these prayers, there is nonetheless a flow to the songs. Often psalms side by side will function as a pair. Psalm 4 is a "going to sleep" prayer (Psalm 4:8), while Psalm 5 speaks of the morning (Psalm 5:3). Where the first half of Psalm 22 conveys anguish, Psalm 23 (which says, "The Lord is my shepherd") answers with reassurance. Traditionally the psalms are divided into five books to reflect the Pentateuch. The first two (Psalms 1–41 and 42–72) have the greatest concentration attributed to David. The end of each book closes with a short doxology of praises to God. The last book, however, ends with five hallelujah psalms in order to close the whole book in a great crescendo.

Primarily the book of Psalms speaks to the day-in-day-out experience of being a believer. When you first read Psalms, you may stand back as a spectator, almost as if you were eavesdropping on the conversations of the ancients. But because the words are so honest, the emotions so uncensored, you may begin to identify with the psalmist. Perhaps you have felt what is being expressed. As the psalmist bares his soul, you observe that something unspoken is happening to the one praying. You become a witness to the transformation of spirit achieved by connecting to God. If you then take the advice of Psalm 1 and meditate on these verses, you may find that you also feel the divine touch within your own soul. What else is there to say but ... *hallelujah*?

Proverbs

We're all familiar with the ordinary use of the word *proverb*, and it's just as likely that we have several proverbs floating around in our heads as we go through life. "Haste makes waste," "A stitch in time saves nine," and "A bird in the hand is worth two in the bush" are but a few. Yet it may seem startling that a book of these aphorisms gets counted as Scripture. Let's take a look at what the book of Proverbs has to offer us.

Both Job and Psalms involve direct address to God and deal heavily in expressing and exploring our emotions. Proverbs departs from this vantage point by turning to the human pursuit of reason in order to offer advice for daily life. As the musician and king David is to Psalms, the wise man Solomon is to Proverbs. Remember what 1 Kings told us about Solomon,

> God gave Solomon wisdom—the deepest of under-standing ... There was nothing beyond him ... Solomon's wisdom outclassed the vaunted wisdom of the wise men of the East, outshone the famous wisdom of Egypt. He was wiser than anyone ... He became famous among all the surrounding nations. He created 3000 proverbs ... He knew all about plants ... and animals. (1 Kings 4:29–33)

What is interesting about Solomon's wisdom is that though it comes from God, it isn't being touted as specific to Israel.

Whereas David's psalms testify to his passionate faith in God, Solomon's intellect is not tied to his knowledge of the Scriptures or the history of the relationship between God and Israel. Instead, his sagacity comes from his astute perceptions of both nature and human nature. When his smarts are compared to the reigning wise men of his day—Ethan, the Ezrahite, Heman, Calcol and Darda, the sons of Mahol (1 Kings 4:31)—he comes out on top. Granted, God gets the credit as the source of Solomon's shrewdness, but the implication remains that Solomon's wisdom stems from his personal acquisition of worldly understanding.

In its introductory verses the book of Proverbs claims to be a "manual for living, for learning what's right and just and fair" cast originally as advice from a father to a son (Proverbs 1:8 NIV) but a book that nonetheless still offers "a thing or two for the experienced to learn" (Proverbs 1:5). Its counsel has not grown stagnant with age but continues to provide excellent navigation tips for negotiating the journeys and inevitable human traffic jams of life. As you read, your may find yourself enjoying these pithy sayings for their obvious common sense and uncommon insight. One of the major themes is that you get out of life what you put in. "Sloth makes you poor; diligence brings wealth" (Proverbs 10:4). "When you're kind to others, you help yourself; when you're cruel to others, you hurt yourself" (Proverbs 11:17). Honesty is extolled. "A good and honest life is a blessed memorial" (Proverbs 10:7). "Honesty lives confident and carefree" (Proverbs 10:9). The book also speaks of humility. "Don't work yourself into the spotlight" (Proverbs 25:6). "Pride first, then the crash, but humility is precursor to honor" (Proverbs 18:12). Proverbs preaches moderation. Avoid gluttony and drinking too much (Proverbs 23:20). Don't be lazy (Proverbs 12:27), but don't worry about getting rich (Proverbs 23:4–5). Some good reverse psychology also makes the list. "A gentle response defuses anger" (Proverbs 15:1). "If you see your enemy hungry, go buy him lunch ... Your generosity will surprise him with goodness" (Proverbs 25:21–22). Wisdom holds marriage in very high esteem. "Enjoy the wife you married as a young man! ... Never take her love for granted! Why would you trade enduring intimacies for cheap thrills with a whore?" (Proverbs 5:18–19). But it does admit that "a nagging spouse is like the drip, drip, drip of a leaky faucet" (Proverbs 27:15). Always doing the *right thing* is paramount. "Far better to be right and poor, than to be wrong and rich" (Proverbs 16:8). "It's wrong, very wrong, to go along with injustice" (Proverbs 24:23).

The proverbs themselves translate well out of Hebrew because rather than rhyme or meter, the primary literary device is parallelism. (Two lines either stating each other's antithesis or two lines restating the same point are the most common patterns.) The collection evinces no particular organizing principles. Sometimes opposing maxims appear side by side. "Do not answer a fool according to his folly" (Proverbs 26:4 NIV); however, "Answer a fool according to his folly" (Proverbs 26:5 NIV). Not even all the proverbs are attributed to Solomon. Chapters 30 and 31 record the sayings of Agur and King Lemuel, men of non-Israelite origin who do not appear elsewhere in Scripture. This last contains what is dubbed the epilogue to the book, the Hymn to a Good Wife (Proverbs 31:10-31). Considering the second-class standing of women in the ancient world, whether in Israel or elsewhere, this ode to the virtues of womanhood reminds us that wise men were not blind to the humanity and giftedness of their mates. The wife described is fully competent in matters of money and business (Proverbs 31:16, 24) as well as homemaking skills (Proverbs 31:13, 15, 19). She shows compassion (Proverbs 31:20), plans for the future (Proverbs 31:21), speaks with good sense and kindness (Proverbs 31:26), and wins the respect of her husband and children alike with her superb home management (Proverbs 31:27–28).

Yet we have still not answered why the book of Proverbs— wisdom that Israel holds in common with other peoples of her day—is part of the Bible. It is not that God is not mentioned in this verses; God actually comes up frequently. The first line following the introduction (Proverbs 1:1–6) makes this clear. "Start with GOD—the first step in learning is bowing down to GOD" (Proverbs 1:7). In the book's first nine chapters where Wisdom and Foolishness are both personified as women (Peterson uses "Lady Wisdom" and "Madame Whore"), Wisdom is always aligned with God. In Proverbs 8:22–31, the voice of Wisdom claims to be the first thing God made, an integral part of the creation process. Although Genesis 1 does not refer to Wisdom directly, we can perhaps interpret God's repeated statements about the goodness of the creation as part of a conversation. Nevertheless, for all that God is invoked here, the tone differs from that of earlier Scripture. It is as if Solomon sees God more intensely through Wisdom than through the sort of relationship arc we observe in the narratives of other biblical personae. Again we have to ask, "Why is this then part of Scripture?"

I suggest this resolution. Proverbs' description of the righteous life completely syncs up with the life lived in obedience to God's Torah. The book of the Law does not do it for us, but when we distill the *spirit* of the Ten Commandments' injunctions and compare it with the guidance for daily living offered in Proverbs, we find that both are describing what makes for good behavior between humans and God as well as humans and one another. It is as if we are seeing the commutative property of mathematics played out (the one that says 2+3 is the same as 3+2). The essence of God's prescription for human conduct can be found in both God's words to Moses on Mount Sinai and the wise observations streaming from humans' minds using their God-given powers of discernment. It is yet another statement that what God has given to Israel is ultimately meant for all humankind.

Ecclesiastes

Did you ever think the expression, "Eat, drink and be merry" came from the Bible? It actually comes from our next book— Ecclesiastes. We get the title for this book from the Greek word for assembly—an attempt to translate the Hebrew word *koheleth*, referring to the one addressing a gathering. Various English translations have used *preacher* and *teacher*. Peterson employs *Quester* to name the person who writes this book. The introductory identification of the author as "David's son and king in Jerusalem" (Ecclesiastes 1:1) would make our Quester appear to be Solomon, but scholars have discounted the idea since the Hebrew used indicates a more modern date. Instead the indirect reference to Solomon works to encourage us to understand the words as coming from Solomon's perspective in that monarch's latter years.[28] In that context we need to remember here that Solomon ruled Israel during her most prosperous period. He had not only fame for his wisdom but also for his wealth and his huge harem. The 1 Kings account of his life views his later years as a disappointment because of his penchant for worshiping the foreign gods of his wives. We never hear Solomon's voice in the narrative version, but we can readily imagine such a man developing the cynical attitude the Quester voices.

Our author launches his work with a simple statement of his theme, "There's nothing to anything—it's all smoke" (Ecclesiastes 1:2). Other translations include the following: "Everything is meaningless" (NIV), and "Everything is vanity" (KJV). Life has boiled down to the same old thing day in and day out. "What happened will happen again. There's nothing new on this earth" (Ecclesiastes 1:9). The Quester calls himself "wiser than anyone before me in Jerusalem" (Ecclesiastes 1:16), so he should know. "What I've concluded is that so-called wisdom and knowledge

---

28 Brevard Childs, *Introduction to the Old Testament as Scripture*, p. 584.

are mindless and witless—nothing but spitting into the wind" (Ecclesiastes 1:17).

Our Quester goes on to explain the basis of his conclusions. As king, he had wealth to afford any pleasure he wanted. "I never said no to myself" (Ecclesiastes 2:10). Yet at the end of his life he reasons that he can't take his wealth with him into death (Ecclesiastes 2:18). What's the point of working hard if you end up with the same fate as someone who hasn't (Ecclesiastes 2:21)? Therefore, "The best you can do with your life is have a good time and get by the best you can" (Ecclesiastes 2:24). God has the say in the end, not humans (Ecclesiastes 2:25–26).

There is much repetition and little organization to the piece. It reads almost like a tirade, except the tone betrays more fatigue and boredom with life than anger. Chapter 3 begins with a beautiful poem professing that there is a "right time for everything on the earth" (Ecclesiastes 3:1). Perhaps you have heard the song using its words titled "Turn, Turn, Turn" by Pete Seeger that the Byrds made into a hit in 1965. But even this poem is followed up with the comment, "I've had a good look at what God has given us to do—busywork mostly" (Ecclesiastes 3:10). God has made the earth beautiful, but "he's left us in the dark" (Ecclesiastes 3:11). Because of our lack of understanding of God, the Quester concludes again, "There's nothing better than to go ahead and ... eat, drink and make the most of your job. It's God's gift" (Ecclesiastes 3:13).

Frequently our author argues both sides of a point. On money he says, "The one who loves money is never satisfied with money" (Ecclesiastes 5:10), or he says, "A rich man's belly gives him insomnia" (Ecclesiastes 5:12). However; "laughter and bread go together and wine gives sparkle to life—but it's money that makes the world go round" (Ecclesiastes 10:19), and "wisdom is better when it's paired with money" (Ecclesiastes 7:11). On work he says, "The fool sits back and takes it easy" (Ecclesiastes 4:5), but he also claims, "One handful of peaceful repose is better than two fistfuls of worried work" (Ecclesiastes 4:6). On pleasure he says, "My verdict on the pursuit of happiness? Who needs it?" (Ecclesiastes 2:2) and then says, "We work to feed our appetites; meanwhile our souls go hungry" (Ecclesiastes 6:7). However, "The only earthly good men and women can look forward to is to eat and drink well and have a good time" (Ecclesiastes 8:15).

This appearance of equivocation is really part of the training in the school of wisdom. The dialectic approach maintains that in order to apprehend truth, "it's best to stay in touch with both sides of an issue" (Ecclesiastes 7:18). On the one hand, the Quester still values wisdom. "There's nothing better than being wise, knowing how to interpret the meaning of life" (Ecclesiastes 8:1) as his inclusion of a number of insightful proverbs attests. In the end, however, wisdom has failed to deliver on its promises. For example, wisdom teaches what amounts to a restatement of the Deuteronomic code. "The good life is reserved for the person who fears God; ... the evil person will not experience a 'good' life" (Ecclesiastes 8:12). But in his experience he has found that reality paints a different picture. "Good people get what's coming to the wicked, and bad people get what's coming to the good. I tell you this makes no sense. It's smoke" (Ecclesiastes 8:14). This is the crux of the author's frustration. He can't make sense of life with his wisdom. "I realized that if you keep your eyes open day and night without blinking, you'll still never figure out the meaning of what God is doing on this earth" (Ecclesiastes 8:16–17). The Quester finds himself in the same boat with Job. No matter how you evaluate life (by wisdom or by good works), the bad news is still that life is unfair.

The Quester feels life's unfairness most when he tries to comprehend death. "It's one fate for everybody—righteous and wicked ... I find this outrageous—the worst thing about living on this earth ... Life leads to death" (Ecclesiastes 9:2–3). The thought takes him back to his original conclusion that you should make the most of life while you have it. In itself this idea is not a negative outlook, but in the context of the Quester's tone it speaks of his disillusionment. He has devoted his life to the pursuit of wisdom, and it has brought no answers. God is impenetrable.

So why is this treatise in the Bible? Does it speak truth? I think we'd have to agree with many of its observations. The ones that the Quester finds disturbing disturb us as well. But what of the refrain that says we might as well eat, drink, and be merry while we can because everything else is meaningless? For all the different lines of discourse taken within the book, all thoughts cycle back to this conclusion until we come to the epilogue at the end of chapter 12. Scholars debate where the epilogue actually begins. The voice of the author appears to end in the middle of 12:8—his final pronouncement being "It's all smoke, nothing but smoke." Then the text shifts to the third person in repetition of that conclusion, "The Quester says that everything's smoke." From here to the close the narrative voice extols the wisdom and teaching of the Quester while it simultaneously frames his work within a more positive theological perspective. Verse 11 notes that "the words of the wise prod us to live well" but adds the explanation, "They are given by God, the one Shepherd." What follows is a word of caution against too much study (Ecclesiastes 12:12). The Quester's excessive pondering has obscured the real bottom line. "Fear God. Do what he tells you" (Ecclesiastes 12:13). Whereas Proverbs' wisdom works to verify the truth of the Torah, the musings of the author of Ecclesiastes threaten to steer off course without the epilogue prompt that "eventually God will bring everything that we do out into the open and judge it according to its hidden intent, whether it's good or evil" (Ecclesiastes 12:14). Wisdom alone cannot discover God's plan for humanity. Human insight has an acknowledged role, but when it attempts to operate independently of God, it flounders. God knows the answers to the great questions the Quester asks. What's the point of life if the good and the evil suffer the same fate? What's the point of life if we all have to die? The Quester appreciates that God is mysterious. The epilogue reminds us that God will eventually make things clearer. In the meanwhile, have faith.

Song of Songs

After tackling all the difficult questions and wrenching emotions expressed in the preceding wisdom books, we come to a treat at the close of this section. The Song of Songs is a beautiful love poem—for the most part a dialogue between two lovers. The Hebrew idiom expressed in "song of songs" implies the superlative—the best of all songs. Let's take a look at what receives this "praise of praises."

Older translations tend to title this book the Song of Solomon because of the heading in the first verse. Like Ecclesiastes, this ascription to Solomon does not require us to consider Solomon the author. Instead it points us to hear the poem in the context of the wisdom tradition that Solomon introduced to Israel,[29] namely that humans can gain much insight into God's creation by careful observation of the interactions of humans. It is consistent with the pursuit of wisdom to examine the value of human love.

Essentially a dialogue between lovers, we could almost read the song as a play, except that the parts are not always clearly delineated. Peterson's translation designates the roles as "the Woman," and "the Man." The NIV employs the titles "Beloved" and "Lover." Occasionally a chorus of women's voices chimes in to back up the voice of the woman. Note that the woman begins this poem and gives us our first taste of its erotic nature. "Kiss me—full on the mouth!" (Song of Songs 1:2). She continues with effusive enthusiasm to praise her *King-Lover*, whose love is better than "vintage wine" (Song of Songs 1:4), and wonders where her man is tending his flocks at the noontime rest so that she can meet with him (Song of Songs 1:7). He answers that she,

---

[29] Brevard Childs, *Introduction to the Old Testament as Scripture*, p. 574

"loveliest of all women" (Song of Songs 1:8), should stay with her flocks for safety's sake. He is coming and bringing her jewelry (Song of Songs 1:11).

The poem continues in this vein back and forth. In chapter 2, they meet in the countryside. The woman compares the man to a graceful gazelle, a virile stag (Song of Songs 2:9). When he leaves her side, she cannot sleep without him (Song of Songs 3:1). In Song of Songs 3:6–10, some readers see the images of a wedding celebration with its reference to Solomon's carriage and its sixty soldiers. The status of the man switches back and forth from the common shepherd to royalty. The man in love can feel like both. The man takes the initiative in chapter 4, praising his beloved's body in detail. Her smile is "generous and full." Her lips are "jewel red." Her breasts are like twin fawns and the curves of her body inviting (Song of Songs 4:1–7). He beseeches her to leave her home and join him (Song of Songs 4:8) and continues to compare her "body and soul" to a beautiful and aromatic garden (Song of Songs 4:12–15). Chapter 5 records what appears to be a dream sequence for the woman expressing her dread of being separated from her lover (Song of Songs 5:2–7). From chapter 6 to the close they are together again, each taking turns to admire the other.

The intensity of the passion expressed in these verses rings true for anyone who has fallen in love. The love described is as emotional as it is physical. The poetry, while highly erotic, marks the antithesis of pornography. The lovers approach each other on equal footing, with the woman in the lead much of the time. Their words celebrate their mutual surrender. The verses also imply the exclusivity of the relationship. The woman exclaims with confidence, "My lover is mine, and I am his" (Song of Songs 2:16). Likewise the man contrasts himself with Solomon who has so many *vineyards*. He is satisfied that "my vineyard is all mine, and I'm keeping it to myself" (Song of Songs 8:11–12).[30] We are taken back to Genesis when God presents the woman to the man because "it is not good for the Man to be alone" (Genesis 2:18). Clearly the Song of Songs gives us a picture of the way love between a man and a woman is meant to be not only from the human perspective but from the divine as well.

Both Judaism and Christianity have often sought to reinterpret this book as a metaphor for God's love for Israel (Judaism) or Christ's love for the church (Christianity). While I would agree that many biblical passages invite multiple layers of understanding, I fear that in the case of Song of Songs these allegorical interpretations emerge because of embarrassment over the sensual nature of the poetry. While I would defend the possibility of these metaphorical readings as a secondary application of the text's meaning, I maintain that the more literal hearing should carry the day. What we have in Song of Songs is a reminder of how precious God's gift of sexuality to humans is. The love expressed here is consonant with the intention of Genesis 2 and all the Torah teaching regarding marriage. In addition, we have in Song of Songs 8:6–7 a consummate observation from the wisdom mind-set about the value and power of human love, one that says, "Love is invincible facing danger and death … The fire of love stops at nothing … Flood waters can't drown love, torrents of rain can't put it out." After all the difficult questions that the wisdom literature has sought and often failed to answer, we must embrace this silver lining with gusto.

The Wisdom Books go a long way to cover terrain untouched by the narrative of Israel's history. Job, many of the Psalms, and Ecclesiastes all complain of breaks in the Deuteronomic code by testifying to the reality of underserved suffering and unpunished injustice. Proverbs holds the line on what normally works in human interaction. Job makes a case of what happens

---

[30] I use Peterson's translation here. Other translations give these words to the woman.

in an extraordinary situation. Ecclesiastes attacks the logic of Proverbs and wisdom in general by reminding us of its inadequacy to make sense of our lives without allowing for the mystery of God. Song of Songs offsets the sourness of the Quester by prompting us to remember the joy God intends for us, even if it is not often realized in marriage. Finally all of these revolve around Psalms, the book that demonstrates that above all else God desires that we talk to our maker with honesty and regularity about what matters to us in our lives.

Let us not be deceived, however. The Wisdom Literature allowed Israel to make worthy observations and ask important questions, but it left many issues still on the table, waiting to be answered. God stands for justice, so what is God going to do about injustice? God wants humans to have the joy of love, so why do humans suffer? God wants us to choose life, but what is the point if we all just die in the end? And what about the promise of the Messiah? What can the Messiah do to change the miserable consequences of living in a fallen world? The baton falls now to the prophets to explore further what God will and will not do to untangle the web that human rebellion has woven.

Chapter 8

Does It Really Say That God Would Send a Messiah?

It's likely that when you hear the word *messiah*, you associate the term with both Christianity and Judaism but are not sure why. Let's try to clarify the biblical use of the title by tracing it through the Old Testament first. We will deal with the Christian interpretation of Messiah in chapter 9.

Messiah is the Hebrew term for the one God anoints to spearhead divine aid. The name can signify a corporate identity as in the *nation* of Israel being God's chosen people. Think back to God's initial promise to Abraham, "I will make you into a great nation ... and all peoples on earth will be blessed through you" (Genesis 12:2–3). But the biblical narrative has also introduced us to the concept of messiah as a specific individual in several examples. God appointed Moses as the Hebrew deliverer who was to go into Egypt and insist that Pharaoh release the Hebrews from slavery. In the period of the Judges God raised up a "savior" (Peterson) or "deliverer" (NIV) when Israel pleaded for help against her enemies. Samuel instituted the ceremony of anointing the king with oil poured over the regent's head when God chose Saul to be king over Israel (1 Samuel 10:1). Every coronation service for the kings of Israel and Judah included the practice. The idea was supposed to be that the anointed one was called by the Lord to facilitate God's help and lead God's people out of their times of distress. We know from the history of the monarchy that kings mostly failed to perform in this capacity. Yet out of the era of the kings, evolving out of God's promise to David to make him a dynasty, emerged the messianic hope—the expectation that a future heir to David's throne would restore Israel and her people and bring them glory. While the Wisdom Literature also fanned the flame of the messianic hope in Psalms, its other books pose questions that augment the scope of the Messiah's mission. Job asks for a mediator between himself and the Deity. The Quester wonders about justice and the fairness of life when everyone does not get their just deserts, especially because good and bad alike die. Is there anything after death? Does it matter whether a person has been obedient to God or rebellious?

As we begin this chapter on Israel's prophets, we note that we will be reviewing much of the same history covered in chapter 6 on the monarchy (see chart on p. 141-143). Although King David comes to serve as the model for the messianic hope, most of the kings of Israel and Judah fall short of their calling to lead God's people in keeping with the Torah. The Lord responded to this dilemma primarily by sending prophets to speak the Word of God as a contradiction to the corrupt leadership of the royal authority. David's prophet Nathan set him straight about his affair with Bathsheba (2 Samuel 12). Two prominent prophets emerged in the books of Kings—Elijah and Elisha. Also in Kings, the prophetess Huldah aided Josiah in his era of reforms. For the most part, however, the prophets working during the period of the monarchy did not answer to God but to the kings themselves, often massaging the royal egos and glad-handing the leadership structure that accelerated Israel's trajectory away from God's ways. For example, during Ahab's reign in Israel the monarch sought advice from his four hundred prophets about whether or not to attack the king of Aram (Syria). Their unanimous pronouncement was, "Go for it ... GOD will hand it over to the king" (1 Kings 22:6). Only under pressure from Jehoshaphat, the king of Judah, did Ahab reluctantly consult the prophet Micaiah. His single voice offered the opposite but correct counsel since Ahab ended up dying in the battle (1 Kings 22:13–38). As we read through the prophets of this chapter, we will observe that they always have to speak against the majority report of royal prophets and priests who ply the people with words they want to hear. God loves Israel or Judah too much to see her suffer. We will find Jeremiah complaining, "Their preachers have been telling them that everything is going to be all right—no war and no famine—that there's nothing to worry about" (Jeremiah 14:13). Both the ubiquity and the popularity of these false prophets create a creditability gap for the prophets that have truly received their vocation from God. As a result, this latter group suffers indignities and persecutions throughout their years of preaching God's message.

The prophets we will read for this chapter have become known as the writing prophets. As already noted, the seventeen books we will cover here overlap the time line of Israel's monarchy, exile, and postexilic periods, giving us a second look at this history from the perspective of the servants whom God called to preach the message of judgment and the crushing consequences of Israel's sins. When you read the strong language and the cutting remarks laid against God's people, you must again wonder why these words were chosen by the community of faith to be preserved—not just because they say bad things about the Jews but also because it would seem that their relevance in predicting the demise of Israel and eventually Judah would end after the fact. But the Jews did hold on to these words because these messages were embedded with God's love, comfort, and hope. In fact, the testimony of the prophets proves that God levies judgment *so that* what is wrong can be made right again. Since the sins that evoke God's wrath are sins that continue to plague humanity—greed, dishonesty, cheating, exploitation, and lack of compassion—there is also an automatic timelessness to their words. Here, echoing back to Genesis 3, the prophets will show us God addressing the quandary that sin creates.

1. God loves His people and the whole of creation, including the other nations of the world.

2. God is holy. When God created the world good, fashioning order out of chaos, holiness was the ingredient that made it good. Consider what damage to human relationships occurs when the prohibitions of the last five commandments are abandoned (murder, adultery, stealing, lying, and envy). This doesn't even address the fallout from faltering in one's duty to God (the remaining commandments). The bottom line is that obedience to the commandments (and to holiness) is necessary for the world to be good. Ignoring sin is not an option for God.

3. God gave Israel the Law so that she might know the way to living rightly before God. Though Israel delighted in this knowledge and perceived the Law as a great gift, her history is riddled with her unfaithfulness to the Torah. Starting with Moses, going through the period of the judges, and continuing on into the monarchy, God's people vacillated between calling upon the Lord for salvation one minute and flouting the divine will the next. From the time Israel entered the Holy Land she struggled to keep from worshiping the gods of the indigenous peoples along with the Lord despite the explicit commandment that she should have no other gods. In his farewell address (Joshua 24) Joshua puts the question before the people as they establish themselves in the Promised Land, "Whom will you serve?" The Hebrews clamor to exclaim their choice is God. Joshua retorts, "You can't do it; you're not able to worship GOD" (Joshua 24:19). The bottom line is that Israel is both unwilling and *unable* to live according to God's commandments in order to be holy.

The dilemma seems to present a dead end. God loves creation. God hates sin. If God overlooks sin in favor of loving humans, the Lord denies His own holiness and gives up on having a good world. If the Deity holds to holiness, there is no way for the Lord to connect to His sin-tarnished people. Supplying miraculous rescues, giving rules, raising up God-loving leaders, and reminding people of their need to repent all have not worked to reverse the progress of sin. God's people continue to reject God's ways once they are out of trouble. As Joshua foretold, humans prove unable to sustain a resolve to love the Lord. The answer must come outside the box of the human mind-set. This will make God's resolution for the problem of sin difficult for humans to grasp. Therefore, God sends the prophets to articulate the dilemma and prepare the people to receive God's answer. To that end, the prophets claim the following with history corroborating their assertions:

1. There are consequences to sin. If Israel does not repent, God will allow enemies to overrun her borders and scatter her people.
   a. Assyria defeats the northern kingdom in 722 BCE.
   b. Babylon defeats Judah in 586 BCE and exiles the Jews from their homeland.

2. God will eventually punish the nations who ravaged Israel and Judah.
   a. Assyria falls to Babylonia in 612 BCE.
   b. Babylon falls to Persia in 539 BCE.

3. The pain of the exile will make God's people feel like their Lord has abandoned them, but Israel and Judah need to remember that they brought this fate on themselves. The author of Lamentations will express it poetically. "He [God] wove my sins into a rope and harnessed me

to captivity's yoke" (Lamentations 1:14). The prophets' general mission is to validate God's blamelessness in the tragedy of the monarchy's defeat. Yet because of the Lord's enduring love, God will not destroy the Jews. The Deity will even restore a remnant of His people to the Promised Land.

    a. The Jews' loss of political autonomy in their homeland accounts for the dispersion of Jews throughout the Mediterranean and eventually throughout the world. Yet they survive to this day.

    b. A small percentage of Jews do return to Jerusalem and Israel in the second half of the sixth century BCE.

4. Finally God will raise up from the Jews a Messiah who will save and cleanse them and all peoples from their sins so that the Genesis-intended order and goodness of creation will be reestablished with the holy city of Jerusalem as the center.

    a. The Messiah does not arrive during the period in which the Hebrew Scriptures are written, but the expectation of His eventual appearance survives. From Isaiah's initial introduction to the *branch* coming from the stump of Jesse who would become the *Prince of Peace* (Isaiah 9:6 KJV) in the eighth century to Zechariah's pronouncement, "Your king is coming!" (Zechariah 9:9), in the fifth, the prophets never back off the promise that God will send the Messiah. Neither do they shrink from their insistence that God's judgment day awaits when evil will be routed and God's good world restored. Malachi ends the Old Testament with God's vow to send the prophet Elijah as a sign before the "Big Day of GOD" dawns (Malachi 4:5).

The Christian canon[31] arranges the prophets somewhat in two sections—the three Major[32] Prophets (Isaiah, Jeremiah, and Ezekiel, with Lamentations inserted between Jeremiah and Ezekiel) followed by the Twelve Minor Prophets with the book of Daniel forming a bridge between the two. Within each section the prophets appear mostly chronologically. In his first thirty-nine chapters Isaiah discourses in Jerusalem during the eighth century, both predicting and then pointing to Israel's fall to Assyria as a lesson for Judah. Scholars believe that chapters 40 to 55 belong to a second Isaiah, with chapters 56 to 66 attributable to a third Isaiah, both sections written after the exile. Thus, Isaiah presents the whole picture of Israel's prophecy in this introductory book. Jeremiah sermonizes in Judah as the fall of Jerusalem is imminent, and Ezekiel speaks to the community in exile. The Twelve revisit this time line as a unit unto themselves, probably because they came to be written on a single scroll. Here the historical pattern recurs more loosely and with a broader range. Hosea and Amos overlap Isaiah with their preaching to Israel before its demise. Jonah is mentioned in 2 Kings 14:25 as prophesying to Israel in this same period, but we will see that the book of Jonah follows a different part of his ministry. Micah serves as a contemporary of Isaiah. Likewise Obadiah, Nahum, Zephaniah, Habakkuk, and possibly Joel coincide with Jeremiah. While not himself a prophet, Daniel's book provides an example of courageous faith sustained outside of Israel, somewhat the way the book of Esther does. Then Haggai, Zechariah, and Malachi continue to bring God's Word to the postexilic community the books of Ezra and Nehemiah describe.

Generally the messages of the prophets fall into the following three categories:

---

[31] See appendix 2 comparing the Hebrew and Christian ordering of the canon.

[32] The designation of *major* or *minor* prophets stems from the length of their writings and does not indicate any priority of importance.

1. **Judgment against God's people for their flagrant sinning.** God wants to go on record that He has given Jacob ample opportunity to repent. But after so many second chances Israel and Judah have developed the attitude that God will never really punish them because the Lord loves them too much. After the fall of Jerusalem the psalmist of Lamentations will remind Judah, "Your [false] prophets courted you with sweet talk. They didn't face you with your sin so that you could repent. Their sermons were all wishful thinking, deceptive illusions" (Lamentations 2:14). On the other hand, Isaiah, Jeremiah, Ezekiel, and the Twelve would valiantly deliver the message God's people didn't want to hear, giving Judah a continual stream of warning from the mid-eighth century forward.

2. **Judgment against the nations that have stood in enmity toward Israel and Judah.** Even though God will use these nations to bring His people to defeat, Jacob's enemies will not escape God's punishment for their atrocities. Almost all the prophets will make a point of predicting disaster for the foes that surround Israel. Isaiah will set the pattern in place by forecasting the fall of Babylon, Assyria, Philistia, Moab, Aram (Syria), Egypt, and Tyre (Isaiah 13–23). Notice how few names are familiar to us in today's world.

3. **Words of comfort and hope.** God's people must not construe the exile as an undoing of God's saving work of the Exodus. God has a plan that will resolve the paradox of the Lord's love for humans and hatred of sin. Hope emerges in the form of the Messiah, the one God will anoint to save not only Israel but all peoples. The Messiah will then usher in a new and ideal kingdom. The prophets do not offer us either a distinct picture of the Messiah or a timetable for the final struggle that will bring the world back to God's intended perfection. Instead each

will provide us with images, hints, and promises of the peace and fullness of glory that waits for those who align themselves with God. It will be left to us, the readers, to determine whether any future person's claim to the title satisfies the prophecies put forth.

Isaiah, Jeremiah, and Ezekiel introduce us to the troubled lives of the prophets. The length and depth of these three books allow us to get better acquainted with these servants of God than the Twelve who follow them. Each will tell us the story of God calling him to become the Lord's mouthpiece. We will see that each labors for a long period of his life and suffers considerable humiliation in order to get God's Word heard. Even among the shorter oracles of the Twelve we will sense each prophet's burden of disgrace from delivering words of judgment against his own people and particularly against the leadership of Judah. God uses the prophets to make the case that Israel and Judah's continuous idolatry and worship of foreign deities as well as their general corruption, dishonesty, and lack of compassion for the marginalized makes them more than deserving of being handed over to their enemies. Yet even as the prophets speak to the specifics of the divided kingdom's sordid history, we will discover that their messages transcend the particular circumstances facing the Israel and Judah that originally heard their words. The postexilic community of faith that received the written record of the prophets' words found in them a theological significance that enabled Jews to weather the political storms and persecutions that followed their return to Jerusalem. It's time we take a look at what the prophets really say.

Isaiah

Positioned in the canon as the first of the writing prophets, Isaiah sets the stage for all those who follow. God has called each one to speak divine words to a people who have grown deaf to the Lord's voice. Writing mostly in poetry, Isaiah presents a multifaceted amalgam of God's justifiable anger and resulting judgment, which springs from both God's holiness and enduring love of His people. This deep passion for the destiny of humanity leads the Lord to proclaim a series of promises that involve redemption of Israel and the nations of the world, a glorious Messiah, a suffering servant, and finally the coming of a new heaven and earth. Among Hebrew writers, Isaiah stands out for his extensive vocabulary and stunning use of wordplay and imagery to bring home his various points. Peterson compares his work to a symphony with its recurring melody of the holiness of God. For our purposes we will focus on his theme that "the deaf will hear and the blind will see."

After a word of introduction (Isaiah 1:1) where we place Isaiah as a prophet to four kings of Judah (approximately 740–681 BCE), Isaiah launches into God's case against the southern kingdom. God brought up His children well, but they have rebelled against their Lord (Isaiah 1:2). To make the point clearer, Isaiah compares Israel to a meticulously built vineyard planted in fertile ground with top-of-the-line equipment that has nonetheless yielded only sour grapes (Isaiah 5:2). He expresses God's disappointment over the harvest with searing Hebrew wordplay, "And he looked for justice, but saw bloodshed; for righteousness, but heard cries of distress" (Isaiah 5:7 NIV). The words for *justice* and *bloodshed* sound alike in Hebrew as do *righteousness* and *distress*.[33]

Isaiah's perception of Judah's corruption rises to a crescendo when he abruptly shifts into prose to describe his formal call to God's service. In a vision he sees the Lord seated on a throne attended by angelic beings known as seraphs. The holiness of God is so palpable that Isaiah shrinks away in shame. "I'm as good

---

[33] Explanation offered in NIV p. 1017.

as dead! Every word I've ever spoken is tainted—blasphemous even! And the people I live with talk the same way, using words that corrupt and desecrate. And here I've looked God in the face!" (Isaiah 6:5). But the seraphs enable Isaiah to go on by cleansing his guilt with a live coal from the altar pressed against his lips. Then Isaiah hears the Master speak, "Whom shall I send?" and without even knowing the mission, he readily replies, "I'll go. Send me!" (Isaiah 6:8). But the message God would have him proclaim to the people is a hard one. They will hear but not understand, look but not see. Like the man-made idols they have chosen to worship in place of God, the people have become deaf and blind to the urgency of repentance that could save them. When Isaiah asks how long this recalcitrance will last, God explains that Judah will have to be hit hard like a forest "with every tree cut down" (Isaiah 6:12). Then from these stumps the "holy seed" (Isaiah 6:12) will send up a shoot from Jesse (11:1). The offspring of Jesse refers to King David, the youngest son of Jesse. Remember that when David came up with the idea of building a house for the Lord, God turned that thought around and promised to build a house (dynasty) for David. The divine vow included the following guarantee: "Your house and your kingdom will endure forever before me; your throne will be established forever" (2 Samuel 7:11–16 NIV).

As we scan the first thirty-nine chapters of Isaiah's book (the section most likely written in Isaiah's lifetime), we can identify the infrequent prose passages with specific events in Isaiah's life, the theophany scene in chapter 6 marking the first. When (in approximately 735 BCE) King Ahaz panics over the possible coalition of Syria (Aram) and Israel (Ephraim) against Judah, Isaiah brings him God's Word that these threats will come to nothing (Isaiah 7:16). Instead Ahaz should put his trust in the Lord, not his own political acumen. When the Assyrian king, Sargon, moves against the Philistines (probably in 711 BCE), Isaiah obeys God's command to go about naked and barefoot for

219

three years as a symbolic warning that Judah's citizens could find themselves refugees like the recently fallen tribes of the northern kingdom. Judah should learn from Israel's defeat not to depend on foreign alliances for security, which only God can provide (Isaiah 20:1–6). Finally forming the climax of this first Isaiah's treatise, we find a second rendition of God's miraculous rescue of Jerusalem in response to Hezekiah's show of faith. In parallel with the narrative offered in 2 Kings 18:13–20:19, we hear Isaiah's assurances that God will prevail against Assyrian King Sennacherib and the taunts of his field commander designed to precipitate the surrender of Jerusalem (Isaiah 36–37). But the narrative of God's fifteen-year postponement of Hezekiah's death (Isaiah 38) illustrates that this 701 BCE salvation of Judah stands as merely a brief reprieve. Isaiah indicates that Hezekiah's subsequent effusive display of the royal treasures to a party of Babylonian envoys foreshadows the spoils that a future king of Babylon (Nebuchadnezzar) would reap from Judah's eventual demise just over a century later (Isaiah 39).

Against the backdrop of this historical iteration, Isaiah speaks largely in poetry. The prophet's oracles of accusation against God's people are braided together with images of the Messiah as well as the end times when all who love the Lord (from Israel and all the nations) will lay down their weapons and convene at the temple on God's mountain (first introduced in Isaiah 2:2). Information about the Messiah comes to us in snapshots at first. After Judah suffers through the consequences of her sins, God's branch (from the stump of Jesse) will appear as the antidote to the poisonous depravity that overtakes a society vanquished by war, where women have lost their husbands and sons to battle (Isaiah 3:25–4:2). Then those who remain, "everyone left behind in Zion, and the discards and rejects in Jerusalem, will be reclassified as 'holy'" (Isaiah 4:3). Likewise the *holy seed* hinted at in God's answer to Isaiah's query about how long the people will stand deaf and blind to God's ways

(Isaiah 6:11–13) explodes into bloom in the passage made famous in Handel's Messiah.

> The people who walked in darkness [blindness] have seen a great light ... For unto us a child is born, unto us a Son is given; And the government will be upon His shoulder. And His name will be called Wonderful, Counselor, Mighty God, Everlasting Father, Prince of Peace ... Upon the throne of David and over His kingdom, to order and establish it with judgment and justice from that time forward, even forever. (Isaiah 9:1–7 KJV).

We should note here that while this passage marks the Messiah as the heir to David's monarchy, it does not describe a traditional ruler. This future leader of Israel will revolutionize government and usher in an ideal kingdom the world has never known.

Cycling back to the immediate future, Isaiah predicts the fall of the northern kingdom to the Assyrians (Isaiah 9:8–10:4)—a fate that befalls Israel in 722 BCE. God makes no qualms about using this foreign power to punish His people because it is their corruption that has left them vulnerable to their enemies. But Isaiah makes it clear that God does not exempt Jacob's enemies from their crimes just because God allows the Assyrian challenge to succeed. The nations that mete out atrocities to Israel will be duly castigated in time (Isaiah 13–23). Yet these pronouncements of judgment against Israel's foes again lead Isaiah to the distant future, particularly the end of the world. In a section known as Isaiah's Apocalypse (Isaiah 24–27), the prophet describes a final battle for the earth that will devastate the planet (Isaiah 24) but leave those who love the Lord safe to attend a magnificent banquet on the Lord's mountain (Isaiah 25). Like the instructions given the night of the first Passover, the people of God must "go home and shut yourselves in ... until the punishing wrath is past" (Isaiah 26:20). Then in a reprise of the vineyard metaphor, God will finally rejoice that His people have returned to Him. The grapes that were sour have become sweet (Isaiah 27).

The road to this point of transformation will be long and hard. Judah should learn from the mistakes Israel made and put her trust in God's protection, not political alliances. But Isaiah speaks to people who are blind and deaf. The leaders of Judah look at fallen Israel and do not see themselves. Isaiah parodies their attitude. "We've taken out good life insurance. We've hedged our bets, covered our bases. No disaster can touch us" (Isaiah 28:15). Because the majority ignores God and His precepts, the exile will come. Yet Isaiah finds that he cannot register God's prescriptions to avoid disaster and the Lord's angry complaints against Judah without continuing to mention God's messages of hope and comfort. The prophet's treatise rocks back and forth between the good news that eventually "a king will rule in the right way" (Isaiah 32:1) and "anyone who looks will see, anyone who listens will hear" (Isaiah 32:3) and his picture of the world after Judah's demise as a barren desert—a return to the pre-Genesis chaos (Isaiah 34). Only the faithful will live to see the desert blossom. "Blind eyes will be opened, deaf ears unstopped, lame men and women will leap like deer" (Isaiah 35:5–6), and all these will embark upon the holy road leading back to Zion (Isaiah 35:8–10).

After the high point of Jerusalem's narrow escape from the Assyrian siege in 701 BCE (Isaiah 36–39), we enter a new phase of Isaiah's ministry—the sections scholars assign to second and third Isaiah. Here we will note a change in the thrust of the message emerging. Whereas in the first thirty-nine chapters Isaiah preaches judgment on Judah's anti-God behavior with the hope that God's chosen might repent and turn back to the Lord, in the latter portions the accent is shifted from accusation to healing. Though God's hand would allow Babylon to lay waste to Jerusalem, the Lord would also stir up Cyrus of Persia (the conqueror of Nebuchadnezzar) to promote the Jews' return to their homeland in a second exodus. But even this reclaiming of Judah will not by itself reverse the damage of the exile. The Jews have suffered not just physically as war refugees living on foreign soil but even more so spiritually. They have had to come to terms with the reality that God has done what they thought their maker would never do, no matter how badly they behaved, namely sacrifice Jerusalem and the temple there. Isaiah must now explain that this, too, is part of God's design—the only way the Lord could get Judah's attention so that she would look and see, listen, and hear and be able to receive God's comfort and eventually the divine restoration.

"Comfort, oh comfort my people!" (Isaiah 40:1) opens this second segment of Isaiah. God instructs Isaiah to remind Judah that the Jews are still His chosen, Israel's sins are forgiven (Isaiah 40:2), and the Lord's covenants remain intact (Isaiah 40:8). Judah must prepare the way for God's reentry to the holy city of Jerusalem (Isaiah 40:3), where God is going to tend His flock like a good shepherd (Isaiah 40:11). Though Isaiah does not mention it specifically, the remnant of Judah that elects to journey to the Holy Land certainly sees God's return in the rebuilding of the temple there. But Isaiah goes on to explain that God has bigger plans than restoring the status quo, especially since, historically speaking, Israel never came close to practicing God's ways in the past. Judah needs something more than rescue from exile. God asserts to Israel, "For a long time now, I've let you in on the way I work" (Isaiah 48:3) and provided the Jews with evidence "confirmed by your own eyes and ears" (Isaiah 48:6). But Israel has not been a good listener (Isaiah 48:8) and has not shared this knowledge with the rest of the world (Isaiah 48:6). Therefore, God is going to do something completely new, "something you'd never guess or dream up" (Isaiah 48:6). Isaiah loosely describes this *new* thing that God is going to do in a series of poems we refer to as the Servant Songs.

The first servant song appears in Isaiah 42:1–4. God presents the servant whom He has chosen and with whom He is pleased because the servant "will set everything right among the nations" (Isaiah 42:1) and will not tire until his work is finished. In the second song (Isaiah 49:1–6) the servant himself speaks and proclaims that God has called him "my dear servant, Israel" (Isaiah 49:3). Even though the servant is equated with Israel, the servant states that his job initially was "to bring Jacob back home to [God]" (Isaiah 49:5), but God found "that's not a big enough job for my servant—just to recover the tribes of Jacob … I'm setting you up as a light for the *nations* so that my salvation becomes global" (Isaiah 49:6). This statement harkens back to the original promise God made to Abraham in Genesis 12:3, "All the families of the Earth will be blessed through you."

The servant continues to address us in the third song (Isaiah 50:4–9). God has taught him to encourage a weary people, and he has remained obedient despite the insults and indignities leveled against him. His confidence in God as his champion does not falter. "Look! the Master, GOD, is right here. Who would dare call me guilty?" (Isaiah 50:9). The fourth song (Isaiah 52:13–53:12), however, quickly turns that expectation on its head. Here in mostly a third-person account, Isaiah tells the story of how the servant must suffer. The once eloquent and exalted servant now appears disfigured (Isaiah 52:14). Isaiah interrupts his discourse to comment, "Who would have thought GOD's saving power would look like this?" (Isaiah 53:1). The prophet goes on to describe a man from whom people turn away, presuming that his unseemliness depicted his own wickedness (Isaiah 53:3–4), but as Isaiah clarifies, "it was our sins … that ripped and tore and crushed him" (Isaiah 53:5). In effect, God has aligned the servant with the Mosaic sacrifice ceremonies associated with the Day of Atonement (see Leviticus 16:5–22). Though completely innocent, the servant bears the transgressions of the people and by his death expiates their sins. The servant is glad that by means of this offering God will make many "righteous" (Isaiah 53:11). God finishes the song with rejoicing, "Therefore I'll reward him extravagantly ... because he looked death in the face and didn't flinch, because he embraced the company of the lowest. He took on his own shoulders the sin of the many, he took up the cause of all the black sheep" (Isaiah 53:12). In this song we begin to see how God proposes to resolve the dilemma of loving His sinful peoples while maintaining His holiness. The servant will do for God's humans what they cannot do for themselves—make them righteous before God.

In one last song the servant shows up implicitly (Isaiah 61:1–2). We presume the person speaking here is the servant because his reference to the Spirit of God resting on him alludes to the introductory description of the servant in Isaiah 42:1, which says, "I've bathed him with my Spirit." Here we also find "because GOD anointed me" linking the servant for the first time with the Messianic figure presented in the first half of Isaiah. God is sending this chosen one to "preach good news to the poor, heal the heartbroken, announce freedom to all captives, pardon all prisoners." We can readily see how postexilic Judaism would have initially cast the people Israel in the role of the servant. Although the remnant of Judah reclaimed the Promised Land despite the loss of political autonomy there and went on to rebuild the temple, its most important achievement was its success in establishing for all future generations a new Israelite identity. From this time forward Jews would be known as a people of the Book (the Scriptures), a culture that kept itself separate from others by strict adherence to Sabbath keeping, a kosher diet, and a strong resistance to marital mingling with outsiders. Moreover, Jews would continue to suffer persecution for their faith for centuries beyond the closing of the Hebrew canon. Yet as we read through the Servant Songs we should notice the tension between equating the servant with the corporate entity Israel in the second song (Isaiah 49:1–6) and the other songs that identify the servant more clearly as an individual. Even when the final song creates a link between the servant and the anointed one, it would be hard for Israel to fathom how the Messiah could be both a triumphant King (9:6) and suffering victim who dies in humiliation (Isaiah 53:6–9).

Coming first among the prophets, Isaiah maps the scope of God's continued Word to His people that the remaining prophets will augment with new details. God will pass judgment on Israel, and Jacob will suffer mightily for her sins. But after the exile God will renew His covenants and lead the Jews in a new exodus, creating a new Genesis project out of this chosen remnant. Hope will spring from the stump of Jesse. The Messiah will come in triumph to reconcile the fallen world to God. "Nations all over the world will be in awe" (Isaiah 52:15). "For what they were not told, they will see, and what they have not heard they will understand" (Isaiah 52:15 NIV). Then God will "gather everyone—all nations, all languages" (Isaiah 66:18) to see His glory and the "new heavens and a new earth" (66:22) that will embody the goodness of the Lord's original intention for creation.

Jeremiah

While Isaiah covers the crisis of the exile in an expansive sweep from the early warning signs of Israel's fall to Assyria through the restoration of the faith in the aftermath of the exile, Jeremiah's ministry zeroes in on the eleventh hour of Jerusalem's imminent collapse. The opening lines of this book inform us that Jeremiah, a priest, preached in Jerusalem from the middle of Josiah's reign (when hope for Judah's spiritual renewal rose momentarily) through the regencies of Josiah's various sons (when Judah was reduced to a vassal state bandied between Egypt and Babylon) up to the destruction of the city and the temple (approximately 626–586 BCE). The prophet's forty years of relentless appeals to his countrymen for repentance testify to God's amazing patience with a people who had grown deaf and blind to their theological roots.

Of all the prophets, Jeremiah stands out as the one most willing to reveal his personal struggle with his vocation. Unlike Isaiah, who reminds us of Samuel in his willingness to answer God's call (Isaiah 6:8, compare to 1 Samuel 3:9-10), Jeremiah protests his assignment much as Moses did (Jeremiah 1:5-6, compare to Exodus 3:10-11). As the Lord did with Moses, God reassures Jeremiah that God will be beside the prophet throughout his ordeal, telling him what to say and guaranteeing his protection (Jeremiah 1:8–9). Although Jeremiah obeys God stalwartly, he vents his frustration with his job on several occasions in what have become labeled his confessions. For instance, he complains how hard it is to be the object of public derision when he speaks God's warnings of impending doom but finds that if he refrains from preaching God's words, they sit like a "fire in my belly" (Jeremiah 20:7–9). It is easy to sympathize with his predicament because Jeremiah has a hard life. God bids him not to marry and have children (Jeremiah 16:2). He is cut off from the community both when it mourns and celebrates (Jeremiah 16:5–9) as a symbolic act to dramatize the coming exile, when the dead will not be properly mourned and no one will feast. The temple priests have him whipped and abused (Jeremiah 20:2) and later thrown into a muddy cistern to starve to death (Jeremiah 38:7) until a royal official of King Zedekiah convinces the monarch to rescue the prophet and merely keep him imprisoned in the palace courtyard (Jeremiah 38:13). God instructs Jeremiah to write down all of his public sermons (Jeremiah 36:2) only to have King Jehoiakim proceed to tear apart and burn the scroll (Jeremiah 36:23). Finally after the fall of Jerusalem he and his secretary, Baruch, get swept off to Egypt with Jews hoping to avoid the ravages of foreign occupation. Jeremiah must continue to preach to these disobedient people that Egypt, too, will fall to Babylon (Jeremiah 42:19–43:10).

Rather than these torments, however, Jeremiah's chief anguish stems from his frustration with the people he both loves and hates. Again like Moses, he suffers between agreeing with God over Israel's offenses yet still wanting to defend and pray for his fellow Jews. In an echo back to Abraham pleading for Sodom and Gomorrah (Genesis 18:26–32), God challenges him to find "a single soul who does what is right and tries to live a true life" (Jeremiah 5:1) so that the Lord can forgive Jerusalem. Jeremiah searches among the common folk but lets them off the hook because "they are just poor people ... They were never taught anything about God" (Jeremiah 5:4). But even among the "best families" and community leaders the prophet sees that all have rebelled from God (Jeremiah 5:5). Since Israel has whored about with other peoples' gods, God is justified in turning her over to foreign powers (Jeremiah 5:19). Yet the Jews refuse to believe that God will really make good on these threats because the priests and royal prophets constantly reassure them that God will never punish Judah (Jeremiah 14:13). Jeremiah tries to explain the hypocrisy of feeling pious because one worships in the temple and makes sacrifices while the same person refuses to live by God's basic commandments of care and concern for one's neighbors (Jeremiah 7:2–11). Still, when God resolves to punish this people who "stubbornly hold on to their illusions, refuse to change direction" (Jeremiah 8:5), Jeremiah laments their fate and asks, "Are there no healing ointments in Gilead? ... Why can't something be done to heal and save my dear, dear people?" (Jeremiah 8:22). On the one hand, Jeremiah swears he "could weep day and night for casualties among my dear, dear people" (Jeremiah 9:1), yet in the next moment he wishes for a "backwoods cabin where I could get away from my people and never see them again" (Jeremiah 9:2). But when God specifically forbids Jeremiah from praying for Judah (Jeremiah 14:11–12),

Jeremiah begs him not give up on His people (Jeremiah 14:20–21) because there is no other God (Jeremiah 14:22).

One of the chief difficulties of reading the book of Jeremiah is its non-chronological arrangement of the prophet's sermons. (For a quick example, note that chapter 32 announces events happening in the tenth year of Zedekiah's reign, while chapter 36 records Jeremiah's words from God received during the fourth year of Jehoiakim, Zedekiah's predecessor.) This observation forces us to discover what principle does organize the arranging of these oracles. We see that the prophet's verbatim preaching (mostly in poetry) gets braided together with narrative accounts about Jeremiah's life and other historical details along with conversations between Jeremiah and God. The effect of reading straight through the book is to feel the constant wrenching of emotions that the prophet endures. For forty years Jeremiah speaks God's words of accusation and makes God's appeals for repentance, predicts the coming destruction of Jerusalem replete with visions of dead bodies everywhere, struggles with the social burden of being a literal "prophet of doom," and pleads with God both on the Jews' behalf and for vengeance against them. After all of Jeremiah's trials, the appendix (Jeremiah 52), in parallel with 2 Kings 24:18–25:21, 27–30, makes a narrative wrap-up that validates all of the prophet's dark predictions. "Judah went into exile, orphaned from her land" (Jeremiah 52:27).

Despite the emphasis on the gloom of both Jeremiah's life and prophecy, we find an abundant sprinkling of hope in references to the eventual return of the remnant to Jerusalem and the rise of the Messiah. When God condemns the current leaders for scattering His sheep (Jeremiah 23:1–2), He reprises the promise from Isaiah to "establish a truly righteous David-Branch, a ruler who knows how to rule justly" (Jeremiah 23:5). God will cut Judah loose from her yoke of "slave labor to foreigners" (Jeremiah 30:8) and bring Jacob's children back from exile (Jeremiah 30:10). Then "one of their own people shall be their leader" (Jeremiah 30:21), which the "David-King [God] will establish for them" (Jeremiah 30:9). To release Israel from this second era of slavery, "God will pay a stiff ransom price" (Jeremiah 31:11). Because Judah broke the covenant God made with her after He led her out of Egypt, God will make a *new* one "when the time comes. I will put my law within them—write it on their hearts!—and be their God … I'll wipe the slate clean for each of them. I'll forget that they ever sinned!" (Jeremiah 31:32–34). We should note how closely the predictions about the Messiah are tied to the idea of the new covenant that will enable God to forgive sins. When Isaiah mentions the *new* thing God will do (Isaiah 48:6), he follows it up with the Servant Songs and the suffering servant whose wounds heal us (Isaiah 53:5 NIV). Jeremiah continues that thought here. When the Messiah comes, God will imprint the Torah within the human heart, and that will dissolve the barrier that sin raises between God and humans.

Jeremiah puts on record God's "down to the last minute" pitch to save Judah from the horrific consequences of the loss of the Promised Land and the holy city of Jerusalem. As late as Jehoiakim's reign (609–598 BCE) God urges Jeremiah to speak in the court of the temple because "just maybe they'll listen and turn back from their bad lives. Then I'll reconsider the disaster that I'm planning to bring on them because of their evil behavior" (Jeremiah 26:3). In the prophet's anguished vacillations between anger and pity as well as despair and hope, we witness God's own frustration with the people He loves. Even after Judaism reestablishes itself back in Israel, Jeremiah's words speak to the community of faith what it needs to remember about how badly its ancestors failed to serve their God and why Israel deserved to lose the land God had given her. The prophet's critiques of Judah's worship (Jeremiah 7) and Sabbath practices (Jeremiah 17), allegiance to idols (Jeremiah 10), and treatment of her fellow humans (Jeremiah 22) keeps successive generations of believers on notice not to abandon

God's ways. But even more, Jeremiah testifies to God's love that outlasts the divine anger. Once the first Jews have been sent into exile in 598 BCE, God has Jeremiah send them a letter of encouragement, urging them to build houses, plant gardens, marry, have children, and even pray for Babylon (Jeremiah 29:5–7). "I [God] know what I'm doing. I have it all planned out—plans to take care of you, not abandon you, plans to give you the future you hope for" (Jeremiah 29:11).

Lamentations

The book of Job examines unwarranted torment. Lamentations takes a look at the suffering Israel brought upon herself. In the Christian canon it follows the book of Jeremiah, causing us to pause and reflect on the cost of the exile to Israel. Written in the style of the psalms, the book consists of five laments, underscoring the obvious reality that pain hurts no matter where it comes from.

Our poet begins presenting the desolate image of defeated and crushed Jerusalem as a reversal of Cinderella. "Once the queen of the ball, she's now a drudge in the kitchen" (Lamentations 1:1). Going on, our speaker proceeds to articulate Judah's sense of loss. "She cries herself to sleep at night" (Lamentations 1:2). "She camps out among the nations, never feels at home" (Lamentations 1:3) "when her people fell … her enemies looked on and laughed" (Lamentations 1:7). But the complaints do not amount to whining. The poet owns up to Israel's culpability. "GOD has right on his side. I'm the one who did wrong" (Lamentations 1:18). What is noteworthy here is that having acknowledged the errors of his ways, he continues to reach out to God for help. "O GOD, look at the trouble I'm in!" (Lamentations 1:20).

The second lament voices the incredulity of Zion's predicament. In righteous fury God "treated his favorite as throwaway junk" (Lamentations 2:1). "The Master became the enemy" (Lamentations 2:5). "GOD abandoned his altar, walked away from his holy Temple" (Lamentations 2:7). Even so, he admits that God had given them all fair warning. "He always said he'd do this ... let your enemies walk all over you" (Lamentations 2:17). Finishing the pattern of the first lament, the poet offers only one viable course of action. "Cry out in prayer" (Lamentations 2:19). Remind the Lord of the horrors the exile has engendered, such as cannibalism, murder, and homelessness (Lamentations 2:21).

As with many of the psalms, in the third lament we witness a transformation. The first twenty verses detail an intensely personal distress ending on the brink of despair with this: "GOD is a lost cause. I'll never forget the trouble, the utter lostness, the taste of ashes, ... the feeling of hitting the bottom." From there the poet pivots into hope. "GOD's loyal love couldn't have run out, his merciful love couldn't have dried up. They're created new every morning. How great is your faithfulness!" (3:22-23). Now our lamenter offers positive counsel.

> When life is heavy and hard to take, go off by yourself. Enter the silence.
> Bow in prayer. Don't ask questions. Wait for hope to appear. Don't run from trouble. Take it full-face. The "worst" is never the worst.
> Why? Because the Master won't ever walk out and fail to return. (Lamentations 3:28–31)

Of course, for all this upbeat advice, the poet can't help also hoping for vengeance against Israel's enemies. Still, he struggles to keep his quest for payback within theologically sound boundaries, remembering the Deuteronomic injunction that it is God's prerogative to avenge (Deuteronomy 32:35).

In a form of inverted parallelism, the fourth lament returns to an iteration of the miseries of the exile, lest they ever be minimized even by the hope held in the future. The final chapter reads more like a confession, with the poet acknowledging that Judah is reaping what she has sown. But now that Jacob has repented ("Would that we'd never sinned!" as written in Lamentations 5:16), our speaker appeals to God's mercy. "Bring us back to you, God … Give us a fresh start" (Lamentations 5:21).

Lamentations is a good example of how Israel works out her sense of abandonment and loss around the suffering of the exile. Here the poet lays out his uncensored pain before the Lord, admitting both that God is the author of the misery but that Israel is also the cause. Defeats even less devastating than Judah's to Babylon have extinguished other cultures throughout world history. Consider how many of the nations Jeremiah foresees falling no longer exist—Philistia (Jeremiah 47), Moab (Jeremiah 48), Ammon (Jeremiah 49:1–6), Edom (Jeremiah 49:7–22), Kedar and Hazor (Jeremiah 49:28–33), Elam (Jeremiah 49:34–39), and of course Babylon (Jeremiah 50–51). As we hear the author of Lamentations sort out Israel's woes, we begin to see why the Jews survived with their faith not merely intact but strengthened through this ordeal.

Ezekiel

Unlike Isaiah and Jeremiah, Ezekiel's testimony has no parallels elsewhere in the Bible. Historically speaking, Ezekiel's treatise takes up where Jeremiah's leaves off. Born into a priestly family in Jerusalem, Ezekiel and his family were in the first wave of Jews deported to Babylon when King Jehoiachin surrendered to Nebuchadnezzar's siege in 597 BCE. In the fifth year of this initial exile (probably about 593 BCE), God commissions Ezekiel to speak the Lord's Word to the people with him there while the ultimate fall of Jerusalem remains some seven years in the future (586 BCE). It seems that many of these more prominent citizens were operating under the delusion that the exile would be temporary. Much of Ezekiel's ministry involves bringing home the reality that these refugees would never see Jerusalem again.

While Ezekiel's prophecy continues God's Word into the exile itself, the literary style of the book departs considerably from the poetic sermons we have found in Isaiah and Jeremiah. First Ezekiel writes mostly in prose, and his logical, analytical tone betrays the systematic legal training of the priesthood. With Isaiah and Jeremiah we get frequent third-person prose insertions into their first-person proclamations of God's words. In Isaiah, biographical information about the prophet obeying God's command to go about naked (Isaiah 20:2) interrupts the oracles against the nations. The entire narrative of the siege of Jerusalem crisis is another example (Isaiah 36–39). Jeremiah's inserts are generally shorter and function to clarify dates and fill in details related to the prophet's sermons (Jeremiah 26:1, 7–12, 16–24). However, the final chapter (Jeremiah 52) is completely written in the third person. Whereas the books of the first two prophets evince a good deal of editing from the postexilic community with these third-person accounts of supplementary information, Ezekiel gives us his story almost exclusively in the first person. In addition, his ministry involves less overt preaching than that of his predecessors. Instead God gives Ezekiel spectacular visions and asks him to perform series of symbolic acts as a means of communicating God's messages to the exilic community. That such a sober, levelheaded man is called to report such fantastical images and act out metaphorical messages in literal body language gives us a good picture of Ezekiel's obedience to the Lord.

Lacking the third-party editorial introduction we find in Isaiah 1:1 and Jeremiah 1:1–3, the book of Ezekiel plunges us immediately into the prophet's vivid and dramatic depiction of his vocation as God's spokesman. Note how he provides his own meticulous dating of the event (Ezekiel 1:1) that is then supplemented by a later editor in the only departure from the first-person narrative for the balance of the book (Ezekiel 1:2–3). As in Isaiah's theophany, Ezekiel sees creatures that attend the Lord, but his vision contains far greater detail. Each cherub has four wings and four faces—that of a man, a lion, an ox, and an eagle (Ezekiel 1:10). Beneath these attendants, the prophet discovers wheels within wheels—full of eyes (Ezekiel 1:18) and above them a fiery radiance that Ezekiel takes to be the "Glory of GOD" (Ezekiel 1:28). Immediately Ezekiel falls prostrate, but a voice dubbing him *Son of man* bids him to stand, and Ezekiel feels the Spirit enter him. Next God hands him a scroll written over with lamentations (Ezekiel 2:10). Ezekiel must eat the scroll (Ezekiel 3:1), acting out the metaphor that God's sorrows will therefore be inside him. Equipped with God's words, Ezekiel is to be the *watchman* of Israel (Ezekiel 3:17). (The watchman is posted at the gates of the city and blows the trumpet to warn the citizenry when danger stirs.) The terms of his duties are as follows: "Whenever you hear me (God) say something, warn them (the people) for me. If ... you don't sound the alarm ... they will die and it will be your fault. But if you warn the wicked and they keep right on sinning anyway, they'll most certainly die for their sin, but *you* won't die" (Ezekiel 3:17–19). The bottom line boils down to this: When Ezekiel obediently does all that the Lord asks, "then they'll know that I am GOD!" (Ezekiel 6:14).

The first series of symbolic acts God requires of Ezekiel work to convince these early deportees of the imminent fall of Jerusalem. To begin, the prophet will strike the pose of a captive being bound hands and feet and unable to speak (Ezekiel 3:25–26). He next must make a model of the military siege of Jerusalem (several years before the actual event) (Ezekiel 4:1–3). Other commands include lying in bed on his left side for 390 days (for Israel) and then forty days on his right side (for Judah) as well as sticking to a special vegetarian diet (Ezekiel 4:4–11). With a sharp sword he is to shave his head and beard and then divide the hairs in thirds to represent the third of the people who will die within the city as it is destroyed, the third that will die outside the city, and the third that will be scattered after the fall (Ezekiel 5:1–4).

Again careful to document the date (Ezekiel 8:1), a year later Ezekiel describes another vision he receives in which the Spirit of God places him invisible within the temple in Jerusalem. From this vantage point he witnesses the blatant idolatry of Israel's leaders as they bow before the pantheon of Egyptian gods and goddesses (Ezekiel 8:10). Elsewhere he sees women weeping for the Babylonian fertility god Tammuz (Ezekiel 8:14) and men worshiping the sun (Ezekiel 8:16). The shock value for Ezekiel's time might equate to us trying to picture generals in the Pentagon making behind-the-scenes deals with terrorists! The initial *glory of GOD* vision returns in Ezekiel 10:9–14, and Ezekiel observes the Lord's glory leaving Jerusalem (and the temple) (Ezekiel 11:23) in a dramatic reversal of the inauguration of the temple under Solomon when the glory first settled in that Holy Place (1 Kings 8:10–11).

After Ezekiel reports on his Jerusalem vision, God commands a second series of symbolic acts designed to simulate the coming influx of refugees driven from the city. The prophet packs his bags and leaves his home at sunset, as one who is seeking the cover of darkness would (Ezekiel 12:3–11). Next he has to tremble as he eats his food (Ezekiel 12:18). Ezekiel also delivers sermons against the false prophets who whitewash the political dangers ahead with lies to give the people false security (Ezekiel 13). God has him compare Israel to an abandoned infant whom God rescues and nurtures back to life (Ezekiel 16:3–7). Later God comes by and sees the foundling grown into a mature woman "ready for love and a lover" (Ezekiel 16:8) and marries her, decking her out like a queen (Ezekiel 16:9–14). But she lets her beauty "go to her head" and becomes a *common whore* betraying God by worshiping other gods, particularly those that included sacred prostitution in their fertility rites (Ezekiel 16:15ff). This reprehensible behavior requires God's judgment and explains why the Lord will allow Judah to suffer in the coming exile. But God's real purpose in delivering punishment is to get His people's attention. The Lord has not forgotten "the covenant I made with you when you were young, and I'll make a *new* covenant with you that will last forever ... You'll remember your past life and face the shame of it, but when I make atonement for you, make everything right after all you've done, it will leave you speechless" (Ezekiel 16:60–63). With this, Ezekiel joins both Isaiah and Jeremiah in speaking about the *new* thing that God is planning—God's solution for making humans holy by atoning for their sins.

Ezekiel's oracles eventually get the attention of the local leaders. When they come to meet with the prophet, God confronts them with Israel's history. Back in the days of their Egyptian slavery, God chose the people of Jacob and pledged to take them out from that country to one flowing with milk and honey. The Lord told them then to get rid of their idols; however, even when they rebelled, "I acted out of who I was, not by how I felt" (Ezekiel 20:9), and after He led them out of Egypt, He "gave them laws for living," including "'Sabbaths,' a kind of signpost ... to show them that I, GOD, am in the business of making them holy" (Ezekiel 20:10–12). When the first generation of freed slaves mutinied against God in the wilderness, God gave their children a fresh start. But these and the generations since have continued to be swayed by the allure of other nations' religions who have gods they can make (idols) and therefore hope to manipulate (Ezekiel 20:32). Since Moses, God has been trying to wean people from the notion that a deity can be placated to grant the wishes of the worshiper. Yet God is confident that in the aftermath of the exile, "you'll remember all that you've done, the way that you've lived that has made you so filthy" (Ezekiel 20:43) and "with open arms" (Ezekiel 20:40) God will gather Israel back from all the places she has scattered.

Seven years after God first approached Ezekiel to call him as a prophet, the exilic community received its first survivor from the fall of Jerusalem (Ezekiel 33:21), vindicating all of Ezekiel's preaching. The Lord reminds the prophet of his continuing role as Israel's watchman. Here God reiterates the urgency of repentance. "As sure as I am the living God, I take no pleasure from the death of the wicked. I want the wicked to change their ways and live!" (Ezekiel 33:11). But now that Jerusalem has succumbed completely to Babylon, God insists that He has had enough of Israel's corrupt leaders. "From now on, I *myself* am the shepherd" (Ezekiel 34:11). "As shepherds go after their flocks when they get scattered, I'm going after my sheep. I'll ... gather them from foreign countries and bring them back to their home country" (Ezekiel 34:12–13). Then, "I'll appoint one shepherd over them all: my servant David" (Ezekiel 34:23).

God brings home the future hope for Israel in another vision. The Lord takes Ezekiel into a valley littered with bones and commands him to prophesy to them. At Ezekiel's words the bones join together and grow muscles and then skin and finally receive the breath of life (Ezekiel 37:4–10). Even though the loss of Jerusalem seems like the end of Judah, God can make even a dried-up, dismembered people whole again. Next God has Ezekiel join together two sticks representing Israel and Judah that God fashions into a single stick in a symbolic unification of the two kingdoms (Ezekiel 37:15-17). "Never again will they be divided into two nations ... I'll save them out of all their sinful haunts. I'll clean them up. They'll be my people! I'll be their God! My servant David will be king over them ... The nations will realize that I, GOD, make Israel holy when my place of worship is established at the center of their lives forever" (Ezekiel 37:22–28).

Ezekiel closes with a final vision—the new temple. After he describes a huge end-of-the-world battle set at some point in the future (Ezekiel 38–39), God again spirits Ezekiel away to Israel where the prophet beholds God's temple in all its architectural detail (Ezekiel 40–42). Next Ezekiel witnesses the *glory of GOD* fill the Holy Place (Ezekiel 43:5). After reviewing the ordinances for the operation of the new place of worship (Ezekiel 44–46), God takes Ezekiel back to the temple entrance and walks with him beside the river. The water from this river will turn the sea it flows into fresh (Ezekiel 47:8). Fruit trees of all kinds that will grow on the riverbank will never wither and will provide both food and healing (Ezekiel 47:12). The land surrounding the temple is Israel's inheritance and will be shared among all twelve tribes (echoing the unification of the kingdoms pronounced earlier). Finally the city will receive a new name, "GOD-IS-THERE" (Ezekiel 48:35).

Ezekiel's treatise documents that the destruction of Jerusalem is not God's vindictive punishment but actually judgment with a purpose. Just as in Genesis when Adam and Eve are expelled from the garden of Eden, God continues to care for them, providing them with clothing (Genesis 3:21). The Lord's "son of man" makes it clear that God has no desire to destroy Israel. After the suffering of the exile, the Lord will breathe new life into the remnant that survives. God not only wants His people to live, but He wants to make them holy too. The divine plan for accomplishing that feat involves a Davidic king who will be a good shepherd, leading the people to live in God's ways. Finally all God's people will convene in the land surrounding His new temple in the city where God lives side by side with humans.

Daniel

In the Christian canon we find the book of Daniel in between the books of the so-called Major and Minor Prophets, and yet Daniel himself is not a prophet. While Daniel contains prophecy, it departs widely from the pattern established in Isaiah, Jeremiah, and Ezekiel where God calls the prophet to become the mouthpiece through whom the Lord's message of both judgment and eventual hope can be delivered. As a book, Daniel divides evenly into two parts. Yet we know these two parts were not written separately and pieced together arbitrarily because the book of Daniel (like Ezra and Nehemiah) also comes to us in two languages that cut across the two sections. Daniel 1–2:3 and Daniel 8–12 are written in Hebrew, but Daniel 2:4–7:28 employs Aramaic. The beginning section (Daniel 1–6) will remind us of Esther in that it tells the story of courageous Jews acting out their faith in life-threatening conditions. The *prophecy* comes in the second half (Daniel 7–12) in the form of four mystifying visions with parallels to images in Ezekiel's testimony, but with a meaning still more inscrutable. Both Judaism and Christianity interpret these dreams of Daniel's as apocalyptic—events that precede the end of the world. While the first three prophets have mentioned a final battle as a prelude to God's transformation of the world into its originally intended goodness, Daniel describes the end times in vivid but mysterious detail.

In contrast to the fantastical visions of the second part of Daniel, the first half reads as a straight narrative told in the third person. Set in a time even earlier than the beginning of Ezekiel's ministry, Daniel tells the stories of some of the elite, well-educated Jews who were handpicked for deportation in the first years of Nebuchadnezzar's assault on Jerusalem. The Babylonians select Daniel and three of his compatriots (Shadrach, Meshach, and Abednego) for special training to prepare them for positions within the foreign king's court. The deluxe treatment the Israelites receive gives them access to the best foods served in the royal kitchen, but these delicacies are not kosher. Despite the risk to his privileged situation, Daniel insists on forgoing the palace cuisine. When the staff fears for his health, Daniel convinces the court attendants to test the recruits on a diet of vegetables and water for ten days and then decide. At the end of the trial the Jews are in better shape than those eating off the royal menu, and Daniel and company earn the right to dine according to their conscience. All find positions of honor within the king's workforce (Daniel 1).

Early on Daniel distinguishes himself as a member of Nebuchadnezzar's court after the example of his ancestor Joseph in Egypt (Genesis 39–50). When the king desires a trustworthy elucidation of a dream, only Daniel (through God's revelation) can oblige his requirement that the interpreter provide not only the meaning but also the content of the original dream itself. The monarch quickly promotes Daniel to a post in his headquarters (Daniel 2). In a lifelong career in government service Daniel maintains his reputation for unlocking mysteries by analyzing a later dream of Nebuchadnezzar (Daniel 4) and by explaining the meaning of the baffling "writing on the wall" that precedes the murder of Nebuchadnezzar's successor to the throne (Daniel 5).

Most memorable of these stories, however, are those that demonstrate tenacity of faith under the threat of death. When Daniel's training classmates, Shadrach, Meshach, and Abednego, refuse to worship the king's golden statue, they face death in a fiery oven. Even when Nebuchadnezzar gives them the opportunity to recant and save their lives, the men respond, "Your threat means nothing to us. If you throw us in the fire, the God we serve can rescue us from the roaring furnace and anything else you might cook up, O king. But even if he doesn't … we still won't serve your gods or worship the gold statue you set up" (Daniel 3:16–18). Notice that their last line demonstrates that our heroes' faith stems from their unconditional allegiance to and love for God, not merely because of what God is capable of doing to help them. Likewise Daniel meets a similar challenge in the early days of his service to Darius, the last of the Babylonian kings. Jealous of Daniel's ascent within the royal power structure, the other palace administrators convince the king to pass a law disallowing prayer to deities other than the monarch himself. But Daniel continues to pray as the Torah prescribed—three times each day. When confronted with his servant's legal breech,

Darius must sentence Daniel to be thrown into the lions' den. Still, even he has faith in Daniel's God. "Your God, to whom you are so loyal, is going to get you out of this" (Daniel 6:16). That faith proves well placed in both examples.

The book's second half shifts significantly in tone and content. Written mostly in the first person, it stands as Daniel's record of four visions he receives in the later years of his life. Generally the first two visions seem to be describing a succession of four kingdoms represented by animal symbols and can be seen as a further analysis of Nebuchadnezzar's dream in chapter 2.

Statue (2:31–25)	Animals (7:2–8)	Animals (8:2–8)
Head of Gold	Lion	
Chest of Silver	Bear	Ram
Belly of Bronze	Leopard	Goat
Legs of Iron/ Feet of Clay	Beast	

Correlating these visions with the kingdoms of history is the subject of an ongoing debate, however. Given Daniel's claim in Daniel 2:37–38 that the first kingdom (symbolized by the golden head in Daniel 2:32 and the lion in Daniel 7:4) represents Babylon, many biblical scholars surmise that the second and third kingdoms indicate the Persians (led by Cyrus who allowed the Jews to return to Jerusalem in 539 BCE) followed by the Greeks (for whom Alexander conquered a large territory in the Middle East from 336 to 323 BCE). However, while both visions climax with the discussion of the rise of the "little horn" that arrogantly blasphemes against God and brutally punishes the Jews, the two accounts differ as to which kingdom engenders this supremely wicked ruler. In Daniel 7:8, this monarch seems to emerge from the fourth kingdom, which many Christians identify with Rome, whereas in Daniel 8:9, this evil king appears to come from the third kingdom, calling to mind the Greek regent Antiochus IV (whom the Maccabees of Hanukkah fame opposed for outlawing Jewish worship in the temple in 167 BCE). That the detailed references to this leader's hijacking of the "daily Temple sacrifice" (8:11-12) most likely indicate the reign of Antiochus IV creates a problem for dating the book of Daniel. Its setting during the Babylonian captivity lays a claim for an early postexilic date, but the vision sequence seems to demand a date after the Maccabean clash with Antiochus. Some scholars propose that basing the initial stories during the exile forms a pretense for calling prophecy what is actually historical reflection. Others counter that Daniel's dream elucidation in chapter 2 represents the prophecy while the visions of chapters 7 and 8 demonstrate the Maccabean author interpreting "history in light of prophecy, not prophecy in light of history."[34] Despite this controversy, the lack of clarity over the "little horn" as well as so much of what Daniel's visions are meant to symbolize serves to maintain the tension the community of faith feels about its ability to forecast these end times. As Daniel himself confesses, "I continued to be upset by the vision. I couldn't make sense of it" (8:27).

The last two visions focus on the endgame alluded to in the first. After the horrific times of the little horn, someone in human form, a *son of man*, will arrive and rule the whole earth in a reign without end (Daniel 7:13–14). The third vision offers complicated calculations concerning the timing of this leader's advent and reveals that the *anointed leader* will be killed (Daniel 9:24–27). The final revelation hints at spiritual warfare among angel princes (Daniel 10:13–21), which is also confusing, and promises the aid of the archangel Michael in the final battle, which will be "the worst trouble the world has ever seen" (Daniel 12:1). Daniel can take heart, however, because his "people will be

---

[34] Childs, *Introduction to the Old Testament as Scripture*, p.620.

saved from the trouble, every last one found written in the Book. Many who have been long dead and buried will wake up, some to eternal life, others to eternal shame" (Daniel 12:2). Again the angel messenger cautions Daniel that "this is a confidential report" to be kept secret until the end (Daniel 12:4). For the time being he should "go about his business without fretting or worrying" (Daniel 12:13).

Taken together the two parts of Daniel present a picture of how one should live in the in-between time after the exile and before the ultimate communion of God's people on the holy mountain of New Jerusalem. The stories of the beginning remind us that God continues to be trustworthy in defending the faithful no matter the odds. The prophecies of the second half, however mysterious, indicate that even though Israel will suffer under foreign empires, God's planned trajectory for His people will be realized according to the Lord's timetable, which is not discernible by humans. Daniel's revelation offers us a sneak peak at the end of the world but self-consciously refuses to be pinned down to anything concrete. Apparently these apocalyptic visions will only make sense when the end times are at hand.

The Twelve

Following Daniel's apocalyptic visions, the Christian canon places the testimony of the twelve Minor Prophets, permitting us to hear again the case God makes for allowing Israel and Judah to fall to their enemies. The primary issue remains Jacob's unfaithfulness to God with the prophets again stressing God's desire not only for sincere repentance but also for the transformation of people's lives in conformity with the spirit of the Torah-prescribed code of loving God and loving one's neighbors. The most obvious difference between the Twelve and the three Major Prophets is the length of their oracles. Even though the original sermons by these shorter preachers were sprinkled historically among the ministries of Isaiah, Jeremiah, and Ezekiel, we should look to their arrangement as a unit (on a single scroll) and read them together as a fourth testimony. The Twelve will walk us again through God's explanation of Israel's loss of the Holy Land. Here, too, we will hear God's judgment levied against Israel and Judah, calling them on their sins. There will also be judgments against the nations, proving God does not condone evil in any quarter. We will gain additional images about the Messiah as well as the end times. Together the Twelve will outline for us the shape of God's final message for His people before we begin the New Testament.

Hosea

Hosea takes us for the first time to the northern kingdom of Israel. During the prosperous and successful (by military standards) reign of Jeroboam II (2 Kings 14:23–29), God calls Hosea to "find a whore and marry her. Make her the mother of your children" (Hosea 1:2). Obediently Hosea marries Gomer and through her has three children, whom God gives symbolic names to represent the Lord's imminent judgment on unfaithful Israel. Because of Gomer's rampant infidelity, Hosea has no trouble finding cause for filing divorce. The argument is, of course, analogous to God's case against Israel. Bu having made the point, God next instructs Hosea to take back his wayward wife. "Start all over: Love your wife again … your cheating wife … the way I, GOD, love the Israelite people" (Hosea 3:1). Hosea has to pay the price of a slave to ransom her back (Hosea 3:2). Likewise "the people of Israel are going to have to live a long time stripped of security and protection … but in time they'll come back looking for their GOD and their David-King … ready for the End of the story of [the Lord's] love" (Hosea 3:4–5). Thus, God uses the story of Hosea and Gomer as an object lesson to explain the paradoxical relationship between the divine anger at and love for

Israel. "That's why I use the prophets to shake you to attention ... I'm after love that lasts, not more religion" (Hosea 6:5–6).

Joel

Scholars have difficulty pinning down a time frame for the book of Joel, but for our purposes we have only to think of it taking place in Judah sometime before the exile. Joel is essentially a single sermon preached in the aftermath of a locust plague. Judah must take warning. As locusts stripped bare the farmlands, so will God's coming judgment devastate the people of Judah. Yet Joel gives strong incentive to repent. "This most patient God, extravagant in love, always ready to cancel catastrophe. Who knows? Maybe he'll do it now" (Joel 2:13–14). But always after God's judgment will come restoration. "I'll make up for the years of the locust" (Joel 2:25). In the time of reconciliation in the future, Joel pictures something akin to Jeremiah's vision of God writing the Law on His people's hearts (Jeremiah 31:32–34). Joel, however, expands the thought to reach outside of Israel. "I will pour out my Spirit on *every kind of people*: your sons will prophesy, also your daughters. Your old men will dream and your young men will see visions" (Joel 2:28), and "whoever calls, 'Help, GOD!' gets help" (Joel 2:32).

Amos

The opening of the book of Amos explains that God calls this prophet out of his life as a shepherd near Bethlehem in Judah to preach judgment in the north kingdom of Israel (Amos 1:1). Amos's ministry predates both Hosea and Isaiah, coming at the height of the monarchy of Jeroboam II when Israel enjoyed both wealth and political clout. God's strategy for piquing the Israelites' attention is to begin by speaking judgment against Israel's neighbors for their great sins (Amos 1:3–2:3) and even

Judah (Amos 2:4–5). Once his audience is cheering for the Lord's retribution against Jacob's enemies, Amos turns the tables and accuses Israel of the same sins, particularly their mistreatment of the poor and their abuse of religious rituals (Amos 2:6–8). Continuing in this rhetorical style (for example, Amos 3:3 says, "Do two people walk hand in hand if they aren't going to the same place?"), Amos forecasts a judgment day for Israel (Amos 4:2). In this vein he compares the kingdom to a bowl of fresh fruit "ripe" for the picking by her neighbors. (Amos 8:2 includes wordplay in Hebrew.[35]) Though Amos pleads on Israel's behalf (Amos 7), God eventually decides, "I've made up my mind to hurt [the Israelites], not help them" (Amos 9:4). "Still, I won't totally destroy the family of Jacob" (Amos 9:8). Judgment day will lead to God's restoration of David's house (Amos 9:11). Then "I'll make everything right again for my people Israel" (Amos 9:14).

Obadiah

As the shortest book in the Old Testament, Obadiah's message is concise. In the main, it stands as a sharp invective against Edom, the nation southeast of the Dead Sea founded by Jacob's brother Esau (Genesis 32:3). In the immediate aftermath of the exile, while the other neighboring nations receive ample judgment for their horrific handling of God's people, Obadiah's charges against Edom stem from its traitorous treatment of a *brother* nation. "On that day ... strangers took your brother's army into exile. Godless foreigners invaded and pillaged Jerusalem. You stood there and watched ... and traitorously turned in helpless survivors" (Obadiah 11–14). Reiterating the judgment day theme of Amos, Obadiah predicts a reversal of Jacob and Esau's fortunes on the horizon. Edom "will go up in flames" (Obadiah 18), but

---

[35] NIV notation p. 1349. The Hebrew *qayits* means *summer fruit* while *qets* means *the end*.

Judah will reclaim Israel. Yet just when we're ready to dismiss Obadiah as another vindictive tirade against Judah's enemies, we find a twist at the end. Instead of the usual political tit-for-tat, "the remnant of the saved in Mount Zion will go into the mountains of Esau and rule justly and fairly, a rule that honors GOD's kingdom" (Obadiah 21).

Jonah

After so many sermons the book of Jonah appears and startles us because we have heard of Jonah. Although 2 Kings 14:25 mentions Jonah as a prophet to Israel preaching God's aid against Assyria during the reign of Jeroboam II, *we* remember Jonah for being swallowed by a whale. Finally we are getting the real story! This narrative begins with Jonah receiving an unusual call from God. God would have him preach to the residents of Nineveh, the capital of Assyria—the enemy! God wants them to repent. Jonah, however, wants no part of aiding Israel's foes and seeks to avoid God's command by boarding a ship sailing in the opposite direction. When God stirs up a storm to threaten the ship, Jonah must confess that he is running from his God and therefore needs to be tossed overboard. Reluctantly his shipmates throw him into the sea. The storm quiets immediately, causing the sailors to worship Jonah's God. In the meanwhile God comes to Jonah's rescue by assigning a large fish to swallow him for three days (Jonah 1). In the belly of the fish Jonah prays what is essentially a psalm of his repentance, and God sees fit to rescue him (Jonah 2). Given the second chance, Jonah obeys the Lord and preaches to the Ninevites, and they do repent. In response, God withholds their destruction (Jonah 3). But now Jonah is angry on two fronts. He doesn't want to appear a false prophet by preaching something (Nineveh's ruin) that doesn't happen (per Jeremiah's definition in Jeremiah 28:9). More importantly he doesn't want God saving Israel's enemies (Jonah

4:2). But God challenges him. Not only does the Lord maintain that the Deity is free to change His mind (a point established as early as Abraham's Sodom and Gomorrah story in Genesis 18:16–33 and as recently as Joel 2:13–14), but God also chooses to highlight divine compassion for Gentiles. "So, why can't I ... change what I feel about Nineveh from anger to pleasure, this big city of more than a hundred and twenty thousand childlike people who don't know right from wrong, to say nothing of all the innocent animals?" (Jonah 4:10).

Micah

The contemporary of Hosea, Amos, and Isaiah, Micah prophesies in Judah before and after the time when Israel falls to Assyria. Like Isaiah 1:2, he utilizes a courtroom venue to present the legitimacy of God's case against Judah (Micah 1:2). Naturally the people have preferred to listen to priests and other religious leaders who reassure them that "nothing bad will happen to us ... Does GOD lose his temper? ... Isn't he on the side of good people? Doesn't he help those who help themselves?" (Micah 2:6–7). Micah warns Judah to beware of people who tell them "how you can get anything you want from God" (Micah 2:11). No matter what people want to hear, God insists that their leaders confront their sinful idolatry (Micah 1:7), contempt of justice, and dishonest abuse of the poor (Micah 3:2). After the judgment the day will come when people will stream to God's mountain where God "will establish justice in the rabble of nations ... and trade in their swords for shovels" (Micah 4:2–3). Moreover, Bethlehem will bring forth a leader, a shepherd ruler who "will save us from old and new enemies, from anyone who invades or violates our land" (Micah 5:2–6). Beyond that, the "day is coming ... when there will be no more war" (Micah 5:10–15). For the time being, God defends the many ways He has made good on the divine covenant with

Jacob (Micah 6:1–5). The only thing the Lord asks in return is for us "to act justly and to love mercy and to walk humbly with your God" (Micah 6:8 NIV).

Nahum

With Nahum we move ahead in time, closer to that of Jeremiah in the seventh century BCE. Nahum preaches an extended judgment of Nineveh at a time when Assyria appears unbeatable. The mighty power had toppled the northern kingdom a century before and would continue to threaten Judah until it would fall to Babylon in 612 BCE. In some ways it stands as the reverse of Jonah. Nahum preaches against Nineveh, but now there is no repentance. Mostly, however, Nahum's sermon explains that no one, not even the great Assyria, is invulnerable to God's verdict. "God is serious business, ... no one gets by with anything. Sooner or later, everyone pays" (Nahum 1:2–3). "No one gets away from God" (Nahum 1:8). Even after the exile and into Judah's ongoing woes in the postexilic period, the Jews would continue to draw strength and find hope in Nahum's reminder that no earthly evil can escape God's eventual punishment.

Habakkuk

Writing closer to the end of the seventh century, when Babylon is emerging as the dominant power, Habakkuk presents us with a new twist. Instead of speaking God's words to Judah, we find the prophet interrogating God. Speaking to the current political chaos in Jerusalem, Habakkuk begins, "GOD, how long do I have to cry out for help before you listen?" (Habakkuk 1:2). When God answers that He will use the "fierce and ferocious, world-conquering Babylon" (Habakkuk 1:6) to punish the sins of Judah, Habakkuk fires back with disbelief, "But you can't be serious! *You* can't condone evil! ... Evil men swallow up the righteous and you stand around and *watch*!" (Habakkuk 1:13). Having essentially accused God of using two wrongs to make a right, Habakkuk stands back to await God's response (Habakkuk 2:1). The Lord explains that the Babylonians will prove unable to keep their gains. Since they operate out of greed, deceit, and violence and have gods who are no more than man-made carvings of wood and stone, they have nothing to sustain their victory over time. On the other hand, Israel has the Lord who outlasts all His people's enemies (Habakkuk 2). Having heard God out, Habakkuk closes with a psalm. Like Job before him, by voicing his honest frustration with the job of making sense of God's actions, the prophet is now able to accept that trust in God is more valuable than understanding. Recalling the witness of his ancestors in the faith, he asks God to "work among us as you worked among them. And as you bring judgment, as you surely must, remember mercy" (Habakkuk 3:2).

Zephaniah

Another contemporary of Jeremiah, Zephaniah lends God's voice of support to reformer King Josiah's attempt to rid the temple and the kingdom of all traces of pagan worship. The major thrust of his oracle consists of the imminent arrival of God's judgment day—the payday of the Lord's anger (Zephaniah 1:15) when God will demonstrate that "I *care* about sin with fiery passion" (Zephaniah 1:18). Any who would avoid the coming punishment must "seek GOD's right ways" (Zephaniah 2:3). In the end, however, the judgment will lead to salvation. God's remnant, "what's left of Israel that's real Israel ... will make their home in GOD" (Zephaniah 3:12). The destruction that spells misery for the godless nations and peoples will become a time of healing and reunion for those who love the Lord.

Haggai

With Haggai we skip ahead to the postexilic period and the homecoming of the remnant of Jews to Jerusalem per the decree of Cyrus of Persia (about 538 BCE). We know from Ezra that rebuilding the temple started off as a top priority for this first wave of returnees. Governor Zerubbabel and the high priest Jeshua oversaw the initial construction of the foundation of the temple and built the altar so that the offering of sacrifices could resume (Ezra 3:2–3; 8–10). The work fell stagnant, however, when those who had remained in the capital during the years of the exile tried to join in the effort. After nearly twenty years of sitting on the back burner, the temple project got a well-needed shot in the arm with the preaching of Haggai. The prophet accuses the people of procrastinating on the job and caring more about their own houses than about God's house (Haggai 1:9). Haggai also takes them to task about the quality of the work, calling for anyone who remembered the old temple to compare it to the new (Haggai 2:3–4). The commitment to rebuild the temple was not just about providing a place for worship. It must stand as a sign of Israel's sincere repentance and return to God. "This Temple is going to end up far better than it started out, a glorious beginning but an even more glorious finish: a place in which I [God] will hand out wholeness and holiness" (Haggai 2:9). With three and a half months of preaching, Haggai manages to spur on the temple rebuilding so that it is complete within four years (about 516 BCE).

Zechariah

Like Haggai, Zechariah prophesies to the generation of Jews almost twenty years reestablished in Jerusalem (about 520 BCE). While he supports Haggai's effort to stimulate the rebuilding of the temple (Zechariah 1:16), his extended message comes cloaked in visions—in sharp contrast to the more straightforward preaching of Haggai. In a series of eight visions filled with symbolic imagery, Zechariah presents flashes of the future God is planning. The godless nations will be punished (Zechariah 2:8–9) but eventually incorporated into God's family (Zechariah 2:11). Next the Lord's servant, called "Branch," will appear and "strip this land of its filthy sin ... in a single day" (Zechariah 3:9). More images, such as a flying book (Zechariah 5:1–4) and a woman in a basket (Zechariah 5:5–11)—highlight God's further determination to do away with sin. The servant Branch will combine the offices of priest (represented currently by Joshua, which is spelled "Jeshua" in Ezra) and ruler (like Zerubbabel) (Zechariah 6:12–13). Unlike Solomon, who rode into his coronation on his father's mule (1 Kings 1:33), this King will come riding on a donkey (Zechariah 9:9) and bringing world peace (Zechariah 9:10). Yet before the restoration of God's intended harmony to the earth, the Lord plans a *big day* of reckoning for all the godless nations (Zechariah 12:9). Next, God "will deal with the family of David and those who live in Jerusalem. I'll pour a spirit of grace and prayer over them. They'll then be able to recognize me as the One they so grievously wounded – that piercing spear-thrust!" (Zechariah 12:10). But on the heels of the people's repentance, "a fountain will be opened ... for washing away their sins" (Zechariah 13:1). After that great judgment day, another "Day is coming—the timing is GOD's—when it will be continuous day [no more nights] ... GOD will be king over all the earth" (Zechariah 14:7–9). Although admittedly wrapped in mystery, Zechariah's oracles charged the task of rebuilding the temple with fresh hope for the eternal resolution of God's people's woes.

Malachi

With Malachi we come to the last of the prophets. Writing in the fifth century BCE (probably parallel to the times narrated in Nehemiah), Malachi speaks to a people who have gotten over both the shock of the exile and the joy of the recovery of Jerusalem and the temple worship. The book operates with a dialectic format outlining God's complaints against His people and their responses.

> GOD said, "I love you."
> You replied, "Really? How have you loved us?"
> "Look at history … I loved Jacob and hated Esau" (Malachi 1:2–3).

God's point is that the people no longer have their heart in their worship. The animals sacrificed are no longer the best. Piety is reduced to going through the motions (Malachi 1:7–14). The leaders are corrupt. People are lax about their marriage vows. Priests quote absurdities like: "GOD loves sinners and sin alike … Judgment? GOD's too nice to judge" (Malachi 2:17). The situation prompts God to advise, "I'm sending my messenger on ahead to clear the way for me" (Malachi 3:1). Judah and Jerusalem need a good cleaning because the judgment day is coming. Only those who return to honoring the Lord will be saved. Therefore, Israel needs to "remember and keep the revelation I gave through my servant Moses … all the rules and procedures for right living. But also look ahead: I'm sending Elijah the prophet to clear the way for the Big Day of GOD" (Malachi 4:4–5). In closing, Malachi provides in the mention of Moses and Elijah what the Jews will use as shorthand for the sum of the Hebrew Scriptures—the Law and the prophets.

Conclusion

Taken as a whole, the Twelve present some noteworthy shifts in emphasis from the previous prophets. While the familiar theme of Israel's sin requiring God's judgment appears immediately in Hosea, the first prophet is equally quick to speak of God's overarching commitment to forgive His people and restore their relationship to Him (Hosea 3:1). Both Joel and Jonah present a strong case that God's promised forgiveness will extend beyond Israel to the Gentile nations. Amos and Micah target social injustice, making a point of how the Law is abused when people go through the motions of worship without attending to the spirit of the Torah, which encourages us to show compassion, especially to those less fortunate. Habakkuk fills in the gap the other prophets leave by giving voice to our natural human struggle to understand God in the midst of suffering. On the other hand, Malachi balances that issue by addressing our tendency to become complacent in our faith. The Twelve add new details to the Messiah description. Micah tells us to look for the promised ruler to be born in Bethlehem (Micah 5:2), and Zechariah informs us that we will recognize the anointed king because he will ride into Jerusalem on a donkey (Zechariah 9:9). For the most part, however, the tenor of the Twelve is one of heightened anticipation of what the Lord will be doing shortly. Now is the time to repent and draw close to the Lord before the coming day of judgment catches up with us. It is a call to be alert and ready for the *new* thing that God is planning.

We have to acknowledge that the prophets drew an unenviable task. They had to tell Israel and Judah news no one wanted to hear or believe. They had to explain that God was going to hurt His people in order to help them, that punishment was actually a sign of the Lord's love. God proves willing to "put everything on the table" for the sake of humans' ability to share in His holiness. Neither the city of Jerusalem nor the temple itself is more sacred than the moral purity of men and women created to enjoy God's intended good world. With the exile, it seemed that the Lord had stripped Israel of everything. It also looked like God had run out of solutions to the paradox of the divine love of humans and hatred of sin. The legacy of the Torah and the Lord's selection of a people for whom God performed many acts of grace and salvation appeared to have come up empty. While the prophets acknowledge this stark reality, they also make it clear that this appearance of defeat is soon to become subject to one of God's great reversals. Just as God told the barren and menopausal Sarah that nothing was impossible for the Deity (Genesis 18:14) and Joseph instructed his brothers that what they had done for evil God had used for good (Genesis 50:20), God will take Israel's very brokenness and transform it. From the wounded and humiliated remnant of the Lord's people, God will bring forth the game-changing "something new" (Isaiah 48:6; Jeremiah 31:31; Ezekiel 16:60). Out of the monarchy for which Israel pleaded but that ended up sabotaging her political autonomy and ownership of the Promised Land, God will redeem the concept of a King for Israel with the promise of a coming Messiah. Whereas kings led God's people away from the Lord, now an anointed King will bring those people back. God doesn't need to do over creation. The Messiah will enable each human to begin anew with God.

We noted earlier that the prophets do not render a clear picture of the Messiah. Likewise they refrain from offering a discernible timetable for his arrival. Rather they provide a series of snapshot images, elusive like bits of remembered dreams. The Messiah will be like David, a triumphal champion for Israel against her enemies (Isaiah 11:10–16; Micah 5:5-6), riding into Jerusalem on a donkey (Zechariah 9:9), but also the "Prince of Peace" who deals "with justice and righteousness" (Isaiah 9:6–7; Jeremiah 23:5). "Blind eyes will be opened, deaf ears unstopped, lame men and women will leap like deer, the voiceless break into song" (Isaiah 35:5–6). In that day God will write His law in people's hearts (Jeremiah 31:33) and bless them with His Spirit (Joel 2:28). The Messiah will be the Shepherd who breaks the Lord's flock out of its slavery (Ezekiel 34:23, 27). Still, this jubilant victory will not come without cost. As Hosea had to buy back his unfaithful wife for the price of a slave (Hosea

3:1–3), Isaiah predicts that the redemption of God's people will be achieved only through the suffering servant (Isaiah 42–53), whose innocent death will heal sinners.

Along with the visions of the Messiah, the prophets tell of the end times. God's day of judgment will arrive as a final horrific battle followed by a magnificent banquet prepared for all who love the Lord. Again the images are blurry, but the final word is good. God will defeat evil, and new heavens and a new earth will replace the broken chaos that is the fallout of humans' choice to reject the Lord's ways.

But how and when this future will come about is never specified. The word of the prophets stands as a reminder to Israel to wait for the timing of the Lord with the courage of Daniel, the honesty of the psalmist, and the obedience of a servant. Like the obscure advice of a folktale's wise man or woman that only makes sense after the story unfolds, Israel will be unable to grasp God's meaning before the Messiah arrives. Until then, she relies on the words of the author of Lamentations, "GOD's loyal love couldn't have run out, his merciful love couldn't have dried up. They're created new every morning. How great your faithfulness!" (Lamentations 3:22–23).

Part Three: The New Testament

One of the major confessions of Christianity is that the Christian Bible consists of two testaments—the Old and the New. When the Christian church emerged as an entity separate from Judaism, she continued to rely on the Hebrew Bible as sacred Scripture. Even when, by the second century CE, the Church had incorporated the New Testament into her Bible, she made no attempt either to shed or change the Scriptures she had inherited from her Jewish roots.[36] Only one alteration of substance occurred, namely the order of the books in the Hebrew canon. As the comparison chart in appendix 2 demonstrates, the Hebrew Scriptures are sorted into the Torah, the Former and Latter Prophets (former being Joshua to Kings, the latter being Isaiah to Malachi), and the Writings. Although the Christian arrangement of the Old Testament derives from the order established in the Septuagint, the Greek translation of the Hebrew Scriptures made centuries before the arrival of Jesus, the Church found as she used the readings that this presentation created a natural connection to the New Testament. The difference boils down to the following: The books included in the Writings section of the Hebrew canon are inserted in various places among the works of the Former and Latter Prophets. Ruth, for instance, follows Judges in order to prepare us for the high point of the monarchy by introducing the ancestors of King David. The Chronicles, immediately following the historical narrative of Samuel and Kings, ask us

---

[36] Childs, *The Rule of Faith,* p. 116.

to reevaluate Israel's monarchy from the postexilic perspective. The placement of the Wisdom Literature between the history books and the writings of the prophets causes us to listen to its content as a complement to the story of Israel. The culture of God's people was richer than the stark recording of their history could reveal. The Wisdom Literature shows us a people deeply aware of all that being human involves emotionally, intellectually, and spiritually. Still, the most significant dissimilarity between the Christian and Jewish canons lies in the Christian assignment of the Latter Prophets as the last words of the Old Testament. These prophets serve to heighten our awareness both of humans' failure to live according to God's Torah and God's simultaneous promise to offer a new solution to the old-as-Eden dilemma of the Deity's love for humans and abhorrence of sin. While it is true that the messianic hope of the prophets is just as important to Jews reading from the Hebrew Scriptures as it is to Christians who believe that Jesus answers that hope, the Christian canon positions the prophets in order to anticipate their message's realization in the New Testament to follow.

When we read the words of the last prophet, Malachi, we hear him speaking to a people grown weary with waiting. Having survived the trauma of exile, they have settled into a status quo that deflates in them any real passion for the promises God has made. Malachi reminds them to be ready for what God will yet do. God will send a messenger to prepare the way for Himself (Malachi 3:1). But it is a long wait—roughly as long as the slavery of the Hebrews in Egypt as the following synopsis will show.

The Persian Empire that graciously allowed the Jews to commence returning to Jerusalem in 538 BCE and shortly thereafter to begin rebuilding the temple eventually, in the fourth century BCE, gives way to the Greek conqueror Alexander the Great. In 336 BCE, as a young man in his twenties, Alexander succeeds his father as king of the Greek city-state of Macedonia and manages in about a dozen years to absorb and exceed the boundaries of the former Persian Empire. After Alexander's early death at thirty-three, his empire splinters among several rulers. The Ptolemaic (Greek-born) Egyptians inherit the rule of Judea in about 322 BCE. The resulting pervasiveness of the Hellenistic culture in the region leads to the translation of the Hebrew Scriptures into Greek (the Septuagint) in the third to second centuries BCE. By the beginning of the second century BCE, the Hellenized Egyptian rule of Judea passes to the more militantly Hellenistic Seleucids based in Syria. The Seleucids' insistence on promoting Greek culture and the religion of the Olympian gods breaks dramatically with the policy of the previous overlords of Judea who had largely tolerated the Jews' temple worship and other religious practices. The tension created by this new administration rolls to a boil in the regency of Antiochus IV. The Seleucid monarch not only bans the practice of Judaism with its temple sacrifices, feasts, and kosher and Sabbath laws but also commandeers the temple for the worship of the Olympian gods, going so far as sacrificing pigs (strictly non-kosher) within the sanctuary and placing an idol of Zeus on the temple altar. The loyal Jewish outrage this action engenders helps the Maccabees to mount the only successful rebellion against Judah's conquerors and to reclaim the rule of Jerusalem from about 165 to 63 BCE. The celebration of Hanukkah commemorates the miracle that a day's worth of lamp oil lasted for eight days while the Maccabees began the cleansing of the desecrated temple. Despite this success, the Maccabean instituted Hasmonean dynasty proves no match against the rising power of Rome when Pompey conquers Judea in 63 BCE.

During this period of Roman occupation, Herod the Great,[37] whose family hailed from the region south of Judea (home to the Edomites in earlier times), emerges as a local leader. Because his

---

[37] See explanation of Herod's family in appendix 4.

family had converted to Judaism during the Hasmonean era, he capitalizes on the temporary political chaos in Rome following the assassination of Julius Caesar in 44 BCE to petition Marc Antony to let him serve as king of the Jews. Although Herod governs at the convenience of Rome, he enjoys enough autonomy to begin renovating the temple in lavish taste by 20 BCE. Nonetheless, he proves a particularly cruel regent, famous for murdering one of his own wives and her sons as well as countless residents of the region. When he dies, close to the birth of Jesus, his kingdom gets divided among his sons, whom Rome redesignates as *tetrarchs* (rulers of fourths) of Judea.

By the time we arrive at the Christian era, Jews live dispersed throughout the Mediterranean in what has become known as the "Diaspora," the result of the original Babylonian exile. Though the faithful continue to make pilgrimages to Jerusalem to celebrate the traditional feasts of Passover, Pentecost, and the harvest festival of tabernacles at the temple, the scholarship of Judaism flourishes in the local synagogues. The centuries following the exile had witnessed the establishment of a new and definitively Jewish order. Whereas the old Israel had focused her pride on the ownership of the land, the politically chastened Jews now clung to their religious traditions rooted in their Scriptures as the source of their identity. Even as the various nations who hosted these "people of the Book" viewed them as a cohesive community holding themselves apart from their neighbors by their strict monotheism and shunning of religious idols, the Jews themselves had begun to diverge into sects in the wake of the Maccabean revolt as early as the second century BCE.

By the time of the Roman occupation, two major sects vied for influence in the management of the temple—Sadducees and Pharisees. While both groups had representatives sitting in the high Jewish council in Jerusalem, known as the Sanhedrin, the Sadducees, comprised mostly of priests with aristocratic backgrounds, had become the primary liaisons with the Roman government. They were willing to make concessions to Roman rule because they believed that keeping the temple open for daily sacrifice and rituals was paramount to Judaism's survival. Though they prided themselves on their purity in worship, their wealth often tempted them to appreciate the finer aspects of Greek and Roman culture.

In contrast, the Pharisees drew their power from the people. Serving mostly as laymen in the synagogues, the Pharisees actively engaged in teaching and discussing Scripture. These forerunners of modern rabbis recognized the authority of oral interpretation and made a habit of wrestling with the specific implications of practicing Jewish laws. Questions concerning acceptable behavior on the Sabbath, the proper way to honor one's parents, the purity of diet, and ritual cleansing absorbed their attention. Their reliance on oral tradition as a complement to the Scriptures stood them in opposition to the Sadducees who recognized the written Law alone as binding. Beyond these legalistic issues, the Pharisees championed the belief in the resurrection of the dead, a point the Sadducees rejected. They criticized the Sadducees for turning theologically soft when trying to curry favor with the Romans.

The remaining sects history tells us about, the Essenes and Zealots, barely receive mention in the New Testament. We know about the Essenes from the discovery of the Dead Sea Scrolls in the midtwentieth century. The Essenes split off from the Pharisees by rejecting the legitimacy of the temple worship. In their dedication to religious purity their practice tended toward asceticism. Many were celibate and lived communally. Some scholars have surmised that Jesus came from this Essene school, perhaps because he was not married, but we will see that the New Testament makes no overt reference to this sect. The Zealots, however, show up as one of Jesus' twelve apostles (Simon, the Zealot) as well as the character Barabbas, a Roman prisoner at the same time as Jesus. These military rebels eschewed religious controversy in favor of political revolution. They sought to purge Judea of her foreign rulers and looked to the promised Messiah to reestablish the nation state of Israel.

The Roman governorship of Judea figures importantly in our understanding of what became the dawn of the Christian era. The saying, "All roads lead to Rome," speaks to Rome's stature as the hub of a semi-global economy. Rome's incredibly efficient military not only brought forth another geographically vast empire onto the world stage but also enabled the construction of a state-of-the-art transportation system that greatly facilitated the administration of her conquered territories. Unlike the area's previous rulers, Rome brought a notable degree of civil stability and legal due process to the region. The *Pax Romana* (literally the "Roman peace"), as it came to be known, began when Caesar Augustus assumed power in 27 BCE and spanned well into the second century CE. Because even non-Roman peoples under the imperial umbrella could enjoy a guarantee of certain rights if they obtained Roman citizenship, it became a valued political status. While the Seleucids had sought to impose Greek culture on its captives, the Romans tended to be liberal regarding occupied peoples' traditions. As long as the natives agreed to acknowledge Roman authority and pay Caesar's taxes, they were free to worship and in other ways maintain their separate cultural identities with tolerance. Roman governors made a point of recognizing local feast days and celebratory traditions. They and most other peoples who encountered the Jews denigrated them for their "unreasonably stubborn" adherence to their religious laws and their unrelenting monotheism with its corresponding reluctance to acknowledge other peoples' deities. Still, Rome's liberality stemmed from its pragmatism, not any ethical system. The empire did not shrink from dealing with enemies preemptively and with brutality. It invented crucifixion as a means of execution precisely because it provided a public spectacle of a slow death by torture. Not only did it deter challenge, but it also confirmed Rome's ultimate control over those she had vanquished.

Into this milieu Jesus is born probably in about 4 BCE. Christianity builds its entire claim to truth on the ground that this man was born, lived, died, and became resurrected as a verifiable fact of human history. Therefore, we note this important difference from the Old Testament: The twenty-seven books of the New Testament are composed and compiled quickly—within about fifty years of the events they describe—during the second half of the first century CE. In his book *Religion on Trial*, Craig Parton explains the significance of the proximity of this documentation. For example, by comparing the four gospels to other works of ancient classical literature by many tests of scholarly authentication, he maintains, "That this material comes with the absolute best manuscript tradition possible, that it comes on top of the events that it records, that it is highly unlikely to have been forged, and that it contains the type of stylistic and factual detail you expect from truthful witnesses."[38]

As we have already noted, we will again observe redundancy in the storytelling. Four gospels provide us with four perspectives of Jesus' ministry, death, and resurrection. Again we will pay attention to the arrangement of these Scriptures because they are not catalogued according to their order of composition. The earliest pieces—the epistles—many written in the 50s and 60s CE, are placed after the Gospels, which were more likely completed between 60 to 85 but possibly as late as 100 CE. Even within the ordering of the Gospels, we will find the two volumes (Luke and Acts) written by Luke, probably our sole Gentile author, separated by the gospel of John. Despite being composed primarily by Jews, the New Testament is written in Greek, not Hebrew. In general, it is not even rendered in very cultured

---

[38] Parton, *Religion on Trial*, p. 57.

Greek either since most of its authors were not classically educated. Instead scholars have found that it is penned in the language of "the common, informal idiom of everyday speech," sharing vocabulary with "shopping lists, family letters, bills and receipts."[39]

As we embark on our journey through the New Testament, let us take in an overview of what lies in store. Of the twenty-seven books, five are narratives (the four gospels and Acts). Twenty-one are letters, and the last is largely poetic. The stories, though not written first, head our list because they need to be read first. First we need to meet Jesus. It will not be enough to hear merely one person's account of this man. We need all four witnesses to speak before we can feel properly introduced to the carpenter from Nazareth. Next we will hear the story of the birth of the church and the response of people who had met Jesus. In the epistles we will gain insight into what it means to become His follower. We will find words of encouragement and caution, comfort and warning, and much clarification of what Christianity entails. Finally a poetic treatise recapping a series of apocalyptic visions and echoing many of the Old Testament prophets offers us a conclusion to the whole of Scripture.

Furthermore, while we read the books of the New Testament, we will notice two ideas that have shifted in the Jewish consciousness during the intertestamental period. The first regards concern for eternal life. We have already remarked on how this had become a point of contention between the Sadducees and the Pharisees. Much of the Old Testament is silent on the subject of life after death. The Psalmist takes for granted the notion that life ends with death and uses it as a bargaining chip with God. "I'm no good to you dead, am I? I can't sing in your choir if I'm buried in some tomb" (Psalm 6:5). "What gain is there in my destruction? ... Will the dust praise you?" (Psalm

---

[39] Peterson, *The Message*, p. 1742.

30:9 NIV). "Let me live that I may praise you" (Psalm 119:175 NIV). On the other hand, Job muses, "If we humans die, will we live again?" (Job 14:14), and he also says, "If all I have to look forward to is a home in the graveyard, ... do you call that hope?" (Job 17:13–15). Likewise the author of Ecclesiastes complains, "It's one fate for everybody ... good people, bad people ... I find this outrageous ... that everyone's lumped together in one fate ... Life leads to death. That's it" (Ecclesiastes 9:2–3). Yet this same speaker notes, "[God] has also set eternity in the hearts of men" (Ecclesiastes 3:11 NIV). By the time we get to the New Testament period, however, more Jews are thinking about the possibility of life after death.

The second idea shift comes in the character of the Devil. There is very little said about Satan in the Old Testament. Remember, the Serpent of Eden is never called the Devil in Genesis. Throughout the rest of the Old Testament we only find the Devil three times. Satan makes a cameo in Zechariah 3:1–2 and serves as the catalyst for Job's miseries in Job 1:6–2:7. But in both of these cases his role is merely that of a designated "accuser," more of the character we now call a "devil's advocate." The third instance comes up in 1 Chronicles 21:1 where Satan incites David to call for a census. Only here does the role of the Devil begin to morph into the character we find familiar to Western culture,[40] the embodiment of the spiritual enemy of God. In the New Testament Satan appears actively attempting to thwart God's purposes. In addition, while we are reading the Gospels, we will find that one of Jesus' primary miracles is to exorcise demons. We can interpret these demons as literal, metaphorical, or even as misnomers for diseases modern science has identified. Even so, when the demons speak, they recognize Jesus as a spiritual being that is both their opponent

---

[40] In addition to what we read in the New Testament, Milton's portrayal of Satan in *Paradise Lost* contributes significantly to the Western vision of the Devil.

and their superior. In the Judaism of the early Christian era, Satan has evolved into a character we now associate mostly with Christianity. It will be important to analyze how this persona figures into the Jesus story.

With these caveats in mind, we are ready to explore the New Testament. Together these twenty-seven books are canonically aligned to provide the answers to the dilemma articulated first in Genesis 3 in the garden of Eden and developed throughout the course of the Old Testament. How will God reconcile love for humans with hatred of sin? By what means will the Deity maintain human free will while providing opportunity for created beings to enter into a permanent love relationship with their maker? What is required of the person who is in such a relationship with God? More than ever, you, the reader, are being called on to piece together the evidence and decide what you think. It's time to find out what the New Testament really says.

Chapter 9

Does It Really Say That Jesus Was the Messiah?

In one sense, the answer to this question is obvious once we have called Jesus the "Christ" because *christ* is the Greek equivalent of the Hebrew *messiah*, meaning "anointed one." While the authors of the four gospels each present their own portraits of Jesus, they stand united in claiming Him as the one promised in the Old Testament. Jesus is the something *new* and "something that you could not guess" that the prophets foretold. But we must remember that the messianic hope as presented in the Old Testament comes to us in a series of snapshots and images—neither a clear picture nor a precise timetable. It left plenty of room for the waiting Jews to speculate about what the Messiah would be like and when He would come.[41] One thought overwhelmed all others, however. The Messiah would surely "restore the kingdom to Israel" (Acts 1:6). What was not expected was that God's Messiah was going to redefine *restoration*, *kingdom*, and *Israel* in ways unforeseen. That Jesus is the Messiah is only the first point. What needs to be explained further is that the Messiah's mission is so much bigger than the prophets could articulate. Once we grasp what the mission is, namely that "he will save his people from their sins" (Matthew 1:21), we must face another conundrum. What kind of human being can perform this kind of salvation?

---

[41] See appendix 5 for how the New Testament interprets Jesus fulfilling the Old Testament messianic hope.

The four gospels each propose to take us on a journey where they introduce us to the man Jesus. In each account we will hear stories of things that Jesus said and taught, miracles that Jesus performed, and claims that Jesus made about who He was and what He had come to do. As we will notice while we are reading, many of these stories are reiterated in more than one gospel. In each gospel Jesus will refer to Himself with the enigmatic title the "Son of Man," probably referencing the messianic figure of Daniel 7:13–14.[42] All four will present the character John the Baptist as the forerunner of the Messiah whom Isaiah and Malachi predicted and the one who also baptizes Jesus. In addition, all gospels speak of Jesus' recruitment of twelve followers, the apostles, whose number serves as an echo to the original twelve tribes of Israel. Again all evangelists cite Jesus' ministry beginning in His hometown region of Galilee and record several of the same miracles (e.g., feeding the five thousand, healing the blind and lame, etc.). Likewise all close with a heavily detailed narrative of His arrest and crucifixion in Jerusalem, where the accounts line up with the most common ground. In the same vein, though each gospel tells its own specific stories of Jesus' after death appearances,[43] all speak resolutely about the reality of His resurrection.

Beyond the above details each evangelist will draw extensively from the Old Testament not only to substantiate Jesus' messiahship but also to demonstrate the myriad ways that Jesus fulfills the promises given to Israel over the whole of her history. But it is here also that we find an interesting and historically disturbing anomaly. While fully embracing the

---

[42] Ezekiel also refers to himself as the "son of man," but for him the title functions to emphasis his humbleness as a human in the presence of the Almighty.

[43] The oldest versions of Mark end at Mark 16:8, before any resurrection appearances are recorded. The expanded version (Mark 16:9–20) includes these appearance stories.

sacred Scriptures of Judaism and being born Jews themselves (with Luke being a probable exception), our witnesses have found that their adoption of Jesus as Messiah has put them at odds with contemporaries in the faith who do not believe. We will see a clearer description of the emergence of the schism between Judaism and Christianity when we read the story of Acts and many of the epistles. For now we simply want to be aware that when the Gospels make blanket statements regarding "the Jews" (statements that have unfortunately been used historically to foment anti-Semitism), they are referring to Jews unlike themselves who stood in opposition to Jesus and His ministry.

Despite these fundamental points of commonality among the four gospels, we next need to remark upon their differences. The major divide lies between the first three evangelists and the fourth. Matthew, Mark, and Luke are known as the synoptic gospels because of their high degree of overlap. Each describes Jesus' active ministry lasting merely a year, beginning in Galilee and then coming to a climax with Jesus' decision to enter Jerusalem, where He meets His death. In contrast, John indicates a three-year ministry in which Jesus travels from Galilee several times to celebrate the various religious festivals in Jerusalem. As we will note when we look at each gospel separately, each evangelist lays claim to a certain amount of material unique to his own account. In the case of Mark, the first gospel composed, this unique element is confined to a smattering of details. Scholars surmise that both Matthew and Luke used Mark as source material for their renderings. They also theorize that Matthew and Luke had additional access to a now-lost written collection of Jesus' sayings. While Matthew and Luke each have a significant portion of his own material, John's gospel stands out for the number of new Jesus stories and sayings it offers. Regardless of these various points of overlapping and singularity, however, we will find as we examine the gospels one by one that each witness has crafted his telling of the Jesus story uniquely. Even when

Matthew and Luke make use of Mark's gospel, it is never a slavish following. Details are preserved but framed with the individual evangelist's particular perspective in evidence. For instance, shortly we will see that while Mark mentions Satan's temptation of Jesus (Mark 1:12–13), Matthew and Luke each expand the story and yet emphasize different aspects in that expansion. Therefore, as we read each, we will want to pay attention not only to the portrait of Jesus but to those of the other characters who factor into the story, such as Peter, Judas, the other disciples, the Jewish religious elite, the Roman governor Pilate, the people who follow Jesus and those who turn against Him. By the time we have looked at all four, we will want to understand both their differences but also how it can be, as Childs asserts, "There was only one Gospel, but it was testified to by Matthew, Mark, Luke, and John."[44] At that point you can decide for yourself if you agree with the evangelists' testimony.

Matthew

The early church fathers assigned the authorship of this gospel to the apostle Matthew, the tax collector, who is called Levi in both Mark and Luke. Although Mark was written first, the New Testament begins with the Gospel according to Matthew. As we read, we will soon see the sense of this placement because Matthew presupposes an understanding of the Old Testament in his audience (suggested because he never stops to explain Jewish traditions) and tells his story with constant reference to Old Testament prophecy in order to expose Jesus' ongoing fulfillment of the messianic predictions. No wonder he begins his testimony with a genealogy of Jesus showing Jesus' direct descent from Abraham as well as His line stemming from the great King David. Interestingly, however, the end point of the genealogy is actually

---

[44] Childs, *The Rule of Faith*, p. 5.

Jesus' earthly father, Joseph, whom Matthew designates simply as "Mary's husband, the Mary who gave birth to Jesus" (Matthew 1:16). As Mary's husband, Joseph is the legal parent of Jesus, and this makes his genealogical heritage relevant to claiming that Jesus is the son of David.[45] The remainder of chapter 1 chronicles the story of Jesus' birth from Joseph's perspective. In that day Jewish tradition charged engaged couples to refrain from sex before marriage. An affair with another partner any time during the betrothal counted as adultery. Likewise a severing of the marriage contract constituted a divorce. When Joseph discovers that his fiancée, Mary, is pregnant, his first thought is to divorce her quietly—in other words, not actively accuse her of adultery, a crime punishable by stoning under Mosaic law. But before Joseph can act upon this resolution, God sends an angel to him in a dream clearing Mary of infidelity because "God's Holy Spirit has made her pregnant" (Matthew 1:20). Here we get the first of Matthew's many Old Testament citations. In Isaiah 7:14, the prophet had testified, "A virgin will get pregnant and bear a son; they will name him Immanuel [Hebrew for *God is with us*]" (Matthew 1:23). From here on Matthew presents Joseph as shouldering the responsibility for the security of Mary and her child. Per the angel's instructions, he names the baby Jesus, a form of Joshua meaning *God saves* "because he will save his people from their sins" (Matthew 1:21). Though Matthew does not explain how Jesus ends up being born in Bethlehem, he notes the fact of it, with its corresponding citation from Micah 5:2, which predicted the small city of David's origin as the birthplace of the Messiah (Matthew 2:6). Only in Matthew's rendering do we receive the tale of the visiting Magi, who have seen a star in the east signifying the birth of the "King of the Jews" (Matthew 2:1–2). When these Gentile astrologers ask Herod the Great how to find this king, Jesus' life is threatened, and Joseph must take his

---

[45] NIV footnote to Matthew 1:16, p. 1436.

family to hide in Egypt (Matthew 2:3–15). Matthew then reports the source of the threat—that Herod will order the slaughter of all boy babies under two in Bethlehem (Matthew 2:16). Once again an angel appears to Joseph to give him the all clear so that the family can return to Israel, this time to the small northern village of Nazareth because Herod's son Archelaus now rules in Judea (where Bethlehem is). It is here in the area of Galilee that Jesus grows to manhood.

Already in this birth narrative, Matthew has laid a foundation for describing who Jesus is. The child bears the prophets' markers for the Messiah with His virgin birth in Bethlehem. Matthew then heralds another God reversal when he connects Jesus to Moses by equating Herod, the titled king of the Jews, with the ancient Israelite nemesis, the Egyptian Pharaoh who ordered the Hebrew boys murdered (Exodus 1:22). Like Moses, Jesus will be a Savior, except that the bondage He will deliver His people from will be "their [slavery to their] sins" (Matthew 1:21). Matthew also reminds us that Isaiah's prophecy for the Messiah included the title Immanuel (God with us), but he is careful not to explain any of this yet. Right now Matthew is laying out clues for us to assemble in order to know who Jesus is.

Next Matthew introduces us to John the Baptist, the one Isaiah prophesied would "prepare the way for the Lord" (Isaiah 40:3; Matthew 3:3). John is already running afoul of the religious authorities of the day (the Pharisees and the Sadducees) with his call to the people to repent of their sins and be cleansed with baptism. John points out that mere Jewish heritage is no guarantee of salvation (Matthew 3:7–9). In his brief narrative of John's activity, Matthew foreshadows the hurdles that Jesus will shortly encounter as His ministry begins. But first John must baptize Jesus, though John acknowledges himself as unworthy of the honor. In this act we will hear God's voice claiming, "This is my Son, chosen and marked by my love, delight of my life" (Matthew 3:17).

After this baptism the Spirit leads Jesus into the desert, where He fasts for forty days. (Remember Moses on Mount Sinai in Exodus 24:18 and 34:28.) Physically weak but spiritually prepared, Jesus faces the Devil's temptation to conform to Israel's expectation of her Messiah. With three different overtures, Satan attempts to convince Jesus that He can achieve His goals if He presents Himself as 1) a prophet (like Moses, who dispensed manna in the wilderness); 2) a priest (who could control the temple worship with God's angels in thrall); and 3) a king (who could restore the might of Israel's golden age).[46] Though the Devil injects scriptural proof into his argument, Jesus has no trouble counter-quoting him. The Lord's anointed will not fall for the easy route to glory. By rejecting Satan's subtle attempts to subvert God's purpose by making Jesus' job easier or more pleasant, Jesus proves His readiness to take on the task God has called Him to do (Matthew 4:1–11).

Like many rabbis before Him, Jesus recruits disciples who follow Him as He begins His teaching and performing of miracles in Galilee (Matthew 4:18–23). Matthew organizes his material using Jesus' speeches as the skeleton, which is fleshed out with the stories of the miracles and Jesus' interaction with the common folk as well as the religious authorities. The first discourse is the most famous—the Sermon on the Mount (Matthew 5–7). Here Matthew has Jesus speaking to His disciples on a mountaintop in parallel to Moses delivering the Law from Mount Sinai. Jesus teaches extensively on the Mosaic law and how God's people have missed the essence of what the Law means. "Don't suppose for a minute that I have come to demolish the Scriptures— either God's Law or the Prophets. I'm not here to demolish but to complete" (Matthew 5:17). Six times Jesus begins a teaching with "You have heard it said—" in order to point out how the common perception of the Torah is neither broad enough nor

---

[46] Robin Griffith-Jones, *The Four Witnesses*, pp. 132–136.

radical enough to uphold God's call to holiness. The teaching against murder is not merely about outlawing the taking of a life physically. Hatred, anger, and insults can kill spiritually. The commandment actually prohibits these deeds as well (Matthew 5:21–22). Likewise the law of retaliation (referencing an eye for an eye in Exodus 21:24 and Leviticus 24:20) needs to be understood as a different mandate. "Do not resist an evil person. If someone strikes you on the right cheek, turn to him the other also" (Matthew 5:39 NIV). Jesus continues, "Love your enemies and pray for those who persecute you" (Matthew 5:44 NIV). Taking up the subject of prayer, Matthew alone records the whole of Christianity's most famous one—the Lord's Prayer (Matthew 6:9–15). Then Matthew concludes the sermon with Jesus' summation—what has become known as the Golden Rule and the guiding principle for human interaction. "In everything, do to others what you would have them do to you, for this sums up the Law and the Prophets" (Matthew 7:12 NIV).[47]

Having delivered this radicalized interpretation of the Law from the mountain, Jesus then descends among the people of Galilee and reveals miraculous abilities as He heals their infirmities (Matthew 8–9). Jesus amazes even His own disciples with His power over nature by calming a storm while they are at sea (Matthew 8:23–27). But after He bids a lame man, "Cheer up, son. I forgive your sins," He scandalizes the teachers of the law. They know that only God can forgive sins. For a man to claim to do so amounts to blasphemy. Yet to His accusers Jesus counters, "Which do you think is simpler: to say, 'I forgive your sins,' or, 'Get up and walk'? Well, just so it's clear that I'm the Son of Man

---

[47] As we noted in chapter 4 under Leviticus, the general concept of the Golden Rule arises in the ethical understanding of many of the world's religions and philosophies as well as within Judaism. While Jesus is not saying something absolutely new here, He is the first person to state the rule in the positive. Compare the pronouncement of Rabbi Hillel in the first century BCE that was eventually incorporated into the Talmud: "That which is hateful to you do not do to your fellow. That is the whole Torah." See also note 17 on p. 98.

and authorized to do either, or both …" At this he turned to the paraplegic and said, "Get up. Take your bed and go home," and the once paralyzed man is now able to walk (Matthew 9:2–8). When the disciples of the currently imprisoned John the Baptist ask whether Jesus is the Messiah, Jesus tells them, "Go back and tell John what's going on: the blind see, the lame walk, lepers are cleansed, the deaf hear, the dead are raised, the wretched of the earth learn that God is on their side" (Matthew 11:4–5). It would not be lost on John's followers that Jesus was making reference to Isaiah (Isaiah 35:5–6; 61:1). In this way Jesus does not overtly claim the role of Messiah but leaves it to John and all within hearing to decide if Jesus' actions match up with messianic prophecy.

Just as John's actions had attracted the attention of the Pharisees, Jesus also continues to come under their scrutiny. Beyond His profession to forgive sins, the Pharisees mostly find fault with His Sabbath purity. When they criticize His disciples for plucking grain from the fields on the Sabbath (Matthew 12:1–8), Jesus rebuts their argument with Scripture, citing the story from 1 Samuel 21:6 when King David and his men ate from the altar bread. Next Jesus goes on the offensive, quoting Hosea 6:6 about the meaning behind the ritual. "I desire mercy, not sacrifice" (Matthew 12:7 NIV). The Pharisees then quiz Him about the legality of healing on the Sabbath, a point that plays to their specialty—oral interpretation of the law. Within this oral tradition the rabbis had decided that giving medical attention on the Sabbath was allowable only if the person was in danger of immediate death. Jesus takes on their challenge. In typical rabbinic fashion Jesus asks if it would be legal to pull a sheep from a ravine on the Sabbath? The Pharisees concede as much. Jesus concludes, "Surely kindness to people is as legal as kindness to animals," and proceeds to restore a man's withered hand (Matthew 12:9–13). Then Jesus withdraws from the Pharisees but continues to heal the sick and afflicted brought to

Him. Although Jesus instructs those He has cured not to reveal who He is, Matthew takes this opportunity to drop another clue about Jesus' identity by quoting Isaiah 42:1–4, the lead servant song (Matthew 12:17–21). This marks the first overt connection between the Messiah and God's suffering servant.

In the meantime, embittered by Jesus' cleverness, the Pharisees have begun to plot how to get rid of Him (Matthew 12:14). Their first tactic is to accuse Him of using black magic to exorcise a man possessed by demons only to have Jesus confront them with their illogic. "If Satan banishes Satan, is there any Satan left?" (Matthew 12:22–28). When the Pharisees try asking Jesus for a sign that God is with Him, He replies that the only "evidence" they will get is the "sign of Jonah." First, like Jonah, the Son of Man will be gone three days in a grave (Jonah 1:17). Second, when Jonah preached to the Ninevites, they repented (Jonah 3:5), but "a far greater preacher than Jonah is here, and you squabble about 'proofs'" (Matthew 12:38–41).

After this round with Jesus' religious opponents, Matthew shows Jesus teaching by parable. In the parable of the sower (Matthew 13:1–9; 18–23), Jesus explains how God's Word takes root in some people and not others. God's call to obedience to the code of holiness will be available to those who pursue it earnestly, but many will reject God. As a case in point, Matthew then turns to the story of John the Baptist's fate—how he is beheaded through Herodias' skillful manipulation of her husband, Tetrarch Herod Antipas (Matthew 14:3–12). Yet despite this example of worldly rejection of God, Jesus shows compassion on the multitudes when He feeds the five thousand, miraculously turning a meal of five loaves and two fish into a banquet that produces twelve baskets of leftovers (Matthew 14:13–21).

Having presented Jesus as teacher of the true Law, miracle worker, opponent of the contemporary religious order, and man of compassion for the many, Matthew draws his gospel to its first climax. Jesus asks His disciples who people think the Son of Man is? They respond, "Some think he is John the Baptizer, some say Elijah, some Jeremiah or one of the other prophets." But Jesus wants to know, "Who do you say I am?" Here Simon Peter demonstrates his leadership. "You're the Christ, the Messiah, the Son of the living God" (Matthew 16:13–16). Jesus states that Peter has received this insight from God and pronounces that Peter, whose name means *rock*, will be the rock on which Christ will build His church. But for now all the disciples are sworn to secrecy. Jesus must go to Jerusalem to suffer, be killed, and then be raised. When Peter protests, Jesus declares, "Peter, get out of my way. Satan, get lost. You have no idea how God works" (Matthew 16:23).

Even as Matthew shows the disciples unable to process what Jesus tells them, his Jesus adds to their confusion when He calls Peter, James, and John to witness His transfiguration. When Jesus and the three go up on a mountain, light radiates from Jesus' face, reminding us of Moses coming down from the mountain after God had restored the stone tablets of the Ten Commandments (Exodus 34:29–30). But now Moses and Elijah stand beside Jesus. Peter asks if they can build shelters for all three when a voice from within a cloud calls out, "This is my Son, whom I love; with whom I am well pleased. Listen to him!" (Matthew 17:5 NIV). The disciples fall prostrate before the Almighty, but Jesus counsels them not to be afraid, just to tell no one about this incident until after His resurrection. When the three look up, only Jesus is with them. The "Law and the Prophets" that Moses and Elijah represent are fulfilled in Him.

Having disclosed this much of His true identity, Jesus returns to His teaching. Moving from the ethical discussions of the Sermon on the Mount, Jesus now offers glimpses of God and God's kingdom. The greatest in the kingdom must be like children (Matthew 18:1–4). God is like the shepherd who, losing one sheep out of a hundred, leaves the ninety-nine in search of the one (Matthew 18:12–14). "Therefore, be like God: work out your disputes and forgive one another" (Matthew 18:15-35). When a rich young man asks Jesus, "Teacher, what good thing must I do to get eternal life?" Jesus responds first with the obvious—obey the commandments. When the man replies, "I've done that. What's left?" Jesus throws him a curve, "Give everything [you have] to the poor ... Then come follow me" (Matthew 19:16–21), and the questioner turns away crestfallen. Jesus remarks how hard it is for those well off to enter heaven. "It's easier to gallop a camel through a needle's eye than for the rich to enter God's kingdom" (Matthew 19:24). To the astonished disciples He explains, "With man this is impossible, but with God all things are possible" (Matthew 19:26 NIV). Then to demonstrate how God has always been presenting reversals of human wisdom, Jesus tells the parable of the workers in the vineyard. Each laborer is recruited for a different number of hours of work and promised a fair wage, yet at the end of the day all the employees receive the same pay (Matthew 20:1–16). Likewise when the mother of James and John asks for special favors for her sons, Jesus tells her she doesn't know what she is requesting (Matthew 20:21–22). But to His disciples He explains, "Whoever wants to be great must become a servant. Whoever wants to be first among you must be your slave. That is what the Son of Man has done: He came to serve, not be served—and then to give away his life in exchange for the many who are held hostage" (Matthew 20:26–28).

After presenting these new insights about the ways of God, Jesus sets His course for Jerusalem. The disciples know now that He is laying claim to the title of Messiah. That He should plan to go to Jerusalem to celebrate the Passover is not unexpected. For a long time Jews have been speculating that the logical time for the Messiah to appear would be during the Passover festival with its story reminding Jews of God's rescue of His people from their slavery in Egypt. Surely the Messiah will be a deliverer like Moses just as Moses predicted in Deuteronomy 18:17–18. When Jesus instructs His followers on the retrieval of a donkey

(Zechariah 9:9) on which He would ride into the city, it seems as though all the prophecies are lining up for them to witness *the restoration of Israel.* After the triumphal entry (Matthew 21:1–11), however, Jesus detours from His people's messianic expectations. Instead of putting aside the Roman conquerors, He raises the ire of the Sadducees and Pharisees by turning over the tables of the moneylenders in the temple (Matthew 21:12). When these religious authorities try to trip Him up in order to turn the people against Him, He turns the tables on them as well. They ask Him by what authority He teaches and does miracles, but Jesus counters by quizzing them about the authority of John's baptism, which the teachers of the law had refused either to endorse or repudiate (Matthew 21:23–27). Likewise the scribes wonder, *Should the people pay taxes?* Jesus cites the image of Caesar on the coinage and replies, "Then give Caesar what is his and give God what is his" (Matthew 22:21). Threatened by the drift of Jesus' teaching, the religious officials plot to rid themselves of his influence. Matthew reveals Jesus' reading their minds when he quotes Jesus musing over Jerusalem, the city that murders her prophets. "How often I've ached to embrace your children, the way a hen[48] gathers her chicks under her wings, and you wouldn't let me" (Matthew 23:37).

The stage is now set for Jesus' final discourse. As He preaches in the vicinity of the temple, Jesus predicts its destruction and warns of the other signs of the end of the age. He harkens back to Daniel's imagery of the end times with the monster of desecration (Daniel 9:27) and the emergence of false messiahs who will lead people away from God with their duplicity. Here Jesus clarifies that the prophets' simultaneous predictions of the arrival of the Messiah and the terrifying day of the Lord when the ungodly will be punished are actually separate events. Jesus will perform the messianic task in the present with His

---

[48]   Note the feminine imagery here for describing God.

death on the cross, but later He will return to usher in the last days. Because no one will know the exact hour and day the Son of Man will return, Jesus warns all future generations to remain watchful and on the ready with the parable of the ten virgins awaiting the bridegroom (Matthew 25:1–13). As we have already learned from the case of Joseph and Mary, the marriage tradition of the day was for formal betrothals to be planned in advance. But the execution of the actual wedding depended on the bridegroom readying a place for his fiancée within his parents' home. The bride and her friends needed to prepare for the wedding, knowing that it could happen at any moment after the engagement, but the time would not be fixed. Therefore, in the parable the bridesmaids (future believers) who await the groom should know ahead of time that they must be armed (with extra oil/patience) against the possibility of the future husband's later-than-expected arrival.

Next Jesus tells the parable of the talents (Matthew 25:14–30). God wants everyone to make the most of what they are given. Those who receive much are expected to produce proportionately. But ultimately what matters to God is how we treat others. In the parable of the sheep and goats Jesus shows God sorting humans by their kindness and understanding of their fellows. He claims that whatever we do to the least ones, we in fact do as though we were caring for Christ Himself (Matthew 25:31–46).

Even though the high priests who plot against Jesus initially decide to wait until after Passover to seek Jesus' life (Matthew 26:3-5), Jesus knows that His end is near. When in Bethany, a small town outside of Jerusalem, a woman anoints Jesus with expensive perfume, the disciples criticize her frivolous expenditure of money that could have gone to help the poor. But Jesus defends her, saying that she has prepared His body for burial. "You will have the poor with you every day for the rest of your lives, but not me" (Matthew 26:11). Matthew notes this as the tipping point that sends the disciple Judas into his betrayal. Judas Iscariot approaches the chief priests with his willingness to turn Jesus in for money and awaits an opportunity to hand him over to the authorities (Matthew 26:14–16). Even though Matthew couches Judas' motivation in terms of monetary gain, we will see as the story unfolds that Judas' expectations are more nuanced than this initial narrative leads us to believe.

From this point of introduction Matthew's narrative accelerates into Jesus' *passion*—the suffering the Son of Man endures from His foreknowledge of the treachery that will erupt among those closest to Him through His death on the cross. As Jesus gathers with His inner circle of disciples in a hired upper room to celebrate the first evening of Passover, He begins by indicating that one among them will betray Him. Each of those assembled fears that he might be the one. Though Jesus acknowledges to a duplicitous Judas that He knows the disciple's plans in Matthew 26:25, He must not do it openly. Instead He leads those assembled in a new rite of thanksgiving—what will become the "Lord's Supper"—pronouncing that the unleavened bread of the Passover is really His body and the wine His blood. They are to become a metaphor of remembrance for how Jesus will allow His body to be broken and His blood spilt as the means by which God will forgive sins (Matthew 26:26–30). Matthew paints this as a truly solemn event, uninterrupted by any response from the disciples. But when the gathering moves outdoors to the Mount of Olives, Jesus again warns that His beloved disciples will fail to stand by Him. He quotes from Zechariah 13:7, predicting that the flock will scatter once the shepherd is struck. Here Peter blurts out, "Even if everyone else falls to pieces on account of you, I won't" (Matthew 26:33). Yet Jesus does not hesitate to disillusion him, "This very night, before the rooster crows up the dawn, you will deny me three times" (Matthew 26:34). Though Peter and all the disciples rush to pledge their loyalty to Jesus, within moments they are already showing signs of weakness.

In the garden of Gethsemane, where Jesus has retreated to pray, He asks Peter, James, and John—the same three who witnessed His transfiguration—to stay awake with Him because "he [has] plunged into an agonizing sorrow and this sorrow is crushing my life out" (Matthew 26:37–38). We hear Jesus' prayer, "My Father, if there is any way, get me out of this. But please, not what I want. You, what do *you* want?" But when He returns for the support of His companions, He finds them all asleep (Matthew 26:39–40). Jesus complains, "Can't you stick it out with me for one hour?" (Matthew 26:40). Bereft of human consolation, Jesus finds strength in further prayer so that He is ready when a gang of religious leaders and their temple police accost Him in the garden. Still it is hard that Judas chooses to identify Jesus to His assailants with a kiss (Matthew 26:49). Because the crew arresting Jesus has arrived armed, the disciples' first response is to fight back, but Jesus puts a stop to this resistance. "Put your sword back where it belongs ... Don't you realize that I am able right now to call to my Father, and twelve companies—more, if I want them—of fighting angels would be here, battle-ready? But if I did that, how would the Scriptures come true that say this is the way it has to be?" After He sets His followers straight, Jesus picks a bone with His foes, "What is this—coming out after me with swords and clubs as if I were a dangerous criminal? Day after day I have been sitting in the Temple teaching and you never so much as lifted a hand against me" (Matthew 26:52–56). Even when it looks as though Jesus is meeting defeat, He maintains the upper hand over all. Nevertheless, the disciples still fall into panic and desert the scene.

Once arrested, Jesus is brought before the Sanhedrin led by the high priest Caiaphas. The testimony presented against Jesus consists mainly of trumped-up charges, none of which seems to hold water. But finally the chief priest poses the question that runs to the root of their conflict. Is Jesus claiming to be the Messiah? Jesus has kept His silence until this point in the inquisition, but now the accusation has come down framed by the priest's appeal to *the authority of the living God*, an oath requiring an answer. Jesus responds, "You yourself said it. And that's not all … the Son of Man [will be] seated at the right hand of the Mighty One" (Matthew 26:64). Within the circumspect language of Judaism, which finds God's name too holy to speak aloud, Jesus is calling Himself not merely God's chosen one but divine like God. Caiaphas tears his robes. This is blasphemy of the worst sort—to equate oneself with the Deity. Under Mosaic law, the priest must sentence such a person to death. No one in the Sanhedrin dares to consider that it is not blasphemy if the accused is speaking the truth.

Peter has followed Jesus to His trial, keeping out of the sight of the religious authorities. As he awaits the verdict, some of the bystanders think they recognize him as a Jesus follower. Nervously Peter refuses to acknowledge his association with the prisoner until the cock crows and Jesus' prediction of denial reduces him to bitter tears (Matthew 26:69–75).

Having first interrupted his narrative with the aside about Peter, Matthew next turns to Judas, who is also feeling remorse after his treachery. Matthew has built the case against Judas carefully first by citing the disciple's desire for payment from the priests and then by putting falsely sweet words in his mouth as he is in the act of betraying his Master. Yet when the religious leaders are carting Jesus off to the Roman governor, Pilate— because they have no authority to execute criminals under Roman law—Matthew now shows us a contrite Judas, one who believes he has betrayed an innocent man (Matthew 27:3–4). As if to confirm this change of heart, Matthew next tells of Judas' subsequent suicide, one of the details unique to his gospel.[49] He opens the door to many questions regarding what Judas thought he would accomplish by betraying Jesus.

---

[49] In Acts 1:16–18, Luke will offer us a different picture of Judas's death.

The representatives of the Sanhedrin who drag Jesus to Pilate recognize that charging the defendant with blaspheming the Jewish God would draw only guffaws from the Roman governorship. In most of the ancient world kings and emperors regularly declared themselves divine. Therefore, the Jewish officials cast their accusations against Jesus in a new light. Posing as satisfied recipients of Rome's imperial protection, they are tattling on one of their own who is calling Himself the "king of the Jews." Surely Pilate realizes the actual situation. The Jewish leadership wants to get rid of Jesus but lacks the political authority to execute Him. He quizzes Jesus about the claims against Him, but Jesus offers only a limp response that He is the king of the Jews "if you say so" (Matthew 27:11). Somehow Jesus' refusal either to defend Himself or throw Himself upon Rome's mercy unsettles the governor, and Matthew proceeds to draw Pilate as a reluctant executioner. First Pilate tries to avoid pronouncing the death sentence by appealing to what the gospel writers deem a Roman tradition of pardoning a single Jewish prisoner out of respect for the Passover. But the accusing parties demand that the infamous Barabbas[50] be released instead of Jesus. Next Matthew stands alone in adding that Pilate's wife warns him not to condemn this man because of a dream she has had. But in the end Pilate, astonished that Jesus fears neither him nor his Roman might, finds that he fears the crowd and its ability to disrupt the Roman order most of all. Unable even to name a crime that Jesus has committed, he nonetheless gives way to the throng's insistence on crucifixion. Ceremonially Pilate washes his hands of responsibility for this judgment, and Matthew allows the voice of the mob to accept the blame in Pilate's place (Matthew 27:25).

If Matthew wants us to believe that Pilate had his reservations, he still has no compunctions about painting the Roman soldiers

---

[50] We will learn later that Barabbas is probably a Zealot who has been actively trying to sabotage the Roman government of Judea.

as sadists. Having gotten wind that Jesus has professed to be a king, they proceed to make a mockery of him. After Jesus has been flogged per Pilate's orders, the governor's brigade strips off His clothing, dresses Him in a red toga, and plaits a crown of thorn brush on His head. Next, positioning Jesus between two robbers also being crucified, they nail Him to the cross complete with the placard proclaiming, "This is Jesus, King of the Jews," which was a joke unto itself—as if Jews were powerful enough to have a king! While the soldiers throw dice for His clothing, the masses, joined by the high priests, while away the time by jeering at Jesus, "He saved others—he can't save himself! King of Israel, is he? Then let him get down from that cross. We'll all become believers then!" (Matthew 27:42). Their words become an echo back to Satan's temptation of Jesus in Matthew 4:5–7. The scene is eerily reminiscent of the misery described in Psalm 22:18 and 22:7–8; however, uncharacteristically Matthew does not cite this allusion. But he is aware of the psalm. After the six hours Jesus spends on the cross, three under a darkened afternoon sky, Matthew records Jesus crying out in Hebrew the first verse of Psalm 22,[51] "My God, my God, why have you abandoned me?" (Matthew 27:46 NIV). The bystanders hear the Hebrew *Eli*, meaning "my God," and think Jesus is calling to Elijah. Instead Jesus gives another loud cry and breathes His last.

Matthew goes on to explain, "At that moment, the Temple curtain [what cordoned off the Holy of Holies—the most sacred place within the temple where only a high priest could enter but once a year] ripped in two, top to bottom. There was an earthquake, and rocks were split in pieces ... tombs opened up ... many bodies of believers ... were raised" (Matthew 27:51–52, compare to Daniel 12:2). The seismic upheaval petrifies the Roman centurion (named because he leads a hundred men) and

---

[51] We have already discussed Psalm 22 in chapter 7. Note that after starting at a point of despair, the psalm transforms halfway through and ends with rejoicing and praise of God.

the guards at the cross whom he commands. They declare, "This has to be the Son of God!" (Matthew 27:54). Jesus' death is a cataclysmic event. It has changed the way humans can connect to God. The sacred purity of the temple is no longer a necessary go-between for God and humans. The earth itself has trembled in response. Death is working backward. Even Gentiles see the truth that Jesus is the Son of God.

But first Matthew must make it clear that Jesus is indeed dead. Of the women who have followed Jesus from His early days in Galilee and have stayed at His side throughout His crucifixion, Matthew names Mary Magdalene, Mary, the mother of James and Joses, and the mother of Zebedee's sons. These women accompany Joseph of Arimathea as he takes Jesus' body from the cross, wraps it in clean linens, and places it in a new tomb with a large stone sealing the entrance. Here Matthew alone adds that the high priests beg Pilate to supply a Roman sentinel so that the tomb can be guarded against the disciples. The Jewish leadership has heard Jesus' claims that He would rise from the dead on the third day and is eager to prevent Jesus' followers from stealing the body in an attempt to fake His resurrection.

Because Jesus' crucifixion has occurred on a Friday and He did not die until the middle of the afternoon, His burial required haste to be accomplished before sundown when the Sabbath would begin. Mary Magdalene and the other Mary, who have both witnessed His suffering, must wait for dawn on Sunday to be able to attend to Jesus' dead body. On their way to the tomb, a second earthquake heralds the arrival of an angel from God who rolls away the stone. The angel shimmers with a lightninglike radiance that scares the Roman guards and the women alike. Addressing himself to the women, the angel declares that Jesus is not there in the tomb but has risen as He had foretold. They are to hurry to tell His disciples. As soon as the Marys are on their way, however, Jesus Himself greets them. The women clasp His knees, worshiping Him, but He repeats the angel's message, "Go tell my brothers that they are to go to Galilee, and that I'll meet them there" (Matthew 28:10).

Next Matthew inserts the fallout from the guards. A few have confessed the truth to the high priests who attempt to spin the story to their own advantage. They bribe the guards to lie that the disciples had stolen the body while the sentinel were sleeping at their post. Then the Jewish leaders agree to speak up for the soldiers with the Roman governor should they be accused of failing in their duty by dozing through their watch. Matthew adds that the Sanhedrin continues to pass this myth around to dissuade people from believing in the resurrection (Matthew 28:11–15).

Finally Matthew returns to Jesus' reunion with the Eleven, the remaining apostles minus Judas, who meet their Master on a mountain in Galilee. In the presence of the risen Jesus most of the disciples (some still doubted as mentioned in Matthew 28:17) respond as the women had in worshiping Him. Matthew closes his gospel with Jesus delivering what has come to be called the Great Commission, which says, "Go out and train everyone you meet, far and near, in this way of life, marking them by baptism in the threefold name: 'Father, Son, and Holy Spirit.'[52] Then instruct them in the practice of all that I have commanded you. I'll be with you as you do this, day after day, right up to the end of the age" (Matthew 28:18–20).

The major thrust of Matthew's presentation lies in his portrayal of Jesus as the Messiah promised throughout the Old Testament. His constant citations of Scripture validate the continuity of the promises God made to Israel in the past with the proclamations Jesus has made about God in the present. According to Matthew, Jesus has not come to abolish the law of Moses but to embody the essence of the Torah teaching that no other human has the ability to put into practice. From the

---

[52] This is the first mention of speaking of God in the three names of Father, Son, and Holy Spirit.

beginning Matthew expresses Jesus' purpose as salvation of God's people from their sins. The cherished hope among Jews that supposed that the Messiah would restore the political kingdom to Israel is now replaced with a Savior who restores humans to their proper connection with their God so that God's kingdom may reign. Although Matthew's Jewish inclination to refrain from speaking directly about God prevents him from wording the notion explicitly, he prepares us to understand Jesus as the incarnation of God—God walking among us as a human. How else does He have the authority to forgive sins? How else does He understand what the Law really means? How else does He expect humans to strive for perfection? How else can He rise from the dead?

Mark

The early church ascribed the Gospel according to Mark to the man named John Mark, whom we will meet in Acts. John Mark worked closely with Peter's ministry, and it has long been thought that his gospel reflects Peter's preaching as that apostle leader sought to spread the message about Jesus. Because about 90 percent of Mark appears in Matthew, this gospel will seem to serve as something of a review of what we have already learned from Matthew. Still we will observe that Mark brings a different kind of energy and urgency to his delivery of who Jesus is and why the world needs to know about Him. As we review Mark, notice the almost frenzied pace of Jesus' ministry and how often Mark uses the word *immediately* or others like it to describe the intensity of Jesus' activity.

Unlike Matthew, who aims to build a case for Jesus' identity, Mark opens simply and boldly, "The beginning of the gospel about Jesus Christ, the Son of God" (Mark 1:1 NIV). Immediately Mark plunges us into a world turned on end because of Jesus. Without any birth narrative, he launches into the ministry of

John the Baptist as the forerunner of the Messiah according to Old Testament prophecy. After John baptizes Jesus, accompanied by the dazzling endorsement of the Holy Spirit (Mark 1:4–11), Mark makes brief mention of Satan's temptation (Mark 1:12–13), and Jesus' calling of His disciples—the fishermen of Galilee He recruits by vowing to teach them "how to catch men and women instead of perch and bass" (Mark 1:17). From there we move to the day Jesus begins preaching in Capernaum, where He amazes the crowds with both the authority of His teaching and the power of His miracles. Curing the fever of Simon Peter's mother-in-law (Mark 1:29–31) results in Jesus spending His entire evening with the "sick and evil-afflicted people … lined up at his door" (Mark 1:32–34). Then in the dead of that same night Jesus escapes to a *secluded spot* to pray only to have Simon Peter and the other disciples search Him out with the plea, "Everybody's looking for you" (Mark 1:35–37). Despite His lack of sleep, Jesus responds, "Let's go to the rest of the villages so I can preach there also. This is why I've come" (Mark 1:38).

Although Mark's gospel is the shortest of the four, he frequently renders his stories in greater detail—another sign that his compilation is written earlier and serves as a baseline reference for the others. We have already heard the story of the crippled man in Matthew 9:2–8, where the emphasis rests on Jesus' power to forgive sins. Where Matthew refers somewhat cryptically to the "faith" (Matthew 9:2) of the paraplegic's friends, Mark spells out what happened. When the crowd prevents the four men from maneuvering their patient close enough to Jesus, the mat bearers think outside the box. They remove the roof of the house so that they can hand the stretcher down to Jesus. With his more thorough explanation, Mark underscores how the resolute faith of all involved profoundly impresses Jesus (Mark 2:2–5) before he makes the point that Jesus can cure both physical and spiritual maladies (Mark 2:8–12).

Showing the local Pharisees looking askance at Jesus' claims to forgive sins allows Mark to transition next to a series of stories that demonstrate Jesus' clash with established Jewish authority. Jesus calls Levi,[53] a tax collector, into His circle of disciples (Mark 2:13–14) despite the pariah status of these Roman collaborators. When the priests criticize the company Jesus keeps, Jesus retorts, "Who needs a doctor: the healthy or the sick?" (Mark 2:15–17). Similarly Jesus answers those who would challenge His Sabbath-keeping by proclaiming, "The Sabbath was made to serve us," (Mark 2:27). "What kind of action suits the Sabbath best? Doing good or doing evil? Helping people or leaving them helpless?" (Mark 3:4).

Unafraid to acknowledge Jesus' divine origin early on, Mark places particular emphasis on Jesus' exorcisms, always including Jesus' admonition to the demons that they refrain from identifying Him as the Son of God publicly (Mark 1:23–25; 3:11–12; 5:1–20). Though the scribes persist in accusing Jesus of serving the Devil even when He expels spirits from the possessed (Mark 3:22–26), not all the religious community disapproves of Jesus. Jairus, the leader of a local synagogue, beseeches Jesus for the healing of his ailing daughter. This request leads to a remarkable presentation of a story within a story. As a crowd follows Jesus to the home of the distraught father, a woman who has for years suffered from a hemorrhaging disorder touches Jesus' cloak. As inconspicuous as she tries to make herself, Jesus knows immediately that power has discharged from His body. He demands to know who has touched Him. She falls to His feet, trembling to tell her story. Jesus soothes her, "Daughter, you took a risk of faith, and now you're healed and whole" (Mark 5:34). In the time this diversion has taken, the household of Jairus intercepts the party coming to the daughter's aid with woe, for the young girl has died. But Jesus persists, "Don't listen to them;

---

[53] In Matthew, Levi is called Matthew (Matthew 9:9).

just trust me" (Mark 5:36). He goes to the bedside where the child lies still. Only Mark records Jesus' words in Aramaic, the common dialect of the day, "*Talitha koum*," meaning, "Little girl, get up" (Mark 5:41). As Elijah (1 Kings 17:17–23) and Elisha (2 Kings 4:32–35) had raised sons from the dead for their mothers, now Jesus brings back a father's daughter. The saving of both females highlights the potency of faith that expects help.

Despite the following Jesus engenders throughout His travels, He finds no respect in his hometown. Initially His neighbors seem to find wisdom in His teaching at their synagogue. "We had no idea he was this good!" (Mark 6:2), but quickly they turn skeptical. "He's just a carpenter[54]—Mary's boy. We've known him since he was a kid. We know his brothers, James, Justus, Jude, and Simon, and his sisters. Who does he think he is?" (Mark 6:3). Jesus expresses little surprise at this outcome. "A prophet has little honor in his hometown, among his relatives" (Mark 6:4). Because he could do no miracles in the face of such doubt, Jesus moves on quickly. He dispatches the Twelve to go out into the countryside in pairs to preach, to heal, and to cast out demons (Mark 6:6–13).

Yet even as the disciples follow Jesus, there are many things they cannot understand. After He teaches the parable of the sower, Jesus must take the Twelve aside in private to explain what the common folk miss (Mark 4:1–20). When a crowd is still gathered at the end of a day, the disciples urge Jesus to send the people away to get their evening meal, but Jesus wants to feed the five thousand. His apostles are incredulous, "Are you serious? You want us to go spend a fortune on food for their supper?" (Mark 6:37). Not only can Jesus still a storm (Mark 4:35–41), but He can also walk on water (Mark 6:45–52). Add to this Jesus' multiple healings of the lame (Mark 2:1–12), the deaf (Mark 7:31–37), and the blind (Mark 8:22–26). Then remember He confounds

---

[54] Matthew calls Jesus the carpenter's son (Matthew 13:55). Only Mark refers to Jesus as a carpenter.

the Pharisees and their preaching about Sabbath purity and ritual cleansing by remarking, "It's not what you swallow that pollutes your life ... It's what comes out of a person that pollutes: obscenities, lusts, thefts, murders, adulteries, greed" (Mark 7:1–23). No wonder the disciples' heads are spinning.

Still it is important to Jesus that He reveal Himself as clearly as possible to His inner circle of followers. Halfway through His gospel, Mark shows Jesus asking these loyal disciples to evaluate all that they have observed. "And you—what are you saying about me? Who am I?" (Mark 8:29). Although Peter answers that Jesus is the Messiah, it is evident that even Peter does not fully *get* Jesus' mission when he rejects the notion that Jesus will have to suffer and be killed (Mark 8:31–32). After the transfiguration (Mark 9:2–8), Mark revisits the gap in the disciples' comprehension with a detailed account of the demon-possessed child whom the apostles cannot cure. All the Synoptics register Jesus' initial frustration with this "unbelieving generation" (Mark 9:19 NIV), but in Mark's telling, Jesus has a full conversation with the father of the boy. Patiently He listens to the father's sad tale—how the son has been beset with episodes of convulsions and foaming at the mouth since childhood. However, when the father finishes his discourse with the plea that's humbly framed, "If you can do anything—" Jesus again takes offense. "If? There are no 'ifs' among believers. Anything can happen." No sooner were the words out of his mouth than the father cried, "Then I believe. Help me with my doubts!" (Mark 9:22–24). Mark's solitary preservation of the father's words about faith mixed with doubt provides hope to all who struggle to believe.

When Mark's gospel follows Jesus' entry into Jerusalem, the narrative is generally more streamlined than Matthew's. On Sunday Jesus enters the city on the colt of a donkey that no one has yet ridden (Mark 11:1–7) and enjoys an enthusiastic reception. Lodging outside the city, Jesus makes forays into Jerusalem every day in order to preach in the temple. While He's in Jerusalem, Jesus rattles the cages of the temple authorities by throwing out the temple moneylenders who have made God's Holy Place a "den of robbers" (Mark 11:17 NIV, compare to Jeremiah 7:11). Jesus continues by telling a parable about some wicked tenants to whom a man has entrusted his vineyard. Periodically the owner (God) has sent servants (the prophets) to collect the proceeds of the vineyard's harvest, but each time the farmhands (Israel/the leaders of Israel) have abused the servants, progressing eventually to murdering them. Finally the owner thinks to appeal to the conscience of his workers and sends his son to collect what belongs to the father. "Surely they will respect my son" (Mark 12:6). But the result is the opposite—the son is killed with the idea that somehow the tenants will inherit the property in his place. And what will the owner do then? "He'll assign the care of the vineyard to others" (Mark 12:9). No wonder the priests felt threatened enough to plot Jesus' death.

Though the Pharisees found much to criticize in Jesus, the Sadducees also had their bones to pick with Him. In typical rabbinic fashion they attempt to trip Him up on the subject of the resurrection, a point of contention between themselves and the Pharisees. Citing the Old Testament tradition of levirate marriage (taking us back to the story of Judah's sons in Genesis 38 and more obliquely to Ruth), they propose the following hypothesis: If seven brothers each in succession marries the same woman and none sires a child on her, which of them will count as her husband when all are raised after death? Jesus has a ready answer,

> You're way off base, and here's why: One, you don't know your Bibles; two, you don't know how God works. After the dead are raised up, we're past the marriage business ... Regarding the dead ... (remember) how God at the bush said to Moses, "I am—not I was—the God of Abraham, the

> God of Isaac, and the God of Jacob"? The living God is the God of the *living*, not the dead. (Mark 12:24–27)

Having parried the attempts of the Jerusalem religious elite to get the better of Him, Jesus closes His Judean teaching with warnings about the end times and the need for the faithful to remain watchful. God's people must think of themselves as having charge of the Master's home. "You have no idea when the homeowner is returning, whether evening, midnight, cockcrow, or morning. You don't want him showing up unannounced, with you asleep on the job" (Mark 13:35–36).

From here Mark guides us straight to Jesus' passion. A woman anoints Jesus with expensive ointment (Mark 14:3), and despite the apostles' criticism, Jesus defends her, promising that her deed of love will always be remembered wherever the gospel is preached (Mark 14:4–9). Again this incident incites Judas to go straight to the chief priests to betray Jesus (Mark 14:10–11). Notice, however, that Mark's Judas does not initiate a request for payment as Matthew's does. In the same mysterious manner He used to lead the disciples to the colt He rode into Jerusalem, Jesus now gives intricate instructions about the procurement of a room where His troop can celebrate the Passover beginning Thursday evening (Mark 14:12–16). As they gather for the holiday supper, Jesus unsettles them all with His prediction of betrayal, but Mark does not add the particular exchange with Judas that we find in Matthew (Mark 14:17–21, compare to Matthew 26:25). In the course of the meal, Jesus initiates the ceremony of Communion (Mark 14:22–25).

As they retire to the Mount of Olives for the evening, Jesus again remarks that all the disciples will fail him—even Peter, despite his protests (Mark 14:26–31). Jesus endures the agony of facing His impending suffering and death without comfort from His companions, and He readies Himself for His ordeal with intense prayer, even calling God *Abba*, the Aramaic familiar form of father (Mark 14:32–42). With His traitor's kiss, Judas identifies Jesus to the ambushing temple priests and their guards. In the skirmish that ensues, where the disciples flee, Mark alone adds an odd detail. "A young man was following along. All he had on was a bedsheet. Some of the men grabbed him but he got away, running off naked" (14:51-52). Some scholars have wondered whether our author, John Mark, might have been this young man.

The temple police proceed to drag Jesus before the Sanhedrin. At the trial's climax, with the chief priest's question, "Are you the Messiah, the Son of the Blessed?" (Mark 14:61), Mark records Jesus breaking the silence He has held throughout the interrogation with a clear, "I am" (Mark 14:62). To speak these words instead of giving a simple yes serves to intensify the crime of blasphemy for the priests because it echoes back to Exodus 3:14 and God's reply when Moses asks for God's name and tells them, "I Am has sent … you."

Next Jesus stands before Pilate on the new charges of claiming to be king of the Jews. As in Matthew, Mark's Pilate finds Jesus' lack of defense startling (Mark 15:4–5), but Mark makes no concerted attempt to present Pilate as unnerved at the prospect of sentencing Jesus to crucifixion. We do learn more information about Barabbas here. "There was one prisoner called Barabbas, locked up with the insurrectionists who had committed murder during the uprising against Rome" (Mark 15:7). This added detail certainly intensifies the irony of crucifying Jesus as a potential usurper of Roman authority while releasing a prisoner already guilty of political murder.

In the main, Matthew has followed Mark's depiction of Jesus' flogging, the mocking of the soldiers (though Mark claims the robe they put on Jesus was purple, not scarlet), the crucifixion itself, and Jesus' last words. But while Matthew takes time to include details about the Roman guards stationed at Jesus' tomb, Mark gives us a better understanding of why the women return to Jesus' burial site on Sunday after the Sabbath. "Mary

Magdalene, Mary the mother of James, and Salome brought spices so they could embalm him" (Mark 16:1). When we come to the story of the resurrection, however, Mark's gospel offers us a scholarship puzzle. The earliest manuscripts include only the verses up to Mark 16:8, making for an abrupt finish of the story. The women approaching the sepulcher encounter a young man dressed in white who shows them the empty tomb and urges them to share the news that Jesus has been raised from the dead with the disciples (Mark 16:5–7). Then "trembling and bewildered, the women went out and fled from the tomb. They said nothing to anyone, because they were afraid" (Mark 16:8). The extended version includes Jesus' actual appearances to Mary Magdalene (Mark 16:9–11) and two followers walking in the countryside who encounter Jesus "in a different form" (Mark 16:12–13). That the apostles fail to believe these first witnesses earns them a scolding when Jesus finally visits the Eleven. Like Matthew's, this longer version concludes with Jesus' exhortation to His followers to go into the world and "announce the Message of God's good news to one and all" (Mark 16:15). Unlike the other gospels, this addendum goes on to sharpen the point by saying, "Whoever believes and is baptized is saved; whoever refuses to believe is damned" (Mark 16:16), and it includes as signs of faith the ability to handle snakes and drink poison (Mark 16:18).

Abrupt as it is, the shorter closing gets my vote for consistency with the character of the gospel as a whole. The images in the longer ending seem borrowed from the other gospels. The shorter version does not deny Jesus' resurrection in any way but rather makes the point of its substance by describing the intense fear the women feel in seeing God's messenger.

Taken as a whole, Mark's testimony bears the force of passion as it races through Jesus' activities and sayings. Jesus is the Messiah and the Son of God. It is essential that the word get out about all that He has done to change the relationship between

God and humankind. Mark's mission is to tell as many as possible about Jesus as quickly as possible. Fear is our natural reaction to confronting the divine. The fear of the women who first learn of Jesus' resurrection confirms the reality of their experience but also demonstrates how high the stakes are. Afraid or not, believers must deliver the message. God has visited earth, forgiven our sins, died, and yet still lives. This is "the good news of Jesus Christ" (Mark 1:1).

Luke

When we turn to the Gospel according to Luke, we notice a difference in narrative style from the start. Although Luke does not mention his own name within the work, we can easily surmise from the companion volume, Acts, that our author is Luke, the "fellow worker" (Philemon 24) whom Paul identifies as "the doctor" (Colossians 4:14). We presume that Luke was born Gentile and received a fairly classical Greek education. At some point he also became fully versed in the Hebrew Scriptures, probably in the form of the Septuagint. His Greek is more sophisticated than that of the other gospel writers, and for those of us imbued in Western culture, his manner of storytelling will seem more familiar. His rendition reads more smoothly with greater transitions from one topic to another. He even opens with a preface and speaks to us in the first person in order to vouchsafe the depth of his research. "Starting from the story's beginning, I have investigated all the reports in close detail, [including those] handed down by the original eyewitnesses" (Luke 1:2). He highlights the purpose of his work: "I decided to write it all out for you, most honorable Theophilus, so that you can know beyond a shadow of a doubt the reliability of what you were taught" (Luke 1:4). From this opening we learn that Luke himself is a believer who has been active in spreading the word about Jesus but that he is not himself an eyewitness.

Although we don't know who Theophilus[55] is, we gather that he is someone who has expressed interest in Christianity. In this way the preface serves not only Luke's original intended recipient but also provides a meaningful introduction to all readers of this gospel.

In Luke 1:5, Luke begins his story in earnest. Note that he does not start just with Jesus' birth but goes before that to the birth of John the Baptist. John the Baptist has a miraculous birth story (Luke 1:5–25) that parallels Isaac's in Genesis 17–21. With this account, Luke keeps John the Baptist in character with those in the Old Testament whose unusual births signaled their special roles in God's purposes. But the tale also makes an excellent transition into Jesus' birth narrative. While the once-barren Elizabeth is still in the seclusion of her pregnancy, the same angel who visited her husband, Zechariah, while he was performing his priestly duties in the temple's Holy of Holies now appears to Elizabeth's much younger cousin, Mary. Mary lives in Nazareth in Galilee, a good journey north of Jerusalem. She and Joseph are betrothed but have not yet married when the angel Gabriel announces to her that she will bear a son to be named Jesus, "the Son of the Most High" (Luke 1:26:32 NIV). While Jewish women had been wondering for centuries whose would be the lucky womb that would cradle the Messiah, no one would have expected the privilege to come in such a way as this. Mary protests, "But how? I've never slept with a man" (Luke 1:34). Gabriel explains that the Holy Spirit will beget the child, but the angel quickly adds this buffer to the shock: "And did you know that your cousin Elizabeth conceived a son, old as she is? ... Nothing, you see, is impossible for God" (Luke 1:35–37, compare to Genesis 18:14). Mary embraces God's calling but also leaves immediately to visit Elizabeth and receive her support. What a relief it must have been to have Elizabeth's welcome include the

---

[55] The name Theophilus literally means "God's friend."

announcement that the child in the older woman's womb leapt at the sound of the virgin's greeting. Luke makes poetry of Mary's response. The song (Luke 1:46–55), known for centuries now as the "Magnificat," Latin for "[my soul] magnifies [the Lord]," parallels the Song of Hannah (1 Samuel 2:1–10), where Hannah praises God for allowing her to give birth to Samuel, a child she gives back to God for divine service. Mary stays the next three months with Elizabeth (Luke 1:56). Although Luke only provides Mary's viewpoint, we can see how his account dovetails with Matthew's presentation of Joseph's side of the story.

When we get to the actual birth of Jesus, Luke adds another important component to his presentation. He dates the event in terms of Roman history. The account of the Roman census also explains how Jesus comes to be born in Bethlehem in accordance with the Scriptures. Even Rome submits to God's plans for the Messiah, however unwittingly. While Matthew has the wealthy, gift-bearing wise men greeting the Christ child, Luke provides us with the image of the local working-class shepherds searching out Mary's baby in an animal manger after hearing an angelic choir. Again he keeps tabs on Mary's perspective. "But Mary treasured up these things and pondered them in her heart" (Luke 2:19 NIV).

For the benefit of his Gentile audience, Luke explains that Jesus is circumcised on the eighth day and given the name that Gabriel had pronounced to Mary (Luke 2:21). Consistent with his ongoing attention to all segments of society, Luke chronicles that Jesus receives the blessing of both a male (Simeon) and female (Anna) prophet. Likewise Simeon and Anna acknowledge that Jesus is indeed the Messiah who is bringing the "redemption of Jerusalem" (Luke 2:38 NIV) as well as "a God-revealing light to the non-Jewish nations" (Luke 2:32). Next Luke even adds the only story we have of Jesus as a young man. On the way home from a Passover trip to Jerusalem, Mary and Joseph discover that their twelve-year-old has stayed behind in the temple, asking questions of the teachers. Jesus responds to his mother's scolding, "Didn't you know I had to be here dealing with the things of my Father?" (Luke 2:49). Chastened, "his mother held these things dearly, deep within herself" (Luke 2:51).

In line with Matthew and Mark, Luke next takes up the story of the adult John the Baptist again, dating his ministry with Roman history markers. Here he also introduces the cast of characters who will feature in Jesus' passion (Luke 3:1–2). After he finishes his discussion of John with the prophet's baptism of Jesus, Luke goes on to offer another genealogy of Jesus' ancestry. Unlike Matthew, who stresses Jesus' Jewish heritage by beginning with Abraham and working forward, Luke traces Jesus' lineage backward through His "publicly perceived father," Joseph, all the way to Adam (Luke 3:37). Clearly Luke seeks to remind his audience that Jesus is the Savior of all peoples.

This same shift of focus from Jewish to universal is apparent in Luke's presentation of Jesus' temptation. The essential story runs the same as Matthew's version, but Luke reverses the final two satanic tests. For a Jew the ultimate affront to God lies in claiming to be king, but Luke sets as his climax what is more likely to impress Gentile onlookers—the temptation to prove the Messiah's divine favor by having Jesus throw Himself from the top of the temple, knowing angels will come to save Him. Here Luke adds that the Devil departs but only "temporarily, lying in wait for another opportunity" (Luke 4:13). As we go forward, we will see Luke expanding the role of Satan in comparison to Matthew and Mark.

While both Mark and Matthew show Jesus launching His ministry by teaching in the synagogue, Luke makes a dramatic event of this preaching by placing it in Jesus' home synagogue. Careful to explain the Jewish worship custom of having the reader unroll the scroll, Luke proceeds to quote the particular verses that Jesus is called upon to read, specifically Isaiah 61:1–2, which is the last of the Servant Songs. After He returns the scroll to the attendant, Jesus sits down (the teaching position in which you stand to read and sit to teach) and announces, "You've just heard Scripture make history. It came true just now in this place" (Luke 4:21). At first His neighbors applaud His eloquence. But Jesus takes the teaching in an unexpected direction. He cites the tales of Elijah (1 Kings 17:1–5) and Elisha (2 Kings 5:1–14), who perform saving acts for people outside of Israel. Now the crowd is unnerved and even seeks to kill Jesus, but Jesus slips away and takes up His ministry still in Galilee but away from his hometown of Nazareth.

Next Luke takes up Jesus' recruitment of disciples. Here he highlights the call to Simon, who will become Peter, with an expanded story. Jesus has used Simon's boat to give Himself some distance from the press of the crowd as He has been speaking. At the conclusion of that teaching session Jesus urges Simon to take the boat out for some more fishing. Usually fishing is done at night, and Simon has already come home that morning with an empty catch. But at Jesus' word he agrees to give it a try. The nets fill so quickly and so fully that Simon has to wave to his partners to come help bring in the huge haul. On shore once more he falls on his knees before Jesus and says, "Master, leave. I'm a sinner and can't handle this holiness" (Luke 5:8). Jesus reassures him, "There is nothing to fear. From now on you'll be fishing for men and women" (Luke 5:10).

Just as he has done with Mark as a reference, Luke brings his own take on the separate material he holds in common with Matthew. Matthew has Jesus delivering the Sermon on the Mount. Luke's Jesus delivers many of the same ideas speaking on the plain (Luke 6:20–49). Both tell the story of the centurion—the Roman officer that seeks Jesus out to save his paralyzed servant. Matthew focuses on the Roman's respect for authority. As a man with soldiers who report to him, he has confidence that when he gives an order, it will be executed. He trusts that Jesus has the same authority in His ability to heal and therefore tells Jesus that He doesn't need to come. "I am not worthy to have you come under my roof"[56] (Matthew 8:8). He tells Jesus that He can say the word and the servant would be well. Luke augments the story with some interesting details. First his centurion never counts himself good enough even to speak directly to Jesus but sends messengers—friends of his who are leaders in the Jewish community—to convey his request. These friends vouch for the Roman pointing out to Jesus that he is God-fearing. "He deserves this. He loves our people. He even built our meeting place [synagogue]" (Luke 7:4–5). Jesus not only heals the slave but registers His amazement. "I've yet to come across this simple trust anywhere in Israel, the very people who are supposed to know about God and how he works" (Luke 7:9).

While Luke develops ideas presented in Matthew and Mark further, he also expands the cast of characters Jesus encounters to include people on the margins of society. Although all the gospels place women at the scene of the cross and as the first witnesses of the resurrection, Luke makes a point to incorporate women throughout his gospel. As we've already seen, he begins with Elizabeth and Mary in primary roles. In addition, he lifts the story of the woman who anoints Jesus with expensive perfume from the beginning of the passion narrative and places it in a new context. Simon, a Pharisee, has invited Jesus for a meal. While they recline together at the table, a woman who is identifiable as a prostitute and who has heard that Jesus is in the house insists on making her way to His side. With her tears she washes Jesus' feet, dries them with her hair, and anoints them with her costly oil. Jesus knows what Simon is saying to himself—that surely a real prophet would know what this woman is and refuse to be contaminated by her sin. But Jesus converts what Simon finds embarrassing into an object lesson that puts the shoe on the other foot. First he tells of two debtors. One owes much more than the other, but neither can pay up. When their moneylender

---

[56] Jews did not visit the homes of Gentiles, as it would make them *unclean*.

forgives both debts, which of the two will be the more grateful? With the answer obvious, Jesus, still speaking to Simon, turns to the woman weeping at his feet and says, "Do you see this woman? I came to your home; you provided no water for my feet, but she rained tears on [them] ... She was forgiven many, many sins, and so she is very, very grateful" (Luke 7:44–47).

Continuing in Luke 8:2–3, Luke credits a number of women with an important role in Jesus' ministry that the other witnesses never mention. Naming several women Jesus has cured of various afflictions, he notes that these "along with many others ... used their considerable means to provide for [Jesus and His] company." Likewise Luke counts two sisters—Mary and Martha—as two of Jesus' very close friends (Luke 10:38–42).

Beyond this attention to women, Luke's Jesus uses images of the poor and outcast to demonstrate how God values what the world typically shuns. We have already noted his choice to highlight the shepherds as witnesses of Jesus' birth. Likewise consider the parables of the rich man and the poor one named Lazarus (Luke 16:19–31), the contrasting prayers of the Pharisee and the tax collector (Luke 18:9–14), and the transformation story of Zacchaeus (Luke 19:1–9).

In addition to these many of Jesus' most famous parables are unique to Luke. The teaching of the Good Samaritan (Luke 10:29–37) stands as an extension of Jesus' encounter with a scholar who asks how he can gain eternal life (compare Matthew 19:16–19 and Mark 10:17–19). Luke poses Jesus as a good rabbi who begins by countering with a question the man can answer for himself, "What's written in God's Law?" (Luke 10:26). The straightforward answer has been preached for centuries in Judaism—love God and love your neighbor as yourself. But Luke's legal expert attempts to challenge the teaching by asking, "How would you define *neighbor*?" (Luke 10:29). This is the perfect set up for the Samaritan parable. Likewise Luke builds on the story comparing God to the shepherd who leaves ninety-nine sheep in order to find one that is lost (Matthew 18:12–14) with two additional *lost* teachings. In Luke 15:8–10, he offers a female example with the tale of the woman who turns her house upside down in search of a lost coin. Then Luke finishes the lost theme with the story known as the parable of the prodigal son (Luke 15:11–32).

Another feature Luke incorporates into his gospel is a generally larger role for Satan. Ironically, however, Luke omits the first place after the temptation story where Matthew and Mark make a point of mentioning Satan, namely Jesus' response, "Get behind me, Satan!" (Matthew 16:23 and Mark 8:33 NIV) to Peter's protest that the Messiah should have to suffer. Going forward, although Luke parallels Matthew and Mark when he tells of Jesus sending the Twelve out into the countryside to preach and cast out demons, he goes beyond the other Synoptics by relating the story of a second commissioning of seventy disciples (Luke 10:1–20). While this extra story has many details in common with the Matthew and Mark accounts, it includes a comment about the Devil we don't find anywhere else. When the seventy return from their assignment jubilant and amazed that even the demons obeyed them, Jesus replies, "I know. I saw Satan fall, a bolt of lightning out of the sky" (Luke 10:18). The import of this comment leaves plenty of room for interpretation. Does it refer to the Devil's temporary impotence while Jesus resides on earth (thus accounting for the disciples' easy successes)? Has Jesus had a vision of what His future act of dying for human sin will ultimately do to Satan's earthly influence? In any event it paves the way for Luke to bring the Devil into the picture when we get to Judas' betrayal. Having already used the story about anointing with oil earlier in his narrative, Luke explains Judas' decision to turn Jesus over to the high priests by simply saying, "Satan entered Judas" (Luke 22:3). While He was preparing His disciples for His imminent arrest, Matthew and Mark's Jesus quotes from Zechariah 13:7, where the striking of the Lord's Shepherd scatters the sheep (Matthew 26:31 and Mark 14:27).

In Luke, however, Jesus explains to Simon Peter, "Satan has tried his best to separate all of you from me, like chaff from wheat. Simon, I've prayed for you in particular that you not give in or give out" (Luke 22:31–32).

As we come to the narrative of Jesus' passion, we find Luke works harder to build our sympathy for Jesus than Matthew and Mark do. Where these evangelists stress Jesus' awareness of Judas' impending betrayal at the opening of the Last Supper (Matthew 26:21; Mark 14:18), Luke begins his scene in the upper room with Jesus declaring, "You've no idea how much I have looked forward to eating this Passover meal with you before I enter my time of suffering" (Luke 22:15). When Jesus prays in the garden of Gethsemane, Luke places an angel at His side, strengthening Him. Jesus prays so intently that "sweat, wrung from him like drops of blood, poured off his face" (Luke 22:44). Next when Jesus appears before Pilate, Luke inflates the charges against Him. "We found this man undermining our law and order, forbidding taxes to be paid to Caesar, setting himself up as a Messiah-King" (Luke 23:2). Moreover, Jesus must also appear before Herod, who happens to be in town from Galilee. Herod remembers Jesus as a local phenomenon from months before in the wake of his execution of John the Baptist (Luke 9:9)[57] but finds his interrogation of Jesus disappointing since Jesus refuses to answer any of his questions (Luke 23:8–12). Quickly the Galilean tetrarch passes Jesus back to Pilate, who, feeling backed into a corner, acquiesces to the crowd demanding Jesus' crucifixion (Luke 23:13–25).

Luke records women weeping in the crowd (Luke 23:28) as Jesus makes His way to the site of His execution. While Matthew and Mark quote an anguished prisoner intoning Psalm 22 once mounted on the cross, Luke's Jesus prays, "Father, forgive them;

---

[57]   Unlike Matthew and Mark, who detail the story behind John the Baptist's beheading, Luke merely alludes to the murder. He frames Herod's interest in Jesus stemming from wondering who this new Jewish holy man was.

they don't know what they're doing" (Luke 23:34). Luke confirms Matthew and Mark's accounts that two criminals were also crucified on either side of Jesus that day, but only he relates the argument between the two. The first hears the jeers of the crowd and grouses, "Some Messiah you are! Save yourself! Save us!" (Luke 23:39). But the other criminal scolds him, "Have you no fear of God? ... We deserve this, but not him—he did nothing to deserve this" (Luke 23:40–41). Then turning to Jesus, he says, "Jesus, remember me when you enter your kingdom" (Luke 23:42). Jesus replies, "Don't worry, I will. Today you will join me in paradise" (Luke 23:43). Finally at the end of His ordeal Jesus loudly pronounces, "Father, I place my life in your hands!" (23:46) and breathes no more. The centurion's response, "This man was innocent!" (Luke 23:47), while less theological than Matthew and Mark's claim, "This has to be the Son of God!" (Matthew 27:54; Mark 15:39), still resounds with genuineness in Luke's telling.

In the same way Luke draws us in to his vision of the resurrection. He begins with the angel visiting the women who have discovered the empty tomb in parallel to Matthew and Mark. But after this he adds a new story—the two walking on the road to Emmaus (also see Mark 16:12). Jesus joins these two men who are in very low spirits and do not recognize him. As they talk together, the unknown Jesus first encourages them to unburden their troubles. Once He hears their dilemma, however, He chides them for not knowing their Bibles well enough. "Why can't you simply believe all that the prophets said ... that the Messiah had to suffer and only then enter into his glory?" (Luke 24:25–26). Jesus proceeds to go through the whole of the Hebrew Scriptures, explaining the many references to Himself. The two invite Him to sup with them and finally recognize Him as Jesus as He breaks the bread for the meal. Instantly Jesus disappears. The friends treasure the moment. "Didn't we feel on fire ... as he opened up the Scriptures to us?" (Luke 24:32). Immediately they are off to share their experience with the Eleven in Jerusalem.

Once there, Jesus appears again, urging them all to touch Him and eat with Him so that they may be convinced that He is no ghost (Luke 24:37–43). Jesus spends some time teaching them. When He must ascend to heaven, He leaves them with two sets of instructions. The first parallels the Great Commission of Matthew. "You can see now how it is written that the Messiah suffers, rises from the dead on the third day, and then a total life-change through the forgiveness of sins is proclaimed in his name to all nations—starting from here, from Jerusalem! You're the first to hear and see it. You're the witnesses" (Luke 24:46–48). But the second is new. "I am sending what my Father promised to you, so stay here in the city until he arrives, until you're equipped with power from on high" (Luke 24:49). Luke here alludes to the arrival of the Holy Spirit, which will serve as the opening of his second volume, Acts.

With Luke's gospel our story of Jesus takes on new nuances. It is Luke's style to write with more focus on the human-interest elements of the events surrounding Jesus' ministry. Matthew gives preeminence to the notion that humans need to value and extend compassion to the least members of our society by positioning Jesus' parable of the sheep and goats as the Master's last teaching before His passion (Matthew 25:31–46). Luke imbues his entire gospel with the same message. And it is Luke who then leads us to the next step. How do the people who have witnessed Jesus' life, death, and resurrection respond to His call to tell others the story? Luke stands ready to reveal what happens next, but we still need to hear from John first.

John

We assume the Gospel according to John is the work of the apostle John,[58] son of Zebedee, whom Mark calls, together with

---

[58] Scholars debate the authorship of all the Gospels, but the discussion of that issue is beyond the scope of this book.

his brother James, the "Sons of Thunder" (Mark 3:17). Since it is likely that this gospel is the one written latest, it is possible that John has seen the work of the other evangelists and writes his testimony in order to offer a new perspective, filling in with stories that do not appear elsewhere and at the same time not reviewing events that the other gospels have already covered. Tradition holds that John was perhaps the only apostle who lived into his old age, and we presume that he writes with that long outlook about what he has witnessed as an apostle of Jesus. Although, like the other evangelists, John never narrates his own name into his work, he seems to refer to himself a half dozen times as the *disciple Jesus loved.*[59] Such a moniker seems at best immodest, implying almost that the other followers were not marked with the same strength of Jesus' affection. On the other hand, perhaps it is the only way John can think to demonstrate the deep bond he feels with the Master. In any event, this is but another piece for you, the reader, to decide for yourself.

Recall that when we began with Genesis, we discovered two creation stories—the first told from God's perspective and the second from the human viewpoint. With the Gospels we find a reversal of this order. The three Synoptic Gospels ground their stories about Jesus within the human sphere, using the backdrop of everyday life to highlight how extraordinary Jesus is. But John zooms out from the human scope and begins his gospel by describing Jesus' entrance into the world of human affairs as the striking of a chord that reverberates throughout the universe. Consciously borrowing from the wording of Genesis 1, John explains that Jesus is the very *word* by which God *spoke* the creation into being. Just as God's first word is *light*, Jesus' life brings *light* to humans.

John goes on to speak about the man named John. He assumes you know he means John the Baptist. Conveying the

---

[59] Again there is no scholarly consensus for the assumption that John is referring to himself as the disciple Jesus loved.

same message as the Synoptics that John is the forerunner of the Messiah, John the evangelist explains John the Baptist's role in terms of these themes of life and light. "John was not himself the Light; he was there to show the way to the Light" (John 1:8). Next he demonstrates that he writes from a time when the separation between Christianity and Judaism has become more distinct. "He [the one John is describing whom we know as Jesus] came to his own people, but they didn't want him" (John 1:11). From here John delivers some consummate theology—the first spelling out of what the other gospels have been pointing to about Jesus. Jesus is the Word made flesh, the incarnation of God living among us (John 1:14). Anyone who believes in him becomes the child of God—not by biological descent but by an act of God's Spirit (John 1:12–13). "For the law was given through Moses; grace and truth came through Jesus Christ. No one has ever seen God," but Jesus, who stands at the Father's side, has made God understandable to us (John 1:17–18) by living beside us as a human. With all this heavy-duty philosophy we can easily see why the canon could never have placed this gospel first. But now that we have read the Synoptics, we find that John, with his high-concept style, expresses ideas that we can begin to work into the Jesus framework that Matthew, Mark, and Luke have helped us to construct.

From the vaunted heights of the prologue (John 1:1–18), John proceeds to lead us through his gospel. He maintains his elevated viewpoint as a baseline and merely *touches down to earth* here and there to connect his elements of Jesus' story to his overarching thesis that Jesus is God come in human flesh to walk among us. His John the Baptist never wonders if indeed Jesus is the one (compare Matthew 11:1–19 and Luke 7:18–35). Instead when he sees Jesus, he declares, "Here he is, God's Passover Lamb! He forgives the sins of the world!" (John 1:29). Here John shows us how, by this later date, the church has come to understand Jesus' mission in terms of Old Testament imagery. Jesus is the Lamb without blemish (Exodus 12:5) that is sacrificed at Passover. The original Passover Lamb's blood smeared on the doorposts of the Hebrews' homes (Exodus 12:7; 13) saved them from the death visited upon Egypt. Jesus' blood prevents the death promised because of our sins. Likewise John's telling makes no climax out of unveiling Jesus as the Messiah. Instead of having Simon Peter breaking ground with this revelation well into Jesus' ministry, John has Simon's brother, Andrew, declaring, "We've found the Messiah" (John 1:41) after listening to Jesus' teaching for one day.

In contrast to Matthew, whose gospel leads us through a series of Old Testament prophecy fulfillments so that we must deduce that Jesus is the Messiah, John begins with that premise and seeks to show how everything Jesus did in His time on earth corroborates that He is the Christ. To this end, John not only offers us several completely new narratives but also describes Jesus' activities as signs of His divine calling. Immediately following his explanation of Jesus' recruitment of disciples, John takes us to a wedding in Cana, where, at His mother's suggestion, Jesus turns water into wine (John 2:1–11). Leaving out the tale of Jesus' raising of Jairus' daughter (Matthew 9:18–26; Mark 5:22–43; Luke 8:41-56), John caps off his discussion of Jesus' ministry with the dramatic story of Jesus reviving Lazarus, brother of good friends Mary and Martha, after he has lain four days in his grave (John 11:1–44).

John is not particularly mindful of the chronology of Jesus' ministry. He tells of Jesus moving back and forth between Galilee and Jerusalem on several occasions. The Synoptics use the tale of Jesus throwing the moneylenders out of the temple (Matthew 21:12–13; Mark 11:15–19; Luke 19:45–48) as the inciting incident leading to the passion. John places the episode early on in his gospel during his first recording of Jesus celebrating the Passover in Jerusalem (John 2:14–16) so that his disciples remember it as a messianic sign—a reference to Psalm 69:9. "Zeal for your house consumes me" (John 2:17). The Jerusalem Jews ask for

Jesus' credentials that give Him authority in the temple. Jesus answers cryptically, "Tear down this Temple and in three days I'll put it back together" (John 2:19). Knowing the whole of Jesus' story, we can comprehend how the disciples later interpreted this statement as a metaphor. The temple is actually Jesus' body, which will be resurrected on the third day after His death (John 2:21–22). The original audience takes it literally and dismisses it (John 2:20).

In the book of John, people are always being stymied by understanding what Jesus says literally when it is meant to be figurative. Jesus' encounter with Nicodemus, a Pharisee serving on the Sanhedrin, makes another case in point. Nicodemus seeks Jesus out in secret (meaning that he visits Him at night as detailed in John 3:2) because Jesus has impressed him with His teachings and miracles. When Jesus replies, "No one can see the kingdom of God unless he is born again" (John 3:3 NIV), Nicodemus wonders how a man could enter a second time to his mother's womb (John 3:4). On another occasion while He is stopping in a Samaritan village, Jesus amazes the woman at the town well with His claim to offer her "living water," water that will quench her thirst forever (John 4:13–14). Jesus must stun her with intimate knowledge of her marital status before she perceives that He is at least a prophet (John 4:19) and not merely someone with a bottomless water pitcher. Yet John uses these incidents as object lessons to make his point that metaphor and analogy are keys to understanding what Christ offers. God's forgiveness of sins grants us a fresh start comparable to rebirth while God's loving grace sustains us spiritually the way water does physically.

Consider next how John utilizes other stories to comment further on sin. The Synoptics all tell of Jesus healing a lame man with the pronouncement that his sins are forgiven joined to the command to pick up his mat and walk (Matthew 9:2–8; Mark 2:3–12; Luke 5:17–26). John frames this healing in a slightly new context, specifically a cripple waiting at a Jerusalem gate and hoping to receive relief from a pool reputed to remedy paralysis (John 5:2–3). Jesus asks the man point blank, "Do you want to get well?" (John 5:6). The man answers that he has no one to lift him into the pool for its cure. Jesus replies immediately, "Get up, take your bedroll, start walking" (John 5:8), proving He has no need for a magical pool to enact miracles. But later Jesus warns the man, "You're well! Don't return to a sinning life or something worse may happen" (John 5:14).

In somewhat the same vein comes one of John's more famous episodes—the woman caught in the act of adultery (John 7:53–8:11).[60] On one level this story resembles those in the Synoptics where the Jewish scribes and teachers try to trap Jesus into speaking against the Law. (For example, they ask, "Is it right to pay Caesar's taxes?") Here the religious authorities bring a woman to Jesus who has flagrantly violated her marriage vows. Given that the Torah punishment for adultery is stoning, they ask Jesus, "What do you say?" (John 8:5). Jesus confounds them with this: "If any one of you is without sin, let him be the first to throw a stone" (John 8:7 NIV). Next Jesus tells the woman He does not condemn her—as the only one without sin He could—but He does caution her to stop her sinning (John 8:11). God's willingness to forgive sins stems not merely from generous compassion but primarily so that humans can change direction and earnestly begin to pursue God's ways.

On another occasion John again employs a familiar healing story to add a different nuance to his examination of sin. The Synoptics feature Jesus giving sight to a blind man in Matthew 20:29–34, Mark 10:46–52, and Luke 18:35–43. In John after Jesus cures a man's blindness, His disciples quiz their Master, "Rabbi, who sinned: this man or his parents, causing him to

---

[60] Like the last twelve verses of Mark, the story of the woman caught in adultery is not included in the earliest manuscripts. I include it because its character is so consistent with John's style and thematic development.

be born blind?" (John 9:2). But Jesus explains contrary to their expectations, "Neither this man nor his parents sinned, but this happened so that the work of God might be displayed in his life" (John 9:3 NIV). Like Job's dilemma, sometimes there is no correlation between suffering and wrongdoing. But where humans have violated God's ways, Jesus demonstrates God's preference for healing over punishment as the way to ameliorate the ravages of sin.

Beyond these one-on-one examples, John also offers a series of Jesus' teachings that shed further light on God's role in redeeming human sinfulness. He expands on the story about the feeding of the five thousand (John 6:1–13)—another tale he revamps from the Synoptics—in order to introduce a series of identity statements that Jesus makes using the formula "I Am." This use of the quasi "name of God" serves to develop the Father-Son relationship between God and Jesus.

The day after feeding the masses, Jesus reflects on the incident with His disciples. They have already made the connection between Jesus sharing of the loaves and Moses providing manna in the desert (John 6:31). But Jesus corrects them, "The real significance of that Scripture is not that Moses gave you bread from heaven but that my Father is right now offering you bread from heaven, the *real* bread ... *I am* the Bread of Life. The person who aligns with me hungers no more and thirsts no more, ever" (John 6:32, 35). John goes on to extrapolate from here the meaning of the Lord's Supper (even though he does not include the ceremony in his discussion of the Last Supper). "Only insofar as you eat and drink flesh and blood, the flesh and blood of the Son of Man, do you have life within you ... By eating my flesh and drinking my blood you enter into me and I into you ... Whoever eats this bread will live always" (John 6:53–58).

John continues with Jesus' *I Am* statements. With "*I am* the light of the world" (John 8:12 NIV) Jesus connects Himself first to God's creation (Genesis 1:3) but also to Isaiah's servant, who is the "light to the Gentiles" (Isaiah 42:6). Jesus ties Himself to the God-as-Shepherd imagery of the Old Testament with the following: "*I am* the good shepherd [who] lays down his life for the sheep" (John 10:11). Typically these assertions draw the outrage of the religious establishment as blasphemy. When the Jewish authorities protest that the *one and only God* is their Father, Jesus counters, "If God was your father, you would love me, for I came from God" (John 8:42). Jesus talks about offering eternal life (John 8:51), but His opponents rebut that Abraham and the prophets all died. "Who do you think you are!" (John 8:53). Here Jesus answers with no-holds-barred fervor, "Believe me, I AM WHO I AM long before Abraham was anything" (John 8:58). Those against Jesus always try to kill Him, but in John's gospel, all these preliminary attempts fail because Jesus' time has not yet come.

It is not until Jesus raises Lazarus from the dead (John 11:1–44) that the threats against His life become real. His final *I Am* claim in His active ministry, "*I am*, right now, Resurrection and Life. The one who believes in me, even though he or she dies, will live" (John 11:25), causes the Sanhedrin to meet in desperation. "What do we do now? This man keeps on doing things, creating God-signs. If we let him go on, pretty soon everyone will be believing in him and the Romans will come and remove what little power and privilege we still have" (John 11:47–48). The high priest, Caiaphas, speaks pragmatically and prophetically at once. "Can't you see that it's to our advantage that one man dies for the people rather than the whole nation be destroyed?" (John 11:50). From this point on the Jewish authorities actively begin to plot Jesus' death, setting out a welcome mat to informers (John 11:57).

John introduces the passion narrative with the woman who anoints Jesus' feet with oil, but for John, this is no random woman from the streets. Instead it is the Mary whose brother Jesus has recently raised. This family of friends is entertaining

Jesus some six days before the Passover. For John, the criticism of the anointing comes solely from Judas who, John claims, is "even then getting ready to betray [Jesus]" (John 12:4). Judas complains of the expense, but John maintains that he is simply a thief already embezzling funds from the common purse of Jesus' followers (John 12:5–6). Jesus counters Judas' disapproval with His praise that Mary is preparing Him for His burial (John 12:7).

The next day John sets as Jesus' triumphal entry into Jerusalem. John doesn't reference any special instructions given to the disciples for the retrieval of the donkey colt. He simply notes that Jesus finds a donkey, and later the disciples recognize that this was a fulfillment of Scripture (Zechariah 9:9). John attributes the size of the crowd to the buzz that had grown surrounding the raising of Lazarus (John 12:17–18). As we will see, John omits the garden of Gethsemane scene, but he inserts an interlude of Jesus' anguish on the heels of this warm welcome. "The time has come for the Son of Man to be glorified … Right now I am storm-tossed. And what am I going to say? 'Father, get me out of this'? No, this is why I came in the first place. I'll say, 'Father, put your glory on display'" (John 12:23; 27–28).

The Synoptics feature Jesus' week in Jerusalem waiting for the Passover as filled with daily visits into the city with Jesus teaching within the temple. John sees Jesus going into hiding during this time (John 12:36). In the same vein John replaces the stirring speeches Jesus makes in public in the other gospels with a far more detailed discourse spoken only to the attendees of the Last Supper. Although along with the garden of Gethsemane, he leaves out the disciples' initiation into the rite of the Eucharist, John makes important additions to our picture of Jesus' last night with His friends. John prefaces his treatment of the evening by noting the depth of Jesus' love for His companions (John 13:1). Jesus demonstrates that love by washing His followers' feet, making it an object lesson echoing the teaching that anyone who would be great must be a servant (Matthew 20:25–28; Mark 10:42–45; Luke 22:25–27). "If I, the Master and Teacher, washed your feet, you must now wash each other's feet" (John 13:14). Next he shows Jesus' distress over His foreknowledge of betrayal (John 13:21), and, like Luke, asserts that it is Satan entering Judas that incites the disciple's treachery (John 13:2; 27).

After He dismisses Judas, Jesus launches His farewell address in earnest. He has warned His disciples recently that the Son of Man must die in order to be glorified (John 12:24), but now He makes it clear that His death is imminent (John 13:33). Therefore, He is giving them a new commandment that will guide and cover them through all the ordeals to come. "In the same way I loved you, you love one another. This is how everyone will recognize that you are my disciples—when they see the love you have for each other" (John 13:34–35). Next He reminds His friends that He is leaving them to go to the Father. They cannot come now, but they will come later. They already know the way to the place where He is going (John 14:4). When Thomas voices the disciples' confusion (John 14:5), Jesus explains, "*I am* the Road, also the Truth, also the Life. No one gets to the Father apart from me" (John 14:6). Now Philip speaks the group concern, "Master, show us the Father; then we'll be content" (John 14:8). Jesus tempers His frustration with patience. "You've been with me all this time, Philip, and still don't understand? To see me is to see the Father" (John 14:9).

Jesus returns to His instructions: "The person who trusts me will not only do what I'm doing but even greater things, because I, on my way to the Father, am giving you the same work that I've been doing" (John 14:12). "If you love me, show it by doing what I've told you" (John 14:15). (You can compare this to the parable of the sheep and goats in Matthew 25:31–46.) Knowing that His disciples feel lost at the idea that He will leave them, Jesus offers His promise of comfort, "I'm telling you these things while I'm still living with you. The Friend, the Holy Spirit whom the Father will send at my request, will make everything plain to you. He will remind you of all the things I have told you" (John 14:25–26). Reiterating the "root command: Love one another" (John 15:17), Jesus calls His followers to testify on His behalf (John 15:27), knowing that they will suffer persecution (John 16:1–4). He compares their current sadness to the travail of a woman in labor where great pain converts to tremendous joy when the baby is born (John 16:21). Likewise Jesus notes, "In this godless world you will continue to experience difficulties. But take heart! I've conquered the world" (John 16:33).

John finishes Jesus' final speech with a long prayer. First Jesus seeks God's blessing for Himself as He faces the death He knows awaits. "I glorified you on earth by completing down to the last detail what you assigned me to do. And now, Father, glorify me with your very own splendor" (John 17:4–5). For His disciples He pleads, "Holy Father, guard them as they pursue this life ... so they can be one heart and mind as we are one heart and mind" (John 17:11). In closing Jesus adds, "I'm praying not only for them [the disciples] but also for all those who believe in me because of them and their witness about me" (John 17:20). This farewell discourse, which only John includes, opens a window for us into how the early church began to interpret Jesus' identity as God's Messiah, who came to accomplish so much more than Israel expected.

When we come to the story of Jesus' arrest, trial, and sentencing, we find John overlapping heavily with the synoptic narratives. John adds a tender moment to the crucifixion scene where he has Jesus looking down from the cross at His own mother (John 19:25). Seeing John standing nearby, He instructs the *disciple he loved* to take her into his own home as his mother and to become the son to her that she is presently losing (John 19:26–27). With this addition to the crucifixion landscape we now realize that John has ended up being the only apostle to witness his Master's dying.

John also records two further remarks that Jesus makes from the cross. Toward the end of His ordeal, Jesus speaks of His thirst. The soldiers oblige him with a sponge soaked in wine vinegar. Like Matthew and Mark, John sees this as a fulfillment of Scripture, probably Psalm 69:21. Then John remembers Jesus' last words as, "It is finished" (John 19:30 NIV). With these words John makes it clear that Jesus' death has accomplished something specific in terms of the mission God has assigned Him. Here John's gospel zeroes in on the connection between Jesus' dying and His having committed no sin and humans receiving forgiveness for their sins.

Like Luke, John's gospel has several resurrection stories. When Jesus appears to Mary Magdalene, she does not recognize Him until He says her name (John 20:14–17), echoing the same phenomenon of delayed identification the two on the road to Emmaus experienced in Luke 24:31. In John, Jesus appears next to all of His disciples save Thomas (John 20:19–23). Thomas refuses to believe their claims about the Master's resurrection until "I put my fingers in the nail holes" (John 20:25). Jesus accommodates his doubts, and Thomas declares, "My Master! My God!" (John 20:28). At this point John appears to write a conclusion to his gospel, essentially saying, "I haven't been able to tell you all the Jesus stories, but I have written what I have 'so that you will believe that Jesus is the Messiah'" (John 20:30–31). But then he can't resist sharing two more resurrection appearances, this time both dealing with Peter. The first of these (John 21:1–14) amounts to a reprise of the episode of the miraculous catch of fish that Luke uses to describe Jesus' original recruitment of Peter (Luke 5:5–11). In the second story, where Jesus asks Peter three times "Do you love me?" (John 21:15-17), we see Peter reaffirming his commitment to Jesus after his three denials on the night of Jesus' arrest. Finally John closes his testimony for good, vouching for its trustworthiness and reminding his readers, "There are so many other things Jesus did. If they were all written down ... I can't imagine a world big enough to hold such a library of books" (John 21:25).

John begins his gospel from the perspective of knowing Jesus not merely as Messiah but as God incarnate. Because of this vantage point, he can present all Jesus' activities, teachings, and miracles through the lens of hindsight. These were the things that Jesus did among us because He was God. The Synoptics employ hindsight as well because each writes from the belief that Jesus is the Son of God. Matthew, Mark, and Luke, however, feel a greater need to ready their audience. They aim to build to an understanding first that Jesus is the promised Messiah—the Savior of Israel—and next that the Messiah's mission is larger than Israel anticipated. Jesus has not come to restore Israel to her former political glory. Jesus has come to restore the children of Israel, God's beloved children, to their proper relationship with their Father in heaven. What is more, the Creator considers the Gentiles God's children as well. Jesus has come to free these too. John uses his gospel to gather up the clues planted in the narratives of Matthew, Mark, and Luke in order to spell out clearly that Jesus, the Son of God, present with the Father at the creation, came to earth as a human born of a human mother for one purpose—to repair what had gone wrong between humans and their maker. Jesus is the solution to God's dilemma of love for humans and hatred of sin.

Remember how the prophets pointed to the previously outlined dilemma. Remember how Isaiah hinted that the Deity's plan involved something *new, something you'd never guess* (Isaiah 48:6). Remember how Jeremiah testified that someday God would make a brand-new covenant with Israel, a covenant that God would "write on their hearts" (Jeremiah 31:33). Together the Gospels show us how Jesus not only carried all the small markers expected for the Messiah (see appendix 5) but also how He addressed this primary concern of reconciling humans to the Lord. The early Christians looked back now to Isaiah's suffering servant, saying, "We thought ... God was punishing him for his own failures. But it was our sins ... that ripped and tore and crushed him ... He took the punishment and that made us whole. Through his bruises we get healed ... God piled all our sins ... on him" (Isaiah 53:4–6), and saw Jesus' death on the cross. While it remains something of a mystery how and why the excruciating death of an innocent man brings about the atonement of sinners, the idea that it works roots deeply into Israel's history. The ancient Mosaic cult with its ritual of blood sacrifices—the blood of a perfect lamb required for Passover—provides a precise metaphor to explain what Jesus is *finishing* when He dies on the cross. The now-recycled Passover imagery works to explain why such a sacrifice includes eternal life. The blood of the lamb prevents death. Jesus' resurrection is the proof. Those who repent their sins receive God's forgiveness and are reconciled to the Father through the death of the Son. To them is given eternal life. This indeed is the gospel to which all four evangelists testify.

Now we can see why it is taken four witnesses to provide a proper introduction to Jesus of Nazareth. While all evangelists quote heavily from the Old Testament, Matthew achieves the best transition in our reading from the Old to the New Testament. Matthew reminds us how much Jesus had in common with Moses so that we can begin to see how big the Messiah's role will be. Jesus will uphold the Torah by teaching its spirit rather than the letter of the Law that had bogged down the religious leaders of His day. Mark goes on to reinforce the vision Matthew has painted by imbuing it with a sense of urgency. The world has changed because of Jesus, and people need to know what the change means. Luke adds to Matthew and Mark's perspective by widening the scope of Jesus' compassion to include people society has forgotten. While he shares material with both Matthew and Mark, Luke also overlaps significantly with John, especially in his treatment of the role of Satan. Finally John presents us with the big picture—the huge gash sin has ripped into the fabric of the universe, starting symbolically with the garden of Eden. This ruinous tear has at last (and for all time) been woven back into a whole cloth. God, who created the world as *good* out of the Deity's holiness, has paved the way out of sin by doing for humans what they could not do for themselves. Because Jesus is God, He can live as a human without sin, making Himself the only sacrifice pure enough to obliterate the gravitational downdraft away from God that sin creates in humans. By offering the means for humans to be reconciled to God, Jesus allows the simultaneous satisfaction of both God's holiness and love for humans—all without violating human free will.

So shouldn't this be the end of the story. Jesus is the answer to God's dilemma. What else is there to say? It turns out there is still plenty to talk about. There is the mandate Jesus has given His disciples to spread the Word among all the peoples of the earth. There is the promise told by both Luke and John that God will send the Holy Spirit to help believers evangelize. And there is still the problem of understanding how to live a life challenged by the example of Jesus and changed by the grace of forgiveness. It's time to see what the Bible continues to say about these new issues.

Chapter 10

Does It Really Say That Christians Should Spread the Gospel All over the Globe?

At first glance Matthew's gospel ending with the Great Commission seems to have already given away the answer to this chapter's question. Jesus has instructed His followers to "go and make disciples of all nations" (Matthew 28:19 NIV). In our modern times, looking back on the two-thousand-year history of the Christian church, we wonder how literally we should understand this commandment. Doesn't proselytizing involve disrespecting the beliefs of others? Doesn't it equate to acting as though we know better than our fellows of different faiths? As we take a look at the book of Acts, you may be surprised to discover that the first Christians also shrank from taking Christ literally regarding this call to evangelism. Their first thought was to witness only to the Jews in all nations. Only gradually did it become clear that Gentiles, all the peoples who are not Jewish, (in other words, everyone else in the world) were also candidates for salvation.

In this chapter we will follow the continued chronicling of Luke as he unfolds the story of how Jesus' disciples, who were scattered and shattered by His crucifixion and then rallied and renewed by His resurrection, step out in faith to tell others about Christ. As we go, we will observe a series of *aha* moments as the early church slowly comes to comprehend the scope, subtlety, and cost of her mission. We will discover how the first believers meet the challenge of explaining who Jesus was and is and what His sacrifice means first to their fellow Jews and then increasingly to Gentiles. In turn, this will lead us to understand how and why Christianity ends up splitting off from its Jewish roots, even while it still embraces the Hebrew Scriptures.

The early church called her initial preachers of the gospel evangelists,[61] literally meaning "messengers of the good news." For those of us living in the Western world in the twenty-first century, Christianity seems more old hat than good news. While nonbelievers generally grant Jesus as one in a line of great moral teachers[62] spread throughout the world's geography and history, the gospel writers would not recognize Jesus in this description. For them His teaching could not be separated from His identity as Messiah/Christ and Son of God. But even if outsiders to the faith count Jesus as good, there is much that is not good associated with Christianity. Consider the sorry legacy of the institution of Christianity—that long list of horrors including the Crusades, the Inquisition, the censoring of scientists, anti-Semitism, the African slave trade and European colonialism that spawned additional racial prejudice, and the denial of basic rights to women (in direct opposition to Jesus' treatment of them). Now contrast the prevailing negative stereotype of missionaries with the fact that Christians have founded so many of the world's hospitals and universities and led so many movements for social reform (e.g., the abolition of slavery). This mixed bag that comprises the public perception of Christianity gives us a pretty good picture of how hard it is to preach the gospel of Jesus

---

[61] Christianity is but one of three major religions that actively seek new converts. Many forms of Islam and Buddhism also proselytize. Judaism and Hinduism tend not to.

[62] Twentieth century Christian apologist C. S. Lewis characterized Jesus this way: "There are only three possibilities. Jesus was a liar, a lunatic, or the Lord. He left us no room to consider him merely a great teacher" (Lewis, *Mere Christianity*, p. 52).

Christ and get it right. Given that Jesus is clear about the call to share His story with others, perhaps the better question for this chapter revolves around how. How can believers speak the message of God's truth while they live within its parameters of God's righteousness? The early Christians were the first to face this dilemma. It's time to look at what the Bible says about how the gospel of Jesus begins to be spread.

Acts

Luke's second volume, known as Acts, or the Acts of the Apostles, opens with an introduction similar to the first, one addressed again to Theophilus. It makes a great transition if read directly from the end of Luke's gospel. Reading it as we are doing after John's gospel, we begin by hearing another Jesus story just as John acknowledged there were more to be heard. At the cross when Jesus commits His spirit into God's hands (Luke 23:46), John records his last thought, "It is finished" (John 19:30 NIV). What is finished, of course, is the bridge of connection between humans and God. Like any new highway, however, it is its use that justifies its cost. People must meet and get to know Jesus in order to travel this new pathway to God. Therefore, though the infrastructure of salvation is complete, God's work of reconciliation with humans continues with both new urgency (because Christ's promised return will mark the end of the world) and revitalizing fervor (because the forgiveness of sins will enable humans to walk in God's intended ways). The risen Jesus appears after His death to many witnesses and for forty days teaches and encourages His disciples in what He wants them to do (Acts 1:3). Now that the Son has done what only God could do, Jesus charges His disciples to do what humans can do, namely to proliferate the Word about God's visit to earth and forgiveness of individuals' sins. But even this commission will continue as collaboration with the divine. The believers must wait in Jerusalem for the promised baptism of the Holy Spirit (Acts 1:5). And here Luke gives us our first reality check. Those gathered with Jesus, listening to these instructions, ask, "Master, are you going to restore the kingdom to Israel now?" (Acts 1:6). It must have been discouraging for Jesus to confront such a complete lack of understanding in His followers. Despite all they had witnessed and learned from Jesus, they were still holding on to the grand vision of the Messiah as a conquering hero who would promote the nation of Israel to political greatness. Jesus is incredibly patient with His reply, "You don't get to know the time. ... What you'll get is the Holy Spirit [who will enable you] to be my witnesses in Jerusalem, all over Judea and Samaria, even to the ends of the world" (Acts 1:8). Neither does Luke let up in expressing these early disciples' cluelessness. He records that as they watch Jesus ascend to heaven, it takes two heaven-sent men in white robes to stir them into the action Jesus has bidden of them. "You Galileans!—why do you just stand there looking up at an empty sky?" (Acts 1:11).

In this way Luke begins to unfold the story of how Jesus' seemingly inept disciples transform into fervent preachers of the gospel, most dying, as tradition declares, in defense of the faith. The evangelist has also given us his outline for discussing this history in Jesus' parting words. The movement will begin in Jerusalem, extend to the Jewish lands of Judea and even Samaria, and eventually reach out among the Gentile nations.

Immediately after Jesus' ascension we find the disciples gathered in Jerusalem in an upper room, presumably where they have been meeting since the resurrection. Luke cites their number at about 120 committed men and women, including the eleven apostles as well as Mary, the mother of Jesus, and His brothers. Mostly they congregate in prayer (Acts 1:14–15). Peter emerges as the group spokesman, and his first order of business is to have those assembled select a new twelfth apostle to replace Judas.[63] Notice how he draws on Scripture to defend this action (Acts 1:20). Prayerfully the believers nominate two men and cast lots (as their ancient Hebrew forebears had done) in order to allow God to choose which should hold the office of apostle (Acts 1:24–26).

The disciples wait in Jerusalem for about ten days before the Holy Spirit arrives during the celebration of Pentecost.[64] While they observe this holy day, the followers of Jesus experience the baptism of the Spirit as a strong wind descending from heaven (Acts 2:2). Suddenly each believer receives the gift of speaking in one of various foreign languages that match up with those spoken by the Jewish pilgrims who have traveled from all over the Middle East and the Mediterranean to attend the festival at the temple. Inspired and enabled by the Holy Spirit, the Jesus followers begin to praise the mighty works of God in these new tongues. As the visiting Jews struggle to understand what is happening, Peter addresses the growing crowd. Again, grounding his sermon in Scripture, Peter quotes from Joel 2:28–32, "I will pour out my Spirit on every kind of people ... on those who serve me, men and women both ... and whoever calls out for help to me, God, will be saved" (Acts 2:17–21). From here Peter proceeds to explain the basic tenets of the faith. Jesus performed miracles and wonders that served as signs that God had sent Him. But even so, His own people betrayed Him to death on a cross. Yet God raised Him up as David predicted in Psalm 16:10 and to which Peter and the other disciples can testify as witnesses. Jesus is God's Messiah. The bottom line is this: "Change your life.

---

[63] Note the variant here in Acts 1:18 from Matthew's story of Judas' suicide (Matthew 27:5).

[64] Pentecost is the Greek name for the Hebrew "Feast of Weeks," which was to be celebrated the day after the seventh Sabbath after Passover, according to Leviticus 23:15–16, making fifty days between the two holidays. Since Jesus died at the beginning of Passover and spent forty days instructing His disciples, that left about ten days between the ascension and Pentecost.

Turn to God and be baptized ... in the name of Jesus Christ, so your sins are forgiven" (Acts 2:38).

Peter's sermon and the Spirit's gift of languages net about three thousand conversions (Acts 2:41) in one day. The new believers merge with the originals, making of themselves a community where all possessions are held in common and all members participate in daily temple worship. Every day more people join the ranks (Acts 2:41–47). The apostles offer instruction and prove able to perform wonders akin to those of Jesus. When a begging cripple asks Peter for money, Peter explains, "I don't have a nickel to my name, but what I do have, I give you: In the name of Jesus Christ of Nazareth, walk!" (Acts 3:6). The miraculous cure raises a commotion that Peter takes care to contain. "Why stare at us as if *our* power or piety made him walk?" (Acts 3:12). The credit belongs to God, who makes these marvels possible through Jesus, the Christ. In this second sermon Peter initially hits even harder on the guilt of God's people who betrayed Jesus to crucifixion (Acts 3:12–16), but he subsequently softens this blow by acknowledging his brothers' ignorance (as Jesus had done from the cross). Next Peter reviews the testimony of Moses, Samuel and the prophets, and Abraham to prove that indeed Jesus is the Messiah foretold in the Scriptures. All this teaching goes to urge his listeners to "change your ways! Turn to face God so he can wipe away your sins" (Acts 3:19).

Despite the influx of temple worshipers the Jesus followers have generated, the temple priests, particularly the Sadducees (who believe there is no life after death), cannot condone all this talk about the resurrection of Jesus. The temple guard arrest Peter and John after the healing of the lame beggar (Acts 4:1–3) and bring them before the Sanhedrin. The ruling elders grill the disciples, "Who put you in charge here? What business do you have doing this?" (Acts 4:7) Could Peter have asked for a better lead-in to preach his testimony? Luke records the amazement of the priests over the eloquence and confidence of these two uneducated laymen (Acts 4:13). Quickly they recognize themselves in a bind. How can they arrest Peter and John for healing someone? They try enjoining the disciples to stop their preaching about Jesus, but Peter rebuts that God's call carries more weight than any human religious authority (Acts 4:19).

Luke sums up the strong start to the evangelists' movement, "The whole congregation of believers were united as one—one heart, one mind! They didn't even claim ownership of their own possessions ... And so it turned out that not a person among them was needy" (Acts 4:32–34). But the honeymoon only lasts for a time. Eventually a couple lies about the proceeds of the sale of their property. While they declare that they are placing all their funds in the community pot, they actually lay aside some of their earnings. When Peter confronts the husband and wife with their falsehood, each one falls down dead. (He acknowledges that no one required them to give away all their money in Act 5:3–4.) This literally puts the fear of God into an otherwise "warm and fuzzy" society (Acts 5:11).

Nonetheless, new believers continue to flock to the regular meetings held on the temple porch (Acts 5:15), and the apostles heal the sick and the demon-possessed (Acts 5:16). The jealousy of the temple elite flares again, and they arrest the apostles. But their attempts to contain the movement fall flat when they discover the Jesus preachers claiming that an angel has released them from their otherwise secure prison cells (5:17–24). Most of the priests want to put the disciple leaders to death for their lack of submission to the Sanhedrin, but a cooler head does prevail. The leading authority in the Sanhedrin of the first century CE was the prominent Pharisee rabbi named Gamaliel. This grandson of the renowned Rabbi Hillel the Elder, who was famous for his negative iteration of the Golden Rule (see note 47 on p. 276), points out that this current movement could be just one in a stream of passing fads that easily die off on their own. Therefore, he says, "Hands off these men! ... If this program or this work is merely human, it will fall apart, but if it is of God, there is nothing you can do about it—and you better not be found fighting against God" (Acts 5:38–39). Gamaliel's argument carries the day. The apostles are released again after a flogging and also uselessly forbidden to speak in the name of Jesus. But the followers of Jesus leave rejoicing that they have had the honor of suffering for their Master's sake. The very men who deserted Jesus in the garden of Gethsemane now have tangible proof of their newfound valor.

The strength of the disciples' courage continues to be tested, however. As the numbers of converts increase, the community begins to factionalize. Although these early believers are all Jews, those native to Jerusalem and the Palestine environs who speak Aramaic (the Semitic dialect of the day and regional language of commerce) begin to clash with those from the Diaspora nations who speak Greek as their common tongue. These Hellenized Jews complain that their widows are being shortchanged in the food lines and petition the apostles to redress this wrong. The apostles' response shows they have attended to the advice Moses received from Jethro, his father-in-law, who cautioned Moses not to try to do everything himself (Exodus 18:13–21). Seven Greek-named men, known for their faith and good sense, are nominated to become the first deacons (Acts 6:3). For a while harmony is restored, and even some of the Jewish priests join the faith (Acts 6:7).

Eventually, however, the deacon leader Stephen falls afoul of another Jewish faction. Finding themselves unable to match Stephen's eloquence in debate, they seek to undermine his authority by accusing him of blasphemy within his Jesus preaching (Acts 6:11). Brought up before the Sanhedrin, Stephen defends himself against the charges by reviewing the history of Israel in order to prove that Jesus is indeed God's promised Messiah. His impassioned speech comes to a crescendo when he begins to vent his frustration against his opponents, "Your ancestors killed anyone who talked about the coming of the Just One. And you've kept up the family tradition … You had God's Law handed to you by angels—gift-wrapped!—and you squandered it!" (Acts 7:51–53). As the crowd begins to disintegrate into a mob, Stephen calls out that he sees heaven opening and the Son of Man standing by God's side (Acts 7:56), the same image Jesus predicts for Himself at His trial before the Sanhedrin (Matthew 26:64; Mark 14:62; Luke 22:69). Continuing the parallel with Jesus' death, Luke records Stephen forgiving his assailants as they stone him to death (Acts 7:59-60, compare to Luke 23:34). Next Luke closes the scene with a bit of foreshadowing by mentioning Saul as an approving witness of Stephen's murder (Acts 8:1).

The martyrdom of Stephen is a game changer, bringing a new sense of gravity to the decision to follow the Way, as the Jesus movement was coming to be called. Fear scatters all but the apostles throughout Judea and Samaria. The Jews who do not accept Jesus as the Messiah begin to push back against what Luke now calls the "church" (Acts 8:1). Saul's name emerges again as one of these Jews who wants to eradicate the Jesus sect. This zealous rabbi goes from house to house, rooting out Christ believers (Acts 8:3–4). But the faithful continue to preach the gospel. Philip, one of the original seven deacons, goes to Samaria where many become disciples. One convert, however, a charlatan named Simon the Magician, seems to believe but shows his true colors when Peter and John arrive to bless and baptize the new community and Simon offers to buy access to their source of power. Peter rebukes him strongly but still urges him to repent as a solution. Although Simon asks Peter for prayer on his behalf, Luke does not reveal what becomes of the one-time wizard's faith (Acts 8:9–24). As the church becomes bigger, it becomes more difficult to distinguish the truly committed from those simply jumping on the latest bandwagon. Despite the Simon setback, Philip continues in his ministry, leaving Samaria for Jerusalem when an angel directs him to go south on the road to Gaza. There he encounters an Ethiopian eunuch who has recently left from worshiping in Jerusalem. The Ethiopian official has been reading Isaiah 53, the Suffering Servant, and invites Philip to explain its meaning. Once Philip tells him about Jesus, the Ethiopian believes and asks to be baptized (Acts 8:26–38). The gospel is spreading further from its hub in Jerusalem.

Next Luke returns to Saul in order to tell the story that explains his relevance to the business of sharing the gospel. On the road to Damascus, again there to hunt down the Christ disciples, Saul hears Jesus' voice and is struck blind. Per the voice's instructions, Saul has his companions lead him into the city, where he fasts for three days. Meanwhile, Jesus contacts a disciple named Ananias and bids him to go to Saul to heal his blindness. Already knowing Saul's reputation, Ananias questions the Lord, but in the end he is obedient to the request and thereby witnesses Saul's baptism. But now Saul finds himself somewhat between a rock and a hard place. He has to sneak out of Damascus to avoid being killed by his former Jewish allies who decry his conversion. Yet when he arrives in Jerusalem, the disciples there do not trust him. Thus rebuffed, Saul retreats to his hometown of Tarsus (Acts 9:1–30).

With Saul on the back burner for the moment, Luke observes that the church next enjoys a period of peace. Returning to Peter's ministry, Luke finds him continuing to visit new communities of believers around the countryside. Miracles persist in propelling the success of Peter's evangelizing. Peter remedies afflictions in parallel to the manner of Jesus' healing. First he commands a paralyzed man to get up from his bed (Acts 9:33-35), and soon after that he raises a beloved seamstress from death (Acts 9:36-42). As always, however, he pronounces his cures "in the name of Jesus Christ," never claiming any personal powers but only those abilities that the Holy Spirit confers upon him. These latest miracles seem to confirm Peter's preeminence as the heir to

Jesus' ministry, much as Joshua's administration of God's parting of the Jordan accredited him as the proper leader to follow Moses, the prophet whom God used to part the Red Sea. (You can compare Joshua 3 to another parting of the Jordan with a similar prophetic transfer from Elijah to Elisha in 2 Kings 2:8, 13–14.)

But Peter's life is about to undergo a surprising course adjustment. Up to now, even as the gospel has extended far from Judea, the evangelizing has been exclusively among Jews. To this point, Luke turns to the story of a man named Cornelius, a Roman centurion stationed in the Italian regiment in Caesarea. He is known as *God-fearing* because he reveres the teaching and practices of Judaism but is not a circumcised convert. One afternoon as Cornelius is praying (per Jewish custom), an angel speaks to him, telling him to send men to Joppa to seek out Peter. Meanwhile, Peter also[65] experiences a vision. Three times a sheet containing kosher and non-kosher animals has descended from the sky, and God has told Peter to eat. Peter has protested that he would never eat non-kosher food, but the Lord has reminded him, "If God says it's okay, it's okay" (Acts 10:15). While Peter reflects on God's words, a voice stirs him to greet the people at the door and to go with them. Peter obeys and travels to Cornelius' home, which is already a big exception to the Jewish practice of keeping clear of the contamination of Gentile dwellings.[66] In due course he baptizes Cornelius and his whole household and witnesses them receive the Holy Spirit. Peter is quick to realize the necessary conclusion from his experience. God means to bring the gospel not merely to the Jews but to everyone in the world. It is interesting to pause here to consider what Peter thought he was saying when he quoted the passage from Joel at

---

[65] Just like Saul's conversion story, where Saul and Ananias receive interlocking messages from God, Cornelius and Peter's divine mandates support each other and confirm the hand of God in their outcomes.

[66] Compare the story of Jesus healing the centurion's servant in Matthew 8:5–13 and Luke 7:1–10.

Pentecost. Joel quotes God saying, "I will pour out my Spirit on every kind of people" (Joel 2:28). At Pentecost, surrounded by Diaspora-scattered Jews from every nation, Peter interprets this reading to mean "every kind of Jew." After the Cornelius incident he has no choice but to interpret the passage in its plainest sense, meaning "every kind of people in the world." But how will the other Jewish Christ believers understand this?

Luke explains that the news of this encounter with the "uncircumcised" reaches Jerusalem quickly and initially the church there is aghast at Peter's behavior (Acts 11:1–3). Once Peter delivers his testimony about his vision from God and his witnessing of the Holy Spirit in the household of Cornelius, the community of believers seems to embrace with joy the idea that "God has granted even the Gentiles repentance unto life" (Acts 11:18 NIV). Meanwhile, surprising reports arrive from some of the believers who have retreated from Jerusalem in the wake of Stephen's murder. Those who began preaching only to Jews have found the gospel taking root among the Greek Gentiles, apparently acting without knowledge of Peter's revelation (Acts 11:19–21). Was this the Holy Spirit again providing another set of interlocking revelations? The Jerusalem church resolves that this activity requires investigation and dispatches Barnabas (one of the first disciples to sell all his possessions after Pentecost as told in Acts 4:36-37) to Antioch, a prominent Roman city in the northeastern corner of the Mediterranean (in current-day Syria). Barnabas confirms the reality of the Gentiles' commitment to Christ for the central church in Jerusalem. Inspired by this new ministry, he seeks out Saul in Tarsus, and together they spend a year building the church in Antioch. Luke notes that it is in Antioch that believers are first dubbed "Christians" (Acts 11:26).

Barnabas is the first disciple to give Saul a chance, trusting him to be a legitimate believer. When a prophet within the Antioch community predicts a famine for Jerusalem, the church there raises funds to aid the home church and sends the offering forth in the hands of Barnabas and Saul. But will the disciples in Jerusalem accept help from Saul and from a church of uncircumcised believers?

Luke leaves this question hanging while he brings us up to date on what is going on in Jerusalem. By now the current King Herod[67] has begun to persecute the church. First putting the apostle James to death by the sword, he also arrests Peter. The night before the apostle leader's scheduled trial, an angel releases Peter from his heavily guarded cell, and the church community rejoices in his deliverance (Acts 12:3–17). Eventually Herod dies. Barnabas and Saul complete their mission without incident and return to Antioch with John Mark,[68] the son of Mary, an early disciple who housed gatherings of believers (Acts 12:12).

Back in Antioch, the Holy Spirit leads the Christian community to commission Barnabas and Saul for missionary work, thus launching the ministry of Saul, who shortly becomes Paul[69] (Acts 13:9) hereafter. At this juncture Luke devotes himself almost entirely to Paul's expansive work in preaching the gospel, an undertaking that will take him on three separate journeys all around the eastern Mediterranean and ultimately land him under house arrest in Rome.

On the first of these expeditions Barnabas and John Mark set out with Paul from Antioch and travel to the island of Cyprus and then go to the city of Perga on the southern coast of modern-day Turkey, where John abandons the mission for undisclosed reasons (Acts 13:13). Luke outlines for us Paul's initial mode of operation by recording the apostle's speech in the synagogue at

---

[67] Rome accorded a tetrarchy that included Judea and Samaria to Herod Agrippa I, grandson of Herod the Great and nephew of Herod Antipas (who beheaded John the Baptist). See appendix 4.

[68] John Mark is possibly the author of the gospel of Mark.

[69] Saul is a Jewish name; Paul is more Roman/Greek. Paul may have Hellenized his name in order to attract believers, but it was not uncommon in that day to have separate names for separate ethnic communities.

Pisidian Antioch in Galatia (modern Turkey). Invited to speak by the synagogue's president, Paul addresses the gathering, "Men of Israel and you Gentiles who worship God" (Acts 13:16 NIV). Right away we learn that in this part of the world it is common for Gentiles to attend Jewish worship services. Next Paul reviews the history of Israel from the Patriarchs, the Exodus, the period of the judges up to the kingship of David (Acts 13:17–22). The mention of David allows him to segue to Jesus as the promised son of David who would come as the Savior of Israel. Paul explains that though Jesus came to His own people, the rulers of Judaism did not recognize Him as the Messiah, and they also arranged to have Him condemned and executed. Nonetheless, this was all in fulfillment of the Scriptures that Paul goes on to quote from various Old Testament sources (Acts 13:33-47). After the sermon many Gentiles flock to belief, particularly warmed by the final quote from one of Isaiah's servant songs, claiming the Servant would be "a light for the Gentiles" (Acts 13:47 NIV quoting Isaiah 49:6). Soon enough the Jews take offense at Paul's message and drive Paul and Barnabas out of the city.

The following becomes a pattern for Paul. When he enters a city, he heads first to the synagogue and delivers the gospel until he gets thrown out. Unfortunately being given the boot is not the only response Paul and Barnabas have to guard against. In Lystra, Paul heals a lame man, and suddenly the people mistake him and Barnabas for the Greek gods Hermes and Zeus. Doing his best to dispel this misperception, Paul ends up beaten nearly to death (Acts 14:3–20). Yet at the next stop, Derbe, the gospel flourishes. Here, however, Paul and Barnabas elect to retrace their steps back to Antioch, visiting the fledgling Christian communities they started on the way in and helping to choose leaders that could sustain these new churches.

As more and more Gentiles become believers, the issue of circumcision heats up again at the church in Jerusalem. The Jerusalem Christians, all also lifelong Jews, feel that their call to Christ has made them even more aware of the pull of the Mosaic Jewish tradition. James, the brother of Jesus, who has emerged as the head of the Jerusalem church, calls a conference for the leaders of the faith to sort out the conflict. Peter speaks eloquently in favor of lifting the circumcision requirement from Gentile converts (Acts 15:7–11). Barnabas and Paul[70] report on the miracles and wonders they have witnessed as they have spread the Word among the Gentiles (Acts 15:12). James then quotes from Amos 9:11–12 to remind the assembly that including the Gentiles has always been part of God's plan. But he does suggest conference members draft a letter to the churches in Gentile lands to limit the possible abuses of this relaxation of Mosaic commands. The chief points of the Jerusalem council's edict are as follows:

1. Circumcision is not required for Gentile Christians.
2. Gentile Christians must abstain from food sacrificed to idols.
3. They must forgo food offensive to Jewish Christians (meat with blood in it, etc.).
4. And they must abstain from sexual immorality.[71]

The council next charges Paul and Barnabas, accompanied by Judas and Silas, to deliver the dictum to the church at Antioch. The members there receive it as an encouragement to their efforts to share the gospel (Acts 15:30–32).

Despite this progress, when Paul decides to return to his missionary travels, he and Barnabas have a falling out over John Mark, whom Paul no longer wants to include in their work. While Barnabas and Mark head back to Cyprus, Paul enlists

---

[70] Note how Luke gives Barnabas top billing only in this Jerusalem setting, indicating that the Jerusalem Christians have still not fully accepted Paul.

[71] In general Gentile societies were liberal in their sexual mores, especially in comparison to Jews.

the aid of Silas and embarks inland back to the city of Lystra, where he recruits Timothy to join him. Timothy's mother is a Jewish Christian, but because his father was Greek, Timothy is uncircumcised. Ironically after he has been arguing forcefully against requiring circumcision for Greeks, Paul goes ahead and circumcises Timothy so that they might still have a level of acceptance among Jews (Acts 16:1–3). Another member added to this party during this second journey is our author, Luke, who announces himself merely by changing from *they* to *we* (Acts 16:10).

On this trip when Paul finds the Spirit blocking his planned route through Asia Minor, he heads across the Aegean for the seaside towns of Macedonia. In Philippi, an earthquake presents Paul and Silas with a miraculous opportunity to escape from prison in parallel to Peter's experience (Acts 12:6–10), but in this case Paul and Silas elect not to flee. Instead they minister to the jailer who would have killed himself for fear of the repercussions of losing charge of the captives. Through Paul's compassion, the jailer and his family become Christians (Acts 16:25–34). The next day, the magistrates are willing to release Paul and Silas quietly, but Paul argues on the basis of his Roman citizenship that they require an official escort out of prison to acknowledge the court's wrongful treatment, specifically their public flogging without a trial (Acts 16:37–39).

As the band of evangelists proceeds south along the Greek peninsula, Paul continues his practice of beginning his ministry in the synagogues. More often now the Jews try to run them out of town after they hear their message and note the number of converts they garner. When Paul sails to Athens, however, he changes his strategy. The Athens of Paul's day is still a university town filled with all kinds of philosophers as well as a wide variety of idol worship. The marketplace serves as a venue for any man who wishes to speak his mind or engage in public debate. After he talks privately with a number of Athenians,

Paul raises his voice in the town center. Thinking about all the different idols, he begins his sermon, "It is plain to see that you Athenians take your religion seriously. When I arrived here the other day, I was fascinated with all the shrines[72] I came across. And then I found one inscribed, TO THE GOD NOBODY KNOWS" (Acts 17:22–23). From this entry point he proposes to introduce his audience to this God—the God who happens to be the Creator of the whole world, including humans. Since we are the Deity's offspring, "it doesn't make a lot of sense to think we could hire a sculptor to chisel a god out of stone for *us*, does it?" (17:29). Thus, for a community unschooled in the history of Israel, Paul finds a new way to talk about humans' need for forgiveness from a credible savior.

Paul rounds out his second missionary journey with a year and a half of ministry in the city of Corinth. There he stays with Priscilla and Aquila, Jewish believers recently expelled from Rome.[73] In time Paul makes significant inroads into the Jewish community, notably the conversion of a synagogue president named Crispus, which draw that establishment's wrath. While he is fending off threats from this Jewish quarter, Paul receives an encouraging vision from the Lord, "Don't let anyone intimidate or silence you. No matter what happens, I'm with you and no one is going to be able to hurt you" (Acts 18:9–10). The revelation proves true when the Roman proconsul, Gallio, refuses to use imperial might to censor Paul on the Jews' behalf (Acts 18:12–16). [74]

---

[72] Paul thinks of these shrines as idols in Acts 17:16 but refrains from using the politically loaded term in his sermon.

[73] Extra-biblical historical sources support Luke's reference here to the expulsion of Jews from Rome at some point during the reign of Roman Emperor Claudius (41-54 CE).

[74] Luke's mention of proconsul Gallio here helps with the dating of Paul's time in Corinth. Extra-biblical sources verify that Gallio served Rome in Corinth in 51 CE.

After he returns to Antioch by way of Ephesus and Caesarea, Paul regroups to prepare for his third missionary journey. Having previously preached a single sermon in Ephesus, he determines to revisit the city and ends up spending two or more years nurturing the Christian community there. His tenure in that city ends when a disgruntled shrine maker incites a riot against Paul as the man who is diminishing his business (Acts 19:23–27). Once affairs in Ephesus return to normal, Paul embarks for Macedonia, where he resides for three months (Acts 20:3). At this point, however, Paul feels the Holy Spirit urging him to get to Jerusalem in time for Pentecost (Acts 20:16). In his travels along the coastline of Asia Minor en route to the Holy City, numerous friends and prophets warn him against entering Jerusalem, fearful for his safety. But Paul is resolute. "I feel compelled to go to Jerusalem ... [even though] the Holy Spirit has let me know repeatedly and clearly that there are hard times and imprisonment ahead" (Acts 20:22–23). Sure that he will never get to visit these churches again, Paul leaves each community with a farewell address, giving encouragement and expressing his steadfast love for the believers. Luke even has him quoting what is for us a new Jesus saying, "It is more blessed to give than receive" (Acts 20:35 NIV).

Once in Jerusalem, Paul and his company meet with James, Jesus' brother and the head of the Jerusalem church. James relates how the local Jewish Christians have become such sticklers for the Mosaic law, including circumcision, despite the edict by the Jerusalem council issued years before. James suggests that Paul perform a ritual purification act to demonstrate that he is still Jewish. Paul agrees, but even before the seven days of purification finish, some of the distrusting stir up a riot against Paul on the false accusation that he had brought Gentiles into the temple (Acts 21:27–29). Rescued by Roman soldiers trying to quell the uproar, Paul asks permission to address the crowd. At first he commands their attention by presenting his rather sterling Jewish pedigree, "I am a good Jew, born in Tarsus ... but educated here in Jerusalem under the exacting eye of Rabbi Gamaliel,[75] thoroughly instructed in our religious traditions. And I've always been passionately on God's side, just as you are now" (Acts 22:3). But as he unfolds the story of his conversion on the road to Damascus, including meeting the risen Jesus and ending with the Lord's call to him to minister to the Gentiles despite his strong Jewish credentials, the mob turns on him (Acts 22:4–21). Immediately the commanding centurion collects Paul and hauls him off to the army barracks. This time Paul's Roman citizenship saves him from a flogging (Acts 22:22–29).

Having convinced the Roman authorities that the day's uprising was a religious matter and not political, Paul again switches strategies to face his next opponent—the Sanhedrin. Here he puts his knowledge of the Jewish council's political structure to good use. When called upon to defend himself, he claims his persecution results from his being a Pharisee (a believer in resurrection), not a Sadducee. This splits the Sanhedrin into its own factions and prompts the centurion to take Paul away again, fearing for this Roman citizen's safety (Acts 22:30–23:10).

That night back in the Roman army barracks, Paul receives another heartening word from the Lord that as good a witness he has been in Jerusalem, he will also be in Rome (Acts 23:11). This boost of confidence serves to sustain Paul through a series of trials. When Paul's nephew clues the centurion into a plot undertaken by some forty Jews to ambush and kill Paul on his way to a second meeting with the Sanhedrin, the Roman officer decides to place his trouble-magnet detainee under Governor Felix's custody in Caesarea (Acts 23:12–24). Felix hears Paul's defense but refuses to decide the matter, hoping for a bribe

---

[75] This is the same Gamaliel we met at the birth of the church in Acts 5:34.

from Paul under the guise of listening to his preaching (Acts 24:24–26).

After two years pass with Paul held under guard in Herod's palace, Festus replaces Felix as governor. Festus reopens Paul's case, and another trial occurs, again with wild accusations from the Jewish contingent sent from Jerusalem pitted against Paul's calm defense. Looking to curry favor with the Jews, Festus suggests taking the complaint back to Jerusalem, but Paul protests and appeals to Caesar (Acts 25:1–11). In court Festus agrees to let him press his suit in Rome, but privately he acknowledges the potential embarrassment of sending a suit to Caesar without credible charges. He invites the current Jewish king, Agrippa, to Caesarea to hear Paul and offer Festus advice. When Agrippa agrees to listen to Paul, he gets more than he bargains for. At this trial Paul again tailors his opening to his audience. "I can't think of anyone, King Agrippa, before whom I'd rather be answering all these Jewish accusations than you, knowing how well you are acquainted with Jewish ways and our family quarrels" (Acts 26:2–3). As he had already done before the crowd in Jerusalem, Paul again presents his résumé as a strict and scrupulous Pharisaic Jew, now augmenting the extent to which he had originally opposed the Way, adding how he had even voted for the execution of Christians (Acts 26:4–11). Then for the third time Luke relates the narrative of Paul's encounter with Jesus on the road to Damascus, the second time in Paul's voice (Acts 26:12–18). Having conveyed this testimony, Paul appeals to the king's supposed familiarity with the ways of Israel's God, "What could I do, King Agrippa? I couldn't just walk away from a vision like that!" (Acts 26:19). At this point Festus, who has not heard this story before, interjects that Paul is crazy (Acts 26:24), but Agrippa admits, "Keep this up much longer and you'll make a Christian out of me!" (Acts 26:28). Though Agrippa does not embrace the faith, he is convinced that Paul has done nothing deserving imprisonment or death and laments that he could have been released had he not demanded a hearing with Rome (Acts 26:32).

In this convoluted manner Paul finds himself en route to Rome, where he knows God will continue to use him as an apostle. The trip is not an easy one, however. Bad weather costs them time, and against Paul's advice they end up sailing in the squally autumn season. In a riveting narrative Luke relates how storms destroy the ship and threaten to drown the crew. Having received an angelic vision confirming the recovery of all hands, Paul, even as a prisoner, ends up managing the crisis. The ship is lost, but all aboard make it ashore to the island of Malta, where they spend the winter. While they are there, Paul heals the sick, never resting from his call to preach the gospel. Eventually a ship takes them to Rome, where Paul receives private quarters—a virtual house arrest with only a single soldier guarding him (Acts 28:16).

Paul makes his first order of business in Rome to meet with the local Jews. While they have not had any letters from Jerusalem concerning Paul to prejudice them against him, they have heard negative reports about the Christian sect. Nonetheless, they prove willing to give Paul a genuine hearing. By appointment a large number shows up to listen to Paul speak all day long, "explaining everything involved in the kingdom of God, and trying to persuade them all about Jesus by pointing out what Moses and the prophets had written about him" (Acts 28:23). At the close some believed. To those who did not embrace the faith, Paul quotes from Isaiah 6:9–10 to demonstrate how God had long ago predicted that not everyone would understand the Deity's actions (Acts 28:26–27). On the basis of this text and his vision from the Lord, Paul focuses his continued ministry on the Gentiles.

Luke closes his second volume on the positive note that Paul lives on under these pleasant circumstances for two years, welcoming all who were curious about the kingdom of God and the Lord Jesus Christ to come to see him. Christian tradition surmises that Paul eventually dies a martyr to the faith, and some of the epistles we will read in the next chapter remind us that his last days were hardly as amiable as Luke concludes them in this narrative. So why does Luke finish his testimony here in Rome instead of Jerusalem and why with Paul and not with Peter or any of the other apostles he has mentioned in the course of his telling?

Perhaps this question holds the key to the overall import of the story of Acts. Luke takes Jesus' commission to his disciples, "You will be my witnesses in Jerusalem, and in all Judea and Samaria, and to the ends of the earth" (Acts 1:8 NIV) and uses this image of the gospel extending outward from the hub of Judaism as the outline for this narrative. Tracking the growth of the church from its birthday at the Jerusalem Pentecost following Christ's ascension, Luke first exposes the post-resurrection transformation of Peter and the original apostles. Right away we see these erstwhile-uneducated fishermen now fully conversant in the Scriptures, thoroughly disciplined in their attention to prayer, and freshly emboldened to preach the story of salvation whenever opportunity presents itself. With their newfound courage, they willingly risk censor and imprisonment from their own temple authorities in defense of their faith, counting it a privilege to suffer for the name of Jesus. In that name they are also able to perform miracle healings as Jesus had done during His ministry on earth. As the church grows, they demonstrate good management skills, electing deacons to handle administrative details so that the apostles could keep preaching. Primarily, however, Luke shows us their responsiveness to the leadership of the Holy Spirit. Though the martyrdom of Stephen underscores the possibly dangerous cost of belief, these early disciples never answer violence with violence, holding fast in practice to the principles that Jesus taught. The Spirit even opens their minds regarding their presumption that the gospel belongs exclusively to Judaism. Originally Peter interprets his call as a ministry to the scattered tribes of Israel, but between his rooftop vision and his encounter with the Gentile Cornelius, God shows him that more than Jews are to be included in this outreach. This is a big hurdle for the early church as we see later with Paul's troubles in Jerusalem, but Peter does not shrink from supporting the welcome to Gentiles at the Jerusalem council.

Into this tableau of the early church, Luke next inserts Paul. In a signature act of making reversals on human expectations, God calls upon Saul of Tarsus, an elite, educated, up-and-coming rabbi and zealous opponent of the Way, and drafts him as the Lord's handpicked apostle to the nations outside Israel. While the opening of the gospel to the Gentiles does not lead Paul, Peter, or any of the apostles to seek to sever their ties with Judaism, Paul particularly suffers the misunderstanding of his fellow Jews as he launches himself beyond the scope of the synagogue. We will hear the anguish of this struggle voiced over and over as we next read his epistles. Luke preserves this context of angry disappointment within the camp of these Christ-believing Jews while he indicates to us that the clash with traditional Judaism will likely result in schism between the two groups.

Devoting more than half of Acts to deal with Paul's ministry, Luke proclaims his assessment that Paul bears the lion's share of the mission to carry the teaching that Jesus is Lord far and wide. His careful record of Paul's various missionary forays also serves to acquaint us with the intensity and versatility of Paul's preaching. After his conversion the vehemence with which Paul originally fights the Way is translated into a relentless vigor with which he pursues the teaching of God's salvation. Luke shows us Paul beginning with the discipline of establishing himself in the synagogues, waiting to be asked to speak, and then explaining to Jews and God-fearing Gentiles that Jesus is the long-sought-for Messiah. Yet as situations change and Paul finds the Holy Spirit leading him further into cities like Athens, where the inhabitants know little to nothing about Israel's God, he adjusts his sermons to connect with these people. As time goes on, he spends longer periods nurturing the churches he has planted. Then despite this success among his burgeoning Christian communities, Paul demonstrates the core authority of his faith by abruptly interrupting his ministry to the Gentiles because the Holy Spirit is calling him to Jerusalem. Once there he complies without argument when James and the Jerusalem church want him to demonstrate his Jewishness by performing ritual cleansings in the temple. When this attempt to reconcile with the Jerusalem church lands him a captive for some two years, Paul holds fast to his faith that God will get him to Rome to continue his mission there.

In addition, Luke shows us a transformation of Paul's character as he pursues God's path. At the start Paul tends toward impatience with his fellow missionaries. We will see this confirmed as we read his letters, but Luke gives us a sample when he tells of Paul's decision to split from Barnabas because of Paul's disapproval of John Mark (Acts 15:37-38). As time goes on, despite a multitude of public beatings, Paul's compassion for others grows. Back in Philippi during the second journey, Paul commands the fortune-telling demon to come out of a young psychic woman mainly because her raving is driving him crazy (Acts 16:16–18). Yet later he ministers to his jailer, preventing him from taking his own life (Acts 16:25–34). On another occasion when Paul has kept his audience up long into the night with his talking, a young man nods off and ends up falling from a third-story window. Thoroughly distressed, Paul throws his arms around the lifeless body and declares, "There's life in him yet" (Acts 20:7–10), and the young man does revive. When Paul determines that he must go to Jerusalem, his various farewell messages to the churches he has planted along the way demonstrate the depth of love for his brothers and sisters in the Lord.

From the *we* passages in the narrative, we know that Luke is allied with Paul both physically and spiritually. We also know from the inclusiveness of Luke's gospel that Jesus' message of God's forgiveness satisfying humanity's debt of sin is meant for all people. How else could the Scripture of Genesis 12:3 (that all the world's peoples would be blessed through Abraham) and Isaiah 49:6 (that God's servant would be a light to the Gentiles) be fulfilled? Luke brings this point home by ending his treatise with Paul working productively in Rome to further the cause of the gospel. As the power center of the known world, Rome will become the necessary launching pad for the church to grow to the ends of the earth. That Luke writes this even as the church suffers the loss of many of its leaders[76] under Roman rule testifies to his faith that the gospel would endure.

Luke has sketched for us the image of the gospel beginning to take root in the lands beyond Israel. The apostles have scattered the seeds of the good news and with the aid of the Holy Spirit begun to nurture the maturation of these infant churches and their new believers. By highlighting Paul, our chronicler has given us a window into the depth of difficulty these early evangelists encountered. Primarily, however, Luke has shown us the answer to our question of *how* the gospel came to be spread. Jesus' disciples dedicated their energy and devotion to the endeavor, but it was their submission to the direction of the Holy Spirit that brought about their mission's success.

But what did Paul and the other Christian leaders actually teach about the Christian life? How does the message that Christ has died to forgive our sins translate into a life change within the believer's heart? How does one sustain faith in the face of

[76] Tradition holds that both Peter and Paul were martyred in the 60s CE, probably during the reign of Nero, who blamed Christians for the great fire in Rome in 64 CE. We will see allusions to suffering for the faith in some of the epistles, but beyond this, the New Testament does not include the chronicles of its martyrs' deaths or other persecutions levied against the church.

disappointment, suffering, and misunderstanding? To answer these questions, we have to go back in time to Christianity's earliest documents—the epistles Paul and others wrote to instruct and encourage these first Christians.

Chapter 11

Does It Really Say That Believing in Christ Is All There Is to Being a Christian?

Have you ever had anyone tell you becoming a Christian is really simple, that all you have to do is believe Jesus has forgiven your sins and you're set to go to heaven when you die? If you've had this experience, hopefully it left you thinking there must be something more to being a Christian than a mere statement of conviction. But what does a belief in Christ involve? Surely we all know people who claim to be Christians behaving in ways that don't conform to what Jesus describes as righteous. On the other hand, we find people we applaud for their self-sacrificing love of humankind who make no confession of faith. Even those who self-identify as Christians know they fail to embody the complete holiness that Jesus teaches. Jesus told His disciples that He is the Way to God, but when they began to preach as we saw in Acts, the road to God opened onto new and surprising territory. The traditional outer markers of Judaism (circumcision, the kosher diet, and the non-association with Gentiles) that used to distinguish God's people from everyone else had to fall away in order for believers to be inclusive rather than exclusive. But the loss of these outside signs of fidelity begged the question: How can we know if a person really believes?

It is in the twenty-one epistles of the New Testament canon that we see the initial mapping of the road to God through Christ. The letters of Paul and several others give us a firsthand look at the front lines where Jesus' disciples exerted themselves to speak the message of God's salvation. Remember that our study here must be confined to an overview. The real sustenance of this material is best digested under close and careful pondering. But we will grasp an impression of what problems erupted within the early church. Paul and the other epistle writers will help us identify the early forks in the Way—roads that veered from the true gospel and led people into misunderstandings and even abuse of the message. Let us follow them now as they parse out the problems and place the first signposts along the highway that is the faith journey of anyone who follows Christ.

The Pauline Letters

With Acts demonstrating the predominance of Paul's ministry it should come as no surprise that thirteen of the New Testament epistles are ascribed to this apostle to the Gentiles. Paul wrote many of these letters to the churches he had planted among the peoples of Asia Minor and the various Greek city-states during his three (or perhaps four)[77] missionary journeys. We will look at each in the order in which it appears in the Bible, an arrangement that has nothing to do with the chronology of its composition. To help us keep our bearings within the time frame that Luke has outlined in Acts, I will attempt to assign a likely date[78] for each missive and to include a sketch of its audience.

---

[77] As we read for the context of these letters, some seem composed during Paul's house arrest that Luke describes at the end of Acts, while others appear to come from a period after Paul's release from that initial sentence when he is doing more missionary work. Finally his last letter to Timothy comes from his final Roman imprisonment preceding his presumed death as a martyr.

[78] All dates I offer are merely an attempt to target a time frame. There is considerable conjecture among scholars about the dating of many of the epistles. In addition, academics debate the authenticity of Paul's authorship of some of these letters. While it is true that issues of intellectual property did not exist in the ancient world, allowing writers routinely to ascribe

Romans

Once we begin reading Paul's letter to the Romans, it will be evident why it appears first among the epistles. Paul writes this letter while in Corinth at the tail end of his third missionary journey (approximately corresponding to Acts 20:2–3) in the mid to late 50s CE (56–57 CE). It represents the apex of his theological thinking—all that he has put together after being a believer for about a quarter century and being a preacher for a good decade or more. Unlike his correspondence with other churches, Paul writes to the Romans as a community he has neither planted nor visited, though the letter expresses his desire to come to the church there. While it ostensibly provides an introduction for the woman who bears the missive, Phoebe, who serves the church in Cenchrea, a suburb of Corinth (Romans 16:1–2), the main purpose of the epistle is to summarize Paul's insights into the faith, initiating a spiritual exchange that Paul believes will mutually benefit both parties (Romans 1:11–12). In the epistles that follow Romans, we will mostly see Paul addressing a particular church's problems and/or celebrating a community's successes. Here, however, Paul presents his consummate analysis of how salvation works in the hope that the church at Rome can follow Paul's thesis to the same conclusions.

Paul gets down to business quickly in this epistle. After he expresses his greetings to the church in Rome, he makes a preliminary statement of his theme. Essentially he says, "We are all believers in God's Son, the one foretold by the prophets to descend from David who gained His identity as our Lord and Messiah when the Spirit raised Him from the dead" (Romans 1:2–4). This is the gospel that Paul is pleased to proclaim: "This extraordinary Message of God's powerful plan to rescue

---

work to a predecessor with a well-known name (like Paul), the Christian canon acknowledges all these letters as Pauline, and therefore, all of them, regardless of actual authorship, hold the authority of Scripture.

everyone who trusts him, starting with the Jews and then right on to everyone else!" (Romans 1:16). As he embarks on his explanation of how God accomplishes this rescue through Christ, Paul lays his groundwork by quoting Scripture. "The righteous will live by his faith" (Habakkuk 2:4 quoted in Romans 1:17). In this way Paul introduces his major thesis that we appropriate righteousness not by accumulating good deeds to our credit and thereby earning our way into God's favor but by *believing* that Jesus' death and subsequent resurrection allow God to wipe the slate of our sins clean once and for all. From here Paul begins a detailed argument for Christianity, anticipating and rebutting the various misconceptions he has encountered throughout his ministry with a series of rhetorical questions.

Why is God angry in the first place? For the Jews it is clear because God has revealed the Torah to them and they know they have sinned. But Paul now calls the Gentiles to account. Even without the revelation of God's Law, creation itself is enough to teach God's existence and nature. Humans had to know that when they made idols, they were worshiping false, unreal gods. But they did it anyway, and look at the chaos the world has become as a result (Romans 1:28–32)! On the other hand, sometimes these outsiders to God's ways "follow it more or less by instinct" and "show that God's law is not something alien, imposed on us from without, but woven into the very fabric of our creation" (Romans 2:15). The bottom line is that humans are sinful whether they know God's Law as a Jew or they perceive it from their own consciences. The mark of righteousness does not appear on the skin (circumcision) but on the heart (Romans 2:29).

Does that mean there is nothing important about being a Jew? (Romans 3:1). God entrusted Israel with the Scriptures. That Jews went on to disobey God does not demean God's words. Rather, the goodness of Jewish law has continued to highlight God's holiness even when Jews themselves fall short of the spirit of that teaching. We need only consider the number of God-fearing

Gentiles already mentioned in Scripture whose ongoing interest in Israel's God was not deterred by Jewish inhospitality.[79] *But doesn't that mean that we can go right ahead doing wrong because that will make God look all the better* (Romans 3:8)? Quite the contrary. It means that all people (Jew and Gentile) have to acknowledge that they have knowingly violated the intended goodness of God's creation and more than earned the sentence of death the Law prescribes (Romans 3:9–20). For God, human trespass on righteousness is so egregious that it cannot be overlooked; however, the Lord is equally aware that sin saddles humans with a debt they can never repay. What humans cannot do, God has done for us. Bearing the weight of human rejection of God's holiness on His shoulders, Jesus paid in our stead the just punishment for sin with His death. It is the amazing generosity of God that allows His sacrifice to atone for our transgressions (Romans 3:23–26).

The beautiful thing about God's grace is that it eliminates human boasting (Romans 3:27). The Lord makes our obsession with trying to be better than our fellows obsolete by removing our success in observing the Law as a credential. *Does that mean that grace nullifies the Law?* (Romans 3:31). By no means, and Paul has the perfect Old Testament story to illustrate how the Law (meaning the Torah here) actually supports the idea of grace. As circumcision has continued to be the "sticky wicket" for Jewish Christians, Paul goes back to Father Abraham to examine how the rite of circumcision emerged in Judaism. Reading the text closely as a rabbi is taught to do, he turns to Genesis 15. Here he reads Abram's first recorded conversation with God. The Patriarch had already received the promise from God of a land and descendants and also obeyed God by moving to the place God showed him (Genesis 12:1–5), but here he talks back to

---

[79] God-fearing Gentiles routinely accepted that their Jewish friends could not invite them into their homes without contaminating themselves (Luke 7:6–7; Acts 10:28).

God. "What use are your gifts as long as I am childless?" (Genesis 15:2). God answers that Abram will have descendants of his own body as numerous as the stars in the sky (Genesis 15:5), and the biblical narrator asserts, "Abram believed the Lord and He credited it to him as righteousness" (Genesis 15:6 NIV). Paul goes on to note that this episode championing Abram's faith precedes the rite of circumcision given in Genesis 17:10 (Romans 4:10–11). Therefore, according to the Torah, salvation—the redemption of our sins that enables us to reconnect to God—which was accomplished by Jesus' death, is a *gift* that God bestows on humans. Paul stresses the magnanimity of this bequest when he observes, "We can understand dying for a person worth dying for … how someone good and noble could inspire us to selfless sacrifice" (Romans 5:7). "But God demonstrates his own love for us in this: While we were still sinners, Christ died for us" (Romans 5:8 NIV).

Since the Lord's grace is such a good thing, should we just keep on sinning so that God can keep on forgiving us? (Romans 6:1). Of course not! Paul refers to the rite of baptism. Immersion under the water simulates the death of our old selves. Our emergence from the baptismal fount corresponds to Jesus' resurrection (Romans 6:5). In our modern parlance our faithful acceptance of God's salvation is like a computer receiving a good virus that begins to rewrite its software. Before Christ, we lived according to the world's standards of "what we could get away with," but now with Christ within us, we abandon those ways and embrace God's holiness. *Without the letter of the Law to judge us, does this mean we can live any old way we want?* (Romans 6:15). It all depends on who your master is. If you serve sin, your life is at the beck and call of a chaotic and broken world with only death as a respite. If you serve God, however, you end up following the *spirit* of the Law, and you get the gift of *real life* with eternal life after death. This is what Paul calls true freedom (Romans 6:15–23).

So does this mean that concern for the letter of the Law caused sin? (Romans 7:7) Paul contends, "The law code started out as an excellent piece of work ... [but] sin found a way to pervert the command into a temptation" (Romans 7:8). Humans find themselves incapable of keeping the Law and obeying God's holiness, even when they know it's the right thing to do. The effort of being righteous seems doomed to failure until we realize that we are not fighting the battle without help. The Law exposed our transgressions. Jesus provides the deep healing of the human compulsion to sin (Romans 8:4). If you think you can make yourself good on your own steam, you end up obsessed with yourself. "Those who trust God's action in them find that God's Spirit is in them," keeping them focused on God (Romans 8:5–6). Paul compares the Christian to an expectant mother getting larger with God's holiness as she awaits the outcome of God's work (Romans 8:23–25). Even when we falter, God's Spirit is beside us, helping us, praying for us (Romans 8:26–27). From this "we know that in all things God works for the good of those who love him" (Romans 8:28 NIV). "With God on our side like this, how can we lose?" (Romans 8:31).

At this high point Paul finds that he must address the source of his deepest sorrow—how traditional Jews have rejected Jesus (Romans 9:1–2). Why has this happened? Again Paul seeks understanding by mining the Scriptures. Abraham had two sons but only one (Isaac, not Ishmael) was the son of the promise (Genesis 17:15–18). While Rebekah's twins were still in the womb and neither was yet guilty of sin, God ordained that the older (Esau) would serve the younger (Jacob) (Genesis 25:23). So Paul asks, "Is that grounds for complaining that God is unfair?"[80] (Romans 9:14). Using the metaphor of a potter and his clay, Paul paints an image of God's sovereignty. It's the potter's choice what kind of vessel he makes. In this way Paul prepares his

---

[80] Even in the examples Paul has cited, we remember that God nonetheless took care of Ishmael (Genesis 21:20) and Esau (Genesis 33).

audience to consider how God sees the Jews' wavering over the question of Jesus. Just because God began His plan with Israel, that doesn't prevent the Lord from choosing the world's other peoples to carry forth the news of salvation. *Does this mean then that God is so fed up with Israel that He'll have nothing more to do with her?* (Romans 11:1). Again Paul consoles himself with Scripture. When Elijah lamented the murder of God's prophets and the attempts on his own life, God reassured him that always there would be a remnant of believers (1 Kings 19:10, 14, 18; Romans 11:3–4). Paul sees the children of God as the branches of God's tree. The Jews who rejected God have been pruned as dead wood, and the Gentile believers have been grafted in (Romans 11:16–18). But nothing obstructs God from cutting off these adoptive shoots if they fail to bear fruit, and likewise God can surely reincorporate the original branches (the Jews) (Romans 11:23–24).

Up to this point in his epistle Paul has carefully made his case for how God's incarnation as Jesus has sent the faith born in Israel into a new trajectory, where the Lord's grace rather than humanity's futile attempt at observing the Law leads to righteousness. But before Paul draws his letter to a close, he has additional nuggets of wisdom to share. In order to caution believers against thinking too highly of themselves, he likens the members of the church to the various parts of the human body. Neither the body nor the church can operate properly unless each member is content to perform the particular operations assigned to each one (Romans 12:4–6). He exhorts Christians to pursue love and all things good and flee from evil. Echoing many of Jesus' earthly teachings, he reminds believers to bless their enemies, show empathy, shun class-consciousness, and live harmoniously with their fellows (Romans 12:9–21). In addition, he urges responsible citizenship, payment of debts, and compliance with the Ten Commandments—what adds up to obeying the Golden Rule (Romans 13:1–10).

But Paul doesn't mean just paying lip service to the Golden Rule. If you think it means merely treating others the way you want to be treated yourself, you are missing an important nuance. We always need to take time to understand each other, to be aware of our differences and make allowances where those differences are not crucial. For instance, what should be the Christian attitude toward meat that has previously been sacrificed to idols? Some Christians will say it is within our freedom to eat anything because idols aren't real in the first place, so nothing has tainted the food. Others would argue that to eat such meat is the same as endorsing the practice of idol worship. If you serve others food according to your own opinions (what would be a shallow practice of the Golden Rule), you risk disrespecting their beliefs and worrying their conscience. "If you confuse others by making a big issue over what they eat or don't eat, you're no longer a companion with them in love, are you?" (Romans 14:15).

Paul wants to hammer home this point as he closes. The Roman church is a blended church made up of Jewish Christians (who probably maintain a kosher diet) and a variety of Gentiles from all over the Mediterranean—some slaves, some free, rich and poor, men and women. There is no way it has escaped the problem that has plagued all the churches Paul has planted and visited—members not getting along with one another. Therefore, he exhorts them, "May our dependably steady and warmly personal God develop maturity in you so that you get along with each other as well as Jesus gets along with us all" (Romans 15:5). We will find that Paul repeats this message frequently in all of his letters.

Although Paul offers a glimpse of his plan to visit Rome on his way to spread the gospel in Spain (Romans 15:24), Acts reminds us that events did not go according to his wishes. His anticipated humanitarian trip to Jerusalem to bring the financial offering from the numerous Gentile churches resulted in a two-year imprisonment in Caesarea, delaying his visit to Rome until about 58–60 CE. When Luke discusses Paul's time with the Roman church, he never refers to the effect the letter had on the members there. Historically, however, the letter has had a profound effect on Christians throughout the centuries. Coming immediately after the stories of Jesus and the saga of the early church, it offers us our first glance at the theology of Christianity—the meaning of Christ's death as the solution to God's plan to win humans back into relationship with their maker without ignoring sin or abolishing human free will. That Paul was able to articulate this understanding in such close proximity to the historical events of Jesus' life and death demonstrates what a clear and strong foundation his witness was able to provide for the faith.

Now that we've read the consummate statement of Paul's theology, it's important to look at the other letters the apostle wrote in the course of his ministry. Many of these earlier epistles will shed light on how Paul came to the theology he expresses in Romans.

Corinthians

From Acts we learn that Paul sojourned in Corinth at least twice, spending eighteen months there in 50–51 CE (Acts 18:1–18) and returning in 56 or 57 CE (Acts 20:1-3[81]) for a season. The first time he arrived in Corinth, the apostle met and worked at tent making with Priscilla and Aquila, both Jewish Christian refugees

---

[81] Technically Luke notes that Paul spends three months in Greece in Acts 20:2-3. Since he refers to the northern part of present-day Greece as Macedonia in Acts 20:1, his term *Greece* signifies the southern portion of the peninsula/archipelago known then as the Roman province of Achaia. Since Acts 17:16–34 seems to indicate there were only a few converts in Athens, the most likely place for Paul to have sojourned would have been Corinth, which was the capital of Achaia and the site of some of Paul's most intense missionary work.

from Rome. As was his custom, Paul began by preaching in the synagogue, but soon enough Jewish opposition there became so frustrating that he resolved to work only with Gentiles (Acts 18:6). As a result, members of these first house churches in Corinth were largely lapsed polytheists. The city also thrived as a commercial hub for Mediterranean trade, and it would have been full of the allure of the latest and greatest products, fashions, and ideas—a virtual hotbed of worldliness. While Jews who converted to Christianity were already inured to living at arm's length from mainstream society, most of the Corinthian Christians struggled with the gospel's call to countercultural behavior (e.g., shunning temple customs and festivals of the Greek gods and goddesses and reining in extramarital sexuality).

Drawing from the two letters that have survived, we see that Paul wrote to this church on at least four occasions. He mentions the first letter in our 1 Corinthians 5:9, and then in 2 Corinthians 2:4, he refers to what would have been a third letter written "with more tears than ink on the parchment." From 2 Corinthians 12:14, where Paul anticipates his *third* trip to the city, we discover that Paul has made an emergency visit to Corinth unrecorded in Acts, probably between our first and second letters. Clearly Paul invested much emotional and spiritual energy in the Corinthian community. It was his first prolonged stay in his missionary work, and the coworkers he befriended there factor heavily in his ministry.[82] But as we will see, the Corinthians incited both love and exasperation in the apostle. As we read Paul's words, we will attempt to picture what was going wrong in Corinth and observe how Paul transformed these difficulties into valuable opportunities to work out the practical application of the gospel message.

---

[82] Priscilla and Aquila end up following Paul to Ephesus (Acts 18:18), and later Paul credits them with saving his life (Romans 16:3–5).

1 Corinthians

Writing from Ephesus, probably in the spring of 54 CE, Paul is responding to Chloe's report of quarrels among the Corinthians (1 Corinthians 1:11). Apparently the faithful have broken into factions, each one espousing the special teaching of his or her particular mentor. Worrying about whose brand of Christianity they follow has sidetracked their focus away from their own growth as disciples. Paul immediately wants to diffuse this tendency. "Has the Messiah been chopped up in little pieces so that we can each have a relic of our own?" (1 Corinthians 1:13). All teachers are but servants of God. "I planted the seed, Apollos[83] watered the plants, but *God* made you grow" (1 Corinthians 3:6). He cautions the Corinthians not to be so easily swayed by other preachers' reputations and their flashy performances but to remember that when he first came to them, he "didn't try to impress you with polished speeches and the latest philosophy [but kept his teaching] plain and simple" (1 Corinthians 2:1–2). Paul had addressed them then as mere babes in Christ who were able only to digest milk and not solid food (1 Corinthians 3:1–2). He is not pleased to find them still so immature in their faith, still so tied to the worldly culture around them (1 Corinthians 3:3). Yet Paul claims to write now not as a scold but as a father who doesn't want his children growing up spoiled (1 Corinthians 4:15). Indeed, the church at Corinth must have felt like a firstborn child to Paul—one that he had originally left, believing it to be ready to grow without him only to find it floundering in his absence.

---

[83] Apollos is first mentioned in Acts 18:24–28. An Egyptian from Alexandria, he was a disciple of John the Baptist until he met Priscilla and Aquila in Ephesus, and from them he learned the gospel of Jesus. He followed up Paul's ministry in Corinth according to Acts 19:1. In 1 Corinthians 16:12, Paul expresses his hope that Apollos will return to Corinth in the future.

Having dealt with the issue of factions, Paul next takes on the other red flags his correspondents have raised about the community. He is appalled to hear that one man in the congregation is sleeping with his stepmother (1 Corinthians 5:1) and that no one has spoken to him about it. He urges them to "hold this man's conduct up to public scrutiny ... It will be devastating to him ... and embarrassing to you. But better devastation and embarrassment than damnation. You want him forgiven before the Master on the Day of Judgment" (1 Corinthians 5:4–5). Paul finds that this example betrays "a flip and callous arrogance" (5:6) in the church leaders that worries him. He is concerned further that the Corinthian Christians are suing each other in secular courts. "When you think you've been wronged, does it make any sense to go before a court that knows nothing of God's ways instead of a family of Christians?" (1 Corinthians 6:1). Both of these situations constitute an abuse of freedom for Paul. "If I went around doing whatever I thought I could get by with, I'd be a slave to my whims" (1 Corinthians 6:12, compare to Romans 6:15–23).

Paul is particularly upset by the extent of sexual sinning and gluttony in the Corinthian community. One of the highlights of Corinth, its temple dedicated to the Greek goddess of love and beauty, Aphrodite, at one time housed as many as one thousand prostitute priestesses. Pagan believers considered a liaison with a temple prostitute an act of worship, and the money paid was an offering to the temple (a tax-deductible charitable contribution in our modern parlance). Some of the Christians in Corinth claimed that their freedom in Christ allowed them to indulge in such activities (1 Corinthians 6:12), but Paul reminds his listeners, "Do you not know that your bodies are members of Christ himself? Shall I then take the members of Christ and unite them with a prostitute? Never!" (1 Corinthians 6:15 NIV). Paul argues against the prevailing Greek thinking that the body and the mind/spirit/soul are separate entities, an idea foreign to Judaism.[84] Some of the Greek philosophies maintained that what one did with the body had no bearing on the spiritual self. This allowed believers to engage in sexual promiscuity and excessive eating and drinking with impunity. Paul counters by explaining that once the Christian has accepted the forgiveness of Christ, one's body itself is a *sacred place* (called a *temple* in 1 Corinthians 6:19 NIV) belonging no longer to oneself but to God. "So let people see God in and through your body" (1 Corinthians 6:20).

Continuing on this theme, Paul turns next to the questions the Corinthians have for him about their sexuality. For himself Paul advocates celibacy. Life is much simpler without a spouse. Paul also expects Christ to return soon and prefers to avoid the encumbrances of marital and familial life so that his energy might be solely devoted to evangelism. Still he recognizes that both the decision to remain single and the choice to marry reflect the gifts and calling that God makes to each individual (1 Corinthians 7:5). In his view the only proper context for sexual expression lies in marriage, and he is clear to prescribe the same fidelity for men as for women (1 Corinthians 7:2–4). Regarding mixed marriages—those between a Christian and a non-Christian—he foresees that the holiness of the believing spouse may ultimately spread to the nonbeliever (1 Corinthians 7:14). Therefore, these marriages should not be dissolved unless the non-Christian chooses divorce (1 Corinthians 7:15).

Another burning issue for the Corinthians regards diet. In the presence of so many pagan temples in Corinth, much of the food for sale in the markets may have been sacrificed to idols. Ought Christians to avoid this meat? For Paul this requires

---

[84] It is from the Greeks that we think of body and soul as separate parts of a human being. The Hebrews remembered Genesis 2:7, where God "formed Man out of dirt … and blew into his nostrils the breath (spirit) of life so that the Man came alive—a living soul!" and always conceived of the human spirit and body as a unit, given life in a single creative stroke by God.

a nuanced response. On the one hand, Christians aver that idols are false so that even food sacrificed to them remains untainted because the gods they represent do not actually exist (1 Corinthians 8:7–8). But what if by eating *idol meat* you cause someone to doubt or misunderstand Christianity? Should you *flaunt your freedom* by attending a banquet in honor of pagan gods and risk confusing someone who is learning to abandon idol worship (1 Corinthians 8:10–11)? Wouldn't it be better simply to abstain from the meal (1 Corinthians 8:12)? Here we see the groundwork laid for the refined teaching of the Golden Rule Paul will exposit in Romans 14.

Paul anticipates that the Corinthians will bristle at his remarks, but he assures them that he has earned the right to pastor them by his work among them. Though he encourages believers to support missionaries and their families, as was always the way that Judaism handled the finances of priests, he reminds them that he paid his own way as a tent maker (Acts 18:3) while he planted the church among them. It pleased him to be able to proclaim the gospel at no cost, and he stands aghast to sense that some Corinthians construe his self-sufficiency as a point of discredit (1 Corinthians 9:15–16). He warns his flock against co-opting religion to suit their own desires. Drawing again on Scripture, he retells the story of Moses—how all the Hebrews witnessed God's miracles of parting the sea and providing food and drink in the wilderness. However, not all remained faithful and got to enjoy the Promised Land (1 Corinthians 10:1–5). "We must never try to get Christ to serve us instead of us serving him" (1 Corinthians 10:9). Whatever trials come that may tempt you to shortcut God's ways, hold to this: "God will never let you down; he'll never let you be pushed past your limit; he'll always be there to help you come through it" (1 Corinthians 10:13).

While addressing some of the disagreements between the sexes, we find Paul both upholding the social norm that privileged men over women and also undercutting it. He begins by asserting the analogy that as Christ reigns over men, men are over women (1 Corinthians 11: 3). Paul makes this the rationale for the already culturally established practice of men baring their heads in worship in contrast to women covering theirs.[85] Probably Paul has mentioned it in response to some challenge of the practice. Despite requiring separate protocols for each sex, the custom nonetheless allowed men and women equally to demonstrate respect for the Deity. As Paul continues to ruminate on the disparity between the genders, however, he observes that it's pointless to make too much of the differences since clearly men and women need each other (1 Corinthians 11:11). "The first woman came from man, true—but ever since then, every man comes from a woman!" (1 Corinthians 11:12).

What concerns Paul more is what he has heard about the pollution of the Lord's Supper with gluttony and drunkenness, especially while others are left to go hungry (1 Corinthians 11:20–22). He repeats the proper administration of the Eucharist for their edification (1 Corinthians 11:23–26) and reiterates, "When you come together to the Lord's Table be reverent and courteous with one another … It is a spiritual meal" (1 Corinthians 11:33–34).

Having dispensed with his major concerns in light of the reports about Corinth he has received while in Ephesus, Paul now turns to insights his continuing work on behalf on the gospel has brought him. First on the subject of spiritual gifts Paul wants to make it clear that God gives out a variety of gifts so that "each person is given something to do that shows who God is" (1 Corinthians 12:7, compare to Romans 12:4–6.) No one gift is better than another. In the same way, God calls each of us to different jobs within the kingdom. Paul compares the church to the human body having different parts yet all dependent on

---

[85] In Paul's day and for centuries before and after, Mediterranean and Middle Eastern tradition dictated that women demonstrate their moral uprightness by covering their heads in public.

one another (1 Corinthians 12:14–31). Then Paul discourses at length on what activates our gifts and our callings. You will likely recognize his passage on love from wedding services, but his description of the nature of love in chapter 13 describes not just marital love but Christian love for all others.

Lastly he cautions the Corinthians not to make too much of the gift of "speaking in tongues," a spiritual language of praise[86] that the community held in particular esteem. Paul admits the value of this praise-speaking in private meditation but doesn't want the gift to predominate the worship service, particularly if no one in attendance can interpret what the speaker is saying (1 Corinthians 14). Here he also adds a word against women speaking in church (1 Corinthians 14:34). Perhaps women were the chief culprits, monopolizing worship time by speaking in tongues. Still, we have to remember how groundbreaking Christianity was for its time. Its habit of having women integrated into worship with men represented a significant break from Jewish tradition where women were routinely relegated to the outside court of the temple or synagogue. Equality between the sexes would not be built in a day!

Paul closes his epistle with a review of the gospel message. Christ died for our sins, was buried, and was resurrected on the third day in accordance with the Scriptures. More than five hundred of His followers witnessed the risen Jesus (1 Corinthians 15:6), and then the Lord appeared to Paul, the only one who wasn't already a believer, so that he could see the Christ resurrected. Paul emphasizes this point because he has heard that the Corinthians have begun to shed doubt on the actual raising of Jesus' body from the dead. We know from other

---

[86] Christians disagree in their understanding of the gift of speaking in tongues. My reading of the context here is that Paul's reference to "speaking in tongues" indicates unintelligible language used to praise God and represents a different gift from that described at Pentecost in Acts 2 when the disciples received the ability to speak foreign languages.

sources that some of the early heresies of Christianity involved the claim that the spirit of Jesus escaped to heaven before His body died on the cross, making the resurrection unnecessary. Paul wants to put any such talk to rest. Jesus really died, and He really rose again. There is no Christianity without this article of faith (1 Corinthians 15).

Paul's final chapter comprises a series of greetings and allows him to end on a high note. Even so, it is clear that he is worried about the state of the church in Corinth. Let us now turn to the second letter that has survived in order to follow up on that community's faith journey.

2 Corinthians

Reading this next letter to the Corinthians is a more difficult task than the first. Paul writes this discourse largely to defend himself against accusations circulating in the Corinthian community. We have to read between the lines in order to ascertain what these criticisms are and how they have undermined both Paul's authority and his relationship with the church. As we read, we'll want to note how skillfully Paul shifts tactics between exposing the wrong thinking in the Corinthians that has led to these allegations on the one hand and affirming his love relationship with the church members on the other.

Paul begins with a positive. He praises God for rescuing him from a recent serious brush with death and adds his thanks to the church for their prayers on his behalf (2 Corinthians 1:8–11). From that foundation he addresses the first complaint against him. When Paul ended up canceling his planned visit to Corinth, word went out that he was capricious with his promises. Paul protests there was nothing glib in his change of plans. Rather he did not want to repeat the pain of his previous visit—the one referred to in the missing letter that caused all parties such anguish (2 Corinthians 2:4). Instead Paul is writing the present epistle in order to clear the air, explain and defend himself, and lay the groundwork for a more pleasant reunion in the future.

Although we don't know the actual situation that created such misery on Paul's interim trip to Corinth, Paul does refer to "the person in question who caused all this pain" (2 Corinthians 2:5). Apparently the apostle had asked the church to discipline this member, but now Paul feels that the punishment needs to end because the man is contrite. It seems the Corinthians have not grasped the nuances of Paul's teaching. The church needs to be mindful of members crossing into sin with their behavior, but any calling into account should be done in order to show the offender the way back to grace, not to augment the level of church overseeing (2 Corinthians 2:5–11). Challenges like this should teach the church to depend more on direction from God rather than their own authority.

Next Paul addresses what is probably his greatest concern about the Corinthians—their penchant for preachers peddling the newest and glitziest message. Paul had already dealt with this problem in 1 Corinthians 1:10–17, but apparently it has only gotten worse. Living in a commercial hub where traders are constantly marketing the next new thing, the Corinthians are easily impressed by *how* ideas are presented. Even though Paul was the first to preach the gospel among them, they now are asking for his credentials (2 Corinthians 3:1). Presumably these other evangelists are supplying letters of recommendation to the churches. We have to wonder what their performances looked like when we hear Paul remind Corinth, "We refuse to wear masks and play games. We don't maneuver and manipulate behind the scenes. And we don't twist God's Word to suit ourselves" (2 Corinthians 4:2). To accentuate the difference between these showmen and himself, Paul sees his ministry as a plain clay pot that allows the gospel to shine all the brighter when compared to his own ordinariness (2 Corinthians 4:7). The purpose of all this preaching after all is to get people to connect to God, not God's spokesmen. In this way Paul makes his point about the Corinthians' infatuation with the "super-apostles" (2 Corinthians 11:5 NIV) while he creates an opening to affirm the gospel anew. That these other evangelists may look impressive only betrays their worldliness. Remember that the world has rejected God; however, God has gone to great pains through Jesus Christ to reconcile humans to their maker. "Therefore, if anyone is in Christ, he is a new creation" (2 Corinthians 5:17 NIV), no longer attached to the standards of a broken world. This is why the Corinthians must beware being "yoked with unbelievers" (2 Corinthians 6:14 NIV). Instead Paul offers this remedy, "Let's make a clean break with everything that defiles or distracts us … Let's make our entire lives fit and holy temples for the worship of God" (2 Corinthians 7:1).

Having restated the essence of the gospel, Paul now feels he can turn to his personal relationship with the Corinthians. He knows his previous letter hurt them but notes that it also helped them. The church's welcome of Titus produced the proof. When Titus was able to confirm that they were still believers, Paul could celebrate his own confidence in the resiliency of their faith (2 Corinthians 7:13–16). Now that Paul has affirmed the Corinthians, he aims to trade on their good will. When he next visits Corinth, Paul will be collecting an offering for the Jerusalem church. The Macedonians, with whom Paul is presently working, have already given generously to the cause, and Paul has assured them that the Corinthians are bound to match their kindness. Of course, Paul claims not to be forcing anyone's hand, "but by bringing in the Macedonians' enthusiasm as a stimulus to your love, I am hoping to bring the best out of you" (2 Corinthians 8:8). Despite his stated confidence in the church's philanthropy, Paul lets the Corinthians know that he will be taking the precaution of sending some of his disciples in advance of his own arrival to remind the church that "God loves a cheerful giver" (2 Corinthians 9:7). (Later we'll see Paul use this same strategy in the letter to Philemon regarding his runaway slave.)

Having prepared Corinth for his imminent return from a positive perspective, Paul now revisits his major bone of contention with the church.[87] Saving the most hurtful allegations for last, he tackles the judgment that he is "wishy-washy when I'm with you, but harsh and demanding when at a safe distance writing letters" (2 Corinthians 10:1). Paul is just not going to take this criticism lying down. People would have him believe he is being conceited when he asserts how surely he knows God has given him the authority to preach the gospel, but Paul isn't rising to the bait. If these "big-shot apostles" (2 Corinthians 11:5) want to compare credentials, Paul encourages them to bring it on! "Do they brag of being Hebrews ...? I'm their match. Are they servants of Christ? I can go them one better" (2 Corinthians 11:22–23). Paul proceeds to fill more than a paragraph chronicling the many hardships he has endured in service to the gospel, concluding, however, that if he has to boast, "I'll boast about the things that show my weakness" (2 Corinthians 11:30 NIV). It's not about who Paul or any apostle is but about who God is. To this point, Paul reveals that God has even given him "a thorn in my flesh" (2 Corinthians 12:8) to keep him grounded in humility. We don't know what this expression means specifically, but it's clear that Paul understood it as an infirmity that God felt Paul needed to keep his focus on the Deity. He quotes God's answer to his prayer for healing, "My strength comes into its own in your weakness" (2 Corinthians 12:9).

As he draws his letter to a close, Paul admits his fear that this third visit, like the second, may not go well (2 Corinthians

---

[87] Some scholars surmise that the abrupt change of tone between chapters 9 and 10 indicates that 2 Corinthians 10–13 is a separate letter. Even if this was the case, the way the canon has preserved the epistle serves to intensify our understanding of Paul's commitment both to defend and believe in his divine call to evangelism.

12:20). Yet that fear will not induce him to either softness or harshness. When he gets to Corinth, Paul is not going to back down in the face of blatant sinning (2 Corinthians 13:3), but his main effort will be to bolster the church. "The authority the Master gave me is for putting people together ... I want to get on with it and not have to spend time on reprimands" (2 Corinthians 13:10). Plainly the church at Corinth cost Paul great pain and not just because they tended to waver in their trust in him. Reflecting earlier in his letter about his general anxiety for all the churches, he observes, "When someone gets to the end of his rope, I feel the desperation in my bones. When someone is duped into sin, an angry fire burns in my gut" (2 Corinthians 11:29). This epistle demonstrates how Paul's understanding of his calling to mentor Corinth and all the churches involved a nuanced stance of identifying wrong thinking and behavior in such a way that the community could see his love behind the criticism. Judging from Acts' report that his third visit lasted three months, it would seem that this letter accomplished its purpose.

Galatians

Paul traveled extensively through the Roman province of Galatia (in Asia Minor, which is modern-day Turkey) on both his first (Acts 13–14) and second (Acts 16:6) missionary journeys. Although the ballpark consensus for dating this epistle is sometime in the early 50s CE, scholars debate where this church might be (given that the Roman province is large and that Luke references many cities that Paul visits within that area) and whether Paul writes before or after the Jerusalem council of Acts 15. For our purposes, however, we need only note that Paul had a specific church that he planted in mind and that he clearly believed that God had called him to preach the gospel *without* requiring circumcision for new converts.

We have just read in 2 Corinthians how Paul had to defend his reputation against the accusations of false apostles. But that was not the first time Paul had to repair damage done to his gospel work by preachers who followed behind him. As one of the preliminary efforts of planting the gospel among Gentiles, Galatia represented a pilot community—one where Christians were not obliged to become Jews (i.e., being circumcised) in order to be counted as believers. Although he does not reference the edict[88] by the Jerusalem council of Acts 15 directly, Paul's mention that his coworker Titus was not asked to be circumcised at the time they visited Jerusalem (Galatians 2:1–3) indicates his understanding that circumcision was to be put aside for Gentile converts. Now he has heard not only that certain preachers (scholars have dubbed this group "Judaizers") have come after him to the church he planted in Galatia, demanding that Christians be circumcised, but also that his new believers have submitted to the practice! In Galatians 4:13–14, Paul reveals the tremendous tenderness he feels for the Galatians who tended him in his illness with compassion and then attended to his preaching with enthusiasm. No wonder this news has wounded him. Therefore, he begins this epistle in honest anger and heartbreak. "I can't believe your fickleness—how easily you have turned traitor to him who called you by the grace of Christ by embracing a variant message" (Galatians 1:6).

Coming out with his fury from the start, Paul assigns himself two tasks for this epistle—to defend the authority of his preaching and to explain why the circumcision issue bears such weight theologically. Addressing his credentials first, Paul reminds his audience, "I wasn't taught [the gospel] in some school. I got it straight from God, received the Message directly from Jesus Christ" (Galatians 1:12). Though he had begun as a star Jew who was zealous to protect Judaism from this upstart

---

[88] The Jerusalem council agreed among other points that Gentiles need not be circumcised.

Christian sect, the only credential he now counts as worthy is that the Lord Jesus had appeared to him and called him to be the apostle to the Gentiles (Galatians 1:13–6). In this way even Paul's résumé is an example of faith eclipsing works. He further testifies to meeting with both Peter and James some three years after his conversion (Galatians 1:18–19) and then fourteen years later, having James, Peter, and John, "the pillars of the church" (Galatians 2:9), corroborate that Paul should be assigned the ministry to the Gentiles. We can only surmise that though the Jerusalem church leaders assented to give up circumcision as a sign of Christianity, many in the early church still felt strongly that the Mosaic code needed to be upheld. We remember that even Paul circumcised Timothy early on in his ministry. Now, however, only a few years later but with much more preaching to the Gentiles under his belt, Paul has found it a terribly unworthy impediment to the gospel. In the first place it encourages Jews to rate themselves ahead of Gentile converts. More importantly it implies that we can connect with God *better* and perhaps *only* by obeying the Law to which circumcision is tied (Galatians 2:11–21). In a fit of uncensored pique Paul goes so far as to suggest, "Why don't these agitators, obsessive as they are about circumcision, go all the way and castrate themselves" (Galatians 5:12).

Yet even as Paul vents his anger, the bulk of this epistle represents his painstaking untangling of what the insistence on circumcision represents. It is here that we will see the genesis of his explanation to the Romans of justification by faith rather than works. Circumcision equates to an allegiance to the Law. But it is not laws that save us. "If a living relationship with God could come by rule-keeping, then Christ died unnecessarily" (Galatians 2:21). It is because no human can keep the Law perfectly that Jesus had to die in our stead, becoming a curse for our sake by submitting to crucifixion, literally "dying by hanging on a tree," an offense that brings a curse according to Deuteronomy 21:23

(Galatians 3:13). In this context Jesus' taking on an unjust curse for which He dies but then lives again creates what amounts to a homeopathic cure for human sinning. Having thus forged a vaccine against sin in His blood, Jesus offers a cure for sin for all willing to receive His inoculation. Citing Abraham's *faith* that "God credited to him as righteousness" (Galatians 3:6; Genesis 15:6), Paul reminds the Galatians that God likewise grants us grace according to our faith, not according to our "moral striving" (Galatians 3:5).

To cement his argument further, Paul continues to mine the Scriptures. He makes an allegorical interpretation of Abraham's two children, Ishmael and Isaac. Ishmael, the son born by "human connivance" (Galatians 4:23) of Sarah's handmaiden (slave), Hagar, represents the slavery of the Law where humans try to achieve righteousness on their own steam. In contrast, Isaac, born according to God's promise to Sarah, a free woman, stands for the freedom God bestows on us through our faith. In the same way that God was able to give Sarah and Abraham the miracle of a child in their old age (with no exertion on their part), God's grace releases us from our doomed-to-failure attempts to gain holiness through our own efforts. "For in Christ Jesus neither circumcision nor uncircumcision has any value. The only thing that counts is faith expressing itself through love" (Galatians 5:6).

This idea that faith and not works is what connects us to God yields many positive consequences for Paul. Historically circumcision served as a means of separating God's people from the rest of the world. But now God has replaced exclusivity with inclusiveness. Paul states this radically by proclaiming, "In Christ's family there can be no division into Jew and non-Jew, slave and free, male and female"[89] (Galatians 3:28). We will

---

[89] A common rabbinic praise prayer thanked God that "I am not a Gentile, not a slave, and not a woman." Paul finds that Christianity turns that thinking on its head.

see throughout his letters how often Paul references Gentiles, women, and even slaves[90] as his coworkers in Christ. While Paul does not attempt to change the culture of his day regarding these injustices, he acknowledges here that God does not identify us by our human-made categories and rankings.

Paul celebrates the equality and freedom God allows by comparing the Law to a boy's tutor—a master for the minor while he is still underage but not the heir that the child will be in adulthood (Galatians 4:1–7). Christians are God's children coming of age, learning how to obey the inner voice of God's Spirit that guides us more precisely and specifically than the black-and-white dictums of the Law. "Christ has set us free to live a free life" (Galatians 5:1). Of course, that freedom is not an excuse "to do whatever you want" (Galatians 5:13; compare to Romans 6). Paul is careful to point out that the abuse of liberty leads to a laundry list of evils (Galatians 5:19–21), but the freedom that engages in serving "one another in love" (Galatians 5:13) yields a cornucopia of goodness (Galatians 5:22–23). Even though salvation comes through faith, belief ushers in a salvation *process* through which God works to transform our nature. Following the advice Paul gives about behavior hastens this transformation because "what a person plants, he will harvest" (Galatians 6:7).

In closing, Paul analyzes the motivation behind those demanding circumcision. "They want an easy way to look good for others [Jews]" (Galatians 6:12), which refers to a virtual halfway house where they can have one foot in Judaism and one in Christianity. Paul sees this practice as a dead end, an illusion of salvation that offers superficial guarantees and promotes the division of humanity into *us* and *them*. Paul is going on record to say that this is not Christianity.

---

[90] See appendix 6.

Ephesians

From Acts we know that Paul spent more time in Ephesus than any other city, staying there as many as three years in the early 50s CE. His ministry thrived until a riot instigated by angry idol makers cut it short (Acts 19:23-41). Paul writes this epistle while imprisoned, presumably in Rome, making this the latest letter we have encountered so far—at least as late as the early 60s CE. Because of the absence of the usual list of personal greetings at the end, scholars conjecture that this may have served as a circular letter delivered first to the Ephesians with the expectation that it would be copied and read aloud in the other churches of Asia Minor. Unlike his correspondence with the Galatians, Paul has no particular bone to pick with the Ephesians and writes primarily to reinforce their understanding of their faith as well as to exhort them to mind that their behavior matches their beliefs. This universal message also supports the claim that Paul was composing what amounts to a theological cover letter for the general church rather than just for the Ephesians.

The letter falls easily into two parts. The first three chapters deal with theology, and the last three offer practical advice for everyday living. The theology section may seem a bit heavy going at first look. Rather than following the step-by-step walk-through of how Christianity works he delivered to the Romans, Paul seems to presume that his audience has some basic understanding of God's rescue in Christ. Instead he utilizes a new image for describing Christ's work on the cross. "In him we have redemption through his blood" (Ephesians 1:7 NIV). The notion of redemption here would resonate in the Ephesians' minds as a reference to the way a slave could earn his freedom. A ransom paid on his behalf would achieve his emancipation. For Christians Jesus pays the ransom that breaks us out of our slavery to sin. Paul contends that God has planned this particular means of saving humankind from the beginning of creation. But God's design went beyond the reconciliation of Creator and created. Christ is the ultimate unifier of humans, allowing God's chosen Jews and Gentiles equal footing before their Lord. Therefore, "it's in Christ that we find out who we are and what we are living for" (Ephesians 1:11). As Paul celebrates the amazing love of the Deity who devised this plan of salvation, he reiterates his ongoing astonishment that God chose him to bring the gospel to the Gentiles, though "I was the least qualified of any of the available Christians. God saw to it that I was equipped, but you can be sure it had nothing to do with my natural abilities" (Ephesians 3:8). In these statements Paul both acknowledges his shame for initially persecuting the church while he expresses again (see Galatians 1:13–16) the notion that it is God in us and not human striving that allows any of us to do good.

On the basis of this theological foundation, in the second half of the letter Paul preaches about what our new life looks like once we have become Christians, much of which will remind us of Romans 12–14. The old habits of sin must be abandoned in order to make way for a life organized by God's love and truth. Paul offers interesting examples. "Be angry—but don't use your anger as fuel for revenge ... and don't go to bed angry; get an honest job so that you can help others who can't work; tell your neighbor the truth, (but) say only what helps; [and always remember to] forgive one another as quickly and thoroughly as God in Christ forgave you" (Ephesians 4:25–32).

Toward the end of the letter, however, Paul launches into some new territory. After he makes generalized statements about human behavior, he targets a series of specific relationships that require special attention—husbands and wives, parents and children, and slaves and masters. At first glance these verses seem to undercut Paul's previous teaching about our equality (Galatians 3:28) in Christ because he appears to uphold the cultural standards of his day. He tells women to submit to their husbands, children to mind their parents and slaves to obey their masters. This is where we have to read more closely. Paul states his thesis for all this commentary in Ephesians 5:21 (NIV), "Submit to one another out of reverence for Christ." Paramount in his advice is the idea that we learn from God's love of us how to love others. His counsel about relationships speaks with insight into the ways that humans tend to fail one another, and he offers solutions that anticipate the fallout of these shortcomings. For example, in his discussion of spousal relationships, he seems to give the typical cultural ascendency to the husband in his specific counsel that wives *submit to* or *respect* their husbands. Doesn't this contradict the notion that there is neither male nor female in Christ? Yet our own language gives us clues to Paul's nuanced understanding here. An unpleasant wife is either a *nag* or a *shrew*. A woman mends this tendency by remembering to respect her husband. On the other hand, husbands often forget to show warmth and tenderness to their wives. Paul frames this teaching by stating that husbands must love their wives no less than Christ loves the church and reinforces it with more than twice the verbiage devoted to advice for wives (compare Ephesians 5:22–24 to Ephesians 5:25–32). He summarizes in Ephesians 5:33 by insisting that in these separate ways, wives and husbands both show reverence to Christ (his original thesis of Ephesians 5:21). In the same way it is noteworthy that he speaks of the fallout of parental disparagement to a society where children have no rights (Ephesians 6:4). On the other hand, his guidance to slaves seems peculiarly complacent in our modern world where slavery is nearly universally abhorred. Here we have to remind ourselves that slavery was a long-established norm in the ancient world. At that time slaves probably had a greater opportunity to impact their individual masters by obeying the Golden Rule than by attempting to abolish the practice of slavery. Overall, however, even as Paul seems to refuse to rock the boat of societal status, his counsel goes far to remind the privileged that the Christian's first allegiance is always to God and that any *perks* that human culture would appear to attach to one's social position are converted to *responsibilities* to show God's love to others.

To close his missive, Paul paints an interesting picture of the Christian putting on armor as a soldier. This military imagery seems incongruous in a movement that preaches turning the other cheek when faced with aggression. Paul, however, still believes that the Christian goes into battle daily. The opponent is Satan, however, rather than humans. He instructs the Ephesians to "take your stand against the devil's schemes [by putting] on the full armor of God: the belt of truth, the breastplate of righteousness, [boots that are] the gospel of peace, the shield of faith, the helmet of salvation, and the sword of the Spirit, which is the word of God" (Ephesians 6:10–17 NIV). The mainstay of the Christian soldier lies in prayer. Paul encourages his beloved Ephesians to *pray hard and long* for each other and for him and his ministry, which continues even in prison (Ephesians 6:18–20).

Philippians

Luke records Paul's first visit to Philippi in Macedonia during his second missionary journey in Acts 16:11–40. Among the local women who attended a Sabbath service Paul held was the dealer in purple cloth named Lydia, who became a stalwart believer. It was here that Paul got himself and Silas imprisoned when Paul called the spirit of divination out of a slave girl, robbing her owners of her fortune-telling powers. But when a miraculous earthquake unlatched their jail chains, Paul passed on their chance to escape by ministering to the warden, who then became a believer. This epistle, presumably written during his Roman house arrest (Acts 28:14–31) in the early 60s CE, echoes this imprisonment in Philippi as Paul mentions how the

Roman soldiers have all heard the gospel because of guarding Paul (Philippians 1:12–14).

Perhaps the most prominent Roman colony in Macedonia (modern northern Greece), Philippi boasted a large population of retired Roman military and other Italian emigrants. Apparently it never had a significant Jewish population. Luke records that in the absence of a synagogue, Paul led Sabbath services outside the city gate by the river (Acts 16:13). Sensitive to the Philippians' lack of Hebrew orientation, Paul uncharacteristically refrains from quoting the Old Testament in this epistle.

The other thing Paul refrains from in this epistle is a recap of the gospel message. He has such confidence in the faith of this church that he feels free merely to encourage and give thanks for their steadfastness. He begins by exhorting the Philippians to *flourish* in loving, learning not only to love more but also to love well (meaning appropriately) in all situations (Philippians 1:9–11). Yet having said that much, he is satisfied to give them an update on his circumstances. Though in prison, Paul wants them to know that their prayers for him have kept him full of high spirits; he cannot even complain about his situation. He hears that other evangelists celebrate his absence from the preaching circuit as a chance to garner the limelight for themselves, but this doesn't bother him because the gospel is being preached (Philippians 1:18). He delights that whether his jail sentence ends in his release or his death, he would be hard-pressed to decide which outcome he desires more. "Alive, I'm Christ's messenger; dead, I'm his bounty. Life versus even more life! I can't lose" (Philippians 1:21). Yet he would like to see the Philippians again and expects that God may well grant that wish (Philippians 1:25–26).

Without having to review the basics of theology, Paul is free here to lend some new insights into the process by which God transforms believers into practitioners of righteousness. Not even the Philippians are exempt from the reminder that the primary element of Christian community involves members getting along with one another. Paul insists that the key to church harmony rests in humility, and he utilizes what could be a modified hymn to express how even Jesus displayed humility. "When the time came, he set aside the privileges of deity and took on the status of a slave, became *human*!" (Philippians 2:6–7). Christ also modeled for us obedience. "He didn't claim special privileges. Instead, he lived a selfless, obedient life and died a selfless obedient death" (Philippians 2:8). By calling Jesus' example to mind, Paul is able to express an important nuance of the Christian journey. Though God has already saved us, salvation continues as a process in which we actively pursue righteousness, seemingly on our own, yet we discover that God is backing up our efforts every step of the way. "Continue to work out your salvation with fear and trembling, for it is God who works in you to will and act according to his good purpose" (Philippians 2:12–13 NIV).

We note as Paul begins to close that he advises steering clear of those who still push for circumcision as a mark of faith (Philippians 3:2). Even though Paul has all the Jewish credentials these Judaizers value, he counts them as worthless compared to what Christ offers (Philippians 3:4–8). Instead Paul takes this opportunity to express in terms of his own life how he is "working out his salvation: I'm not saying that I have this all together ... but I am well on my way, reaching out for Christ, who has so wondrously reached out for me" (Philippians 3:12). Making a contrast with those who preach conformity to the Mosaic code, Paul reminds the Philippians that Christians are *citizens* of heaven (Philippians 3:20)—a concept that surely resonated with a population where Roman citizenship figured importantly.

Before signing off, Paul demonstrates his ongoing concern for individuals in the community by asking the church's help in repairing the relationship between two women "who worked for the Message hand in hand with ... me" (Philippians 4:3). The

Philippian representative, Epaphroditus, whom Paul references in Philippians 2:25–30, has likely brought him up to date on the situation. Still, even voicing this concern is not enough to dampen his bright spirits. Reminding the Philippians once more to celebrate God and "instead of worrying, pray" (Philippians 4:6), he seems to be pronouncing a benediction when he intones, "And the peace of God, which transcends all understanding, will guard your hearts and minds in Christ Jesus" (Philippians 4:7 NIV). But he has more to say! He cannot leave off his great thanks for all the gifts that the Philippian church has contributed these many years of Paul's ministry. Apparently they stand alone among the churches Paul planted in this respect (Philippians 4:15).

The epistle to the Philippians enjoys a reputation as the most joyful of Paul's writings. Certainly the warm spot Paul has in his heart for this church is a contributing factor in the letter's upbeat tone. From Philippians 3:1, we learn that Paul has written on several occasions to this community, and clearly they have remained engaged in his ministry for more than a decade at the time of its composition. But the sense of rejoicing that Paul exudes throughout the epistle goes beyond mere simpatico between the apostle and his converts. In this letter we find Paul in a place where his faith journey has led him to a level of confidence in the Lord and peace about how God is using him that presents Christianity in perhaps its most attractive light. As Paul himself concludes, "I've found the recipe for being happy whether full or hungry … Whatever I have, wherever I am, I can make it through anything in the One who makes me who I am" (Philippians 4:12–13).

Colossians

Like Rome, the church at Colossae is not one that Paul planted. Colossae lies east of Ephesus in Asia Minor, and Paul names his disciple Epaphras as the sower of the gospel there (Colossians

1:7). Trusting Epaphras to have preached accurately, Paul begins this epistle (another probably written from his first Roman imprisonment in the early 60s CE) rejoicing in the faith of the believers there and building rapport with a congregation who knows him only by reputation. After reiterating the basic tenet of the gospel, namely that Christ reconciles humans to their maker by means of His death and resurrection, Paul comes around to his main concern for the Colossians. He has heard rumors of heretical ideas floating into the community—a hierarchy of spiritual beings (angels and so forth), an insistence on special rites, diets and holy days, as well as the exploration of *mysteries* and *secrets* known only to a select group. These notions were probably an early expression of the heresy known as gnosticism, its name connoting the *special knowledge* of its initiates. Paul seeks to reinforce that what the Colossians learned about Christ at first was correct. Co-opting the language of these interlopers, he maintains that Jesus is *the secret* and *mystery* (Colossians 1:27) that God has now chosen to reveal to the whole world. The salvation that the Lord has provided through Christ is sufficient. The Colossians should not listen to people who want to "add to the Message" (Colossians 1:28). Calling these folk bullies who urge Christians to worry about "details of diet, worship services, [and] holy days" (Colossians 2:16), Paul reminds the troubled Colossians, "You're already *in*—insiders—not through some secretive initiation rite but rather through what Christ has already gone through for you, destroying the power of sin" (Colossians 2:11).

As Paul continues to voice his sincere concern for the Colossians, he sprinkles this epistle with several ideas he has expressed in other letters. He expands the thinking first offered in Galatians 3:28, saying here, "Words like Jewish and non-Jewish, religious and irreligious, insider and outsider, uncivilized and uncouth, slave and free, mean nothing. From now on everyone is defined by Christ, everyone is included in Christ" (Colossians

3:11). Likewise he repeats the teaching about household relationships that we read in Ephesians 5:21–6:9 (see Colossians 3:18–4:1). Still, he presents a relatively new image to bring his point home. Paul compares the decision to follow Christ to the choice of a new God-designed wardrobe. The Christian clothes him or herself in "compassion, kindness, humility, quiet strength, [and] discipline … And regardless of what else you put on, wear love. It's your basic all-purpose garment. Never be without it" (Colossians 3:12–14). As a sign of how Paul has already put into practice what he preaches, we find in his closing chapter that he sends greetings from Mark, whom we know as John Mark, the author of the second gospel. In Acts 15:38, Luke notes that Paul and Barnabas split up their ministries because Paul thought Mark was a quitter. Here we find Paul and Mark reconciled[91] (Colossians 4:10). Embedded also in this closing list of greetings, the canon serves us a snippet of foreshadowing with the name Onesimus, "a trusted and dear brother" (Colossians 4:9) about whom we will hear more in the letter to Philemon.

As we move beyond the letter to the Colossians, we should note how much gentler and more nuanced Paul's response to wrong thinking has become. In Galatians, we see the same articulate intellect at work exposing the fallacies of the errant arguments—in that case, the need for circumcision—but Paul can scarcely contain his temper as he writes. Here, however, Paul works consciously to format his line of reasoning so that it will not be construed as accusatory. While he is quick to condemn the heresies of *secret knowledge* and *mysterious rites*, Paul does not indict the Colossians for abandoning their faith. Instead he shows them how they need to remain vigilant when it comes to ideas that seem at first blush similar to Christianity but are actually antithetical to it. His upbeat tone displays his confidence that

---

[91] Paul continues to mention the ongoing devotion of Mark in 2 Timothy 4:11.

the Colossians only need some careful repetition of the gospel message to be back on track in their faith.

Thessalonians

Luke chronicles Paul's visit to Thessalonica in Acts 17:1–10. As part of his second missionary journey, the stay in Thessalonica began with Paul preaching in the local synagogue. After three Sabbaths some of the Jews took action to oppose Paul. Luke claims they were jealous of the number of converts Paul had quickly garnered across the social spectrum—some Jews, many God-fearing Greeks, and even several of the prominent women of the community. Eventually these malcontents caused enough trouble to prompt Paul and Silas to move on. Paul writes these two letters in the early 50s while he is still in Corinth. We suppose that about six months separate the writing of the pair. Most academics dating these epistles believe they represent Paul's earliest missives.

Having had to leave the city abruptly, Paul has continued to worry about the state of the church he planted there. Unable to travel there himself, he has dispatched Timothy to check on the situation. He sends his first letter to the Thessalonians after he receives Timothy's glowing report (1 Thessalonians 3:1–2). Much of the first letter reflects Paul's joy in having his sense of the strength of the community's faith confirmed. He remembers them taking the gospel to their hearts from the first and notes that much of their growth in the faith was owing to their willingness to imitate the ways of the evangelists preaching to them (1 Thessalonians 1:6).

One point of the gospel that seemed to resonate particularly with the Thessalonians was the prediction of Christ's return. We know that this message was always part of the evangel preached because all four gospel writers include Jesus making this promise. Its mention here indicates its early and integral inclusion in Paul's ministry as well. The anticipation of Christ's imminent return was especially strong in the early years, and the Thessalonians remind us that it easily became an occasion for confusion. Paul takes pains here to relieve the Thessalonians' fear that those who have died before Jesus' second coming will miss out on their heavenly reward. In fact, Jesus will call the dead to rise first before He gathers up the living to join him in "one huge family reunion with the Master" (1 Thessalonians 4:15–17). Paul follows up this teaching with a reminder that no one will know the timing of this event.

Half a year later Paul addresses the Thessalonians a second time. Again he is full of praise for their ongoing faith, especially in the wake of persecution. The issues surrounding the second coming continue to plague the community, however. Having received word that the Thessalonians are now afraid that they have missed the day of Christ's return, Paul hastens to reassure them. First he counsels them not to listen to rumors indiscriminately. Then he reminds them that before Jesus arrives, the Anarchist—a man of lawlessness—will descend upon the scene and set himself up in God's temple as "God Almighty" (2 Thessalonians 2:3–5). Of course, once this Anarchist enters, Christ will not be far behind. They need not worry. Here we get an early glimpse of the enemy the church anticipated coming in the end times. We will see these visions expanded when we come to the last book of the Bible.

But another fallout of this obsession with Jesus' return is that some members of the society have given up their jobs in anticipation of the end of the world. Paul refuses to mince words about this lot. They are lazy. He reminds the Thessalonians of the example he and his coworkers set while he lived among them. "We worked our fingers to the bone, up half the night moonlighting so you wouldn't be burdened with taking care of us" (2 Thessalonians 3:8), and he restates the rule he gave them, "If you don't work, you don't eat" (2 Thessalonians 3:10).

These concerns in the Thessalonian church give us our earliest picture of the teaching of Christ's return and how easily it set believers off track from the real business of learning the life of faith. Although the church has never let go of the doctrine of Jesus' promised second coming, we can begin to understand why much of the time[92] it has been judiciously delegated a back seat to the teaching of developing Christian behavior among humans. On the other hand, we should note how expertly these letters also expose Paul's pastoral abilities. Evenhandedly he infuses his message with both compliments and exhortations to the Thessalonians to continue on their faith journeys with kindness and patience and a willingness to confront wrong within a context of love. As in all his letters, Paul urges prayer for himself and his ministry along with all members of the community (1 Thessalonians 5:16–28; 2 Thessalonians 3:1–3). His closing benediction of the first letter sums up his aspirations for these brothers and sisters in Christ, "May God himself, the God who makes everything holy and whole, put you together— spirit, soul, body—and keep you fit for the coming of our Master, Jesus Christ" (1 Thessalonians 5:23).

The Pastoral Letters

Paul addresses his remaining four epistles to individuals rather than churches. Dubbed the Pastoral Letters, the first three of these, two to Timothy and one to Titus, represent his coaching of the next generation of evangelists. We first met Timothy in Acts 16 when Paul recruited him for his second missionary journey (Acts 16:1–3). At the time we noted the

---

[92] During periods of crisis, however, concern for the return of Christ intensifies. Historically we have many examples of this, such as the various Roman Empire persecutions in the first three centuries CE, the Black Death of the fourteenth century, the Great Disappointment of the Adventist movements in the nineteenth century, and most recently the flurry over the second millennium.

irony of Paul's decision to circumcise Timothy after he had so strenuously argued against the necessity of imposing Jewish customs on Gentile converts. But Timothy was only half Gentile. Though his father was Greek, his mother and grandmother were both Jews who became Christians (Acts 16:1 and 2 Timothy 1:5). Timothy stands out as Paul's right-hand man through much of Acts, and then Paul names him his "son in the faith" (1 Timothy 1:2). Not only did he accompany Paul on his various missions, but Paul also relied on him to make return visits to churches Paul had planted. In addition, Paul lists him as a co-sender on six of his letters.

1 Timothy

Since scholars continue to debate a date for 1 Timothy, we will not concern ourselves with when the letter was composed. Instead we derive from the context that Paul writes Timothy after he dispatched him to lead the church at Ephesus (where he and Paul had worked for so long in the 50s CE), not merely in Paul's absence but as a semi-permanent assignment. News of false teaching in that church has reached Paul, and he instructs Timothy to turn the community back to the basics of the gospel, "love uncontaminated by self-interest and counterfeit faith" (1 Timothy 1:5). Paul seeks to grow Timothy's self-confidence about his own work for the church by recapping for him what God has been able to accomplish in Paul's life. "Even though I was once a blasphemer and a persecutor and a violent man ... I was shown mercy so that in me, the worst of sinners, Christ Jesus might display his unlimited patience" (1 Timothy 1:13, 16 NIV). Paul's first piece of advice is prayer, "Pray everyway you know how, for everyone you know" (1 Timothy 2:1). He follows up with the reminder, "[God] wants not only us but *everyone* saved" (1 Timothy 2:4). This is why Timothy's ongoing work is so important.

This idea that *everyone* should be saved casts the idea of the immediacy of the gospel in a slightly new light. Let us say that in the beginning the evangelists saw themselves as booking agents for a boat (Christianity) that at first seemed ready to launch (with Jesus' return) any day. Their priority was to get as many people *saved* as possible. By the time we get to 1 Timothy, however, while Paul continues to reference the promise of the second coming (1 Timothy 6:14), he now frames this event within the bracket that "God will bring about in his own time" (1 Timothy 6:15 NIV). More than ever the evangelists realize they are not merely *selling tickets* to God's kingdom but actively building it here on earth. The goal of evangelism has morphed from a focus on the quantity to the quality of conversions. If the *boat* that is Christianity is to strike the balance between being launch-ready while remaining indefinitely dockside, it is all the more important that everything and everyone on board be shipshape. Therefore, the church must diligently embrace the teaching and nurturing of her members. It should come as no surprise that the balance of this letter serves up specific advice about the art of being a pastor.

As is evident from the Pauline letters we have already read, Paul has never shrunk from the challenge of teaching Christian behavior. Here, however, his focus will rest less on individual conduct and stress the maintenance of a cohesive and stable social order within the church. Apparently factors have emerged that threaten the church's equilibrium. Men have become embittered and argumentative (1 Timothy 2:8), while women have been asserting their ascendency (1 Timothy 2:11-12). Even though we have numerous examples of Paul treating women as leaders and referring to churches that meet in the houses of women, here Paul seems to backpedal on his previously claimed lack of difference between men and women (Galatians 3:28). Much of what the apostle advises here seems aimed at restoring order to a church that has erupted into a certain amount of chaos. His criteria for selecting church leaders (1 Timothy 3) reveals a presumption that these leaders would be male, not a surprising expectation for his day. Similarly his admonishment to slaves to maintain their respect for their masters (1 Timothy 6:1–2) demonstrates his predisposition to work within the established social order rather than challenge it. It is understandable that women and slaves would have seen in the gospel a remedy to their society's oppression. While Paul has previously seemed to position himself as on board with the freedom of the gospel, perhaps these passages represent his concern that these under classes are moving to change too much too quickly. Remembering how relatively recently in world history the evils of slavery and the inequality between the sexes have begun to be addressed goes some way in explaining Paul's tactic here.

Other ways Paul finds to guide Timothy in reducing chaos involve his concern that various members of the church receive appropriate compassion for the meeting of their needs. Here he takes pains to remind Timothy to encourage families to take care of their own so that the church can direct her efforts to those who have no safety net for aid (1 Timothy 5:8, 16). In general, his further comments about women, especially widows, reflect the common expectations of the ancient world that young widows will want to remarry and continue to have children whereas older women (those older than sixty) should be content to devote themselves to *all kinds of good deeds* (e.g., babysitting and washing the feet of the saints) (1 Timothy 5:9–10).

Primarily, however, the tone of Paul's letter is one of loving encouragement. As pastor, Timothy ought to treat all the church as members of his family—older men like fathers, young men as brothers, older women as mothers, and younger women as sisters (1 Timothy 5:1-2). More personally he counsels Timothy, "Don't let anyone put you down because you are young" (1 Timothy 4:12), and he reminds him it's okay to "go ahead and drink a little wine" (1 Timothy 5:23). His closing remarks display his profound affection for and faith in this young man to whom he is passing his mantle. "Pursue a righteous life—a life of wonder, love, steadiness, courtesy" (1 Timothy 6:11). "Oh, my dear Timothy, guard the treasure you were given" (1 Timothy 6:20).

2 Timothy

In his second letter to Timothy, Paul reinforces his original message. He encourages Timothy to be bold in spreading the gospel, cherishing the gift of faith nurtured in him by his grandmother and mother (2 Timothy 1:5). He compares the tough work of church-building to the relentless dedication required of soldiers, athletes, and farmers (2 Timothy 2:3–6). Timothy is to keep to the essentials of the faith while he tries to curtail *pious nitpicking* from cropping up among the believers. Above all else Paul warns him to elect leaders who practice what they preach (2 Timothy 2:14–17). Even though the gospel has landed Paul back in a Roman prison (2 Timothy 1:12, 16–17), he reminds Timothy that the privilege of serving the Master in this way is more than worth the hardship involved. The best antidote for trouble lies in reading Scripture (2 Timothy 3:15–16).

Even as Paul repeats his encouragement, however, his tone is different here, much more personal. He opens with a clear statement of his affection, "To you, Timothy, the son I love so much (2 Timothy 1:2), and he recalls their "last tearful good-bye" (2 Timothy 1:4). Acknowledging the imminence of his own passing, Paul asks Timothy more pointedly to take his place in the spreading of the gospel (2 Timothy 4:6). Timothy has been a good apprentice. He has shared in Paul's teaching and troubles and witnessed the power and rescue of the Holy Spirit in numerous ways (2 Timothy 3:10–11). While Paul laments the recent desertion of some of his disciples, he is thankful that Luke has stayed by his side (2 Timothy 4:11). Though in Philippians

1:22–24, Paul claimed indifference to life or death because both allowed him to rejoice in Jesus, here he begs Timothy twice (2 Timothy 4:9, 21) to visit him before the end, making it clear how much he craves their reunion on this side of the grave. This letter, cast as the apostle's last, displays not only Paul's ongoing fervor for the gospel but also the depth of his emotional attachment to men and women who have shared his calling.

Titus

As we have read through Acts and into the Pauline epistles, it becomes apparent that Paul mentored many disciples. Although Timothy stands out as Paul's right-hand man, it is clear that Paul had deep relationships with many in the early church. We first hear of Titus in Paul's letter to the Galatians, where he holds this young Greek up as an example of an early, uncircumcised Christian (Galatians 2:1–3) against the claim of subsequent preachers who demanded circumcision for Christians. Reading between the lines, we gather that Titus accompanied Paul and Barnabas on their first missionary journey when the idea of including Gentile converts was relatively new. Titus shows up again in Paul's 2 Corinthians as someone Paul entrusted to work with the difficult Corinthian church (2 Corinthians 8:8, 16). Second Timothy places him on assignment in Dalmatia (2 Timothy 4:10).

Paul's letter to Titus, his "legitimate son in the faith" (Titus 1:4), seems to be sent around the same time as his first letter to Timothy. Here Paul has left Titus on the island of Crete with the difficult task of dealing with a rather stubborn and rebellious group of new Christians. Paul admits to leaving Titus "in charge in Crete so that you could complete what I had left half-done" (Titus 1:5). Apparently a group of rebels who sound like the Judaizers of Galatia have sown a lot of discord in the Cretan community. Their concerns have extended beyond circumcision, and they worry the new Christians about the purity of ceremonies (Titus 1:13–16) and even their genealogies (Titus 3:9). Paul's advice, similar to what we read in 1 Timothy, rests specifically on Titus selecting strong leaders of good reputation and ongoing practice and generally on Titus urging basic, upstanding decorum on all members of society. The idea remains that Christians should put forward a lifestyle unimpeachable by outsiders. Against this end Paul confides that Titus' personal example will carry the most weight, "Show them all this by doing it yourself, incorruptible in your teaching, your words solid and sane. Then anyone who is dead set against us, when he finds nothing weird or misguided, might eventually come around" (Titus 2:7–8). Paul goes on to remind Titus that all believers, himself included, began "stupid and stubborn, dupes of sin, ordered every which way by our glands, going around with a chip of our shoulder, hated and hating back" (Titus 3:3), but "our loving Savior God, stepped in, ... gave us a good bath, and we came out of it new people" (Titus 3:4-5). With this vision and teaching in mind, Titus is to take a firm stand against the rebels. "Warn a quarrelsome person once or twice, but then be done with him" (Titus 3:10). Like Timothy, Titus needs to remember "you're in charge. Don't let anyone put you down" (Titus 2:15). By all we can see in the New Testament, Titus kept at his mission, having started early under Paul in Galatia and still hard at work as a proven leader in Dalmatia as Paul's words end.

Philemon

This last letter of the Pauline epistles is merely a short note by comparison to Paul's other works. Paul claims Philemon as a "good friend and companion in this work" (Philemon 1) of spreading the gospel. On the basis of this rapport Paul writes to Philemon to ask an unusual (for the time period) favor, namely forgiveness of a runaway slave. Under the laws of the Roman

Empire it was not considered murder to kill one's own slave. Generally masters refrained from capital punishment because it rendered a poor return on their financial investment. But a runaway slave would easily be worth the loss given how difficult it would be to sell him to others. Add to that the accusation that the slave was also a thief, and the death penalty would have been the common response. Given these social norms, we must remark on Paul's audacity (and Onesimus' courage!) to have sent the missive by this same slave's own hand (Philemon 10), entrusting him with this note as well as his epistle to the Colossians (Colossians 4:9). Paul describes Onesimus by making a pun of his name, which means *useful*. "He was 'useless' to you before [when he ran away]; but now [that he has become a Christian] he's 'useful' to both of us" (Philemon 11). Paul would prefer to keep Onesimus with him, but has sent the slave back to his master to make reconciliation.

What a contrast this request makes with the teachings about slavery we have read in Ephesians, 1 Timothy, Colossians itself—the very letter Onesimus bears along with this one to Philemon. Here Paul honors the legal norm of his era by convincing Onesimus that he needs to make amends to his master for the suggested ways he has wronged him. "If he owes you anything" (Philemon 18) probably means *if he has stolen from Philemon*. But at the same time Paul's tone with Philemon as much as insists that the master welcome Onesimus no longer as a slave ("I don't need to remind you, do I, that you owe your very life to me?" as it says in Philemon19). It would seem that Paul is of two minds about slavery (and the issue of women as church leaders). When he is giving advice of a general nature as he does in the above letters, he seems inclined not to buck the social system already in existence, but when he's dealing with particular cases like this one, not to mention the many instances where his greetings to women imply their leadership in the church, he ends up affirming his statement of equality summed up in Galatians 3:28, which indicates that God refuses to acknowledge the ways human label one another. How are we to understand this?

What can help us here is to note how Paul makes a clear distinction between God's vision of who we are and the way the world sees us. Because Paul accepts the fallenness of the world, he expects it to abound with injustice. Christianity anticipates transforming the world not by legislating change from the powers that be downward but from the groundswell of individuals and their communities being made over from the inside out and the bottom up. This is how Paul and other early Christians choose to put certain battles—major changes in the societal framework—aside for another time. But we should note how Paul handles the case of Christians married to nonbelievers as an example. While he advises believers to accede to the wishes of those not yet converted, he still expects that faith will have a leavening effect on most of these marriages (1 Corinthians 7:12–14). Clearly this is the tact he takes with Philemon—believing that the man who is a master according to the world's reckoning will by faith be able to rise above the standards set by his day and treat his slave as a brother in Christ.

The nuances of this closing letter of Paul's present a good platform from which to launch a summary of the Pauline corpus. What are the themes that Paul brings to our understanding of Christianity?

Summing up Paul's Contribution

Of primary importance in Paul's work is his consistent interpretation of Jesus' death on the cross as the ultimate act of God to reconcile the breach between humans and their Creator caused by human sin. Paul goes to great pains to explain how this phenomenon occurs using as many different images as possible. Speaking in religious terms, he presents Jesus as a temple sacrifice offered as expiation for human sin (Romans 3:23–25).

In Galatians 3:10–14, he pictures Christ becoming a curse (by hanging on a tree) and thus producing a *vaccine* to sinning for anyone who would receive inoculation. Using the parlance of the slave markets, he names Jesus the one who ransoms us from the slavery of sin (Ephesians 1:7). Often he refers to believers as legally adopted sons and daughters of the Almighty. Together these various metaphors help us to grasp what is essentially a mystery—how Christ's death removes the impediment of our sin that was such an affront to the Deity's holiness. With our sin accounted for, God and humans are connected again in the love relationship that was the Lord's original intention at creation. Christ's actual resurrection from the dead stands as the proof of God's consummate plan for humans to live in eternity with their maker. Humans receive their redemption from God *solely through faith*, not by any accumulation of good works to their own credit. That they should become doers of good works is the necessary consequence of their faithful acceptance of God's grace in absolving them of sin. Paul aids the action of the Spirit working within believers by exhorting Christians toward constant prayer and the maintenance of loving relationships without concern for socially defined barriers. Always he reminds churches to resist petty disagreements and to value one another in their differences because each member of the church has a God-given role to play. Likewise Christians must consider the effects of their actions on others (whether it be in what they eat, say, or do) so that their deeds do not become the occasion for another to sin.

Although Paul proclaims the Christian a *new creature* called to abide by *God's* and not humans' standards of righteousness, he never speaks of revolution. His directive lies in living *within* the established order, not *coercing* others to change but behaving in such a way that attracts respect and possibly provokes the nonbeliever's contemplation. The Christian should not seek persecution but nonetheless should be prepared for it.

Christ submitted Himself to extreme suffering and even death. Many Christians will likewise suffer. Committing violence is never even raised as an option, however, because vengeance belongs to the Lord alone. Instead Paul challenges Christians to accept political authority and live as good citizens, paying their debts and not abandoning their jobs even in anticipation of Christ's return. Paul never preaches a recapturing of the Acts 4:32–36 momentary utopia, where new believers held all things in common in order to meet everyone's needs. Rather like Jesus' lesson of "turning the other cheek," Paul envisions the coming of God's kingdom through the transformation of individuals and the communities they populate from the inside out. Therefore, though he advises women not to upstage men in the sanctuaries, he simultaneously encourages the ministries of the numerous women he befriends in the course of his mission. In turn, even as he asks slaves to keep their place before their masters, he asks Philemon to embrace his runaway as a brother in Christ.

To me, however, the most disarming aspect of Paul's ministry still lies in the personality that shines through these letters offering us about as thorough a depiction of Paul's character as we get of any biblical figure. First Paul's life is an object lesson in redemption. The man, to whom Luke casually alludes in Acts 8:1 as approving of Stephen's murder, becomes the lynchpin in the initial dissemination of the gospel after Jesus' death. Yet what is perhaps most interesting about his conversion rests in how Paul's character is not so much altered as redirected. The zeal that he once held against Christians becomes channeled into a relentless pursuit of evangelism. The intellectual prowess he honed as a rabbi enables him as an apostle to explain the gospel over and over again to converts of varying backgrounds and understandings. Walter Wangerin, writing a novel about Paul's life, supposes, "When problems arose in his churches, he wasn't so much aggrieved as glad for the chance to think and write. He said that in solving problems, the Spirit taught him things he hadn't known before."[93]

In these letters we have seen Paul appear boasting and humble, eloquent and dogmatic, impatiently furious and peaceably acquiescing. Yet taking the corpus as a whole, I find both his manifest love of Jesus and his fellows fueling his passion for ministry. Biographer John Pollock wonders if Paul's treatise on love in 1 Corinthians 13 isn't in some way autobiographical— that the chief learning Paul gleans from his evangelizing is the importance of love.[94] While Paul proves himself willing to endure anything for the sake of spreading the Word of God, his letters also testify mightily to his deep affection for the men and women with whom he works. In sum, we observe how Paul's concern for the survival of the truth and clarity of the message commands his painstaking attention as he maps out the details of how to convert espoused faith into day-to-day living. Even as the centuries have passed, his words continue to speak to the heart of what faith means.

While vital to the establishment of the church, Paul's voice is not the only one marking the signposts on the Christian's journey. We now need to turn to the remaining eight epistles in the Christian canon. What do they have to add to Paul's message?

Hebrews

No one knows the identity of the author of Hebrews.[95] Neither do we know the location from which he (or she) writes nor the specific church addressed. For a while people supposed Paul

---

[93] Walter Wangerin, Jr. *Paul, a Novel*, p. 352.

[94] John Pollock, *The Apostle*, p. 46.

[95] Scholars (including Martin Luther) conjecture that the author may have been Apollos, the Alexandrian Jew initially discipled by Priscilla and Aquila in Acts 18:24–28. In recent times Priscilla herself has been suggested as the author.

as the author, but even reading in English we can tell that this work does not resemble Paul's literary style. As a first point it is not really formatted as a letter. Believers are addressed but never named. Rather it reads as a presentation of the author's well-thought-through analysis of how Christianity stands as the fulfillment of the Hebrew Scriptures. Its heavy use of Old Testament imagery and Scripture as well as its reliance on an intimate understanding of Mosaic worship and sacrifice rituals testify to an individual well versed in Judaism, probably initially a Jew converted to Christianity. As we will see, evidence of Pauline influence exists, but the line of reasoning is the author's own. The work represents this evangelist's insight into how the Hebrew Scriptures foreshadow and foretell the coming of Jesus as the resolution of God's dilemma of love for humans and hatred of sin.

As the book's title implies, our author approaches his audience as a Jewish Christian speaking to other Jewish Christ believers. He seeks to draw from his disciples' knowledge of Scripture and Jewish custom to help them interpret both their Christian faith and the present hardship that now accompanies their belief in Christ. His first point rests on the primacy of Jesus. True, in the past God sent prophets and even angels to proclaim the Lord's words, but Christ surpasses all of these. As important as Moses was to God's chosen people Israel, in his obedience to the Lord he built a house (the framework of Judaism) as God's servant, "getting ready for what was to come whereas Christ as Son is in charge of the house" (Hebrews 3:5–6).

Jews of the first century were well acquainted with the importance of the priesthood to the faith. Up until the Romans' destruction[96] of the temple in 70 CE, priests would daily perform the ritual sacrifices and conduct worship services for the

---

[96] The author never mentions this event. Is this because he writes before 70 CE or because he is trying to diminish the loss of the temple worship for Christians?

children of Israel. The author of Hebrews seeks to access his listeners' understanding of those practices in order to explain how Jesus is actually the high priest above all those operating in the Levite and Aaronic tradition. Jesus, he asserts, is a priest after the order of Melchizedek—the priest Abraham encounters in Genesis 14:18.[97] In Genesis, Melchizedek appears only briefly, and he is described as both the king of Salem (meaning peace, the root of the name for the Holy City) and the priest of the "Most High God" (Genesis 14:19 NIV). When Abram gave him one tenth of his battle plunder (Genesis 14:20), he acknowledged Melchizedek as aligned with the same Lord he himself served. Mosaic law would later draw on this precedent in its mandate for the laity to offer tithes as support for the clergy (Numbers 18:21). These Levite priests' duties involved highly prescribed conventions that allowed them to cleanse their own sins while they also attended to the transgressions of the children of Israel. But Jesus is a wholly different kind of priest. Our author points to the absence of any genealogies qualifying Melchizedek (Hebrews 7:2) as a connection to Jesus, who also did not descend from the traditional Levitical line. (Jesus hails from the tribe of Judah.) The temple rites that the Levite clergy oversaw represented a temporary arrangement put in place until the time ripened for God to put in motion the divine plan for addressing the world's evil. Jesus' death on the cross obliterates the need for the elaborate sacrificial rituals of Judaism. Instead of goat or calf blood, which never could expunge sin in reality, He spills His own blood, and because He committed no wrong, His sacrifice absolves all human sin once and for all (Hebrews 9:12). In addition, like Melchizedek, Jesus is both priest and king. As priest, He purifies believers; as king, He invites them into the everlasting life of heaven.

---

[97] Melchizedek is also mentioned in Psalm 110:4 (NIV). Given a messianic interpretation, the psalm predicts the Chosen One will be "a priest forever, in the order of Melchizedek."

We do hear echoes of Paul's teaching when this writer complains that his readers are still immature in the faith, needing milk when they should be ready for solid food (Hebrews 5:12–14, compare to 1 Corinthians 3:2). Also like Paul, he roots his line of reasoning in Old Testament imagery and the close scrutiny of Scripture. Still, while his explanation of Christian theology does not contradict Paul, his selection of biblical texts and his arguments themselves demonstrate a fresh approach. Though proclaiming the same message, our writer has been set free to preach the gospel in his own style. Even more than Paul, the author of the book of Hebrews sees a natural flow from the promises of the Old Testament to their fulfillment in Jesus. In Hebrews 11:1 (NIV), he defines faith as "being sure of what we hope for and certain of what we do not see." Then he walks us through a recitation of the various Old Testament Hebrews, whose trusting service to the Lord allowed the Deity's purposes to unfold, even though they themselves did not behold the fruition of God's promises. Unlike Paul, he does not focus on the issue of faith replacing the Law but instead draws heavily on Jeremiah's prediction that God would exchange the old failed *covenant* with a new one written "on [the people's] hearts" (Hebrews 8:10 NIV and Jeremiah 31:31–14). In addition, some of his imagery reflects Platonic[98] philosophy. He claims, "The law is only a *shadow* of the good things that are coming, not the realities themselves" (Hebrews 10:1 NIV).

It is possible and maybe even likely that the author of the book of Hebrews writes before the time when Judaism and Christianity began to identify themselves as separate religions. As he closes his work, our writer offers some typical pieces of advice. He suggests we should get along with one another (Hebrews 13:1), be hospitable to the needy (Hebrews 13:2–3), honor marriage

---

[98] Plato, writing in the fourth century BCE, puts forward his theory of forms that an object like a table that we see in our world is but a "shadow" of the "real table" or the *form* table that exists beyond this world.

(Hebrews 13:4), and avoid strange teachings (Hebrews 13:9–10). But the major thrust of his work remains a reminder to these Jewish Christians to stay the course. Even in the face of an increasing number of Gentile Christians, Jewish Christians must not doubt what they have been taught about Christ. Jesus is the fulfillment of everything the Hebrew Scriptures promised. In this way the book of Hebrews makes a great illustration of why Christianity never sought to turn its back on its Jewish scriptural roots but rather embraced the Old Testament as the necessary context for understanding Jesus.

James

Before we discuss this book, we do well to review what we know about James, the half brother of Jesus[99] from the gospels, Acts, and Paul. The gospels paint a rather unflattering portrait of a brother out of sync with Jesus. The Synoptics see him as misunderstanding and wanting to interrupt Jesus' preaching (Matthew 12:46–50; Mark 3:31–34; Luke 8:19–21). On the other hand, John has the brothers trying to urge Jesus to make his ministry more public (John 7:3–5). Despite this, Acts 1:14 shows Jesus' brothers along with his mother, Mary, gathering with the faithful in Jerusalem after Jesus' ascension, then clearly on board with his mission. Then Paul singles out James specifically as one to whom the risen Christ appears (1 Corinthians 15:7). In Galatians, Paul mentions meeting James in Jerusalem some years after his own conversion (Galatians 1:19) and refers to him as a *pillar* of the church in Galatians 2:9. Acts 15:13–29 confirms Paul's assessment of James's stature as James emerges as the leader of the Jerusalem church and orchestrator of the Jerusalem council's letter to Gentile believers regarding circumcision. But later in Acts, we find James worrying over Paul's missionary

---

[99] In Matthew 13:55 and Mark 6:3, James appears first in a list of Jesus' brothers.

activities, especially to the extent that they clash with Jewish Christians' perception that Paul is eschewing the law of Moses in order to garner Gentile converts. Paul attempts to make amends with the Jewish Christian sector by taking a vow of purification according to Jewish custom, but as Acts 21:17–36 attests, it ends badly with Paul arrested. Unlike Paul, James seems able to maintain the respect of both Christian and traditional Jews while he nonetheless devotes himself to following Jesus.

The book of James begins the last seven letters, known as the General Epistles because they do not address a particular church and deal with universal advice to Christians everywhere and in all times. Scholars tend to assign a later date to many of these letters, especially those that allude to Roman persecution, which was not rampant throughout the empire until the latter part of the first century. As we read, we immediately notice the Jewish flavor in the greeting, "To the twelve tribes scattered among the nations" (James 1:1). Much of what James writes sounds very similar to the words of Christ recorded in Matthew's gospel. It's a gift when life tests us. Trials cause us to mature in our faith (James 1:2–4, compare to Matthew 5:12). When we feel lost, we must ask for God's help "boldly, believingly" (James 1:5–8, compare to Matthew 7:7–8). Take care to obey the "Royal Rule of the Scriptures: 'love others as you love yourself'" (James 2:8, compare to Matthew 22:39 and Leviticus 19:18). In the same way, James' advice echoes Jewish wisdom literature. He cautions strenuously against the uncontrolled tongue and the trouble thoughtless words can ignite (James 3:3–10, compare to Proverbs 16:27–28). He challenges those who would be wise to live humbly, not trying to be better than others but striving always to respect and honor and make peace with one's fellows (James 3:13–18, compare to Proverbs 11:2, 18).

Over the centuries what has brought James his renown, however, lies in his discussion of faith and works. Like Paul, he employs Abraham to make his point. While Paul uses Abraham to emphasize *faith* and how God credited Abraham's faith as righteousness before there was any law (Genesis 15:6; Romans 3:28; Galatians 2:15–16), James harkens back to Abraham's binding of Isaac (Genesis 22:1–19) as the *work* that proves his faith (James 2:21). Again reminding us of Jesus' parable of the sheep and the goats in Matthew 25:31-46, James asserts, "Real religion … is this: reach out to the homeless and loveless in their plight" (James 1:27). This allows him to conclude, "Faith without deeds is dead" (James 2:26 NIV). Strictly speaking, James' outlook does not contradict Paul's thesis that it is through faith alone that we receive God's forgiveness, but Martin Luther took a dim view of James' emphasis on works, calling the book an "epistle of straw" in his *Preface to the New Testament*, which was published in 1522. A close reading of James, however, makes it clear that he believes where there is faith, works necessarily follow; however, he does not believe the converse that good works indicate the presence of faith.

By tradition, James' chief claim to fame lay in his persistent prayer. We see evidence of this in his final chapter. Here he recommends prayer at all turns, "Are you hurting? Pray. Do you feel great? Sing. Are you sick? Call the church leaders together to pray" (James 5:13–14). Why? "The prayer of a person living right with God is something powerful to be reckoned with" (James 5:16). To me, his words resound with the voice of Jesus' teaching, and his style of address shows all the markers of a patient pastor tending his flock. This book provides a fascinating record of not only how Jesus' teaching was preserved but also how profound an impact Christ's life, death, and resurrection made on His followers.

Peter

We are familiar with Peter from the gospels and Acts. The gospels show us a common fisherman who's initially rather rough around the edges and who was nonetheless a natural leader. (His name appears first in every list of the apostles.) A study in contradictions, Peter along with James and John, the sons of Zebedee, stood in awe while they witnessed Christ's transfiguration on the mountain (Matthew 17:1–8; Mark 9:2–8; Luke 9:28–36), yet they faltered in the garden of Gethsemane when Jesus especially asked them to stay awake with Him (Matthew 26:37, 40; Mark 14:33, 37). As the first to pronounce Jesus the Messiah (Matthew 16:13–28; Mark 8:27–9:1; Luke 9:18–27), Peter received Jesus' designation as the rock on which He would build His church. But his faith turned rocky at Jesus' arrest, and he ended up denying his Master three times despite his earlier confident promises of steadfastness (Matthew 26:69–75; Mark 14:66–72; Luke 22:55–62; John 18:16–18, 25–27).

When we encounter Peter in Acts, however, we find a changed man. Still very much the leader of the fledgling group of believers as Acts opens, Peter now emerges preaching forcefully and able to quote appropriate texts from Scripture readily. In addition, he performs healings similar to those of Jesus with the important distinction that he cures in the name of Christ. While Paul makes it clear in Galatians 2:8 that Peter was to be apostle to the Jews as Paul would be to the Gentiles, it is Peter's vision on the rooftop in Joppa (Acts 10:9–18) that awakens the home church in Jerusalem to the astounding reality that God meant salvation for the Gentiles as well as the Jews.

The two letters ascribed to Peter must be dated from the 60s or later and speak to a second-generation church that seems to see herself as both separate from Judaism yet also the inheritor of the promises God made to Israel. The first letter combines an articulate summary of the essentials of the Christian faith with an enthusiastic exhortation to believers to demonstrate the truth of the gospel in exemplary living. Full of appropriate references to Scripture and clear theological insight into the meaning of the gospel, it bears evidence of Pauline influence while it maintains its own voice. In contrast, the second letter communicates in a more personal tone and comes across as more of a farewell letter.

1 Peter

Addressing himself like James to "exiles scattered to the four winds" (1 Peter 1:1), Peter begins this epistle likening Christians to a new wave of God's people dispersed into the world and exiled as the Jews had been in the Diaspora after the fall of Jerusalem in 586 BCE.[100] These represent a new generation of Christians—ones who "never saw [Jesus], yet ... love him" (1 Peter 1:8). In accordance with John's gospel, Peter explains Jesus as the *unblemished* paschal lamb whose sacrificial death redeems the sin of humans (1 Peter 1:19, compare to John 1:29). Like Paul, he grounds his message in the understanding of Christ's death as God's plan conceived before creation (1 Peter 1:20–21, compare to Ephesians 1:4–10). The new life Jesus brings the Christian is not a biological rebirth but a spiritual one coming forth from "God's living Word" (1 Peter 1:22). Peter offers us some fresh images of this new life in Christ. He compares believers to "living stones" (1 Peter 2:5 NIV) who together with Jesus as the cornerstone (1 Peter 2:6; Psalm 118:22) build a sanctuary—a replacement for the Jerusalem temple. The church is now the metaphorical temple, and all Christians are now priests whom God has "chosen to be a holy people" (1 Peter 2:9). In this analysis Peter implies that because traditional Jews have not accepted Christ, their mantle as God's chosen now falls to Christianity. As Israel suffered (through the exile and Diaspora), so will the

---

[100] This comment about the *scattering* begs the question whether this epistle is written after the Roman destruction of Jerusalem in 70 CE. The author seems to see Christians in a parallel situation to the displaced Jews of the first exile in 586 BCE when Babylon razed Solomon's temple.

church—the new Israel—endure trials in the present age and the future.

Like Paul in Ephesians and Colossians, Peter raises the issue of household relationships but adds his own nuances. He counsels slaves to show their faith by continuing to offer good service even when their masters treat them unjustly (1 Peter 2:18–20). In the same way, Jesus fulfilled the role of God's suffering servant from Isaiah. "He suffered everything that came his way so you would know it could be done" (1 Peter 2:21). Speaking to women married to unbelievers, he advises, "Be submissive to your husbands so that, if any of them do not believe the word, they may be won over without words by the behavior of their wives" (1 Peter 3:1 NIV). With husbands he reminds, "Honor [your wives] ... As women they lack some of your advantages" (1 Peter 3:7). With these examples he makes a general rule: Christians must live humbly, not making demands on others but being a blessing to their communities. He entreats Christians *not* to challenge the authorities and their likely injustices but instead to impact the world by living the standards of holiness Jesus conveyed through His teaching and His life, turning the other cheek, as it were, to the world so that the unbeliever may be "conquered" by their goodness (1 Peter 2:13–17). "Most of all, love each other as if your life depended on it ... Be quick to give a meal to the hungry, a bed to the homeless—cheerfully" (1 Peter 4:8–9).

In the early days of the faith outsiders had a difficult time understanding whether those who followed Jesus were Jews or believers in some new religion. It requires the authority of Peter, the man whom Jesus charged with founding His church, to articulate the identity of the faith. Christians are a new kind of Jew. As the new Israel, Christians must embrace afresh God's Old Testament call to be a people set apart (Exodus 19:6). Yet unlike the Jews of the first exile, they need not mourn the loss of a physical temple and its worship and sacrifices. Instead they must see themselves as a spiritual temple, a beacon to the world to light the way to God. Though Christians should always be ready to testify about their faith to anyone who asks, Peter admonishes them to "do this with gentleness and respect" (1 Peter 3:15 NIV). Preaching must never supplant the primary means of witness—to live humbly according to God's holy ways of compassion and truth.

2 Peter

The second letter speaks to us most clearly as a farewell address. Here the author identifies himself humbly as *Simon Peter* (2 Peter 1:1) allowing us the recall from the gospels how many times Jesus reverted to the apostle's original name when Peter stumbled. Peter begins in a personal mode, "I know that I am to die soon ... and so I am especially eager that you have all this down in black and white so that after I die, you'll have it for ready reference" (2 Peter 1:14–15). By way of corroboration Peter reminds his readers they can trust his words because he was an eyewitness to Christ's transfiguration (2 Peter 1:16–18). Continuing, the apostle admonishes the faithful to rely on Scripture because "prophecy resulted when the Holy Spirit prompted men and women to speak God's Word" (2 Peter 1:21). This will be their primary defense against lying prophets and their heretical teachings. Perhaps Peter refers here to some incipient forms of gnosticism as we observed in Paul's letter to the Colossians. He also warns about fallout from the delay of Jesus' second coming. While Peter affirms that the Lord will return, it will be as Christ foretold it, "Unannounced, like a thief" (2 Peter 3:10, compare to Luke 12:39) coming in the night. Believers need to remember that "with the Lord a day is like a thousand years, and a thousand years are like a day" (2 Peter 3:8 NIV, compare to Psalm 90:4). "God isn't late with his promise ... he is restraining himself on account of you, holding back the End because he doesn't want anyone lost" (2 Peter 3:9).

Before he signs off, Peter even mentions the work of "our good brother Paul, who was given much wisdom in these matters ... [and] in all his letters, has written you essentially the same thing (2 Peter 3:15–16). While he admits that some of what Paul writes is "difficult to understand" (2 Peter 3:16), he implies that what Paul has written is Scripture. With these comments we hear the church acknowledging the formation of the canon that will be added to the Old Testament. In addition, this letter works to indicate that Peter sees himself working in concert with everyone God has called to spread the gospel, not worrying about his own legacy of evangelism. It speaks volumes about the inception of the Christian movement that its original leaders did not seek to promote themselves but rather envisioned themselves as servants entrusted with the building of God's kingdom on earth.

John 1, 2, and 3

While the fourth gospel is credited to the apostle John, neither it nor the other three testimonies about Jesus' life shed much light on his personality. We know that along with his brother, James (the son of Zebedee, not the James of our previous epistle), and Peter, John was among those closest to Jesus in the latter's earthly life. Jesus invited the three to witness His transfiguration and pled with the same trio to keep watch with Him in the garden of Gethsemane the night before His crucifixion. On the other hand, his mother caused a stir when she tried to parlay her sons' proximity to the Master into a tangible reward, asking that Jesus promise the pair a seat on either side of His throne (Matthew 20:21). (Mark 10:35–40 puts the request in the brothers' mouths.) Jesus also denied these "Sons of Thunder" (Mark 3:17) when they offered to rain destruction on some Samaritans who refused to receive the Master (Luke 9:51–56). Nevertheless, his own gospel claims him as the only one of the Twelve to observe the crucifixion; his presence there affords Jesus the opportunity to place His mother into John's care (John 19:25–27). In Acts 4, he emerges as Peter's right-hand man, and in Galatians 2:9, Paul refers to him as a *pillar of the church.*

Beyond this, most of what we know about John we must infer from his writing. Again, whether the same man who wrote the gospel also contributed the three letters ascribed to the evangelist is a matter of scholarly debate. As we read, however, we quickly recognize John's literary style from the gospel. He refers to Jesus as the *Word* (1 John 1:1) and makes heavy use of contrasting images, such as light and darkness, truth and lies, and love and hate. Like Peter, John confirms himself as an eyewitness of Jesus' life (1 John 1:2). He continues his practice of refraining to name himself but clearly states his reason for writing: in the gospel, "So you will believe that Jesus is the Messiah" (John 20:31). In the first epistle his purpose is "that you who believe in God's Son will know beyond the shadow of a doubt that you have eternal life" (1 John 5:13).

In his first letter John follows James in emphasizing the importance of our words matching our actions. "If someone claims, 'I know [God] well!' but doesn't keep his commandments, he's obviously a liar" (1 John 2:4). Another example of liars are what John calls the antichrists who abound in their midst (1 John 2:18). These heretics, likely early Gnostics, are denying that God incarnated Himself in Jesus, that Christ was both the Son of God and still a flesh-and-blood human (1 John 2:22–23; 4:2–3). John affirms that Jesus actually died and rose again. These facts are the basis of our faith in God's forgiveness of our sins and promise of our eventual resurrection in heaven. Still, the major thrust of his message remains love. Because "God is love" (1 John 4:16), we are not just enabled to love but required. "Loving God includes loving people. You've got to love both" (1 John 4:21).

John begins his second and third letters identifying himself as *the elder* (NIV) or *pastor* (Peterson). Here he is writing to specific people and their churches whose identity is now lost. The format of both epistles is similar. John commends the faith of the addressee, warns them against the same heretics he debunked in his first letter, and reminds both communities to focus on the commandment to love one another. In both letters he applauds their general hospitality to familiar and unknown Christians alike. Yet he makes note of certain exceptions. In the second letter he takes care to admonish the community from taking in deceivers and giving them a forum for their lies (2 John 10–11). Still, he reserves his stiffest criticism for a certain Diotrephes, who has engaged in malicious gossip and refused reception to Christians (3 John 9–10). Having mentioned these points of concern, the elderly pastor concludes saying that he prefers to meet in person rather than discuss these issues in *pen and ink.*

These three letters of John give us yet another picture of the activities of those whom God asked to spread the gospel across the earth. In John's case it seems that beyond telling the story of the gospel, he, more like James, realized his call primarily as a pastor to the communities of faith he had planted.

Jude

Calling himself the brother of James (which, presuming he means James, the brother of Jesus, makes him a half brother of Christ as well), Jude offers us the last epistle of the Bible. In this short letter Jude writes to an unnamed community about the danger of heretics. Using examples from both the Old Testament and the Apocrypha,[101] Jude offers cautionary tales about people who abandoned God and suffered because of it. He reminds his audience that the apostles of Christ foretold that false teachers like these would plague believers "in the last days" (Jude 18). Therefore, he writes to encourage the faithful to stay strong in

---

[101] The Apocrypha is a collection of books written during the period between the Old and New Testaments.

their beliefs. "Be tender with sinners, but not soft on sin" (Jude 23). Jude closes, "To him who is able to keep you from falling and to present you before his glorious presence without fault and with great joy—to the only God our Savior be glory, majesty, power and authority, through Jesus Christ our Lord, before all ages, now and forevermore" (Jude 24–25 NIV). This benediction incorporated into the text points to how worship reinforced belief in the earliest years of the church. In addition, this book is yet another reminder of how seriously the fledgling church felt the threat of false teaching and how determined the first-century evangelists became in their efforts to keep the message of the gospel uncorrupted.

In Conclusion

The letters that complete the New Testament's epistles corroborate the teaching of Paul, but they also widen the window through which we can view the issues the church confronted in the first century CE. While all attest to the primacy of Jesus' actual death on the cross and literal resurrection from that death as the foundation of the Christian assertion that God has forgiven human sins, each new author provides a fresh perspective based on his particular ministry. The writer of Hebrews underscores the seamless progression from the Old Testament to the New as the ongoing revelation of what God is doing for humans. James highlights the measure of true faith as a harvest of good works. While 1 Peter establishes Christianity as heir to the promises and requirements God made of Israel, 2 Peter lends understanding to the delay of Christ's second coming. John reiterates the preeminence of the love commandment. Jude brings in the last word by echoing all the above in their warnings against heretical teachings.

The upshot of all these letters is that the early evangelists, though separate personalities, adhere to a remarkably unified set of basic beliefs. Jesus Christ—His life, death, and resurrection—is the ultimate proof of God's love for humanity. Christ's sacrificial death allows God and humans to enter into a relationship that, though something God always desired, was impossible for God to enjoy while sin stood in the way. It is this relationship, which is available to humans by faith and not works and which grants new life as an ongoing transformation of character, that allows humans not by their own efforts but by their connection to the Lord to approach God's *goodness*. But the process of transformation is neither automatic nor easy. The Christian must actively follow Jesus by maintaining the relationship through prayer, worship, fellowship, and the reading of Scripture. These letters demonstrate how quickly wrong teachings, inside rivalries, and outside persecutions can distract the believer from this course. Primarily, however, they offer a salve to these human shortcomings—advice for the forgiven who still find themselves sinning. The earnest Christian will find in these epistles the encouragement to press on toward the goal of living righteously before the holy God.

Chapter 12

Does It Really Say That the World Will End?

Maybe not emotionally but intellectually we all know the geophysical universe that we inhabit will end someday. Scientists offer a host of possibilities for how it might happen. Some of these project the ending to come millions or billions of years from now, while others caution that it could be sooner than later if we're not careful with our environment. It is still possible with nuclear weapons and biological warfare for humans to bring about their own demise. Yet as we saw with the creation story, what the Bible has to say about the end of the world is not in answer to the questions when and how but rather why. Why the world will end someday and what will happen after it ends are significant issues the book of Revelation addresses. But even these queries are not the primary focus. Instead we find that this last book is all about closure—framing the biblical testimony with ultimate meaning. Just as Genesis gave us the beginning, Revelation offers us the ending of the story the Bible has been telling throughout the Old and New Testaments—the summation of all that God has accomplished in this grand act of creating humans in the image of the Deity to people the earth. As we begin this final stop on our introductory tour of the Bible, let us prepare to find two familiar finishing themes brought to life in this apocalyptic discourse. The first is what makes the ending of a crime drama so satisfying. The evildoers are brought to justice, and the innocent are properly vindicated. The second reaches deep into our experience of childhood storytelling. What began as "once upon a time" will now end with "and they lived happily ever after" (when we understand the *they* to mean those who love God).

Most scholars date the book of Revelation to 95 CE when the persecution of Christians under the reign of Roman Emperor Domitian reached its height. Our author, John[102] of Patmos, identifies himself at the outset (Revelation 1:2) as a servant of Jesus Christ under trial for the kingdom's sake (Revelation 1:9). He reports that "on the Lord's Day"[103] he has had a vision while praying "in the spirit" (Revelation 1:10) and that God has commanded him, "Write on a scroll what you see and send it to the seven churches" (Revelation 1:11). The book's title, Revelation, is a translation of the Greek *apocalypse*, meaning, *unveiling*. We have seen examples of apocalyptic literature in the Old Testament, including Isaiah 24–27, Daniel 7–12, Ezekiel, and much of Zechariah. In the New Testament we have heard Jesus describe the end times in the synoptic gospels—Matthew 24, Mark 13, and Luke 21. The images from these past visions added to sayings and themes drawn from throughout the Bible supply the palette from which John will paint the progression of his vision. To the person unfamiliar with the Bible, all this borrowing makes Revelation almost the antithesis of its name— more like a muddying of the waters than a book of unveiling. For this reason, like the last chapter of any novel, Revelation makes little sense read apart from the context of the books that precede it. Yet even within the framework of the whole of the Bible, Revelation is not going to be easily understood. Let me

---

[102] It is unlikely that John of Patmos is actually the same John who writes the gospel and the three epistles. In the first place he names himself forthrightly from the beginning, something the gospel writer never does. In addition, his style, vocabulary, and imagery differ significantly from that of the evangelist.

[103] By the end of the first century Christians have added worship on the first day of the Jewish week, Sunday, in celebration of the day of Jesus' resurrection.

offer some tips for gaining a preliminary understanding of what Revelation aims to say to us.

Firstly we must avoid seeing Revelation as a coded riddle that will provide the solver with an inside scoop about when and how the world will come to a close. Every generation has its self-acclaimed prophets who insist they can match up the symbols of Revelation with persons and events of their own day. We have only to look to the many failed predictions of the end of the world to see that Revelation is not meant for this purpose.[104] Instead as we read, we will have better luck understanding John's work if we think of it offering closure to the great themes the Bible has raised throughout its text. In *Reversed Thunder*, Eugene Peterson sums up the essence of Revelation as "famous last words," God's parting remarks on all subjects that relate to the Deity and the Lord's salvation of humans, judgment of evil, and ultimate plan for eternity. In order to perceive what final words God is saying to us through John, we need to read with a heightened awareness of our author's literary acuity. John shifts deftly from poetry to drama, utilizing hyperbole, symbols, and vivid imagery. He will cue our sensory organs—eyes, ears, nose, tongue, and fingertips—to communicate his images while he still engages us cognitively. As the first chapter of Genesis displayed God as artist, creating the earth with the spoken word, this opposing bookend expands this portrait of the Almighty, exposing God's meticulous attention to details and patient proffering of second chances. Prepare for Revelation to bombard you in every way you can process information. Like the whole of the Bible, this is not a book we can digest in a single bite! Therefore, let us

---

[104] A quick Internet search will yield a couple of pages of failed predictions for the second coming of Christ and/or the end of the world. Noteworthy among those of relatively recent history were the Great Disappointment when Baptist preacher William Miller calculated the end of the world in 1844 and Hal Lindsey's book, *The Late Great Planet Earth*, published in 1970 and predicting the end times within a generation of the 1948 establishment of the state of Israel.

attempt simply a *taste* as we take a *first look* at what Revelation really says.

Revelation

The book of Revelation begins as though it were a letter. An angel appears to John on Patmos and charges him to write down all that Christ will reveal to him in the vision to follow (Revelation 1:1–2). Blessings will come to everyone who reads this prophecy (as with the Old Testament prophets, think of prophecy as "forth-telling"—speaking the words of God, not "foretelling" the future) (Revelation 1:3).

First up is a magnificent picture of the glorified Christ. When we read the synoptic gospels, we found Jesus introduced as a man, and through the course of the narrative, we were led to discover Him as something more—the Messiah. The Gospels closed with Jesus being executed and then resurrected, but the risen Christ still bore the stigmata—the scars of his crucifixion—so that the witnesses to His renewed life would remember that He was a human who had definitely suffered death. Writing some sixty years later, John must refine that mental perception of Christ to include the image of Jesus glorified.[105] Drawing on the theme of *seven* indicating *completeness* with which the Bible begins in the first creation story (Genesis 1–2:3), and which John utilizes throughout Revelation, John then imbues Daniel's "son of man [arriving in a whirl of clouds]"[106] (Daniel 7:13) image with seven attributes of grandeur, including (1) white hair, (2) flaming eyes, (3) feet of bronze, (4) a voice like rushing waters, (5) right hand holding the seven stars, (6) a mouth like a sharp sword, and (7) a bright shining face (Revelation 1:14–16). Speaking out of this radiance, Jesus gives Himself new titles: "I'm A to Z [alpha and

[105] Peterson, *Reversed Thunder*, p. 31.

[106] Jesus makes use of this Daniel image at his trial before the Sanhedrin (Matthew 27:64; Mark 14:62; Luke 22:69).

omega in the Greek alphabet]. I'm THE GOD WHO IS, THE GOD WHO WAS, AND THE GOD ABOUT TO ARRIVE.[107] I'm the Sovereign-Strong" (Revelation 1:8). In the end *this* is how we need to think about Jesus.

Next John records what Jesus has to say to the seven churches to which the prophet is to send this message. John transitions to this section by highlighting a different aspect of the above glorified Lord (Revelation 1:4–8; 13–16) when addressing each church in the following format:

1. Identification of Jesus
2. Affirmation of the church's virtue
3. Correction
4. Promise

In this way John shows the transcendent Jesus commending the perseverance against evil (of Ephesus), the patient and steadfast suffering under persecution (of Smyrna and Philadelphia), the bold witness (of Pergamum), and the persistent service (of Thyatira). At the same time Jesus vehemently chastises the churches that forget *love* while they pursue justice (in Ephesus), overlook heresy (in Pergamum), tolerate immorality (in Thyatira), relax into apathy (in Sardis), and most emphatically, indulge in the pursuit of material riches (in Laodicea). The Lord encourages these efforts by giving us a glimpse into the glorious banquet God has planned for those who have *ears awake* to the Spirit's words (Revelation 2:7, compare to Matthew 11:15, Mark 4:23, Luke 14:35, and Isaiah 6:9–10). Note the sensory cues John scatters within the messages to the churches. The Laodiceans' defection to worldly values renders them tasteless, "stale … stagnant," making Christ "want to vomit" (Revelation 3:16),

---

[107] God's special name given in answer to Moses' query in Exodus 3:14: I-AM-WHO-I-AM (YHWH) is expanded here to include all three tenses of the verb *to be*.

but those who *hear* will *taste* "Tree-of-Life fruit" (Revelation 2:7, compare to Genesis 2:9) and *sacred manna* (Revelation 2:17, compare to Exodus 16:31). They will also *feel* the weight of the *Life crown* offered to Smyrna (Revelation 2:10) and the "clear, smooth stone" (Revelation 2:17) pressed into the hand of those in Pergamum, and they will *see* the white garments of the Christians remaining in Sardis (Revelation 3:4 NIV).

This section culminates with the image of knocking at a door, which we first saw in the Sermon on the Mount/Plain when Jesus told His listeners to "ask ... seek ... knock and the door will be opened" (Revelation 3:20, compare to Matthew 7:7 and Luke 11:9 NIV). Here, however, the initiative from Jesus' sermon is reversed. It is Christ who knocks and waits to invite the ones who answer to His banquet. This shift in nuance is typical of John's allusions to Scripture. He never merely quotes the biblical literature, though surely he knows it well enough. Instead he recycles the images and ideas and tweaks them to express the new truths being revealed to him.[108] Using this image of a door of invitation, John transitions to the next aspect of his vision—a door opening into heaven (Revelation 4:1–2).

From this privileged vantage point we now gaze on the throne of heaven that Isaiah beheld as part of his call to prophecy (Isaiah 6). Encircling the Lord's throne are twenty-four others— twelve for the tribes of Israel and twelve for Jesus' apostles. In the center are four animals reminiscent of Ezekiel's initial vision from his vocation (Ezekiel 1:4–14). Everyone is singing praises to God, celebrating the Lord's holiness (Revelation 4:8) and creation of the world (Revelation 4:11).

As he looks more closely at this scene, however, John spies a scroll "in the right hand of the One Seated on the Throne" (Revelation 5:1). The scroll is secured with seven seals, but an angel's voice cries out in lament, "Is there anyone who can open

---

[108] Peterson, *Reversed Thunder*, p. 23 and footnote on corresponding page.

the scroll, who can break its seals?" (Revelation 5:2). Now John is distraught, weeping because there is no one to open the seals until one of the throned elders consoles, "Don't weep. Look—the Lion from Tribe Judah, the root of David's tree, has conquered" (Revelation 5:5). John's initial distress parallels the state of human bondage to sin that dominated the landscape of human history until the coming of Christ. With the incarnation, that bondage has finally ended, the seal against humans' fellowship with their maker broken. Now the choir of heaven can augment their praise of God with three new hymns commending the worthiness of the slain Lamb (think of the original Passover sacrifice) who breaks the seals (Revelation 5:9–10, 12, 13).

Echoing the ugliness and misery reverberating throughout human history, the opening of the seven seals unleashes a host of evils. Perhaps you have heard of the four horses of the apocalypse. They make their appearance (Revelation 6:2–8, compare to Zechariah 1:8–17; 6:1–8) as the Lamb rips open the first four seals and war, bloodshed, famine, and disease spread throughout the earth. The fifth seal uncovers the suffering of those persecuted for their faith, while the sixth lets loose an avalanche of natural disasters (Revelation 6:9–13). Amid all this chaos, the ones who love the Lord will remain standing strong, *sealed* against this evil (Revelation 7). Finally the Lamb opens the seventh seal, and heaven pauses in silence (Revelation 8:1). The crucifixion has accomplished God's task. Humans are free to live in peace with the Lord.

Even as Jesus' death has provided for human forgiveness, however, God's work with the creation is not complete without the promised judgment against the wrongdoers. John now uses seven trumpets to announce the punishment of evil. Again six trumpets blast in succession, and all manner of horrors visit the earth. Characteristically the people who survive these catastrophes do not see in them the opportunity to repent of their sins (Revelation 9:21).

As John waits for the seventh trumpet to sound, an angel hands him a little scroll that John must eat (Revelation 10:9–10, compare to Ezekiel 2:8–3:3). The honey tasting words become bitter in John's stomach, but he is nonetheless required to "prophesy again over many peoples and nations and languages and kings" (Revelation 10:11). At this eleventh hour when God is ready to make the final judgment, the gospel must still be proclaimed as widely and fully as possible so that all people have the opportunity to believe. As part of this last chance for repentance, God will provide two witnesses to preach for about three and a half years[109] (Revelation 11:3). Then the Beast from the Abyss will kill them and leave their bodies exposed for three and half days, after which time they will be resurrected. When the unbelievers fail to respond to this miracle, the seventh trumpet will signal the finality of judgment (Revelation 11:15). With this verdict pronounced all of heaven begins rejoicing. The real celebration of God's saving acts cannot begin until justice is rendered. God will take the vengeance promised back in Deuteronomy 32:35.

If we compare this section of Revelation to a courtroom scene, we could say that we have just heard the ruling of the jury. The judge must now pronounce a sentence. Before doing so, however, the judge chooses to recap the crimes committed. This is what we see next in John's vision. John takes us back to Jesus' birth but gives it a cosmic setting. A beautiful woman labors to give birth. Crouching beside her lies "a huge and fiery Dragon ... with seven heads and ten horns ... poised to eat up the child" (Revelation 12:1–4). God saves the child and the woman, but "the great Dragon—the ancient Serpent, the one called the Devil and Satan, the one who led the whole earth astray"—is thrown down from heaven to earth (Revelation 12:9). Whether this scene describes Jesus' earthly birth or merely the birth of God's plan

---

[109] Three and a half is one-half of seven. Since seven stands for completeness, three and a half is a symbol of incompleteness.

to save humankind at the beginning of creation, the key factor John highlights here is Satan's extreme effort to sabotage God. The Dragon recruits two beasts—one from the sea and one from the land. The second Beast uses magical signs to dupe people into worshiping him. He demands humans bear his mark in order to conduct any business. His number is 666—three numbers and each one short of the perfect seven (Revelation 13:18).[110] But all the while the Beast seems to enjoy dominion on earth, the true ruler, "the Lamb standing on Mount Zion" (Revelation 14:1) rejoices along with all who love the Lord over the perfect culmination of God's plan, which is ready to occur.

The sentence is set. For all that Satan and those humans who have followed him have done to dismantle God's good intentions for the world, seven angels stand forth to "dish out [of seven bowls]" (Revelation 16) the last seven plagues that will satisfy God's ordinance of justice. Notice the similarity between these disasters and the ones visited upon Egypt as the prelude to the Passover. As the seventh bowl is poured out a voice from the throne declares the judgment "done!" (Revelation 16:17). Reminiscent of Jesus' death on the cross ("It is finished" as said in John 19:30 NIV and the seismic activity in Matthew 27:51–54), lightning, thunder, and an earthquake punctuate the accomplishment of God's punishment of evil (Revelation 16:17–18). More images enhance our understanding of God's righteous indignation against the unholy. The great whore holds a "gold chalice in her hand, brimming with defiling obscenities, her foul fornications ... Drunk on the blood of God's holy people she has mounted the Beast with seven heads and ten horns [who] once was, is no longer, and is about to ascend from the Abyss and head straight for Hell" (Revelation 17:1–8). The Beast's name is an antithesis of God's, "THE GOD WHO IS, THE GOD WHO WAS, THE

---

[110] A number of commentators also equate the number 666 with Nero, emperor of Rome from 54-68 CE and the first imperial persecutor of Christians. Nero blamed Rome's great fire of 64 CE on Christians.

GOD ABOUT TO ARRIVE" (Revelation 1:4). Along with the whore and the Beast, we catch a glimpse of the fate of the once great city of Babylon, the name stemming from the nemesis of Israel's exile (and probably a thinly coded name for Rome). The place has now become a symbol of political force opposing God's people. What will happen to Babylon bustling with the latest fashions and innovations? She will be "sunk in the sea" (Revelation 18:21). Only the blood of God's martyred saints and prophets will testify to her memory (Revelation 18:24).

As John shuts the door on the earth and its evils, he finds the whole of heaven in glorious celebration. The heavenly hosts applaud God's justice but quickly turn from it to make ready for the wedding feast, the marriage of the Lamb to His bride: Christ and the church (Revelation 19:7–8). In prelude to the marriage the battle between Christ and the Devil replays. Satan is chained up for a thousand years and then loosed once more. Quickly he squanders his freedom by reengaging in the ways of deception, leading the nations astray. This time God banishes him to "Lake Fire and Brimstone" forever. Following him there are all those whose have shunned God and whose names are not in the Book of Life (Revelation 20).

Thus, we have had our satisfying ending to a crime drama. Evil, which has run rampant throughout the world's history, has met more than its match. Not only has it been fairly judged and duly punished, but it has even thrown away a second chance at redemption. With its lack of substance exposed, evil simply ceases to factor into the equation of God's redeemed universe. All that is left is what is holy and completely in sync with God. This paves the way for our fairy-tale finale, "And they all lived happily ever after."

What John sees next came to us first from Isaiah—the new heaven and new earth (Revelation 21:1, compare to Isaiah 65:17). A new and holy Jerusalem descends from heaven, and a voice announces, "God has moved into the neighborhood, making his home with men and women! They're his people, he's their God" (Revelation 21:3). No more tears, no more death—nothing can mar the beauty and peace of life in God's country. The New Jerusalem shines with precious gems and streets of gold but offers neither temple nor sun and moon because God and the Lamb provide constant light.

Here is where John's vision closes. The angel speaking to John reminds him of the trustworthiness of what he has seen. "Time is just about up. Let evildoers do their worst … but let the righteous maintain a straight course and the holy continue on in holiness" (Revelation 22:11). John must use his record of this sight to encourage the faithful to be ready for Jesus to return as promised. In addition, he warns against anyone seeking to add or subtract from the prophecy herein (Revelation 22:18–19). Though John has experienced terrors in this full body and mind unveiling of God's plan for the end of the world, the vision of the new world to come has overwhelmed his fears and planted in him a tremendous hunger. When Jesus assures him, "I'm on my way! I'll be there soon!" John fervently prays, "Yes! Come, Master Jesus!" (Revelation 22:20).

In Conclusion

Probably most of us do not share John's yearning for this second coming of Jesus. We admit that the world is far from perfect, but many of us are comfortable *enough* here. It is what we know and understand. Our world still affords us certain pleasures and aspirations. And we would judge ourselves blind and callous to the world's shortcomings if we were not eager to make the world better *before* the end comes. Here, however, is the crux of the difficult tension the call to follow Christ creates. On the one hand, the believer must busy himself with the building of God's kingdom—the breaking out of holiness into a sin-soaked and chaos-wracked world. On the other hand, there is the promised second coming described here in Revelation as the foregone conclusion of God's plan. Jesus charges His followers to be fully engaged at their posts at all times but still expectant that at some point the battle will be suspended and the glorious time of eternal peace will begin. Yet it is hard to maintain this mind-set of readiness for an event that has not occurred two thousand years since its prediction. We want to ask if it's really necessary for God to end the world after all.

At the beginning of this chapter I stated that Revelation, like its counterpart Genesis 1, never claims to offer a human perspective on the world's end. Instead, like the whole of the Bible, what we read is God's side of the story of our world. In Genesis, God creates a good earth and fills it with the goodness that is life. But when the Lord designs humans in the image of the Deity, endowing men and women with free will, God's intended goodness falls offline. The resulting dilemma seems to paint the Almighty into a corner. The Lord must either maintain the integrity of His holiness and abandon the sin-sullied humans or choose to love the men and women He made and necessarily pollute His righteousness. As we know, God found a way to avoid any such compromise. The Way is Christ whose death on the cross somehow atones for human sin and makes it possible for Creator and created to join in loving relationship. When we talk about the amazing grace of God's forgiveness, it is easy to make light of sin. It's like a huge debt that we could never repay, and once erased, it is easily forgotten. Revelation checks this human tendency of ours. The world must end at some point because there must be an accounting for evil. In fact, knowing that God will ultimately deal with the sins perpetrated on us actually frees us to forgive others as the Lord's Prayer instructs. Revelation assures us that the Lord does not turn a blind eye to *unrepented* sin. It matters to God when people pervert justice, manipulate the weak, betray trust, and indulge greed and self-absorption. Yet as abhorrent as sin is to the Almighty, it is no match for the relentlessness of God's love. Revelation also shows us the Lord's willingness to forgive even the most grievous of transgressions, only requiring that we confess and own them. In John's vision we see how judiciously God treats evil and how many times judgment is stayed so that sinners may observe and learn from the consequences of their misdeeds before God pronounces a final verdict.

But in the end there comes a time when second chances are no more. Evil is a consequence of free will—not something God created. Having no substance of its own, it finds no foothold in the new heaven and earth. The humans who come to live in the New Jerusalem are new beings who are still free but now immune to the allure of sin. They have utilized their free will to choose God and now find themselves heirs to all of the Lord's originally intended goodness. God's plan for humankind is complete. We are to live happily ever after. No wonder John prays, "Come, Lord Jesus."

Afterword

In the introduction I asked what kind of carrot could the Bible offer that would make the tackling of this very long and not simple book worthwhile. Given the Bible's own claim that it represents God's self-disclosure to humans, I proposed that we think of our reading as providing *insider information*, giving us God's side of the story of human existence. Now that we've finished our tour of the sixty-six books of the Christian Bible, we can *begin* to assess what the Bible is showing us about who God is and what the Lord's expectations are with regard to humans.

Genesis 1–2 reveals a God who defines goodness by creating the world and charging humans both to care for and flourish in it. Genesis 3 explains the hitch. The world can only remain good if the humans, out of their free will, elect to follow God's prescription for holiness—the code set down in the Torah that amounts to the operating instructions for the human machine. Human violation of the Deity's ordinances—what the Bible labels *sin*—inevitably leads to a disintegration of relationships between human and maker as well as persons and their neighbors. While our world offers glimpses of God's originally intended beauty and goodness, the pervasiveness of sin continually sullies the picture with the horrors of hatred, greed, and selfishness.

If we postulate the Deity's omniscience, it only makes sense that God must have anticipated sin as a natural consequence of free will. Many people draw their anger with the Lord from this very point. Why would a good God allow the evils that abound in the world? But this is where the Bible really serves its reader.

The whole of the Bible tells the story of the Lord's stratagem to combat sin without compromising on either human free will or the standard of holiness.

The Old Testament shows God's plan unfolding within the history of the people Israel—the people to whom the Lord reveals Himself both in a code of holy living (Torah) and as an agent who acts in history to rescue His beloved. Yet despite these demonstrations of God's love and faithfulness, Israel cannot live into the calling God has set for her. Again the Lord both anticipates this failure and has a means to nullify it. A Messiah will come who will reconcile Creator and created.

The New Testament attests that Jesus was and is this Messiah. In His life we see enacted the paradox of God's relentless hatred of sin contrasted with His dynamic love for sinners. His death on the cross certifies our redemption before God, freeing us to pursue a new life in harmony with our maker and our fellows. Here I lay it out as though it were a simple thing. But the Bible helps us by reminding us of the trials and missteps that so often belabor the spiritual journey of the Christian pilgrim. And it also assures us that if we stick with God, all will be right in the end.

As you have spent this time investigating what the Bible really says, I hope that you have seen sights that you will want to visit again. I guarantee you will find new things in the Scriptures no matter how many times you open the pages. John the evangelist has told us there are so many stories about Jesus that all of the world's books could not contain them. Still, the Bible remains the key to them all. I proclaimed at the start that God wants to reveal Himself to us. I believe that we can summon the Holy Spirit to show us God's story here whenever we honestly seek it from these texts. But in my experience the Spirit is particularly responsive to our individual state of mind and faith. While there may be times when we can open the Bible at random and find just the right words of inspiration, more often God will ask us to wrestle with these stories. How do they teach us about God? More importantly, what do they offer us as we struggle to understand the meaning of our individual lives? In this introductory sightseeing I have tried to help you grasp a sense of the biblical terrain. But it is my real hope that on these pages you have encountered the true guide who will continue to accompany you on your own particular faith journey. This one will not answer every question you have on cue but will, with your permission, prove to you the reality of God's love for you and the meaningfulness of your existence. Don't expect your proof to convince someone else. As the biblical story line demonstrates, God meets us one-on-one. But do expect it to change your life and how you live.

Appendix 1: Literary Devices

Allegory: An *allegory* is a narrative that functions on at least two levels. The first or primary level makes sense as a literally understood story. In the secondary level the characters and setting work together to symbolize a larger idea the author desires to correlate with the action of the story. Paul *allegorizes* the Genesis story of Abraham's two sons, Ishmael and Isaac, in Galatians 4:22–31. There he calls for Ishmael, the son of a slave woman, to correlate to God's old covenant of the Law enacted at Mount Sinai. Isaac, the son of a free woman, corresponds to the new covenant of forgiveness that God puts forth in Christ.

Allusion: An *allusion* is a subtle reference an author makes either to something mentioned earlier in a narrative or an echoing back to another narrative with which the author assumes the reader is familiar. In this way the author calls up some of the associations built into the reader's understanding of the first reference and incorporates them into his new train of thought. The narrator of the second creation story *alludes* to the first creation story with the word *good.* In Genesis 2:18, God is quoted as stating that it is "not good" for the man to be alone. Because in Genesis 1:1–2:3 everything God creates is "good," our new narrator can use allusion to alert us to God's attention to this discrepancy.

Analogy: An *analogy* is a general means of comparing two seemingly different things in order to highlight something they have in common. Both similes and metaphors are varieties of analogy.

Antagonist: The *antagonist* is the villain of a story who tries to cause difficulty for the narrative's hero.

Climax: The action or *plot* of a story generally follows a pattern. It begins with a complication or problem that the main character is forced to resolve. The mounting difficulties the hero encounters through the course of the story comprise the rising action, which then culminates in the *climax*—the high point of the plot and the resolution of the character's problem. In Western literature the climax tends to come almost at the end of the story with only a small amount of falling action after it. In Hebrew literature, however, sometimes the climax is given emphasis by being placed at the center or the story, with the rising action parallel to the falling action. See also *inverted parallelism.*

Character: *Characters* are the people who play out the action of a story or narrative.

Dialogue: *Dialogue* is the recording of the conversations between characters.

Foreshadowing: An author uses *foreshadowing* when he or she drops a hint early on in the plot that indicates something that will be important later on in his or her narrative. For example, Luke merely mentions Saul at the conclusion of his narrative of Stephen's martyrdom in Acts 8:1 and then waits to tell the story of his conversion until Acts 9.

Hyperbole and Understatement: Frequently an author will exaggerate a point in order to emphasize its meaning. The purposeful use of exaggeration in literature is *hyperbole.* In 2

Kings 18:17–35, the narrator of Kings infuses the speech of the Assyrian's commander with hyperbole in order to heighten the fearfulness of his attack on Jerusalem. In contrast, sometimes emphasis is achieved by *understating*. Nathan uses this device with dramatic effect to call David to account for his sins in 2 Samuel 12:7.

Image/imagery: When an author is able to conjure in the reader a mental picture or snapshot of an idea with words, we name it *imagery*. Frequently the devices of simile and metaphor aid the creation of imagery. Consider how Psalm 8 reiterates the imagery of the creation story in Genesis 1 by speaking of the *heavens* as the *work of [God's] fingers*.

Inverted parallelism: With this device, an author highlights an idea by building a series of parallel points both before and after the discussion of his or her central thesis. A prime example is the narrator's report of Solomon's reign in 1 Kings 1–12 where he highlights Solomon's construction of the temple (Kings 5–9).

Irony: An author creates *irony* when he sets the reader's expectations in one direction and then delivers an outcome opposite to those expectations. Paul speaks of the irony of the cross in 1 Corinthians 1:23 when he states that what is a *stumbling block for Jews and foolishness for Greeks* is actually the *power and wisdom of God.*

Metaphor: A *metaphor* is an analogy or equation made between two objects commonly considered dissimilar usually by utilizing a linking verb. In Song of Songs 2:1, the lover uses *metaphor* to claim, "I am a rose of Sharon, a lily of the valleys."

Narrative: This form of writing is used to tell a story. A *narrative* varies by the perspective of the narrator. In the Bible most of the narratives are told in the third person with the author recording events that he did not himself experience. In Acts, however, Luke employs both third- and first-person narratives, indicating that in some of the events he records he was also a participant. In all cases of narrative, however, it is important to analyze the attitude of the narrator to the story being told.

Parable: A *parable* is a form of allegory delivered in a short but dramatically effective story. Jesus is a champion of this art form.

Parallelism: *Parallelism* is the means of making a point by stating an idea and then restating the same idea with slightly different words. Consider Proverbs 19:6. Alternatively sometimes juxtaposing two opposite ideas in parallel makes the point as well (compare Proverbs 19:4). This technique is particularly common in Hebrew poetry, making biblical poetry more readily translatable than that of other languages.

Personification: *Personification* involves treating an inanimate object or animal as though it has the characteristics of a human. In Job 38:7, the *morning stars* are said to be *singing.*

Poetry and Prose: *Poetry* is the form of literature that communicates ideas primarily by inciting our senses and emotions rather than our cognition. Whereas *prose* generally restricts itself to grammatical sentences in order to express complete thoughts, poetry relies more heavily on imagery and the sounds words make, conveying its ideas largely in phrases or verses.

Protagonist: The *protagonist* is the hero of a narrative.

Rhetorical Question: At its most basic level a *rhetorical question* is one that does not expect an answer, usually because the implied answer is obvious. An author uses this device for its dramatic effect. Paul makes great use of this technique in his letter to the Romans.

Setting: In a narrative the *setting* reminds us where and when the action of the story takes place. For instance, in Ruth, the setting is stated explicitly as "in the days of the judges, in Bethlehem" (Ruth 1:1) and helps us to interpret the meaning of the story.

Simile: A *simile* is an analogy or comparison between two seemingly dissimilar objects using *as* or *like*. The lover in Song of Songs states that her beloved is "like a gazelle or like a young stag" (Song of Songs 2:17).

Symbol: In literature an object or idea becomes a *symbol* when it is used to signify more than the simple and specific meaning of its immediate context. The primary symbol of Christianity has become the cross. In its original context the cross merely signified the ancient Roman Empire's means of execution. Since Jesus' crucifixion, however, the *cross* is now imbued with the wide range of meanings revolving around Jesus' willing sacrifice of His life for the redemption of humanity (e.g., undeserved suffering, God's undying love, hope for humanity).

Appendix 2: Comparing the Hebrew and Christian Canons

Hebrew Scriptures	Christian Old Testament:
Law	**Law**
Genesis	Genesis
Exodus	Exodus
Leviticus	Leviticus
Numbers	Numbers
Deuteronomy	Deuteronomy
Prophets	**History**
Former	Joshua
Joshua	Judges
Judges	Ruth
1 and 2 Samuel	1 and 2 Samuel
1 and 2 Kings	1and 2 Kings
Latter	1 and 2 Chronicles
Isaiah	Ezra
Jeremiah	Nehemiah
Ezekiel	Esther
The Twelve (Minor Prophets)	

Writings	Wisdom
Psalms	Job
Proverbs	Psalms
Job	Proverbs
Song of Songs	Ecclesiastes
Ruth	Song of Songs
Lamentations	
Ecclesiastes	**Prophets**
Esther	Isaiah
Daniel	Jeremiah
Ezra-Nehemiah	Lamentations
1 and 2 Chronicles	Ezekiel
	Daniel
	The Twelve (Minor Prophets)

Rabbis describe the arrangement of the Hebrew Scriptures as a wedding cake. The five books of the Torah form the bottom layer, the foundation. The prophets come next, signifying the second layer, and the writings top off the cake. While all layers are important and authoritative, the books of the Law bear the most weight theologically followed by the prophets, leaving the writings as more of a flourish at the end.

The Old Testament, taking its arrangement from the Septuagint, the Greek version of the Hebrew Scriptures translated in the third century BCE, begins by gathering the mostly narrative works and organizing them chronologically (the Torah and the history). Then it fleshes out the history first with the Wisdom Literature and then with the latter prophets, into which Lamentations and Daniel are inserted. This divergent arrangement parallels several theological differences in Jewish and Christian interpretation of the same Scriptures.

Appendix 3: Deities of Israel's Neighbors

God's command to destroy the native inhabitants of the land of Canaan—the land Israel was to claim according to God's promise—rested on the premise that the religion of the Canaanites would prove an insurmountable temptation to the Hebrews to stray from their faith in the one God. The history of Israel certainly corroborates that prediction. But what was the faith of the various Canaanites? We see only glimpses of their deities' names and rituals mentioned in the Bible. Archeology confirms that the people native to the land Israel conquered practiced a religion stemming from its geographic neighbors of Egypt and Mesopotamia and represented something of an amalgam of their belief systems. We have already found *El*, the creator God, showing up in the first creation story of Genesis. According to the Canaanite pantheon, El, the supreme god, fathered several gods, but two of these figure predominantly in the clash with the Hebrews. The first of these is the son of El, *Baal*, who governed weather—rains and storms—an important and understandably common function in any agricultural society. Yearly Baal died and became resurrected, corresponding to the dry and wet seasons. His name connotes *Master* or *Lord* and was even initially synonymous with the Hebrew *adonai*, meaning Lord, until the Israelites found it shameful to equate the lord of another faith with their own Lord. Because rain brought fertility to the ground, idols for this deity most often took the form of the bull (probably because these animals plowed the fields). Baal had consorts that were also sisters whose names come into the Old Testament as *Asherah* or *Ashtoreth* or *Astarte*. These female deities also dealt with fertility, and their worship usually involved sacred prostitution rites. Trees and poles became the symbols of the female deity. Together Baal and Asherah allowed the Canaanites the balance of male (lord) and female (lady) in their worship.

In addition to these primary deities, we learn from the Samson story in Judges that the Philistines worshiped a god named *Dagon*, who was most likely a grain or agricultural god. In several places the Old Testament chronicles with horror the rites of *Molech*, a fire god whose worship demanded the supreme sacrifice of children being put through the fire. My guess is that he represented the god of last resort.

What made the Canaanite religious practices so irresistible to the Hebrews, however, revolved around the idea that the purpose of human worship amounted to the placation of the deities. These sacrifices and other religious observances afforded humans the comfortable and convenient sense of controlling their own destiny by being able to buy the blessings of their gods. In contrast, the God of Israel emerged as a deity who refused manipulation. Micah summarized God's agenda, "And what does the Lord require of you? To act justly and love mercy and to walk humbly with your God" (Micah 6:8).

Appendix 4: Herod's Dynasty

The first Herod mentioned in the New Testament is *Herod the Great*, who ruled Judea for Rome in the last half of the first century BCE (Matthew 2:1–19; Luke 1:5). According to historians trying to date this period, he died in about 4 BCE, probably shortly after Jesus' birth. This King Herod had ten wives and multiple sons, some of whom Herod had killed. Upon Herod's death Rome divided his jurisdiction among at least three of his sons—*Archelaus*, governor of Judea from 4 BCE to 6 CE (Matthew 2:19–22); *Philip*, tetrarch of the northern territories of Iturea and Traconitis from 4 BCE to 34 CE (Luke 3:1); and *Herod Antipas*, tetrarch of Galilee from 4 BCE to 39 CE (Luke 3:1). Herod Antipas comes into the gospel witness as being manipulated into ordering the execution of John the Baptist (Matthew 14:1–12; Mark 6:14–29). Antipas' second wife, Herodias, had first been married to his half brother, *Herod II*, also called *Herod Philip I* or simply *Philip* (in Matthew 14:3 and Mark 6:17), who, while a son of Herod the Great, did not rule in succession to his father. It is Herodias' daughter Salome from her marriage to Philip who dances for her stepfather, Antipas, and cons him into offering her the Baptist's head on a platter. Antipas also figures into Jesus' passion in Luke 23:7–12 when Pilate asks him to weigh in on the charges against Jesus.

We find the third generation of Herod's dynasty in Acts 12:1–23. Here the ruler Luke refers to as King Herod is actually *Herod Agrippa I*, grandson of Herod the Great, who served as king of Judea from 37–44 CE. He had James, the brother of John the evangelist, put to the sword and Peter imprisoned during the early years after Jesus' death and resurrection. Finally in Acts 25:13–26:32, Paul argues his defense and pleads to go to Rome before *Herod Agrippa II*, great-grandson of the first Herod, who came to rule as king of Judea in the middle of the first century CE.

Appendix 5: Jesus' Fulfillment of Messianic Markers

While the Old Testament fails to offer a precise picture of the Messiah and when he will arrive, it does supply a number of markers that stand out as clues for God's people to help them identify the savior of Israel when they meet him. First we will look at several definite statements the Old Testament makes about the Messiah. Next we will look at additional passages that Israel understood as messianic. Finally we will compare some of the images found in the Psalms and Isaiah's suffering servant songs that Christians linked to Jesus' ordeal on the cross.

The Hebrew Scriptures offer some concrete statements about the Messiah:

The Messiah will be a Jew from the tribe of Judah and the house of David.
OLD TESTAMENT: In his farewell address Moses stated that God promised Israel, "I'll raise up for them [Israel] a *prophet* like you [Moses] from their kinsmen" (Deuteronomy 18:18). Earlier on in Genesis, Jacob's blessing on Judah said, "The scepter shall not leave Judah; He'll keep a firm grip on the command staff until the *ultimate ruler* comes and the nations obey him" (Genesis 49:10). God's pledge to build a dynasty for David saying, "Your house and your kingdom will endure forever before me; your throne will be established forever" (2 Samuel 7:16 NIV) narrowed the candidates to *a son of David.* Amos confirmed that this descendant

would embody the messianic hope when he pronounced, "In that day [when the Messiah comes] I [God] will restore David's fallen tent" (Amos 9:11).

NEW TESTAMENT: All four gospels acknowledge Jesus as a Jew. Both the Matthew and Luke genealogies document Judah (Matthew 1:3 and Luke 3:33) and David (Matthew 1:6 and Luke 3:31) as Jesus' ancestors.

God will send a messenger as preparation for the Messiah's arrival.
OLD TESTAMENT: Isaiah predicted a predecessor of the Messiah who will beseech God's people, "In the desert prepare the way for the Lord; make straight in the wilderness a highway for our God" (Isaiah 40:3 NIV). This language recalled the arrangements any community would need to make in anticipation of a royal visitation. Malachi echoed Isaiah, "Look! I'm sending my messenger on ahead to clear the way for me" (Malachi 3:1).

NEW TESTAMENT: All the gospels name John the Baptist as the forerunner of the Messiah (Matthew 3:1–12; Mark 1:2–8; Luke 3:2-18; John 1:19-27). His message of repentance and baptism for the cleansing of sins readied God's people to hear Jesus.

The Messiah will be born in Bethlehem, David's birthplace.
OLD TESTAMENT: Micah prophesied, "But you, Bethlehem ... from you will come the leader who will shepherd-rule Israel" (Micah 5:2).

NEW TESTAMENT: The angels proclaim to the shepherds, "Today in the town of David a Savior has been born to you; he is Christ the Lord" (Luke 2:11 NIV). Matthew joins Luke in claiming this location for Jesus' birth and also quotes from Micah to corroborate Bethlehem's importance as a fulfillment of Scripture (Matthew 2:1, 5-6).

The Messiah will make a triumphal entry into Jerusalem on a donkey.

OLD TESTAMENT: Zechariah testified, "Your king is coming! A good king who makes all things right, a humble king riding on a donkey, a mere colt of a donkey" (Zechariah 9:9). The reference to the "good" and "humble" king earmarked him as a messianic figure.

NEW TESTAMENT: All the gospels testify that Jesus made His triumphal entry into Jerusalem on a donkey, openly acknowledging Himself as the Messiah (Matthew 21:1–7; Mark 11:1–17; Luke 19:28–35; John 12:12–15).

Israel understood several prophecies as references to the Messiah:

The Messiah will reign as King establishing God's justice and righteousness.

OLD TESTAMENT: Isaiah's messianic prophecy acclaimed, "For to us a child is born, to us a son is given, and the government will be on his shoulders. And he will be called Wonderful Counselor, Mighty God, Everlasting Father, Prince of Peace. Of the increase of his government and peace there will be no end. He will reign on David's throne and over his kingdom, establishing and upholding it with justice and righteousness from that time and forever" (Isaiah 9:6-7 NIV).

NEW TESTAMENT: Throughout the gospels Jesus preaches about God's justice and righteousness in fulfillment of this prophecy. Mark, Luke and John reference many times where Jesus teaches about the "kingdom of God," (Matthew shows Jesus using the phrase "the kingdom of heaven"), again keeping the context of this picture of the Messiah. Likewise, all the evangelists dub Jesus the "Son of God." John confirms that Jesus is literally God with us: "The Word became flesh and made his dwelling among us" (John 1:14 NIV).

The Messiah will demonstrate God's compassion with healings.

OLD TESTAMENT: Isaiah described what would happen when, "Your God will come ... Then will the eyes of the blind be opened and the ears of the deaf unstopped. Then will the lame leap like a deer, and the mute tongue shout for joy" (Isaiah 35:4–6 NIV).

NEW TESTAMENT: All the gospels speak of Jesus' numerous occasions of physical healing. "Great crowds came to him, bringing the lame, the blind, the crippled, the mute and many others, and laid them at his feet; and he healed them" (Matthew 15:30 NIV). Luke uses Jesus' statement of His many healings as a reply to John the Baptist's queries about His Messiahship: "Go back and report to John what you have seen and heard: The blind receive sight, the lame walk, those who have leprosy are cured, the deaf hear" (Luke 7:22 NIV).

The Messiah's arrival is good news for the world's downtrodden.

OLD TESTAMENT: In Isaiah's final servant song, the servant spoke, "The Spirit of God, the Master, is on me because God anointed me. He sent me to preach good news to the poor, heal the heartbroken, announce freedom to all captives, pardon all prisoners" (Isaiah 61:1).

NEW TESTAMENT: The Beatitudes, part of the Sermon on the Mount, recorded in Matthew 5:3–12 along with its parallel in Luke 6:20–22 illustrate this Isaiah passage well. In addition, Luke 4:16–21 relates Jesus reading this verse during worship in His hometown synagogue and proclaiming its fulfillment in Him.

The Messiah will usher in a new covenant, including the forgiveness of sins.

OLD TESTAMENT: Jeremiah proclaimed that in the future God "will put my law within them [my people]—write it on their hearts! ... I'll wipe the slate clean for each of them. I'll forget that they ever sinned" (Jeremiah 31:32–34). Through Ezekiel, God promised Israel in exile, "I'll make a *new* covenant with you that will last forever ... when I make atonement for you" (Ezekiel 16:60–63).

NEW TESTAMENT: All the gospels assert that Jesus' primary mission on earth was to forgive human sins. Matthew 1:21

explains that Jesus' very name reflects this mandate, "Give him the name Jesus because he will save his people from their sins." John the Baptist cries out, "Look, the Lamb of God, who takes away the sin of the world" (John 1:29 NIV). The author of Hebrews summarizes, "The time is coming ... when I (God) will make a new covenant with the house of Israel ... I will put my laws in their minds and write them on their hearts ... I will forgive their wickedness and remember their sins no more" (Hebrews 8:8-12 NIV).

The Messiah's work will include everyone in the world.
OLD TESTAMENT: Back in the beginning God promised Abram, "All the families of the Earth will be blessed through you" (Genesis 12:3). The Psalms testified, "All the ends of the earth will remember and turn to the Lord, and all the families of the nations will bow down before him" (Psalm 22:27 NIV). God spoke His plan to the servant, "I will make you to be a covenant for the people and a light for the Gentiles" (Isaiah 42:6 NIV). Joel added that God would "pour out my Spirit on *every kind of people*" (Joel 2:28).
NEW TESTAMENT: After his eye-opening vision in Acts 10:9–32, Peter reports to the early believers in Judea in Acts 11:1 that the Gentiles have also received the gospel. After expressing their initial disbelief, Luke records the reformed sentiment of the Jewish Christians as a praise, "So then, God has granted even the Gentiles repentance unto life" (Acts 11:18 NIV).

Christ's death by crucifixion reverberated with images from the Hebrew Scriptures:

From Psalm 22
"My God, my God, why have you forsaken me?" (Psalm 22:1 NIV). "But I am a worm and not a man, scorned by men and despised by the people. All who see me mock me; they hurl insults, shaking

their heads: 'He trusts in the Lord: let the Lord rescue him'"
(Psalm 22:6-8 NIV)

"I am poured out like water, and all my bones are out of joint"
(Psalm 22:14 NIV).

"A band of evil men has encircled me, they have pierced my hands
and feet. I can count all my bones; people stare and gloat over
me. They divide my garments among them and cast lots for my
clothing" (Psalm 22:16-18 NIV).

NEW TESTAMENT: Matthew 27:46 and Mark 15:34 testify that
Jesus quoted the first verse of Psalm 22 while on the cross. While
these words give voice to Jesus' momentary despair, the rest of
the psalm echoes with other elements of the execution scene that
the gospel writers narrate. Matthew 27:39–44; Mark 15:29–32;
Luke 23:35–37, 39; and John 19:3 all record the mocking that
Jesus endured. While the gospels presume their readers are
familiar with the mechanics of a crucifixion, the Old Testament
verses that describe the hands and feet being pierced and the
sheer physical pain of the maligned man's ordeal match up well
with what someone condemned to be crucified would feel. In
addition, all four attest to the Roman guards' gambling over
Jesus' clothing (Matthew 27:35; Mark 15:24; Luke 23:34; John
19:23–24).

From Psalm 69
"They put gall in my food and gave me vinegar for my thirst"
(Psalm 69:21 NIV).

NEW TESTAMENT: All four gospels note that the soldiers
offered Jesus a kind of wine that was meant to be somewhat
anesthetizing for his pain (Matthew 27:34; Mark 15:23; Luke
23:36; John 19:28-30).

From the Suffering Servant Song of Isaiah
"He was despised and rejected by men, a man of sorrows, and
familiar with suffering ... Surely he took up our infirmities

and carried our sorrows, yet we considered him stricken by God, smitten by him and afflicted. But he was pierced for our transgressions, he was crushed for our iniquities; the punishment that brought us peace was upon him, and by his wounds we are healed ... The Lord has laid on him the iniquity of us all. He was oppressed and afflicted, yet he did not open his mouth; he was like a lamb led to the slaughter" (Isaiah 53:3-7 NIV).

"He was assigned a grave with the wicked, and the rich in his death, though he had done no violence, nor was any deceit in his mouth. Yet it was the Lord's will to crush him and cause him to suffer, and though the Lord makes his life a guilt offering, he will see his offspring and prolong his days, and the will of the Lord will prosper in his hand. After the suffering of his soul, he will see the light of life and be satisfied; by his knowledge my righteous servant will justify many, and he will bear their iniquities. Therefore I will give him a portion among the great ... because he poured out his life unto death ... For he bore the sin of many and made intercession for the transgressors" (Isaiah 53:9-12 NIV).

NEW TESTAMENT: Christians look to these verses from Isaiah as particularly indicative of Jesus' crucifixion. The passage juxtaposes the irony of how at first humans understood what happened to Jesus as a sign that God had abandoned him, but later believers saw Jesus' suffering as a redemptive and atoning act for humanity's sins. In particular, the gospels show Jesus making very little effort in defending Himself. (Compare Isaiah 53:7 to Matthew 26:63, "But Jesus remained silent," and Mark 15:5, "But Jesus still made no reply.") After Jesus' death, Pilate granted Sanhedrin member (and opponent of the bid to get Jesus executed) Joseph of Arimathea, the right to bury Jesus, thus placing Christ in a wealthy (though not wicked) burial place (Matthew 27:57–60; Mark 15:43–46; Luke 23:50–53; John 19:38–41).

Appendix 6: Women and Slaves Mentioned in Paul's Epistles

I have already noted that at times in his epistles, Paul seems to hold contradictory ideas about women and slaves. While he proclaims, "There is neither Jew nor Greek, slave nor free, male nor female for you are all one in Christ Jesus" (Galatians 3:28), he also tells women to "submit to their husbands" (Ephesians 5:22 NIV) and to "learn in quietness and full submission ... [and not to] teach or have authority over a man" (1 Timothy 2:11-12 NIV). Likewise, he instructs slaves to "obey your earthly masters with respect and fear" (Ephesians 6:5 NIV), but nonetheless encourages his friend Philemon to treat his runaway slave Onesimus "as you would welcome me" (Philemon 17). Confusing as these apparent vacillations are, I find that it has helped my thinking about Paul to take a look at the number of women and slaves he mentions in his letters as being partners or co-workers in spreading the gospel.

Paul and Women:

Let's begin in the epistle to the Romans, which devotes much of the sixteenth chapter to greetings. Of the twenty-nine people listed in the first fifteen verses, twelve are women (and another ten are likely slaves). Writing from Corinth, Paul begins with his courier, *Phoebe*, a deacon. Paul exclaims, "I heartily endorse both her and her work. She's a key representative ... She deserves anything you can do for her. She's helped many a person, including me" (Romans 16:1-2). Next he asks about his long time friends, *Priscilla* and Aquila (note that the wife's name appears first). He describes, "[They] have worked hand in hand with me in serving Jesus, [and even] once put their lives on the line for me" (Romans 16:3-4). He names the *hard working Mary* and a fellow Jew named *Junias – an outstanding leader* who became a Christian before he did (Romans 16:6-7]. *Tryphena, Tryphosa,* and *Persis* all make the list, noted for their *diligence* in serving the Lord (Romans 16:12). When greeting the family of Rufus, Paul makes special mention of Rufus' mother who "has also been a dear mother to me" (Romans 16:13). In his final greetings the names of four more women emerge: *Hermas, Julia, Nereus' sister,* and *Olympas* (Romans 16:14-15).

The names of women appear scattered in some of Paul's other epistles. *Priscilla* surfaces most often: in 1 Corinthians 16:19 (an earlier letter where her husband Aquila's name is placed first) and in 2 Timothy 4:19 (Paul's farewell letter where she is back to top billing). It is on the basis of *Chloe's* reports about Corinth that Paul writes 1 Corinthians. We find *Euodia* and *Syntyche* in Philippians 4:2-3. Though Paul exhorts them to reconcile here, he nonetheless praises their work on behalf of the gospel. *Nympha* and the church that meets at her house receive greetings in Colossians 4:15 as well as *Claudia* at the end of 2 Timothy 4:21. Also in 2 Timothy, Paul makes a point of crediting the faith of Timothy's grandmother *Lois* and mother *Eunice* as nurturing Timothy's own *honest* belief (2 Timothy 1:5). Finally, Luke makes mention of several women involved in Paul's ministry in Acts: *Eunice* (Timothy's mother, in Acts 16:1); *Lydia,* a God-fearing (i.e. Gentile) businesswoman dealing in *expensive textiles* who became an early convert (Acts 16:14-15, 40); the prominent women Paul converted in Thessalonica (Acts 17:4); *Damaris* of Athens (Acts 17:34); *Priscilla* (Acts 18:2-3, 18-19, 26); and the four prophesying daughters of Philip, one of the original seven deacons selected in Acts 6:1-6, (Acts 21:9).

Paul and Slaves:

Although scholars are less certain which people Paul greets are slaves, some of the names we find are common slave names. In this way, we conjecture that *Ampliatus, Urbanus, Stachys, Apelles, Asyncritus, Phlegon, Hermes, Patrobas, Philologus,* and *Nereus* are either slaves or freed men (Romans: 16:8-10, 14-15). Of course, the whole of Paul's letter to Philemon discusses the runaway slave, *Onesimus,* whom Paul claims as a son (Philemon 10).

Bibliography

Childs, Brevard S. *Introduction to the Old Testament as Scripture.* Philadelphia: Fortress Press, 1979.

Childs, Brevard S. "Jesus Christ the Lord and the Scriptures of the Church." *The Rule of Faith.* Harrisburg: Morehouse Publishing, 1998.

Childs, Brevard S. "The Nature of the Christian Bible: One Book, Two Testaments." *The Rule of Faith.* Harrisburg: Morehouse Publishing, 1998.

Griffith-Jones, Robin. *The Four Witnesses.* New York: HarperCollins, 2001.

Lewis, C. S. *Mere Christianity.* New York: HarperCollins, 2001.

Lewis, C. S. *Reflections on the Psalms.* New York: Harcourt, Brace & World, Inc., 1958.

Parton, Craig A. *Religion on Trial.* Eugene, OR: Wipf & Stock, 2008.

Peterson, Eugene H. *The Message.* Colorado Springs, CO: NavPress, 2002.

Peterson, Eugene H. *Reversed Thunder.* New York: HarperCollins, 1991.

Pollock, John. *The Apostle*. Colorado Springs, CO: David C. Cook, 2012.

Wangerin, Jr., Walter. *Paul: A Novel*. Grand Rapids, MI: Zondervan, 2000.

Yancey, Philip. *Prayer: Does It Make Any Difference?* Grand Rapids, MI: Zondervan, 2006.

NIV Study Bible, 10th Anniversary Edition. Grand Rapids, MI: Zondervan, 1995

Acknowledgements

Although writing is a largely solitary activity, no one writes a book alone! This work was little more than an idea I casually referenced in my Christmas note when Charlie Scalise offered to read it for me. Over the last six and more years he has patiently plowed through each chapter, bringing his expertise as a scholar and teacher and his experience as a Christian to bear on my ideas and their expression. I am so grateful for the countless times he saved me from saying what I didn't mean to say! Digesting Charlie's comments always left me happier with my writing. Charlie, I am so grateful for both your early faith in me as well as your constructive prodding that always forced me to find ways of making the text clearer and my points sharper. I could not have finished this without you!

Next, I must thank all the people – from Wayne Presbyterian and Wayne United Methodist Churches – who came to my Bible studies and joined me in this great exploration of the Bible. You were the fathers of this child/book of mine: your questions and confusions and comments sowed the seeds that germinated in my mind giving me the impetus to take on this project. And you have also been my biggest cheerleaders!

Much gratitude goes to my spiritual direction group who prayed me through the entire composition of this book. In the same vein, I thank all the dear friends who kept tabs on my progress and supported me with their encouragement.

A special thank you to my pastor, Joe DiPaolo, whose thoughtful sermons, insightful teaching, and candid sharing and living out of his faith continue to inspire and guide me. In addition, I thank Eugene Peterson who has served as a literary minister to me through his books. When he granted me permission to use *The Message* early on in this project, he added, "Keep writing . . . it is work that you must do simply to stay obedient to our Lord." God knows how many days those words kept me from abandoning my efforts!

A shout out to my children who clued me into many mysteries of working the computer, cheered as I progressed through my chapters and even volunteered to read the raw manuscript. Special gratitude to my husband who tolerated my work space strewn with large books and papers and, when we traveled, suitcases heavy with Bibles and other texts over the last several years. When we were first married and I was staying home with our children, he always told people I was a writer. I'm glad to have delivered on that vote of confidence at last!

In my dedication, I recognize Brevard Childs who was my professor at Yale who planted in me this passion I have for the Bible, and Irené Wagner whose invitation to help teach her Bible survey course to the Women's Bible Study conjured the vision for this book. In their memory I hope to have produced a work worthy of their great inspiration.

About the Author

Katie Hoyt McNabb graduated from Yale with a BA in religious studies and went on to teach high school English until she and her husband began their family. While raising four children and volunteering in many school programs she maintained her "secret identity" as a student of the Bible and adult Christian educator.

Does It Really Say That in the Bible? is the outgrowth of sharing her passion for the Scriptures with many students over the last dozen and more years of her teaching in churches.

CPSIA information can be obtained at www.ICGtesting.com
Printed in the USA
BVOW07s1114180814

363104BV00002B/2/P